ATLAS

OF

⭐

AMERICAN

⭐ MILITARY HISTORY ⭐

ATLAS
OF
★
AMERICAN
★ MILITARY HISTORY ★

Edited by James C. Bradford

OXFORD
UNIVERSITY PRESS

2003

OXFORD
UNIVERSITY PRESS

Athens Auckland Bangkok Bogota Buenos Aires Calcutta
Cape Town Chennai Dar es Salaam Delhi Florence Hong Kong
Istanbul Karachi Kuala Lumpur Madrid Melbourne Mexico City Mumbai
Nairobi Paris Sao Paulo Singpore Taipei Tokyo Toronto Warsaw
and associated companies in
Berlin Ibadan

Published by Oxford University Press, Inc.
198 Madison Avenue
New York, New York 10016
www.oup.com

Library of Congress cataloging-in-publication data available upon request

1 3 5 7 9 8 6 4 2

Printed in Italy by Centro Poligrafico Milano S.p.A.

Produced by Cynthia Parzych Publishing, Inc.
732 Broadway, 3rd floor
New York, New York 10003

Design and Typesetting by Dorchester Typesetting Group Ltd.

Maps by Advanced Illustration Ltd.

Page 2-3: *This contemporary French print captures the moment on 19 October 1781 when the United States was assured of ultimate victory in its battle for independence from Great Britain. On that day, at Yorktown, Virginia, the English army commanded by Lord Cornwallis surrendered to the combined armies of the United States and France under orders given by General George Washington and General de Rochambeau .*

Contents

List of Maps

Key to Maps

Military units/types

⊠ Infantry
⊘ Cavalry
◼ Armored
◪ Armored cavalry
⊠ Mechanized infantry
⊖ Airborne/Parachute
⊼ Airforce command
TF 38 Task force
YAMAMOTO Name of commander/ Force
Artillery/Battery

Size of military units

Army group
Army
Corps
Division

Size of military units (continued)

Brigade
Regiment
Battalion
Company
–xxxx– Army operations boundary

General military symbols

◁ Air strip
⊛ Airfield
✳ Battle site
⚓ Naval battle site
⊗ Surrender site
⚓ Naval base
▣ Military base
■ Fort
Fortifications, Siege, Blockade
Engagement/Explosions/ Bombardment/Bombing

A Signal tower
⊡ Radar station
Fighter
Bomber
Ship sunk
Submarine
Aircraft carrier/ Carrier battle group
8 Fleet carrier
4 Light carrier
Battleship
Cruiser
Destroyer
Other warship
Transport
→ Movement
- -▶ Retreat
Front line

Fighter flight path
Bomber flight path
Helicopter flight path

Other symbols used on maps

• Town
○ Capital city
▲ Oilfield
═ Bridge
Mountain/High ground
Rivers
Seas and lakes
Roads
Railroad
Borders

7

The Colonial Wars: 1512-1774

merican Indians from warrior-hunter societies may have felt both curiosity and apprehension at the arrival of the first, small groups of Europeans from Spain, France, the Netherlands, and England. Ostensibly, there seemed little to fear from these men who arrived from Europe without knowledge of Indian regional languages, customs, power relations, or geography. There were few bow men among these newcomers and they arrived without women or adequate stocks of food. The colonizers' metal-edged tools and weapons were impressive, however, and their matchlock muskets could be frightening novelties, as in the Battle of Lake Champlain (1609), and devastating when massed in ambushes like those at Mystic, Connecticut (1637) and Siwanay, New York (1644). Used individually, however, matchlocks were inaccurate, unreliable, and useless in the rain or the dark. Surprise, so essential to hunter-warrior combat, was impossible because of the burning matchcords of this style of musket, which gave away position because of the smell, sound, and light they produced.

Confronting New and Ancient Enmities

Some American Indian communities, like the Calusa of southern Florida who probably encountered the Spanish first in their role as slave traders, consistently drove off the Spaniards with showers of arrows. Other communities, like the confident

Tuscaloosa Choctaw, were soon destroyed by the Spanish explorer Hernando de Soto's well equipped army (1539-42), which won its only pitched battle at Mabila, near the confluence of the Tombigbee and Alabama rivers (1541) and unknowingly introduced diseases, including smallpox, measles, and dysentery, which killed thousands. Major tribal confederacies, like the ancient alliance of the Huron and Iroquois in the eastern Great Lakes area, confidently attempted to enlist the Europeans as dependent allies in their own warfare and diplomacy. Smaller groups, like the Roanokes and Wampanoags, sought the support of Europeans in struggles with their more powerful neighbors.

Ancient enmities between American Indian nations continued to take precedence over any concerted "racial" wars against the European arrivals until the middle of the eighteenth century. The population of eastern North America continued to fall until about 1700, due primarily to American Indian deaths from transplanted European diseases. Losses were heaviest in the more densely populated corn-growing societies like the Massachusetts, the Iroquois, and the Huron. One less obvious consequence of this tragedy was that it reduced competition for land and game, contributing to the relatively peaceful initial European settlements at both Québec (1608) and Plymouth (1620). The Iroquois, on the other hand, counteracted population decline by launching a

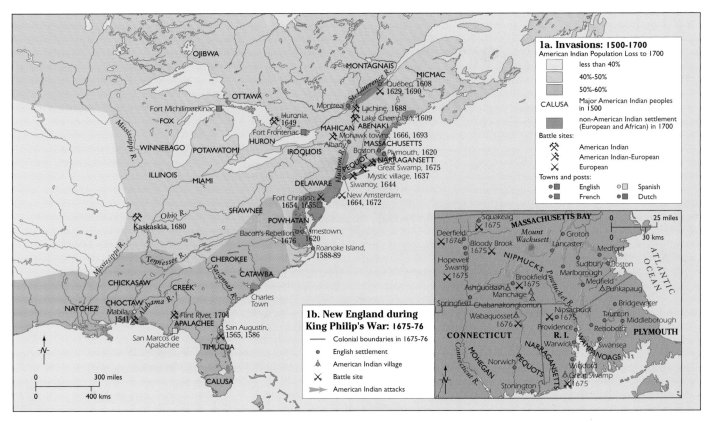

series of successful "mourning wars" to replace their dead with adopted captives taken while destroying or dispersing Iroquois-speaking Huron (1649), Petun (1650), Erie (1657), and Susquehannock (1680) neighbors.

European Aggression

Although most American Indians remained preoccupied with their traditional enemies, European settlement among the Indians accounted for a succession of local wars between 1600 and 1675. These struggles continued throughout the colonial period. Among the more persistent were the Anglo-Powhatan wars of 1609-14, 1622-32, and 1644-46 which ended in conquest by the English. The Mohawk-French wars of 1609-24, 1650-67, and 1687-1701, and the Mohawk wars in the St. Lawrence, Lake Champlain, and Lake Ontario regions were all conflicts which ended in a draw. As aggressive confiscators of American Indian land or as trading partners and allies willing to prove themselves in intertribal conflict, Europeans readily fought American Indians. The Dutch of New York fought Keift's War (1639-45) against the Mohawk, and the Peach War (1655-57) and Esopus wars (1659-60, 1663-64) against the Delaware in the Hudson River Valley. From the Anglo-Powhattan and Pequot wars (1637) to Bacon's Rebellion, and King Philip's War (1675-76) to the Tuscarora (1711-13) and the Yamasee (1715-28) wars, colonial Englishmen belligerently expanded alliances, landholdings, and slaveholdings by assaulting neighboring Indians, supplying arms, or buying Indian slave captives.

Europeans, like the American Indians, always gave their own rivalries precedence and did not unite with other Europeans in conflicts against the American Indians. From the time of the Franco-Spanish battle over San Augustín in present-day northeast Florida (1565), to the Swedish-Dutch conflict over Fort Christina in present-day southern New Jersey (1654-55), and the English capture of Dutch New Amsterdam, modern-day Manhattan (1664, 1672), Europeans routinely exported their wars to the New World but, before 1685, seldom carried the peace settlements they reached elsewhere to the North American continent.

European aggression in North America had many roots and purposes, but initially one prominent motivation was the hope of intercepting precious metals from American mines that were bolstering Spanish power in Europe. The French (1564) and English (1586) ventures in northeastern Florida, as well as those by Humphrey Gilbert in Newfoundland (1578-83) and Sir Walter Raleigh on Roanoke Island off North Carolina (1585-89), centered on the purpose of obtaining Spanish-American silver and gold.

Between 1689 and 1714, European powers generally left their colonial fighting to their settlers. Although outnumber-

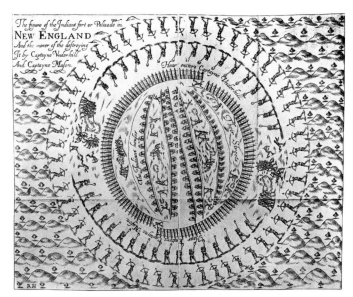

English expansion into the Connecticut River Valley led to Pequot Indian raids on Saybrook and Wethersfield, Connecticut. Captain John Mason and 280 colonists retaliated by setting fire to the Pequot fortified village of Mystic near present-day Groton, Connecticut, on 25 May 1637. The 100 Mohican allies accompanying the English did not participate in the assault on the village, but joined in killing 600-1,000 Pequots as they fled the flames. This illustration of the attack accompanied Captain John Underhill's memoir published in London in 1638.

ing the French in Canada by sixteen to one, English colonists were divided and faced two major disadvantages. Any overland attack on the St. Lawrence Valley heartland of New France funneled invaders into the Lake Champlain-Richelieu River waterway, while the French could raid a wide variety of targets using that same route. New France also had an extensive fur trade alliance with unknown numbers of Algonquin-speaking hunters, trappers, and customers, as well as mission villages with hundreds of Iroquois and Abenaki converts and refugees. To counter this alliance, the English forged their "covenant chain" alliance with the Iroquois, building upon the latter's long-standing rivalry with the Huron, Mohican, and Montagnais allies of New France. Similarly, South Carolina supported the Creek in the destruction of the Apalachee-Spanish missions of northwest Florida (1702-04), culminating in the decisive victory at Flint River (1704), near where the river meets the Chattahoochie.

Making Alliances

By 1689, most eastern American Indians were armed with improved flintlock muskets and needed to be linked to a European supply of gunpowder. Their best chance to halt or reverse white settler encroachment was to stage guerrilla wars

On 29 February 1704, the French with Indian allies attacked Deerfield, Massachussetts, killing or carrying into captivity over half of the village's 291 residents in one of the bloodiest events of Queen Anne's War. Reverend John Williams' eyewitness account in The Redeemed Captive *was published in 1707.*

against the English, whom they fought as allies of New France. With the exception of the Yamasee War (1715–17) and Pontiac's War (1763–66), American Indian tribes never confederated effectively to conduct war against colonial Europeans who had been deprived of all their Indian allies.

In each of the first two Anglo-French wars, King William's War of 1689–97 and Queen Anne's War of 1702–13, a certain equilibrium developed. New France and her American Indian allies struck the first serious blows in each war, and the English colonies responded with the more conventional sieges of Port Royal, Nova Scotia (1690, 1707, 1710), and Québec (1690, 1711). The sieges exhausted English colonials' enthusiasm and resources and seriously threatened New France. Belligerence subsided or was diverted towards American Indians, as in the English wars with the Tuscarora (1711–13) and the Yamasee (1715–28) in the Carolinas, French attacks on the

Iroquois (1693, 1696) in New York, and on the Fox tribe at Detroit (1712).

The Anglo-French Peace of Utrecht (1713) did not bring a lasting peace to North America. New England settlers fought the eastern Abenaki again in Dummer's War (1722–27), after New Englanders had attacked villages at Penobscot and Norridgewock, in present-day Maine, in 1722. On their southern frontiers, English settlers were spasmodically fighting both the Spanish (1702–13, 1718–21, 1726–28, 1739–44) and their allies, the Yamasee (1715–28). San Augustín's formidable Castillo de San Marcos withstood English sieges in 1702, 1728, and 1740. The Anglo-Spanish frontier was relatively calm during the twenty years after 1743, and it was the British conquest of Havana, Cuba in 1762 that prompted Spain to cede Pensacola and Florida to the British the following year. During the same era, the French challenged the Spanish at Pensacola (1719), and fought major wars with the Fox (1711–38) and the Natchez (1729–30) in the Mississippi Valley, and with the Chickasaw (1736, 1739–40) in present-day Mississippi and Alabama.

French Fortifications

The French also used this time to build major fortifications. The best of the forts were massive, earth-filled walls faced with logs or stone and vulnerable only to artillery fire. By 1744, these forts forced a fundamental change in North American warfare: Artillery trains were now needed, as were roads on which to haul them, and armies to escort them. Besides building four forts in Louisiana country, the French tried to secure what was now an overextended St. Lawrence-Great Lakes frontier. They began rebuilding Fort Niagara in 1720 and started building the massive defenses at Louisbourg on Cape Breton Island that same year, adding Fort St. Frédéric on Lake Champlain in 1731. The English responded feebly by stockading small forts at Oswego (1727) and Saratoga (1738) in present-day New York State.

When the Anglo-French struggle resumed in 1744, the North American portion of the conflict was launched from Louisbourg, with a successful surprise attack on the small, regular British garrison that protected the New England fishery at Canso, Nova Scotia. New England's response was the conquest of Louisbourg, where New England land forces were complemented by a British naval squadron that blockaded Louisbourg harbor. The next year the French sent an unprecedented armada of seventy-six ships to recover Louisbourg, but these were destroyed on the North Atlantic by storms, calms, and diseases. Meanwhile, Canadian and Indian forces balanced these disasters by capturing English outposts at Saratoga, Fort Massachusetts, and Grand Pré, Nova Scotia in 1746. There were signs of increasing imperial commitment to North American war: The French fleet sent and lost in 1746, British government funding of American provincial forces who mustered that year, and even the impressment riot in Boston late in 1747 which resulted from an enlarged British naval presence to protect the maritime frontier of New England. The British also began to build their naval station and military colony at Halifax, Nova Scotia, the year after the Peace of Aix-la-Chapelle (1748) returned Louisbourg to the French.

The French and Indian War

The climactic struggle known as the French and Indian War in the British colonies and the Seven Years' War in Europe, began as a local, intercolonial struggle for trade and land in the upper Ohio country. After hastily constructed Virginian stockades at the forks of the Ohio River and nearby at Fort Necessity were surrendered to Canadians in 1754, Britain and France began to reinforce their colonists with unprecedented numbers of regular troops from Europe.

In the first four years of fighting (1754-58), the Indians, Canadians, and French successfully defeated British armies and garrisons and brought demoralizing guerrilla warfare to British colonial farms in New York, Pennsylvania, Maryland, and Virginia. Three of four British initiatives of 1755 failed.

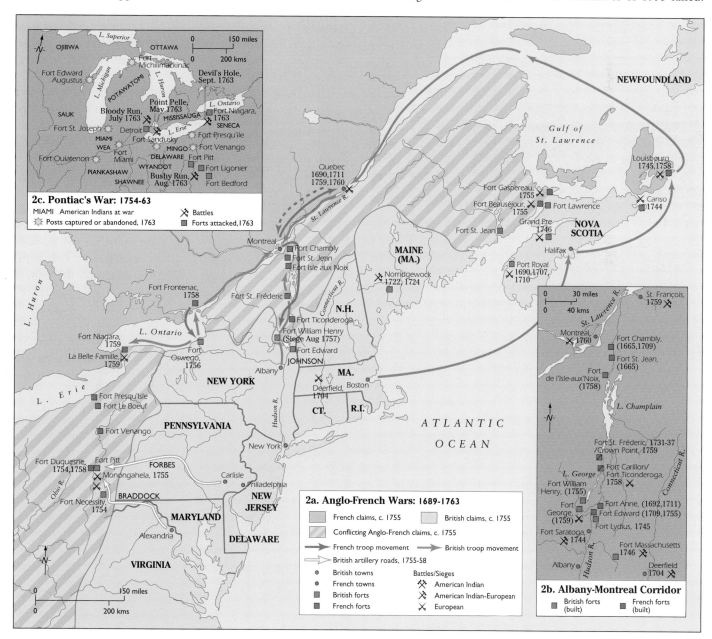

2c. Pontiac's War: 1754-63
MIAMI American Indians at war
☼ Posts captured or abandoned, 1763
✕ Battles
■ Forts attacked, 1763

2a. Anglo-French Wars: 1689-1763
French claims, c. 1755
British claims, c. 1755
Conflicting Anglo-French claims, c. 1755
→ French troop movement
→ British troop movement
▷ British artillery roads, 1755-58
● British towns
● French towns
■ British forts
■ French forts
Battles/Sieges
✕ American Indian
✕ American Indian-European
✕ European

2b. Albany-Montreal Corridor
■ British forts (built)
■ French forts (built)

General Edward Braddock's army was destroyed near its target, Fort Duquesne on the Ohio River. British colonial armies sent against Fort Niagara and Fort St. Frédéric failed to reach their objectives, though they won a ragged defensive battle at Lake George. Only the tiny French fortifications of Fort Beauséjour and Fort Gaspereau on the isthmus that linked Acadia to the mainland fell, due to a surprise attack by overwhelming numbers. Indian raids paralyzed the back country of Pennsylvania and Virginia from 1755-57, driving frontier settlements eastward by as much as 200 miles. French forces made quick work of the sieges of Fort Oswego in 1756 and Fort William Henry in 1757, both in present-day New York State. From that time, British naval blockades hindered French reinforcement of Canada while more British regulars continued to arrive. General Louis Montcalm's defensive preoccupations came into increasing conflict with the more aggressive strategy of the Governor of New France, Pierre-François de Rigaud, Marquis de Vandreuil; and the disgusted American Indians withdrew most of their support after 1757.

The British and colonial response had, until 1758, been slow, inadequate, and divided. Under British Prime Minister William Pitt's leadership, the British government massively increased direct spending on the American war and subsidized more of the colonial contributions. The British regained the offensive for the first time in three years and this time their armies took three of their four objectives: Louisbourg, Fort Frontenac, and Fort Duquesne. Montcalm's victory at Fort Carillon (Ticonderoga) was a surprising success in what was becoming a defensive French strategy in the face of more numerous and better supplied opponents. In July 1759, a major Canadian-American Indian relief force was sent from the Ohio country to help the besieged Fort Niagara. The relief force was destroyed in the Battle of La Belle Famille and the fort was surrendered the next day. That month the last siege of Québec also began, ending three months later with British victory on the adjoining Plains of Abraham. Although French and Canadian forces returned to win a battle there the next spring, their victory was nullified when a British naval squadron managed to reach the St. Lawrence in May, a week before the arrival of the French naval forces. In September 1760, within forty-eight hours of each other, three British armies led by the Brigadier General James Murray, Colonel William Haviland, and General Jeffrey Amherst converged on Montreal in a feat of logistics that brought the prompt surrender of New France.

A Shift in Alliances

Most American Indian communities had been quick to read the signs of increasing English strength and to accept British and Six Nations advice to remain neutral. The Shawnee, Delaware, and Mingo tribes withdrew from the French before Fort Duquesne fell in 1758. A thousand American Indians in the Fort Niagara relief force withdrew support just before their Canadian allies were defeated in July 1759. Few American Indians, even from French missions, fought with the final defenders of Québec and Montreal. In contrast, the Cherokee, who had been active British allies, began a three-year war against the British in 1759. The British sent increasingly powerful invasion forces into the mountainous Cherokee country of eastern Tennessee in each of the three summers of the war. Reinforcement failed to prevent the surrender of the starving two-hundred-man British garrison at Fort Loudon, but the British eventually destroyed nineteen evacuated Cherokee towns. The Cherokees eventually won a negotiated peace, but, in view of multitribal cooperation in the Indian wars against the British in 1763, it is striking that the Cherokee did not find any Indian allies.

The Peace of Paris (1763), unlike the three preceding Anglo-French peace settlements, was decisive because the French government surrendered North America. No longer able to pit French against English, the American Indians soon found that the English were not accommodating. The British reneged on their promises to withdraw from the Ohio country and white hunters and settlers flooded into Indian land. Britain ended its extravagant war spending. When the military budget was drastically cut, the result was open mutiny among a few regular British regiments. Additionally, there was widespread Indian discontent because of the end of traditional tribute gifts, because liquor sales were banned, and because gunpowder became scarce and expensive.

Indian War

Disillusioned American Indians launched what is inaccurately called Pontiac's War (1763-66), against British forts in the Great Lakes and Ohio country. Such a name implies a level of leadership that Pontiac did not possess. In fact, the conflict erupted when warriors of fifteen tribes captured nine widely dispersed western British posts in May and June 1763. The stronger and well-provisioned posts of Fort Pitt, Fort Detroit, and Fort Niagara were besieged in vain, but reinforcements for the last two of these posts were destroyed at Point Pelee on the shore of Lake Erie; Bloody Run, four miles north of Detroit; and Devil's Hole, ten miles south of Fort Niagara. In raids against the Maryland, Virginia, and Pennsylvania frontier settlements, Indians killed and captured about two thousand settlers. The only major British success came when Colonel Henry Bouquet was sent to relieve Fort Pitt. His troops won the only field engagement of the war, a ferocious two-day battle at Bushy Run, in August 1763. The Royal Proclamation of 1763, with its provision of a clear line dividing the European colonies from Indian-controlled land came too late to avert the conflict, but it became part of the negotiated settlement.

The next decade was peaceful despite relentless colonial intrusion on Ohio Indian lands, but in 1774 the Shawnee fought the brief Lord Dunmore's War against the Virginians. After an indecisive military campaign in which the Shawnee killed 81 and wounded 140, but failed to rout 2,400 militia at Point Pleasant, where the Kanawha River meets the Ohio, an uneasy truce settled over the region. In the subsequent chaos of the American Revolution, Virginians came to interpret Point Pleasant as their conquest, and the truce that followed as Shawnee surrender of Kentucky.

The expansive territory Britain had just won in North America would not be held for long. Despite the royal proclamations, the migrant invasion of American Indian country accelerated. The British government was deeply in debt, its army was too reduced to police the new American frontiers, and its colonists soon proved unwilling to accept additional imperial taxes to pay for such policing. Britain's conquest of French Canada had ended the Indian strategy of playing one European power against another, but the white men were about to divide again, when thirteen of Britain's North American colonies rose in rebellion against the mother country.

The climax of the Anglo-French struggle in North America came when the French General Louis de Montcalm (above) and 16,000 defenders of Québec were forced into an open engagement on the Plains of Abraham and defeated by the British General James Wolfe (below) with only 4,400 troops on 13 September 1759. Both commanders were mortally wounded in this decisive, thirty-minute battle.

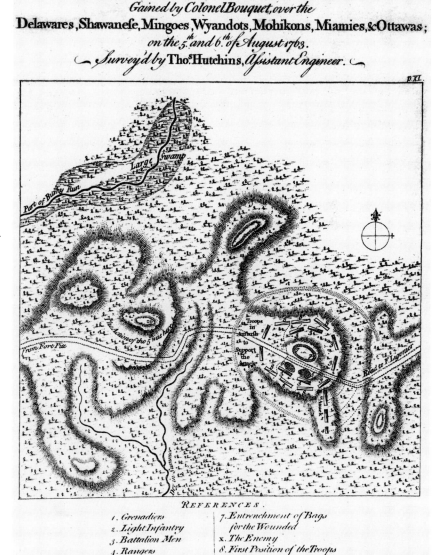

PLAN OF THE BATTLE NEAR BUSHY-RUN,
Gained by Colonel Bouquet, over the
Delawares, Shawanese, Mingoes, Wyandots, Mohikons, Miamies, & Ottawas;
on the 5th and 6th of August 1763.
Survey'd by Tho.s Hutchins, Assistant Engineer.

REFERENCES.
1. Grenadiers
2. Light Infantry
3. Battalion Men
4. Rangers
5. Cattle
6. Horses
7. Entrenchment of Bags for the Wounded
x. The Enemy
8. First Position of the Troops
□ □ Graves

This contemporary map (right) illustrates the Battle of Bushy Run. Colonel Henry Bouquet's forces won the two-day engagement, 26 miles east of Pittsburgh, Pennsylvania in 1763.

The American Revolutionary War: 1775-83

At dawn on the morning of 19 April 1775, a column of 700 British regulars was fast approaching the village green at Lexington, Massachusetts. There, a band of seventy militia waited. They were not looking for a fight; rather, they intended to protest the presence of these British soldiers on the soil of freeborn English subjects during peacetime. As the British advance line neared the green, a mysterious gunshot rang out. The regulars responded with a flurry of musket fire that left eight patriot militia dead and ten wounded. This action ignited the eight-year war for independence waged by Great Britain's thirteen colonies. With the formal signing of peace accords in Paris in September 1783, those colonies—Connecticut, Delaware, Georgia, Maryland, Massachusetts, New Hampshire, New Jersey, New York, North Carolina, Pennsylvania, Rhode Island, South Carolina, and Virginia—emerged victorious as the United States of America. The war resulted from tensions which had grown for more than a decade between Britain and thirteen of its North American dominions. Between the years 1763 and 1775, issues of taxation and political liberties drove the two sides farther apart, and the skirmish at Lexington provided the final spark resulting in Anglo-American civil war.

The Origins of the War: 1763-75

Britain's participation in the French and Indian War in North America (1754-63) and in the Seven Years' War in Europe (1756-63) brought the nation a brilliant victory as well as a new set of problems. The British acquired the North American colonial possessions of France and took east and west Florida from Spain. While the conquest of Canada eliminated the French as a threat to England's North American colonies, the government of the British king, George III, also had to grapple with the costs of administering and policing its newly expanded empire. The wars had caused the British home government's debt to skyrocket from seventy-five million to one hundred thirty-seven million pounds. George III's ministers and parliament did not expect their American brethren to contribute to the decrease of this debt, but they fully expected them to absorb an increased proportion of the ongoing costs of imperial administration, such as paying for regular troops and royal officials working in the colonies. The Americans paid few local taxes, compared to British subjects living in Great Britain, who bore very heavy tax burdens. In March 1765, the king and his parliament adopted the Stamp Act, which placed taxes on a long list of goods ranging from newspapers and pamphlets to legal documents, with the purpose of gaining revenue from the colonists.

Americans reacted with levels of rage that stunned leaders in Britain. From the beginning of the eighteenth century, the colonies had conducted their own affairs with little assistance or interference from London, especially from 1700 to 1760, the so-called "era of salutary neglect." The Stamp Act and other actions, such as the Royal Proclamation of 1763, that stopped the colonists from expanding further into American Indian lands to the west, represented a reversal in British policy that seemed to threaten the colonists "rights as Englishmen" to liberty and property. Colonial leaders, pointing out that the colonies had no representation in the British Parliament, raised the cry of "no taxation without representation." Riots and violence erupted in several North American cities. In March 1766, the king and parliament gave into American

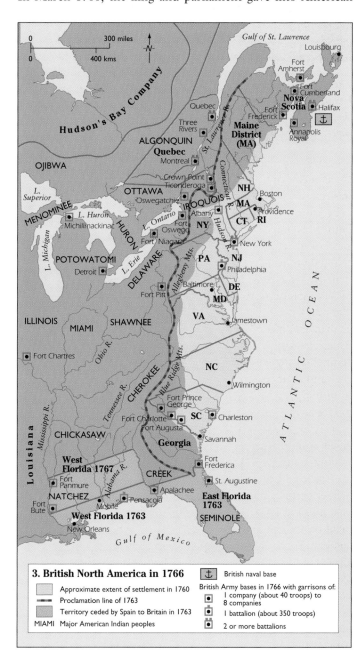

3. British North America in 1766

⚓ British naval base

▢ Approximate extent of settlement in 1760

▬ Proclamation line of 1763

▢ Territory ceded by Spain to Britain in 1763

MIAMI Major American Indian peoples

British Army bases in 1766 with garrisons of:
▣ 1 company (about 40 troops) to 8 companies
▣ 1 battalion (about 350 troops)
▣ 2 or more battalions

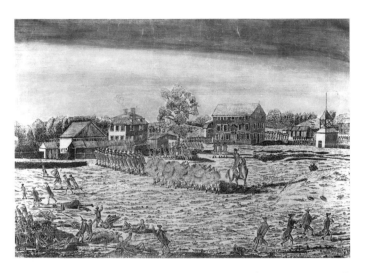

The American artist Ralph Earl made this sketch for an engraving of Lexington Green and the events that marked the beginning of the American Revolutionary War in April 1775, among the first American historical prints.

pressure and repealed the Stamp Act, but also passed the Declaratory Act, in which Britain's right to tax the colonials was reasserted, a measure which contributed to further tension.

In June 1767, the British Parliament passed the Townshend Duties revenue act placing taxes on a variety of goods such as glass, lead, and tea. This measure sparked a new round of colonial protest. As before, the inhabitants of Boston were particularly rancorous. In response, London sent British regulars to Massachusetts to enforce its will. On 5 March 1770, soldiers and Bostonians clashed in the streets, resulting in five civilian fatalities. The so-called "Boston Massacre" provided American patriot leaders with a powerful weapon that featured compelling images of impending tyranny unless British officials and their red-coated soldiers desisted. As the 1770s began to unfold, Americans were increasingly vigilant about watching for any new imperial assaults on their rights and liberties.

In 1773, Britain's problems with the American colonies dovetailed with another issue. The British East India Company, a trading company operating in India founded in 1600, was on the verge of bankruptcy and blamed the loss of its American market partially on the cheap Dutch tea which was being smuggled into the colonies. To help the company, the British Parliament passed the Tea Act, which lowered the price of the British company's tea in the American marketplace to make it more attractive to customers, even with the addition of duty. Patriot leaders saw this as yet another threat to American rights. On 16 December 1773, Bostonians disguised as American Indians boarded docked merchant ships and dumped 342 chests of tea into Boston Harbor. From March to May 1774, the British Parliament responded with the Coercive Acts, which among other

things, closed the port of Boston until the locals could pay for the discarded tea and also altered the charter of the Massachusetts government. General Thomas Gage, British military commander in North America was appointed the colony's new governor and he was sent there accompanied by hundreds of troops. Tyranny became the colonists' watchword.

That summer, delegates from every colony except Georgia gathered at the First Continental Congress in Philadelphia, where radical leaders dominated the proceedings. Among its actions, this congress approved a plan that would lead to a boycott of British trade and called upon colonists everywhere to prepare themselves for defensive military actions, unless some means could be found to get the British to change their policies. In Massachusetts, the militia began drilling troops and building up military supplies. In February 1775, King George III declared that Massachusetts was in a state of rebellion and General Gage began to send expeditions into the countryside to seize patriot weapons caches. The British column intercepted by the Lexington militia on 19 April 1775 was on such a mission.

Commanded by Lieutenant Colonel Francis Smith, the British soldiers regrouped on Lexington Green and they continued on toward Concord, another five miles down the road. As they began to destroy military stores the patriots had failed to remove, provincial militia began to converge on Concord. At the town's North Bridge, militia clashed with British light infantry, and the outnumbered British troops retreated. Smith soon ordered a general withdrawal to Boston. As the column limped back to the city, Massachusetts militia harassed the British soldiers, firing from behind trees and stone fences. During the course of the operation, the 1,800 British troops engaged that day, including a relief column commanded by Hugh, Lord Percy, suffered 273 casualties before regaining the safety of Boston. The Massachusetts citizen-forces, eventually aided by militia from other New England colonies and nominally commanded by Artemas Ward, began an impromptu siege of Gage's force in Boston.

From Skirmish to War in the Northern Theater

The Massachusetts Committee of Safety began to act as an administrative body to help cope with the situation. Acting on advice from Connecticut militia Captain Benedict Arnold, this body concocted a plan to seize Fort Ticonderoga on Lake Champlain, with the idea of capturing dozens of artillery pieces there. Captain Arnold was selected to lead the expedition against Fort Ticonderoga, but Ethan Allen of Vermont and his Green Mountain Boys were already organizing an attack force. The two men quarreled, but then agreed to share command prerogatives. Under cover of darkness on 10 May 1775, they succeeded in surprising the small British garrison

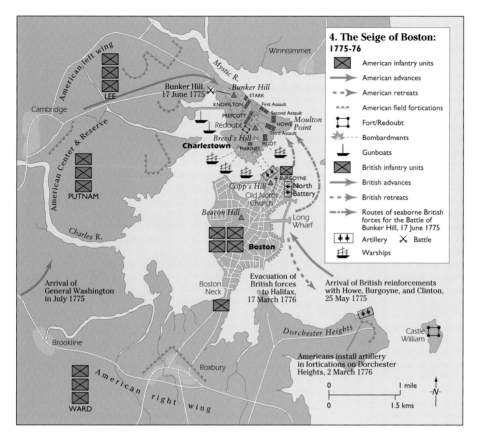

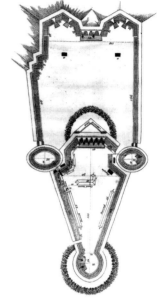

After dislodging American forces from Charlestown near Boston, the British erected fortifications which they occupied until their withdrawal from Boston in March 1776. This plan of the British redoubt on Bunker's Hill was drawn by a British officer who was serving in the area.

at Fort Ticonderoga. Another bit of daring action resulted in the capture of Crown Point, twelve miles to the north, two days later. Their control of the two forts netted the patriots about one hundred serviceable pieces of ordnance as well as a clear route for a possible invasion of Canada by moving north through Lake Champlain.

The British did not remain idle. In late May, British reinforcements, along with generals William Howe, John Burgoyne, and Henry Clinton, arrived in Boston to bolster Gage's command. On June 16, the patriots got the attention of the British by digging in on Breed's Hill on the Charlestown peninsula north of Boston. Originally, the American forces under William Prescott and Israel Putnam planned to fortify the higher promontory of Bunker's Hill, but they inexplicably took up a position on the lower hill. On June 17, Gage and Howe landed 2,500 soldiers to drive off the patriot forces, but rather than employ a flanking movement and seize the neck of land behind Breed's Hill, the British generals opted for a frontal assault in a ploy designed to impress the Americans with the impossibility of their standing against British regulars. The Americans repulsed two charges with bloody results for the British, but on the third attempt, the regulars carried the position as the patriots withdrew for want of ammunition. Technically, the British had scored a victory by winning the

field, but at a terrible price. To Howe's mortification, their loss was 1,054 casualties, forty percent of those engaged. He never forgot the cost of directly assaulting entrenched patriot troops.

As the summer of 1775 progressed, some American rebels sought to expand the conflict. At first the Second Continental Congress, which began to convene in Philadelphia in May, rebuffed any idea of mounting an expedition into Canada to secure Québec as the fourteenth colony. By midsummer, however, the notion of taking Québec to strengthen the patriot cause while sealing off the St. Lawrence River-Lake Champlain-Hudson River corridor as a natural highway of invasion, had gained majority support in the Continental Congress. Two forces undertook the mission. One, under the command of General Richard Montgomery moved northward from Lake Champlain along the Richelieu River. This attempt to seize Montreal failed in September, but succeeded two months later on 13 November. Another column of 1,100 men commanded by Benedict Arnold forged its way on an epic march through the Maine wilderness. In mid-November he arrived outside the walls of Québec with 650 bedraggled survivors. On the night of 31 December, Arnold and Montgomery launched an attack on the fortress city during a severe blizzard. Montgomery was killed and Arnold was badly wounded as the British repulsed the assault. Arnold doggedly maintained a

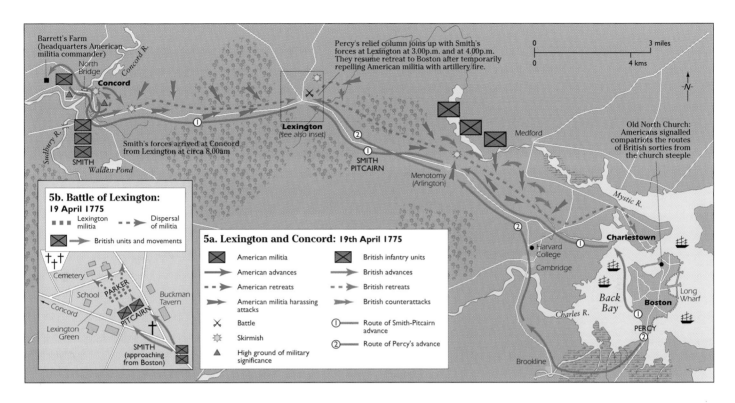

Barrett's Farm (headquarters American militia commander)

North Bridge

Concord

Smith's forces arrived at Concord from Lexington at circa 8.00am

SMITH

Walden Pond

Sudbury R.

Concord R.

Percy's relief column joins up with Smith's forces at Lexington at 3.00p.m. and at 4.00p.m. They resume retreat to Boston after temporarily repelling American militia with artillery fire.

Lexington
(see also inset)

SMITH
PITCAIRN

Menotomy (Arlington)

Medford

Mystic R.

Old North Church: Americans signalled compatriots the routes of British sorties from the church steeple

Harvard College

Cambridge

Charlestown

Back Bay

Charles R.

Boston

Long Wharf

PERCY

Brookline

0 ——— 3 miles
0 ——— 4 kms
-N-

5b. Battle of Lexington:
19 April 1775

- ▪▪▪ Lexington militia
- - - ▶ Dispersal of militia
- ⊠ ▶ British units and movements

Cemetery

PARKER

School

Buckman Tavern

Concord

Lexington Green

PITCAIRN

SMITH (approaching from Boston)

5a. Lexington and Concord: 19th April 1775

⊠ American militia	⊠ British infantry units
▶ American advances	▶ British advances
- -▶ American retreats	- -▶ British retreats
▶ American militia harassing attacks	▶ British counterattacks
✕ Battle	① Route of Smith-Pitcairn advance
☀ Skirmish	② Route of Percy's advance
▲ High ground of military significance	

siege for a few months, but patriot forces, ravaged by smallpox, were run out of Canada by British relief forces in June 1776.

As it approved this action to seize Canada, the Continental Congress also supported the colonial army besieging Boston, authorizing companies of Pennsylvania, Maryland, and Virginia riflemen to bolster its ranks and involving more of the colonies in the defense of liberty. John Adams of Massachusetts proposed the appointment of George Washington of Virginia to the post of commander-in-chief. A move that was intended to guarantee intercolonial support for the cause also provided an individual of strong character and commitment to the fledgling Continental Army's top post.

By July 1775, Washington was in Massachusetts, taking on the difficult task of imposing discipline and order on the citizen-soldiers besieging Boston. His immediate objective was to forge an army which could drive the British from the city. He also dispatched his artillery chief, Colonel Henry Knox, to bring the ordnance captured at Fort Ticonderoga to bolster the siege. After a harrowing winter march, Knox brought the badly needed guns, and the Continentals went to work placing them in fortifications on Dorchester Heights, south of Boston. As the morning of 5 March 1776 dawned, Howe, who had replaced Gage in October as the overall British commander in North America, found his position untenable, and decided to evacuate his forces to Halifax, Nova Scotia. This bloodless triumph did much to bolster American spirits, but the summer of 1776 brought new difficulties to the patriot cause.

The ministers in London, now realizing they had a full-scale rebellion on their hands, began to put Britain's rusty machinery of war into motion. Both the army and the Royal Navy had fallen into disrepair since the Seven Years' War, with the army claiming 48,000 troops and the navy listing 139 ships of the line. Although the army began recruiting, training, and equipping new regiments, this was a time-consuming process when a ready supply of troops was needed. The ministry of Lord Frederick North obtained the services of regiments from several of the petty princelings of northern Germany. These "Hessian" soldiers eventually totaled approximately 30,000 soldiers. Even so, the strategic task facing the British military establishment was formidable. The eastern seaboard of the North American continent stretched about 1,500 miles from Maine to Georgia, and the American colonies had no center of political or strategic gravity whose capture would break the rebellion. Subduing and controlling such an immense, sprawling area would seem to be beyond the ability of any of the limited European forces. To its credit, the North ministry developed a reasonably sound strategy; namely, to send an expeditionary force consisting of 30,000 soldiers under General William Howe and a fleet of about 450 vessels under his brother, Admiral Lord Howe, to New York City. The city would provide a central base from which British forces could operate, either across New Jersey to seize Philadelphia, or northward up the Hudson River Valley to sever New England from the rest of the colonies.

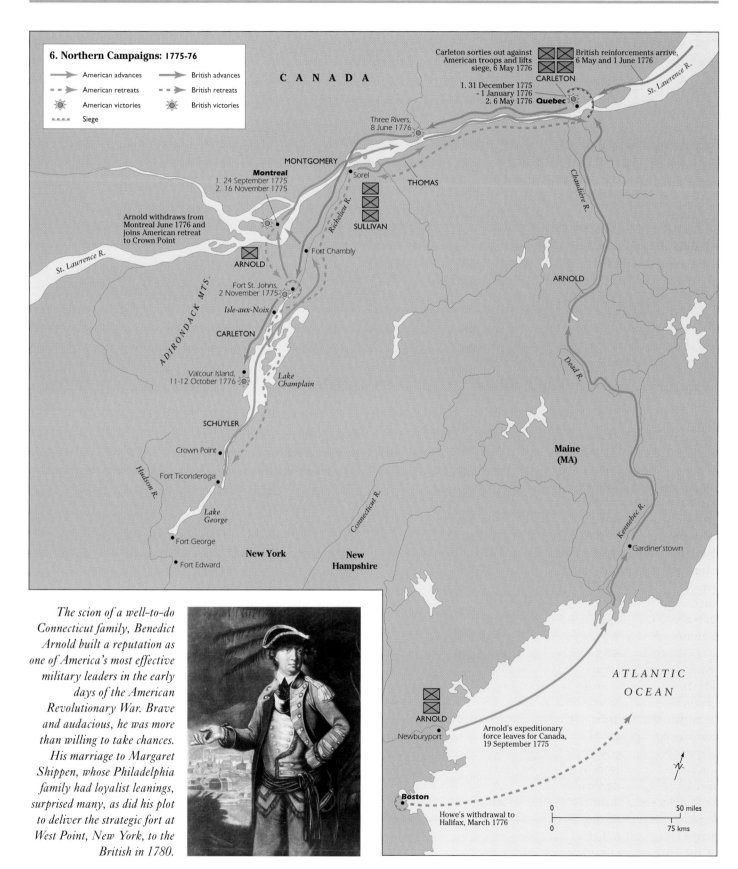

6. Northern Campaigns: 1775-76

American advances
American retreats
American victories
Siege
British advances
British retreats
British victories

C A N A D A

Carleton sorties out against American troops and lifts siege, 6 May 1776

British reinforcements arrive, 6 May and 1 June 1776

CARLETON

1. 31 December 1775 - 1 January 1776
2. 6 May 1776 **Quebec**

St. Lawrence R.

Three Rivers, 8 June 1776

MONTGOMERY

THOMAS

Montreal
1. 24 September 1775
2. 16 November 1775

Sorel

Chaudière R.

Arnold withdraws from Montreal June 1776 and joins American retreat to Crown Point

SULLIVAN

Richelieu R.

St. Lawrence R.

Fort Chambly

ARNOLD

ARNOLD

Fort St. Johns, 2 November 1775

Isle-aux-Noix

CARLETON

ADIRONDACK MTS.

Valcour Island, 11-12 October 1776

Lake Champlain

Dead R.

Maine (MA)

SCHUYLER

Crown Point

Fort Ticonderoga

Hudson R.

Lake George

Connecticut R.

Kennebec R.

Gardiner'stown

Fort George

New York

Fort Edward

New Hampshire

ATLANTIC OCEAN

ARNOLD

Newburyport

Arnold's expeditionary force leaves for Canada, 19 September 1775

Boston

Howe's withdrawal to Halifax, March 1776

0   50 miles
0   75 kms

The scion of a well-to-do Connecticut family, Benedict Arnold built a reputation as one of America's most effective military leaders in the early days of the American Revolutionary War. Brave and audacious, he was more than willing to take chances. His marriage to Margaret Shippen, whose Philadelphia family had loyalist leanings, surprised many, as did his plot to deliver the strategic fort at West Point, New York, to the British in 1780.

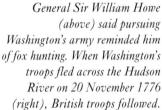

General Sir William Howe (above) said pursuing Washington's army reminded him of fox hunting. When Washington's troops fled across the Hudson River on 20 November 1776 (right), British troops followed.

Washington also understood the importance of New York, and despite the hindrance of short-term enlistments, he managed to scrape together a force of 28,000 men by August 1776 to defend the city. Despite the boost to morale that the issuing of the Declaration of Independence in July provided, this army was ill-prepared to face the British onslaught. Washington's force lacked experience and training and it was split between Manhattan and Long Island, a potentially fatal predicament in the face of an enemy with naval superiority. These weaknesses were exposed with a vengeance during the Battle of Long Island (27 August 1776), when Howe's multipronged attack inflicted 1,500 casualties on the rebels and forced a rout which left Washington with his back to the East River. The British did not press their advantage, however, and the patriot army escaped across the river under the cover of a fortuitous fog.

This pattern of defeat, retreat, and escape continued during the ensuing weeks and months. Washington withdrew from Manhattan while leaving some 6,000 troops in forts Washington and Lee to guard the Hudson River. On 28 October, Howe brushed aside the rebel army at White Plains, then doubled back to seize the forts. On 16 November, Fort Washington fell and the British took 2,000 American prisoners. Two days later, a force led by Major General Charles Lord Cornwallis captured Fort Lee. Meanwhile, after detaching a force of 8,000 under General Charles Lee to guard the Hudson highlands, Washington crossed the river with 5,000 troops and fell back across New Jersey. Hounded by Howe's columns, the remnant of the rebel army escaped across the Delaware River and into

Pennsylvania in early December. At the same time, a British force under Sir Henry Clinton seized Newport, Rhode Island, for use as a naval and foraging base.

As defeat dogged Washington's forces in the New York-New Jersey theater through the summer and fall of 1776, patriot forces in northern New York scrambled to prevent a British thrust through the Lake Champlain-Hudson River corridor. By mid-June, the ragged, smallpox-ravaged survivors of Montgomery's and Arnold's commands had evacuated Canada under the command of John Sullivan. Britain's military governor of Canada, Sir Guy Carleton, with 10,000 regulars, Canadians, and Indians at his disposal, planned to lead a force south along Lake Champlain, to seize Fort Ticonderoga, and proceed to Albany. To check the attack, Benedict Arnold hastily constructed a small patriot flotilla to defend the waterway. After some months of ship building, the rival fleets clashed off Valcour Island on Lake Champlain on 11 October 1776. Arnold's makeshift squadron fought gallantly, eventually sustaining significant losses, before withdrawing under the cover of fog and darkness. The damage American forces inflicted, along with the lateness of the season, convinced Carleton to suspend operations and retreat to Canada. Arnold's boldness secured the northern frontier for the winter of 1776-77, thus freeing Washington to concentrate on the immediate problem of Howe's occupation of New Jersey.

After driving the Continentals across the Delaware River, the British commander-in-chief concluded that he had accomplished enough and ordered his forces into winter quarters. With New York in British hands, the Continental Congress in flight, and Washington's army reduced to a threadbare 2,400 troops, Howe seemed to have every justification for this decision. Yet, he underestimated the persistent temperament of his opponent. Washington instinctively understood that as long as he had an army in the field, the rebels could claim the cause was still alive. He also knew that the enlistments of many of the troops under his command were due to expire on 31 December. Thus, bold action was essential to keep any semblance of an army in the field and to bolster the patriot cause.

Fortunately for the rebels, the advance outpost at Trenton offered an inviting target. The three Hessian regiments, 1,500 troops led by Colonel Johann Rall occupying the town, had neglected to prepare fortifications. With information about the garrison's condition provided by spies, Washington planned a quick strike across the Delaware River under the cover of darkness on Christmas evening to surprise the Hessians after their holiday celebration. With his available strength desperately low, Washington could not move until Charles Lee's forces arrived. For his part, Lee was dithering to the north, spending much of his time criticizing his superior. Fortuitously, the former British major fell into the hands of a British patrol, and John Sullivan was able to assume command and link up with Washington. Thus reinforced, the Americans moved to surprise the Hessians. Though only Washington's main body made it across the icy Delaware, this column succeeded in catching the Hessians, full of holiday drink, completely off guard. The rebels captured some 1,000 troops, and Washington's forces slipped back across the river. On 30 December, the Americans crossed the Delaware again to engage British forces under General Charles, Lord Cornwallis. After a skirmish near Assunpink Creek on 2 January, Washington slipped away from Cornwallis and smashed a British brigade at Princeton. This victory obliged the British to withdraw from much of New Jersey and enabled Washington to establish winter quarters in Morristown, where he could both observe the British forces in New York and guard the approach to Philadelphia.

The Campaigns of 1777

Though they had suffered several serious reverses, the patriot forces had survived their opponent's strongest blows. Conversely, although British forces had scored seemingly significant victories, they had failed to extinguish the rebellion. Thus, stopping the conflict during the 1777 campaign fell upon the British. Lord George Germain, the American secretary and minister in charge of operations in North America, proposed coordinated operations by the armies then in New York and Canada. Howe's force would drive northward up the Hudson, while the army in Canada, now commanded by General John Burgoyne, would drive south. The two forces

would meet in Albany, severing New England from the rest of the colonies. A third force of 1,700 British regulars, Tories, and Indians under Colonel Barry St. Leger would drive from Oswego on Lake Ontario eastward down the Mohawk River, hopefully crushing patriot resistance in central New York.

General Sir William Howe, however, had other ideas. Desiring another crack at Washington after the embarrassing defeats at Trenton and Princeton, the British commander chose to sail his army around the Virginia coastline, land south of Philadelphia, and march on the city. Howe may have thought that seizing the rebel capital would bring about a patriot collapse, as such a stroke would usually prove decisive in a European conflict. Whatever his motivation, Howe did not operate in concert with Burgoyne, and in July he set sail from New York with 15,000 troops, leaving Clinton in New York with a garrison of 7,500 men, too weak to render any assistance to Burgoyne.

At the operational level, Howe's campaign proved a success. After landing at Head of Elk at the northern end of the Chesapeake Bay, about fifty miles southwest of Philadelphia, on 25 August he drove toward the city, obliging Washington to march to meet him with 11,000 troops. The two armies collided at Brandywine Creek on 11 September, with a flanking movement carrying the field for the British. Though forced to evacuate Philadelphia, the rebel army had fought well, leaving Washington eager for a rematch. On 4 October, the rebel commander struck at the British forces at Germantown with an elaborate plan involving four converging columns. The attack came apart in a fog, enabling the British to rally and defeat the Continentals, who suffered 1,000 casualties. This reverse, together with the loss of the Delaware River forts, obliged Washington to withdraw into winter quarters at Valley Forge, where the Continental Army spent a hard winter which would pass into legend. Yet these setbacks proved to be only superficial for the patriot cause. Howe's army had gained merely a comfortable city in which to pass the winter, little compensation for the consequences of Burgoyne's campaign.

The general known as "Gentleman Johnny" set out from St. John's in Canada in June 1777 with 10,000 troops and Indians. After Burgoyne's capture of Fort Ticonderoga and a strike at the retreating Americans at Hubbardton, his army's progress was soon slowed to a crawl once they left the southern end of Lake Champlain. An assortment of camp followers and baggage trains encumbered Burgoyne's force, and patriot troops under General Philip Schuyler felled trees across roads and blocked fords with boulders. The delay of Burgoyne's offensive enabled Schuyler's successor, Horatio Gates, to assemble a considerable force of New England militia. In August, the British advance began to collapse. On 16 August, a Hessian column detached from the main force to seize supplies of food

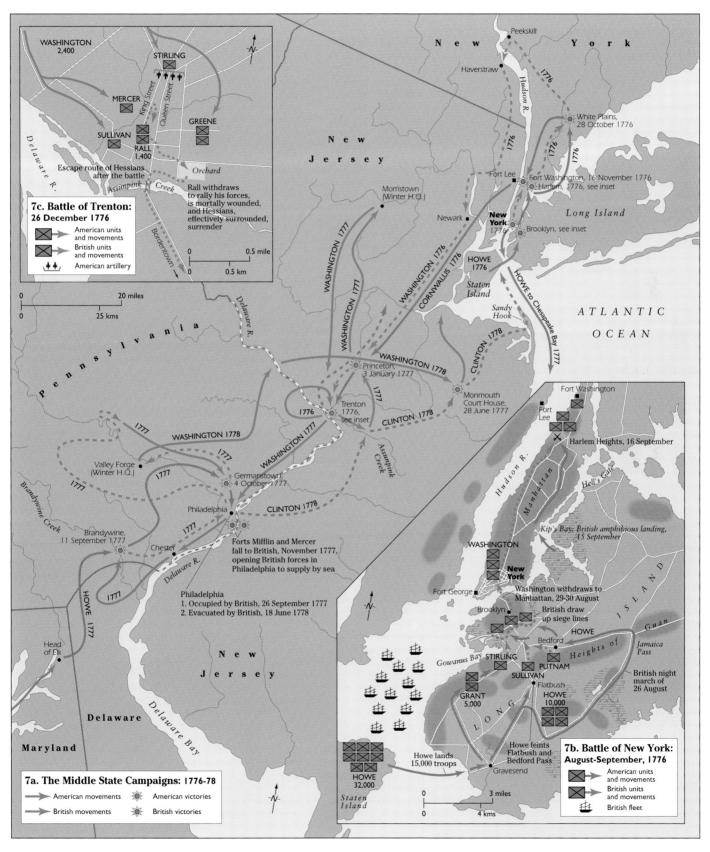

7c. Battle of Trenton:
26 December 1776

WASHINGTON
2,400

STIRLING

MERCER

GREENE

SULLIVAN

RALL
1,400

King Street

Queen Street

Orchard

Escape route of Hessians
after the battle

Assumpink Creek

Bordentown

Rall withdraws
to rally his forces,
is mortally wounded,
and Hessians,
effectively surrounded,
surrender

Delaware R.

American units
and movements

British units
and movements

American artillery

0   0.5 mile

0   0.5 km

0   20 miles

0   25 kms

Pennsylvania

Delaware R.

Valley Forge
(Winter H.Q.)

1777

1777

1777

WASHINGTON 1778

1777

1777

WASHINGTON 1777

Germantown,
4 October 1777

Philadelphia

Brandywine Creek

Brandywine,
11 September 1777

Chester

Delaware R.

HOWE 1777

1777

Head
of Elk

Delaware

Maryland

Delaware Bay

New Jersey

CLINTON 1778

Forts Mifflin and Mercer
fall to British, November 1777,
opening British forces in
Philadelphia to supply by sea

Philadelphia
1. Occupied by British, 26 September 1777
2. Evacuated by British, 18 June 1778

Trenton
1776,
see inset

1776

1777

Assumpink
Creek

WASHINGTON 1778

Princeton,
3 January 1777

WASHINGTON 1778

Monmouth
Court House,
28 June 1777

CLINTON 1778

CLINTON 1778

New Jersey

WASHINGTON 1777

WASHINGTON 1777

Morristown
(Winter H.Q.)

Newark

CORNWALLIS 1776

WASHINGTON 1776

New York

Peekskill

Haverstraw

Hudson R.

1776

1776

1776

1776

White Plains,
28 October 1776

Fort Lee

Fort Washington, 16 November 1776
Harlem, 1776, see inset

New York
1776

Brooklyn, see inset

Long Island

HOWE
1776

Staten
Island

Sandy
Hook

HOWE to Chesapeake Bay 1777

ATLANTIC
OCEAN

Fort Washington

Fort
Lee

Harlem Heights, 16 September

Hudson R.

Manhattan

Hell's Gate

Kip's Bay: British amphibious landing,
15 September

WASHINGTON

New York

Fort George

Washington withdraws to
Manhattan, 29-30 August

British draw
up siege lines

Brooklyn

Gowanus Bay

STIRLING

SULLIVAN

PUTNAM

HOWE

Bedford

Heights of Guan

Jamaica
Pass

British night
march of
26 August

GRANT
5,000

Flatbush

HOWE
10,000

LONG ISLAND

Howe lands
15,000 troops

Howe feints
Flatbush and
Bedford Pass

Gravesend

HOWE
32,000

Staten
Island

7b. Battle of New York:
August-September, 1776

American units
and movements

British units
and movements

British fleet

0   3 miles

0   4 kms

7a. The Middle State Campaigns: 1776-78

American movements   American victories

British movements   British victories

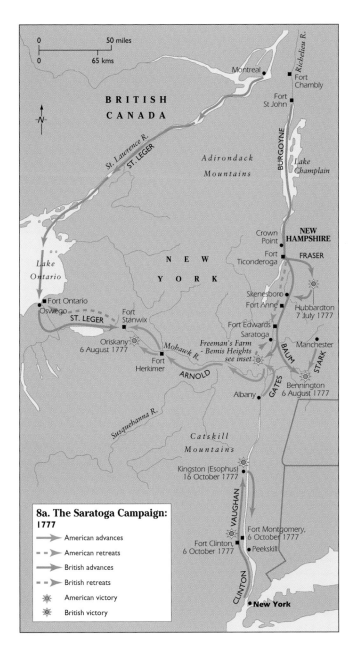

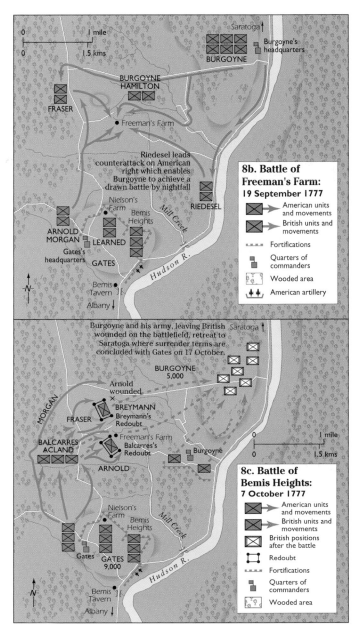

and horses, was crushed at Bennington, New Hampshire, by New Hampshire militia under John Stark, costing Burgoyne 900 troops. St. Leger's column in the Mohawk River Valley suffered serious losses at the battle of Oriskany, New York, on 6 August, helping to oblige its retirement.

Burgoyne's fate was to be sealed at the two-part Battle of Saratoga. The first clash occurred on 19 September at Freeman's Farm, where patriot forces under Benedict Arnold and Daniel Morgan checked a British thrust. On 7 October, Burgoyne again challenged the Americans. Defying Gates's orders relieving him of command, Arnold rallied the patriot army and led the charge which carried the British positions. Burgoyne's

army staggered in retreat and, having suffered 1,000 casualties in the two engagements and with its supplies practically gone, surrendered on 17 October. The Saratoga campaign proved a decisive turning point in more ways than one, for the rebel capture of an entire British army convinced the French monarch, Louis XVI, and his chief minister, the Comte de Vergennes, that the American cause had proved its viability. In February 1778, they signed an agreement with Benjamin Franklin, the American representative in France, to enter the war as a formal ally.

This development changed the nature of the war at a stroke. The conflict was no longer a civil war in British North America.

This 1858 painting depicts Benedict Arnold leading the charge against Breymann's Redoubt, the closing action of the Battle of Bemis Heights and the second phase of the Battle of Saratoga. The dual failure of the British campaign to divide its rebellious colonies in half and to hold the American capital at Philadelphia, led Britain to shift operations to the South.

Britain found itself threatened by its chief European rival with no Continental allies to deflect French pressure. Germain and the North ministry were compelled to redeploy their military and naval forces and refocus their strategy. Troops and ships had to be withdrawn from North America to protect both Great Britain and the West Indies from invasion. Likewise, the strategy of concentration against the patriot armies had to be abandoned as dispersion of precious resources to different places became the norm. The British, now on the defensive, were vulnerable to allied counterstrokes, provided that the French and Americans could coordinate their operations.

The immediate effect of this shift in strategy came in the form of instructions to evacuate Philadelphia sent from Whitehall to Sir Henry Clinton, who had succeeded Howe as commander-in-chief in North America. His force of 10,000 troops departed for New York on 18 June 1778. Since Washington's army had received some European-style training from the Prussian soldier-of-fortune Friedrich von Steuben, Washington eagerly sought to engage the retreating British column. On 28 June, the patriot forces engaged the British at Monmouth Court House in New Jersey. A sharp fight in excessive heat produced a tactical draw, yet the Continentals claimed a triumph by virtue of Clinton's withdrawal to the safety of New York.

The clash at Monmouth proved to be the last major engagement in the northern theater. The British launched periodic raids into Connecticut; a joint Franco-American attempt to recapture Newport, Rhode Island, in August 1778 ended in

fiasco; and in September 1780, when Benedict Arnold's plot to hand West Point over to the British fell apart, he defected to the British side. Yet, the operational focus of the war shifted to the southern colonies, as the British tried to exploit supposed loyalist sentiments there to bring about the collapse of the rebellion.

Warfare in the West

The frontier of the thirteen colonies provided the stage for confused, irregular warfare among patriot forces, loyalists, and American Indians during the American War for Independence. For the Indians, the war was a turning point. One of the colonists' primary grievances against Britain was the so-called Proclamation Line of 1763, which barred further white settlement west of the Trans-Appalachian region. American Indian tribes, particularly the Six Nations of the Iroquois Confederacy, realized that their existence would be threatened if the rebels succeeded in their bid for independence. Thus, most of the tribes gave their support to the British and their fight proved to be a struggle for survival.

The first outbreak of American Indian resistance occurred on the frontiers of North and South Carolina. The Cherokee nation sought reprisals for a long history of affronts by the colonials. During the summer of 1776, warriors, led by a chief named Dragging Canoe, raided several white settlements. The patriot governments of the two colonies responded by mustering their militia and conducting a series of brutal campaigns. They destroyed Cherokee villages, food supplies, and broke the Cherokee resistance by late fall. Though further skirmishes occurred throughout the war, the whites had secured the southern frontier.

In a larger sense, however, the Cherokee War of 1776 proved to be only the first round of conflict between the patriots and the American Indians. On the northern frontier, the tribes posed the strongest threat to rebel expansionist ambitions. The Indians were aided by the British, especially by the officers and agents at the trading post and fortress of Detroit. Under the direction of Henry Hamilton, the lieutenant governor of Canada, the British sought to employ the Indians in harassing raids along the frontier. The most devastating Indian retribution came in 1778, when Iroquois warriors led by the Mohawk chief, Thayendanegea (known to whites as Joseph Brant), joined forces with a troop of loyalist rangers commanded by Major John Butler and terrorized the Pennsylvania and New York back country. In early July, they exterminated a band of militia in the Wyoming Valley, who had foolishly left the protection of the local stockade. The carnage culminated in the Cherry Valley Massacre in the Mohawk Valley region of New York in early November. Despite the protests of Brant, the loyalists indiscriminately slaughtered thirty-two men,

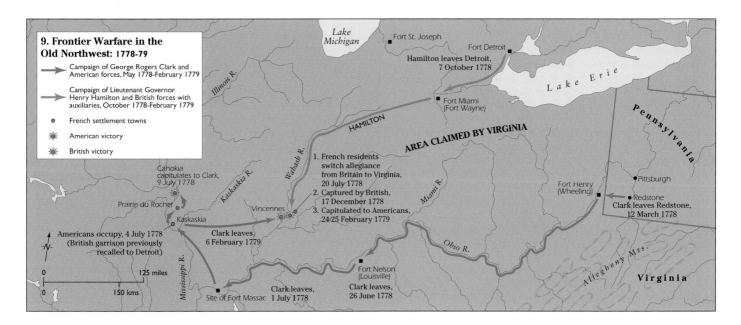

9. Frontier Warfare in the Old Northwest: 1778-79

→ Campaign of George Rogers Clark and American forces, May 1778-February 1779

→ Campaign of Lieutenant Governor Henry Hamilton and British forces with auxiliaries, October 1778-February 1779

● French settlement towns

✷ American victory

✷ British victory

Lake Michigan

Fort St. Joseph

Fort Detroit
Hamilton leaves Detroit, 7 October 1778

Lake Erie

Fort Miami (Fort Wayne)

HAMILTON

Illinois R.

Wabash R.

Kaskaskia R.

AREA CLAIMED BY VIRGINIA

Pennsylvania

Cahokia capitulates to Clark, 9 July 1778

Prairie du Rocher

1. French residents switch allegiance from Britain to Virginia, 20 July 1778
2. Captured by British, 17 December 1778
3. Capitulated to Americans, 24-25 February 1779

Vincennes

Miami R.

Fort Henry (Wheeling)

Pittsburgh

Redstone
Clark leaves Redstone, 12 March 1778

Kaskaskia

Clark leaves, 6 February 1779

Ohio R.

Americans occupy, 4 July 1778 (British garrison previously recalled to Detroit)

Mississippi R.

0 ___ 125 miles
0 ___ 150 kms

Site of Fort Massac

Clark leaves, 1 July 1778

Fort Nelson (Louisville)
Clark leaves, 26 June 1778

Allegheny Mts.

Virginia

women, and children. For patriots on the frontier, the year had been one of horror, and they called for vengeance.

Retribution was not long delayed. In Virginia, the state government commissioned a young frontiersman, George Rogers Clark, to take action. Clark believed that the Indian threat could be neutralized if his force of irregulars could gain control of the Illinois-Indiana country. With a force of only 175 troops, Clark descended upon the French settlements of Vincennes, Kaskaskia, and Cahokia in the Illinois country. In response, Lieutenant Governor Hamilton marched south with a force of 235 men comprising Indians and Frenchmen, and recaptured Vincennes in October. He settled into winter quarters before moving against Clark in Kaskaskia. Clark took advantage of the lull to seize the initiative. In February, he executed a daring march to Vincennes and proceeded to besiege Hamilton. To persuade Hamilton to capitulate, Clark had his men hack to death four Indian prisoners using tomahawks, in full view of the garrison. Hamilton hastily surrendered and was sent to Virginia as a prisoner. Clark's band continued to campaign in the west, succeeding in curbing Indian activity and reinforcing patriot claims to the region between the Appalachians and the Mississippi River. This small force could not act effectively against the British base at Detroit, however, which enabled the British to exercise *de facto* control over the area north of the Ohio River until the 1790s.

The problem of Joseph Brant's warriors and Major John Butler's Rangers, who were leading guerrilla style attacks against colonial settlements, still remained. In May 1779, Washington dispatched a force of 3,000 Continentals, led by John Sullivan, to the western frontier in New York against

these Indian-loyalist raiders. At Newtown, New York (near present-day Elmira), in the heart of Iroquois country, Brant and Butler made their stand. During the engagement of 29 August, however, the Indians and the loyalists chose to withdraw. For the next month, Sullivan's troops burned crops, ransacked villages, and savagely murdered their inhabitants. This operation secured the region for the patriot cause, but also resulted in the near-extinction of the Iroquois.

This fate was to be shared by all of the Indian nations east of the Mississippi River in the coming decades. Without the protection of the British government, whose support was not motivated by sympathy for the Indian cause, but by a desire to monopolize the lucrative fur trade formerly controlled by the French, the tribes could do little more than fight to delay the American encroachment on their lands and destruction of their culture. While the revolt against Great Britain would eventually lead to independence for the white colonials in North America, it also spurred on the conquest and destruction of the native occupants of the continent.

The War at Sea

During the American Revolution, sea operations were of great strategic importance. The patriot forces, lacking adequate resources, were dependent on foreign sources for military supplies, particularly France. Since the British armies in North America were forced to draw reinforcements and equipment from Great Britain, 3,000 miles across the Atlantic Ocean, after France's entry into the conflict naval operations took on a new dimension. Britain was threatened now in new theaters, such as the West Indies and India. Thus, the American Revolution at sea, which began with small but effective operations

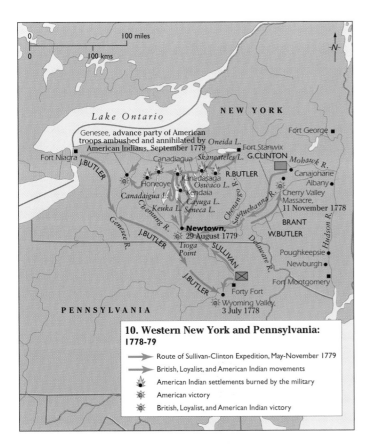

10. Western New York and Pennsylvania: 1778-79

→ Route of Sullivan-Clinton Expedition, May–November 1779

→ British, Loyalist, and American Indian movements

✿ American Indian settlements burned by the military

✿ American victory

✿ British, Loyalist, and American Indian victory

Raids led by the Mohawk Chief Joseph Brant terrorized settlers in western New York and Pennsylvania until 1779, when George Washington dispatched troops under Major General John Sullivan with the mission of "total destruction and devastation." The Iroquois homeland was not to be "merely overrun but destroyed."

mounted by patriot naval forces, evolved into a full-blown struggle for naval superiority between Europe's leading naval powers.

The Continental Congress made its first tentative foray into naval affairs in October 1775, when it began to see the need to mount some sort of defense of its exposed American coastline and established the Continental Navy. It purchased eight small merchant vessels for conversion into warships and authorized the construction of thirteen frigates during the war. Financial problems, however, prohibited large-scale naval construction. Then, as now, warships were the most technologically complex, and thus expensive, weapons systems, requiring large sources of manpower, raw materials, and capital. The primary naval vessel of the period, the ship-of-the-line, could carry as many as 120 guns and 1,000 sailors. The fledgling patriot government had no such resources at its disposal, hence, its emphasis on the smaller and less expensive frigates of about 40 guns and 300 sailors. Given its precarious financial situation throughout the war, the Continental naval program was destined to remain a modest affair.

This does not mean, however, that the patriots did not have the means of waging war at sea. They also relied on the state navies and privateers to raid British merchant shipping and transports. The state navies never had more than forty ships at their combined disposal. Privateering, which amounted to legalized piracy during wartime, became the patriots' primary naval weapon. The Continental Congress and the state governments issued letters of marque to ship owners, who then attacked enemy commerce. Captured and condemned vessels became prizes and the property of the owner, captain, and crew, among whom the spoils were divided according to proportion of investment and crew rank.

Privateering proved to be both an effective weapon against the enemy as well as a profitable source of income for those involved in this business. For the British, the American privateers proved to be a major source of trouble, as their efforts, combined with later naval activity by the French, Spanish, and Dutch, led to the seizure of approximately 3,300 ships of the total 6,000 British vessels involved in overseas trade during the war. Though the British transport system avoided collapse during the war, the privateers compounded British supply problems and made its land operations in the far-flung theaters of North America, the Caribbean, and India all the more difficult.

Commerce raiding also made for good propaganda, as the exploits of individual captains made news both in America and in Europe. In March 1776, a squadron of eight Continental Navy vessels under Commodore Esek Hopkins raided New Providence in the Bahamas and captured the British governor, thus exposing the vulnerability of London's possessions in the

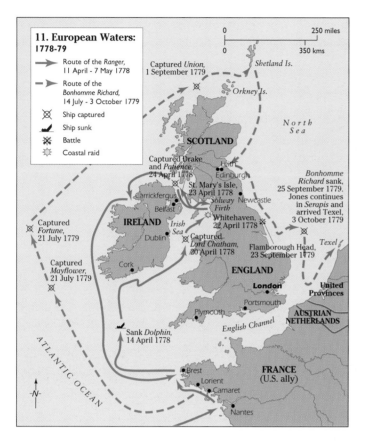

11. European Waters: 1778-79

→ Route of the *Ranger*, 11 April - 7 May 1778
--→ Route of the *Bonhomme Richard*, 14 July - 3 October 1779
⊠ Ship captured
🦅 Ship sunk
✳ Battle
☀ Coastal raid

Captured *Union*, 1 September 1779
Shetland Is.
Orkney Is.
North Sea
SCOTLAND
Captured *Drake* and *Patience*, 24 April 1778
Leith
Edinburgh
Bonhomme Richard sank, 25 September 1779. Jones continues in *Serapis* and arrived Texel, 3 October 1779
St. Mary's Isle, 23 April 1778
Carrickfergus
Solway Firth
Newcastle
Belfast
Whitehaven, 22 April 1778
Captured *Fortune*, 21 July 1779
IRELAND
Irish Sea
Dublin
Captured *Lord Chatham*, 20 April 1778
Texel
Captured *Mayflower*, 21 July 1779
Cork
Flamborough Head, 23 September 1779
ENGLAND
London
United Provinces
Portsmouth
Plymouth
AUSTRIAN NETHERLANDS
English Channel
ATLANTIC OCEAN
Sank *Dolphin*, 14 April 1778
Brest
FRANCE (U.S. ally)
Lorient
Camaret
Nantes

and Philadelphia. The summer of 1776 had witnessed Sir Henry Clinton's abortive attempt to seize Charleston, South Carolina, and later the British successfully occupied Newport, Rhode Island. Throughout the war, British forces conducted small-scale operations against American ports to curb privateering activities, such as the British raids on Nantucket and Martha's Vineyard in the late summer and early fall of 1779. Yet, the ever-widening conflict stretched the Royal Navy's resources and jeopardized its superiority. A particularly acute problem was that of chasing down the American vessels carrying military supplies from the West Indian islands, especially from the neutral Dutch island of St. Eustatius. The Royal Navy was forced to divert ships from operations against the North American coastline to pursue these elusive vessels.

The decisive point in the naval war was France's entry in 1778. The combination of the French fleet, considerably refurbished and upgraded since the disastrous Seven Years'

Born in Kirkudbright, Scotland, John Paul Jones was apprenticed to a Whitehaven merchant and went to sea at age thirteen. He entered the Continental Navy in 1775 and returned to the Solway to raid Whitehaven and to try to kidnap the Earl of Selkirk from St. Mary's Isle in 1778. In 1779, his capture of the Countess of Scarborough *and the* Serapis *earned him a knighthood from Louis XVI of France. After the American Revolutionary War, Jones served as an admiral in the Russian navy, winning victories in the Black Sea.*

Caribbean. The most distinguished American captain, however, was John Paul Jones, a native of Scotland who joined the Continental Navy and made an early name for himself capturing prizes off the coast of Canada.

In early 1778, Jones arrived in France with the sloop of war *Ranger*, fortuitously timing his arrival with the Franco-American alliance. From there, he proceeded to raid British shipping off the coast of the British Isles, crowning this achievement by raiding the Lake District port of Whitehaven. This bold act unnerved a population isolated from the conflict and incited a wave of antiwar protest, underscoring the harassing role the American navy could play. For his part, Jones continued taking the war at sea to the British. In 1779, he captured a French merchant hulk and converted it into a forty-two-gun sloop, the *Bonhomme Richard*. That September, he challenged the Royal Navy frigate *Serapis* off the coast of England at Flamborough Head. Though his ship was sunk from under him, Jones's mariners successfully boarded and seized the British vessel, again making Englishmen nervous and demonstrating the overextended condition of Britain's military and naval forces.

Until this turn of events, the Royal Navy had enjoyed an enormous superiority in the war. Its command of the sea enabled the British fleet to land forces anywhere they were required, as demonstrated by Howe's landings at New York

Painted after an etching by Moreau made from life in 1780.

Robert Cleveley's painting depicts the occupation of Newport, Rhode Island, by the British in 1776. By 1777, Newport was the only British outpost in New England.

War, and patriot privateers severely taxed their British opponents. Cooperation between these allies, however, proved to be difficult and was marked by distrust. At the time of the Battle of Monmouth in June 1778, a French fleet under Charles Hector, the Comte d'Estaing, arrived off the coast of New York, but the French admiral did not want to risk running his ships over the sand bar at Sandy Hook and opted instead for an attack against the British garrison at Newport, Rhode Island. This first attempt at joint operations ended in fiasco at Newport in August 1778. D'Estaing's fleet put to sea to meet a relief force commanded by Admiral Lord Howe. When a storm inflicted more damage on both the fleets than either did to its opponent, d'Estaing sailed to Boston without naval support to make repairs. General John Sullivan's Continentals consequently had to withdraw, leaving Newport in British hands. As the war shifted south, this pattern was repeated, causing much friction between the allies. These difficulties aside, the French presence in the war was a turning point, for the multiple threats posed by French military and naval forces compelled the British to rethink their strategy and redeploy their own troops and ships in a war which had already stretched Britain's resources to the breaking point.

The War in the South: 1779-81

One of the most important ramifications of the change in British strategy was the decision to shift the focus of military operations to the southern states. The leadership in London believed that loyalist sentiment was stronger in the South, and if supported by sufficient military forces, the British could take control of the region. They also believed that reclamation of the South might cause a ripple effect which would undermine the rebel cause in other areas. The capture of Charleston and Savannah also would provide British forces with bases for operating against the French in the Caribbean. Clinton was wary of dispatching large numbers of troops southward, because of his concern about his position in New York. He did send 3,500 troops under Lieutenant Colonel Archibald Campbell to occupy Savannah in December 1778, but a major British effort in the South was not organized until early 1780.

The South had already seen fighting, but of a different nature from that conducted by the conventional field armies in the northern theater. The first eruption of violence occurred in Virginia in 1775, when the fugitive royal governor, John Murray, Lord Dunmore, offered freedom to Virginia slaves who joined the tiny loyalist force he was assembling. Local

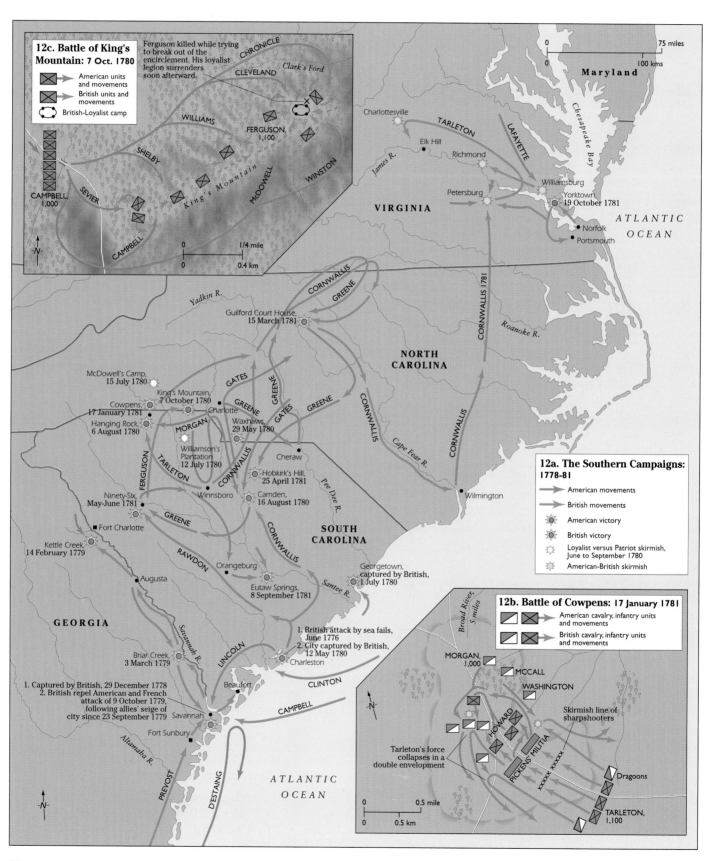

12c. Battle of King's Mountain: 7 Oct. 1780

American units and movements

British units and movements

British-Loyalist camp

Ferguson killed while trying to break out of the encirclement. His loyalist legion surrenders soon afterward.

CHRONICLE

CLEVELAND

Clark's Ford

WILLIAMS

SHELBY

FERGUSON, 1,100

King's Mountain

McDOWELL

WINSTON

SEVIER

CAMPBELL, 1,000

CAMPBELL

0   1/4 mile
0   0.4 km

-N-

0   75 miles
0   100 kms

Maryland

Chesapeake Bay

Charlottesville

TARLETON

Elk Hill

Richmond

LAFAYETTE

James R.

Williamsburg

VIRGINIA

Petersburg

Yorktown, 19 October 1781

ATLANTIC OCEAN

Norfolk

CORNWALLIS 1781

Portsmouth

Roanoke R.

Yadkin R.

CORNWALLIS

GREENE

Guilford Court House, 15 March 1781

NORTH CAROLINA

CORNWALLIS

McDowell's Camp, 15 July 1780

GATES

GREENE

King's Mountain, 7 October 1780

Cowpens, 17 January 1781

GREENE

GATES

GREENE

Cape Fear R.

CORNWALLIS

Charlotte

Hanging Rock, 6 August 1780

MORGAN

Waxhaws, 29 May 1780

Williamson's Plantation 12 July 1780

Cheraw

FERGUSON

TARLETON

CORNWALLIS

Hobkirk's Hill, 25 April 1781

Wilmington

Ninety-Six, May-June 1781

Winnsboro

Camden, 16 August 1780

Pee Dee R.

■ Fort Charlotte

GREENE

SOUTH CAROLINA

Kettle Creek, 14 February 1779

RAWDON

CORNWALLIS

● Augusta

Orangeburg

Eutaw Springs, 8 September 1781

Santee R.

Georgetown, captured by British, 1 July 1780

12a. The Southern Campaigns: 1778-81

American movements

British movements

American victory

British victory

Loyalist versus Patriot skirmish, June to September 1780

American-British skirmish

GEORGIA

Savannah R.

LINCOLN

Briar Creek, 3 March 1779

1. British attack by sea fails, June 1776
2. City captured by British, 12 May 1780

Charleston

1. Captured by British, 29 December 1778
2. British repel American and French attack of 9 October 1779, following allies' siege of city since 23 September 1779

Beaufort

CLINTON

CAMPBELL

Savannah

Fort Sunbury ■

Altamaha R.

PREVOST

DESTAING

ATLANTIC OCEAN

-N-

12b. Battle of Cowpens: 17 January 1781

American cavalry, infantry units and movements

British cavalry, infantry units and movements

Broad River, 5 miles

MORGAN, 1,000

MCCALL

WASHINGTON

Skirmish line of sharpshooters

HOWARD

PICKENS' MILITIA

Tarleton's force collapses in a double envelopment

xxxx

xxxx

Dragoons

TARLETON, 1,100

0   0.5 mile
0   0.5 km

planters and the patriot militia savagely crushed the resulting slave insurrection. The Cherokee War of 1776 saw rebel militia and irregulars confront Indians in a brutal partisan struggle. In late June of that year, British forces under Clinton attempted to take Charleston by sea. They were repulsed when two British ships ran aground under the guns of Fort Moultrie at the entrance to the harbor and troops landed on Long Island, off Charleston, were unable to cross to Sullivan's Island to attack Fort Moultrie from the rear. The first British success in the South came in late 1778, when an expeditionary force of 3,500 captured Savannah and, with the aid of loyalist partisans, reestablished British rule in Georgia.

Throughout 1779, Clinton proved reluctant to detach forces from his already reduced army for further southern operations, so as not to weaken his base in New York. In the meantime, patriot forces in the South took action. In late September, the Americans and the French made another attempt to launch a combined effort, as an army of 1,400 troops under General Benjamin Lincoln and Admiral d'Estaing's fleet descended on Savannah and began siege operations. On 9 October, a premature attempt to take the city by storm ended in failure, as the British repulsed the attack with heavy losses for the allies. D'Estaing, concerned about the safety of his ships in the turbulent autumn weather, set sail for France, obliging Lincoln to retire with the battered remnants of his command to Charleston.

With the news of this success, and convinced New York was safe from attack, Clinton set sail for Charleston with 7,600 troops. For his part, Lincoln, with 3,000 Continentals and 2,500 militia, prepared a defense. In May 1780, the British attacked the city and Clinton sent a flanking force to cut off Lincoln's escape route. When a heavy bombardment convinced Charlestonians that they should surrender, Lincoln capitulated. This defeat proved to be one of the most catastrophic for the patriot cause, as the entire southern department of the Continental forces had been captured. Indeed, it was the second largest surrender of U.S. forces to a foreign enemy in history, ranking behind only the surrender of U.S. troops to the Japanese at Corregidor in World War II.

The triumph at Charleston encouraged the British to pursue their strategy for the reconquest of the South. Clinton returned to New York and left this task to Lord Cornwallis, cautioning his aggressive subordinate to secure his lines of supply and ensure that the territory to the rear of his army was free of rebel irregulars and controlled by loyalist auxiliaries. Cornwallis ignored Clinton's advice, particularly the last point. Indeed, it was the partisan war between loyalists and patriots which largely determined the outcome of the campaign in the South. On 29 May 1780, loyalist dragoons, commanded by Banastre Tarleton, overtook a battalion of Virginia Continentals at the Waxhaws near the North Carolina border. When the Continentals attempted to surrender, Tarleton's troops massacred them. Encouraged by this example, loyalists threatened by the rebels took reprisals against their oppressors, with Tarleton's legion in the forefront of these operations. Southern patriots replied in kind, as bands of irregulars under Thomas Sumter, Francis Marion (the "Swamp Fox"), and Andrew Pickens retaliated against their Tory enemies and harassed the flanks of Cornwallis's army, activity which complicated immeasurably the task of the British commander.

In the wake of the disaster at Charleston, the Continental Congress charged Horatio Gates, the hero of Saratoga, with the task of reorganizing the southern department, despite George Washington's objections. When Gates's army of 3,000 collided with Cornwallis's regulars at Camden, South Carolina, on 16 August 1780, the patriot force disintegrated and Gates fled the field in disgrace. In spite of continuing partisan resistance, the patriot cause was in crisis in the South as Cornwallis prepared to press his advantage.

Cornwallis's thrust into North Carolina in the autumn, however, gave the patriots an opportunity to gain some ground in the South. As British columns pressed northward, the left wing led by Major Patrick Ferguson was engulfed by rebel irregulars. With a force of 1,100, consisting mostly of loyalists, Ferguson fell back and prepared a defense at King's Mountain in northern South Carolina. On 7 October 1780, 1,000 frontiersmen attacked Ferguson's force from all sides, killing or wounding 340 of their enemy. Ferguson was killed and 698 prisoners were taken. This debacle obliged Cornwallis to retire to South Carolina. When patriot irregulars followed up the victory at King's Mountain by trying and hanging several Tory leaders, many of the loyalists became convinced that the British regulars could not protect them and they abandoned Cornwallis's campaign.

When the Continental Congress asked George Washington to replace the disgraced Horatio Gates, he appointed Nathanael Greene, the ablest of his subordinates. Despite limited troops and materials, Greene took bold countermeasures against Cornwallis. He dispatched the 280-man cavalry force of Colonel "Light Horse" Harry Lee southeast to operate jointly with Francis Marion's partisans. To follow up the victory at King's Mountain, he sent 600 Continentals and militia led by Daniel Morgan to strike at the British post at Ninety-Six in western South Carolina. Greene proposed to face Cornwallis's main body with only 1,000 of his own men. This unorthodox plan was designed to deflect British attention away from the undermanned main body led by Greene and simultaneously render the British forces vulnerable to irregular action. The gamble paid off. When Cornwallis sent Tarleton with 1,100 troops to halt Morgan's advance, the British were lured into a trap at Cowpens on 17 January 1781. The battle was a tactical masterpiece in which the British were defeated by a double envelopment. Tarleton's force was decimated, with only 140 survivors, and the patriot losses were minimal. The Battle of Cowpens struck another blow at the British campaign to control the South.

The patriots did not rest on their laurels. Morgan, pursued by Cornwallis, linked up with Greene, and the combined rebel force continued to draw the British after them. Cornwallis abandoned his heavy baggage, but failed to catch the rebel force in an effort which wore down his own army. On 15 March, Greene, his army reinforced, offered battle at Guilford Courthouse in central North Carolina. Tactically, the engage-

ment proved inconclusive, as the two armies battled on even terms throughout the day. Greene, concluding that he had done enough damage, withdrew, technically giving Cornwallis a victory by conceding the field. The casualty lists, however, told a different story. His losses compelled Cornwallis to retire to the port of Wilmington, North Carolina, leaving most of North Carolina in rebel hands.

Thus, the patriots thwarted the British attempt to subdue the southern states. Through risk, daring, and doggedness, Greene and Morgan turned Cornwallis's aggressiveness against him and undermined the loyalist will to fight in the process. In spite of these patriot successes, substantial British forces remained in the region. Beginning in December 1780, a

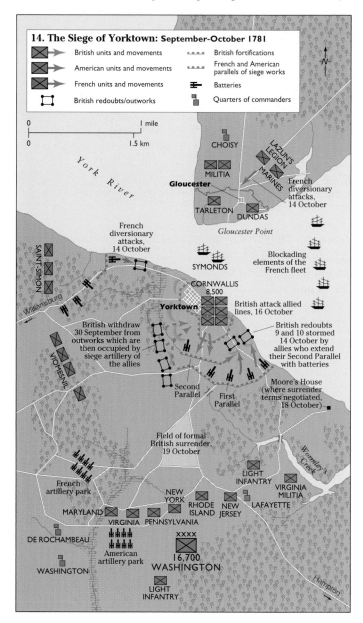

13. The Approach to Yorktown:
August – September 1781

American and French military units and movements

American military units and movements

British military units

British naval units (number of ships of the line indicated) and movements

French naval units (number of ships of the line indicated) and movements

Battle site

Hudson R.
HEATH
CLINTON
WASHINGTON
DE ROCHAMBEAU
New York
Princeton
Sandy Hook
New Jersey
Philadelphia
Chester
Pennsylvania
Maryland
Elkton
Graves and Hood with a combined British Fleet sail from New York to find and engage French Fleet in the Chesapeake area
Baltimore
Annapolis
Mount Vernon
Delaware Bay
Delaware
GRAVES
Potomac R.
Rappahannock R.
Virginia
York R.
LAFAYETTE
Williamsburg
James R.
Yorktown
ATLANTIC OCEAN
Hood arrives Chesapeake, 25 August, and not finding the French Fleet there sets sail for New York
HOOD
Battle of the Chesapeake, 5 September 1781
CORNWALLIS
Portsmouth
DE BARRAS DE ROCHAMBEAU
De Barras arrives Chesapeake on 10 September from Newport, Rhode Island, bringing de Rochambeau's siege artillery
De Grasse arrives Chesapeake 30 August from the West Indies with 4,000 French troops
DE GRASSE
0   50 miles
0   75 kms

14. The Siege of Yorktown: September–October 1781

British units and movements

American units and movements

French units and movements

British redoubts/outworks

British fortifications

French and American parallels of siege works

Batteries

Quarters of commanders

0   1 mile
0   1.5 km
York River
CHOISY
LAZUN'S LEGION
MILITIA
MARINES
French diversionary attacks, 14 October
Gloucester
TARLETON
DUNDAS
Gloucester Point
French diversionary attacks, 14 October
SAINT-SIMON
Williamsburg
SYMONDS
Blockading elements of the French fleet
CORNWALLIS 8,500
Yorktown
British attack allied lines, 16 October
British withdraw 30 September from outworks which are then occupied by siege artillery of the allies
VIOMESNIL
British redoubts 9 and 10 stormed 14 October by allies who extend their Second Parallel with batteries
Second Parallel
First Parallel
Moore's House (where surrender terms negotiated, 18 October)
Wormley's Creek
Field of formal British surrender, 19 October
LIGHT INFANTRY
VIRGINIA MILITIA
French artillery park
MARYLAND
NEW YORK
RHODE ISLAND
NEW JERSEY
LAFAYETTE
VIRGINIA
PENNSYLVANIA
DE ROCHAMBEAU
American artillery park
xxxx
16,700
WASHINGTON
WASHINGTON
LIGHT INFANTRY
Hampton

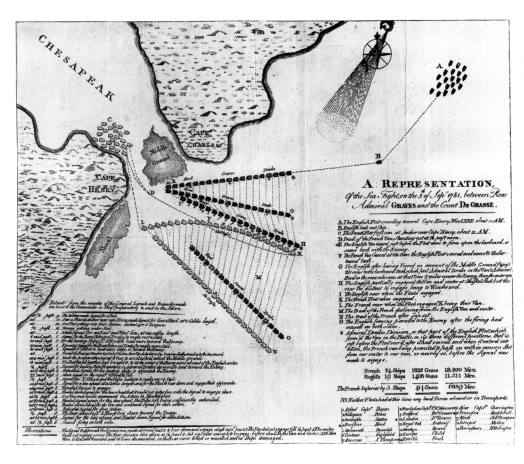

Although tactically a draw, the Battle of the Chesapeake was a strategic victory for the French and Americans because it blocked the British from reinforcing or evacuating Lord Cornwallis's army at Yorktown. This contemporary English representation of the engagement traces the maneuvers of the opposing fleets, lists the names of the nineteen British ships and their commanders, and details the observations and commands sent to those captains by British Admiral Thomas Graves. After the British surrender at Yorktown, French Admiral de Grasse and his twenty-four ships returned to the West Indies, where he was taken captive at the Battle of Isles des Saintes the following April.

force of 1,500 British soldiers under the renegade Benedict Arnold conducted raids in Virginia as a prelude to operations in the Chesapeake Bay. Washington dispatched Continental forces under the Marquis de Lafayette to stop Arnold and give cover to Greene's rear. With Cornwallis contained, Greene advanced into South Carolina. On 25 April, he was checked at Hobkirk's Hill by British General Charles Rawdon's army. Heavy British losses, however, compelled Rawdon to retire to Charleston, enabling Greene's Continentals, with the help of the partisans, to destroy the British garrisons in South Carolina. By July, only Orangeburg, Charleston, and Savannah remained in British hands. In September, the British force at Orangeburg made a break for Charleston. Greene caught them at Eutaw Springs on 8 September. Though the engagement was tactically inconclusive, the British were left bottled up in Charleston and Greene had stopped Britain's attempt to conquer the South. As decisive as this blow was, events in Virginia would provide the fatal thrust to Britain's war in North America.

The ground for Washington's triumph at Yorktown was prepared when Benedict Arnold's force invaded Virginia in December 1780. When de Lafayette and his troops entered the fray, Clinton sent 2,000 troops under General William Phillips

to reinforce Arnold's army. Cornwallis, still positioned at Wilmington, saw an opportunity to regain the initiative. In April, he ventured north with the intention of meeting up with Phillips (Arnold had returned to New York) and assuming overall command. In a single stroke, Cornwallis set the stage for a double catastrophe. First, he abandoned the British forces located in the deep South. Then, in August, Cornwallis selected Yorktown, Virginia, as a base for further operations and he instructed his 8,500 troops to establish defensive positions there. Isolated on the York-James peninsula with his back to the sea, Cornwallis placed the British southern army in an exposed position of which the Franco-American allies took full advantage.

At first, George Washington viewed these developments as an opportunity to recapture New York and avenge the humiliation of 1776. He counted on the French expeditionary force under the Comte de Rochambeau, quartered at Newport, Rhode Island, since July 1780, to provide the numbers he felt were necessary for the operation. When the two commanders met in May 1781, de Rochambeau suggested that the imminent arrival of the French fleet under the command of Comte de Grasse in Chesapeake Bay would suggest that operations in Virginia should go forward first. But Washington preferred to proceed with his original plan and set the date of the attack on New York for 2 July. When Clinton received reinforcements in New York, however, the attack was called off. In August, Washington finally received confirmation that de Grasse's fleet was headed for the Chesapeake. Aware of Cornwallis's movements, Washington seized the opportunity. With a screening force left in New York to throw Clinton off the scent, Washington and de Rochambeau swiftly marched to Yorktown. On 5 September, de Grasse's fleet drove off the British fleet under Admiral Thomas Graves in the Battle of the Chesapeake. By the end of September, 7,800 French regulars, 5,700 Continentals, and 3,200 militia had surrounded Cornwallis. On 14 October, daring night assaults captured the two prominent British redoubts. Two days later, a British counterattack failed to retake these key positions. Because the French navy had cut off escape by sea, the British commander was obliged to ask for surrender terms on 17 October. Two days later, as their band played "The World Turned Upside Down," the British laid down their arms in a formal capitulation ceremony. French and American casualties for the Yorktown campaign amounted to 232 compared to 552 British dead and wounded.

Although the war formally dragged on for two more years, Yorktown proved to be the decisive blow to Britain's desire to subdue the rebellion in North America. Cornwallis's surrender, coupled with defeats in India and the West Indies, brought down the ministry of Lord North. His eventual successor, the Earl of Shelburne, redirected Britain's efforts against France, Spain (which entered the war in June 1779), and the Netherlands (Britain declared war on the Dutch in December 1780 in retaliation for clandestine arms shipments sent to the American rebels). Simultaneously, the British opened negotiations with the American commissioners in Paris. Although Washington's army was threatened with mutinies and the Continental officer corps discussed mounting a coup, the Shelburne ministry's decision to concentrate its military efforts elsewhere ensured the survival of the patriot cause.

Final Operations: 1780-83

It is ironic that a war which began with shots exchanged on Lexington Green would see its concluding engagements fought off the coast of India. When viewed in the context of European power politics, however, it is no surprise that Britain's civil war in North America led to conflicts with its rivals. All of its continental adversaries had something to gain by challenging Britain's position of supremacy as a result of the Seven Years' War. France saw the opportunity to avenge its losses from its own disastrous defeat in the earlier conflict. The other naval powers, Spain and the Netherlands, sought to reduce the threat the British posed to their declining empires.

In 1780, Catherine the Great of Russia, outraged by British action against neutral shipping, organized the states of the Baltic into the League of Armed Neutrality. This action served to deny Britain access to the Baltic Sea region and critical raw materials it needed for ship construction, further exacerbating Britain's precarious situation at the time of Yorktown. As a result, the Shelburne ministry moved to recover Britain's military position in the Caribbean and Indian theaters and to negotiate with its former American subjects.

Measures had been undertaken to carry out these plans even before the resignation of the North ministry in March 1782. In late 1779, Admiral Sir George Brydges Rodney set sail for the Caribbean in response to the threat posed by d'Estaing's seizure of several islands there. In April and May, Rodney fought a series of actions with the French fleet of Comte de Guichen, which, although indecisive, curtailed French naval activity in the islands. One of his most significant successes came in February 1781, when he seized the Dutch-held island of St. Eustatius, the primary clearinghouse for shipments of military stores to the American rebels. Rodney neutralized the island as a source of American supplies, despite losing St. Eustatius to the French in November.

Threats to its security compelled Britain to stretch its already thin resources to cover a variety of contingencies. Because of the presence of 30,000 French troops at Cherbourg and in Britanny, a large British naval squadron was dispatched to guard the Channel. Britain's Mediterranean bases at Gibraltar and Minorca were vulnerable to Spanish attack. Gibraltar withstood a siege from 1779 to 1782. A Franco-Spanish force captured Minorca after another long siege in February 1782. In America, Bernardo Gálvez, the Spanish governor of Louisiana, moved to exploit British weakness in west Florida. In March 1780, troops under Gálvez's command captured the British post at Mobile, and in May 1781, his forces seized Pensacola, thus providing the reason for Florida to be returned to Spain with the peace settlement of 1783. The Dutch posed another threat, which manifested itself in August 1781, when a Dutch squadron, escorting a fleet of merchantmen to the Baltic, set sail into the North Sea. At Dogger Bank, the site of many European naval clashes, the Dutch ships encountered a British squadron under the command of Admiral Hyde Parker. After an engagement of over three hours and many casualties, the Dutch withdrew, leaving the Royal Navy master of the North Sea.

The final major naval engagement of the war came in April 1782. Admiral de Grasse, fresh from his triumph in the Chesapeake Bay, spent the first months of 1782 sparring with the British under Admiral Samuel Hood for control of several Caribbean islands and succeeded in taking Nevis, St. Christopher, and Montserrat. In April, de Grasse's fleet moved to

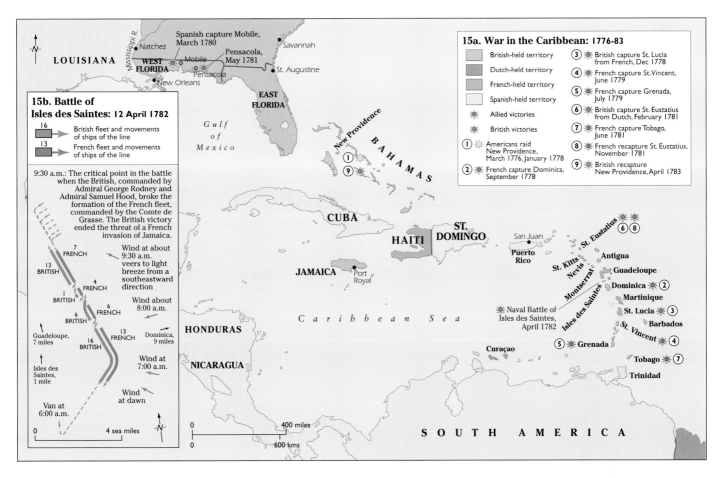

15a. War in the Caribbean: 1776-83

British-held territory
Dutch-held territory
French-held territory
Spanish-held territory
Allied victories
British victories

① Americans raid New Providence, March 1776, January 1778
② French capture Dominica, September 1778
③ British capture St. Lucia from French, Dec 1778
④ French capture St. Vincent, June 1779
⑤ French capture Grenada, July 1779
⑥ British capture St. Eustatius from Dutch, February 1781
⑦ French capture Tobago, June 1781
⑧ French recapture St. Eustatius, November 1781
⑨ British recapture New Providence, April 1783

15b. Battle of Isles des Saintes: 12 April 1782

16 British fleet and movements of ships of the line
13 French fleet and movements of ships of the line

9:30 a.m.: The critical point in the battle when the British, commanded by Admiral George Rodney and Admiral Samuel Hood, broke the formation of the French fleet, commanded by the Comte de Grasse. The British victory ended the threat of a French invasion of Jamaica.

attack Jamaica with 10,000 French troops. On 12 April, the British, reinforced by Rodney's fleet, engaged the French near the Isles des Saintes, in the channel between Dominica and Guadeloupe. Rodney and Hood smashed de Grasse's fleet, winning one of the most decisive naval victories of the eighteenth century. Though there would be minor operations in both the Caribbean and in India, the Battle of Isles des Saintes proved to be the last major action of the war on either land or sea. By mid-1782, all the participants were involved in negotiations to resolve any issues still unsettled by seven years of fighting.

Concluding the Peace

Ending the war could only be achieved by negotiating through the Machiavellian maze of European diplomacy. For the American representatives that meant avoiding the machinations of their French and Spanish colleagues. Both of these European powers were well aware of the threatening implications of the successful creation of a strong New World republic. Both of the Bourbon states sought to keep the new nation subordinate to their interests. For their part, the American commissioners—John Adams, John Jay, and Benjamin Franklin—moved to conclude matters with the British. In the

articles signed 30 November 1782, Britain recognized American independence as well as its claim to the territory between the Appalachian Mountains and the Mississippi River, while the Americans were obliged to relinquish claims to Canada and cease the confiscation of loyalist property. For their part, the French and the Spanish were in no position to protest, as the defeats at Isles des Saintes and Gibraltar, as well as impending French bankruptcy, left both nations eager to end the war on whatever terms they could get.

In the final analysis, what began as an armed protest by colonials against the perceived abuses by the mother country became a major war involving most of Europe's powers, ending with the exhaustion of all the participants. For the infant United States of America, such an outcome was the most fortuitous of all possibilities. Not only was the nation able to secure its independence from its former British masters, it also avoided being trapped in the orbit of its European allies, while struggling with potentially fatal internal dissension from many sources. Free from these Old World influences and protected by vast oceans, the new country could concentrate on its own future conflicts, foreign and domestic, and eventually expand across the continent.

Foreign Wars of the Early Republic: 1798-1815

After establishing its independence, the United States was eager to isolate itself from the conflicts of Europe, but this proved impossible. The French Revolutionary Wars (1792-1801) and the Napoleonic Wars (1803-15) threatened the new nation's commerce and neutral rights around the globe and, as a result, the United States was drawn into wars with France and England. The nation was compelled to defend its interests against the Barbary States of North Africa which included Algiers, Morocco, Tripoli, and Tunis. These wars tested the ability of the United States to wage war under widely different circumstances. Each war also provided a vindication of early American naval power.

The Quasi-War: 1798-1801

The Quasi-War was an outgrowth of the French Revolutionary Wars. Although the United States sought to remain neutral, it was formally linked to France by a pair of treaties signed in 1778. When the United States appeared to tilt its foreign policy toward England with the Jay Treaty of 1794, by which the United States gave preferential status in trade to England, France felt betrayed and in 1796 unleashed a war on American commerce. France's aim was to bully the United States into renouncing the Jay Treaty and to loot American trade in the process. The United States responded by authorizing its warships and armed merchantmen to attack armed French vessels

in American waters as well as on the high seas. The result was the Quasi-War, an undeclared naval war that lasted two-and-a-half years.

The United States commissioned forty-nine warships during the conflict. Although concentrating in the Caribbean (where most of the French depredations took place), the U. S. Navy also showed the flag in the Wine Islands in the eastern Atlantic and the Mediterranean as well as beyond the Cape of Good Hope and in the East Indies. The U. S. Navy performed particularly well in the contest. The American *Constellation* captured the French frigate *l'Insurgente*, the *Boston* took *le Berceau*, and the *Pickering* seized *l'Egypte Conquise*. In addition, the *Constellation* hammered *la Vengeance* into submission although the French frigate escaped capture. The U.S. Navy also took eighty-two French privateers and recaptured seventy merchant vessels. The U.S. Navy's only loss was the *Retaliation*, a French vessel originally taken off the American coast by the *Delaware*, but later recaptured by *l'Insurgente* and *Volontaire*.

Over 1,000 American merchant vessels armed for defense during the conflict. Although some of these ships were captured despite their armaments, many others fought or frightened off French cruisers. In addition, armed American merchantmen captured six French privateers and retook eight American vessels that had been taken by the French.

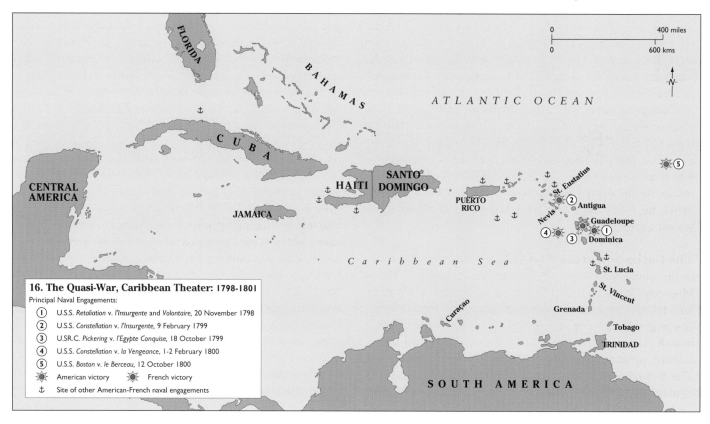

16. The Quasi-War, Caribbean Theater: 1798-1801

Principal Naval Engagements:

① U.S.S. *Retaliation* v. *l'Insurgente* and *Volontaire*, 20 November 1798

② U.S.S. *Constellation* v. *l'Insurgente*, 9 February 1799

③ U.SR.C. *Pickering* v. *l'Egypte Conquise*, 18 October 1799

④ U.S.S. *Constellation* v. *la Vengeance*, 1-2 February 1800

⑤ U.S.S. *Boston* v. *le Berceau*, 12 October 1800

☀ American victory   ☀ French victory

⚓ Site of other American-French naval engagements

Lieutenant Stephen Decatur became a national hero when he led a group of American sailors in a dangerous night raid in the harbor of Tripoli in February 1804. They burned the captured frigate, the U.S.S. Philadelphia, *to prevent its use by Tripoli against the U.S. squadron in the Mediterranean. The construction of the 36-gun frigate at Southwark near the city of Philadelphia is depicted in this engraving published by Birch & Son in 1800. The vessel's construction was paid for by the citizens of the nation's capital, Philadelphia, and presented to the U.S. Navy.*

As a result of American operations in the Caribbean, insurance rates for vessels trading between the United States and the West Indies dropped dramatically, from 25 to 33 percent in mid-1798 to 10 percent at the end of 1799, which was not much above the peacetime rate of 5 to 7 percent. The vigorous American response not only saved much American property but also induced France to sue for peace. The Convention of Mortefontaine, also known as the Convention of 1800, was signed 30 September 1800 in France and brought the war to an end in 1801. It freed the United States from the Franco-American treaties in exchange for waiving any claims against France for the depredations it had committed. For the United States, the Quasi-War was a remarkably successful limited war against a great power.

The Barbary Wars: 1791-1815

In the eighteenth century the North African states of Algiers, Morocco, Tunis, and Tripoli regularly used war as an excuse for raiding merchant ships, taking captives for ransom, and exacting tribute from foreign governments. Although the British flag protected American merchant ships during the colonial period, after independence they became fair game. The United States ended the first round of depredations by signing treaties with the Barbary States in the 1780s and 1790s.

On 10 May 1801, Tripoli declared war on the United States in the hope of exacting tribute. In the ensuing Tripolitan War, the United States sent four successive squadrons to the Mediterranean. One squadron, under the command of Commodore Richard V. Morris, established a blockade of Tripoli and destroyed or captured four enemy cruisers. Another squadron, under Commodore Edward Preble, borrowed gunboats and bomb ketches from the Kingdom of the Two Sicilies, which was also at war with Tripoli. Preble planned to bombard the city of Tripoli, but disaster struck when the U.S.S. *Philadelphia* ran aground in the harbor of Tripoli and was captured and refloated by enemy forces. This loss might have tipped the naval balance toward Tripoli, but a group of American seamen led by Lieutenant Stephen Decatur burned the ship in a daring night raid. An attempt to destroy Tripoli's ships with a bomb ship failed when the vessel blew up prematurely, killing all thirteen Americans on board.

A more powerful squadron under Commodore Samuel Barron renewed the blockade of Tripoli in 1804. At the same time, U. S. Navy agent and American consul to Tunis William Eaton led seven U. S. Marines and a motley and mutinous army of 400 Arabs and Greeks from Alexandria, Egypt, across 600 miles of Libyan desert to threaten Tripoli by land. Supported by U. S. naval fire, this force captured the city of Derna in Tripoli. The threat by land as well as by sea induced Tripoli to sign a peace pact on 4 June 1805, that ransomed American

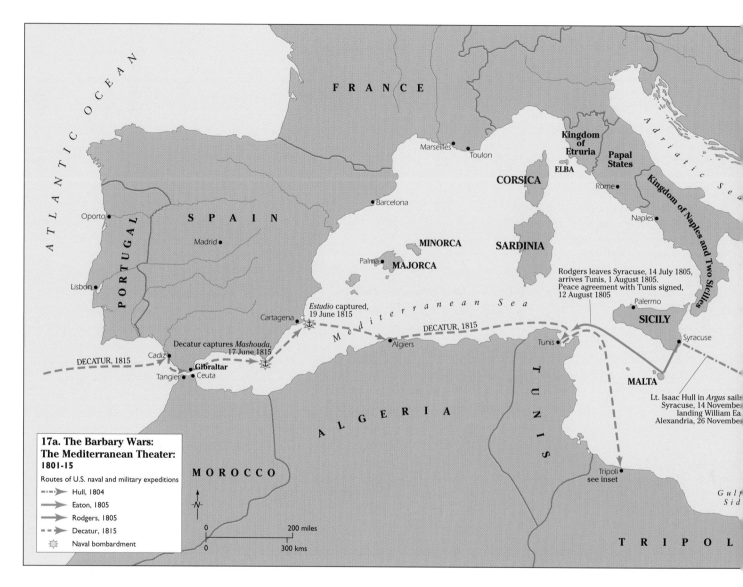

17a. The Barbary Wars:
The Mediterranean Theater:
1801-15

Routes of U.S. naval and military expeditions

- ---→ Hull, 1804
- ——→ Eaton, 1805
- ——→ Rodgers, 1805
- - -→ Decatur, 1815
- ✵ Naval bombardment

0 — 200 miles
0 — 300 kms

Estudio captured,
19 June 1815

DECATUR, 1815

Decatur captures *Mashouda*,
17 June 1815

DECATUR, 1815

Rodgers leaves Syracuse, 14 July 1805,
arrives Tunis, 1 August 1805.
Peace agreement with Tunis signed,
12 August 1805

Lt. Isaac Hull in *Argus* sails
Syracuse, 14 November
landing William Ea
Alexandria, 26 November

Tripoli
see inset

prisoners but explicitly forswore tribute payments.

An uneasy peace followed, with the Barbary States periodically seizing American ships for ransom, especially during the War of 1812 when the U.S. Navy could not respond. On 2 March 1815, the War of 1812 now over, the U.S. Congress declared war on Algiers and the administration dispatched a powerful squadron under Decatur to the Mediterranean. Decatur captured two Algerian warships and compelled Algiers to make peace without tribute, to free captive Americans without ransom, and to pay damages. Decatur forced similar treaties on Tripoli and Tunis. The Algerian Expedition concluded this chapter of warfare with the Barbary States.

The War of 1812: 1812-15

The War of 1812 was a direct result of Britain's involvement in the Napoleonic Wars (1803-15) clashing with America's

national interests. The United States declared war on England on 18 June 1812 to force the British to give up the orders in council which regulated American trade with the Continent and impressment, the British practice of removing seamen from American ships. The war lasted two and a half years.

The United States targeted Canada because this was the only place where the British were vulnerable to American power. The United States could have concentrated its forces against one or more of the three cities that anchored British defenses on the St. Lawrence River. The resulting conquest of Québec, Montreal, or Kingston in Canada would have given the Americans effective control of everything to the west in Canada. But instead, the United States chose a western strategy to take advantage of American enthusiasm for the war in the west and to end depredations by Britain's Indian allies in the region.

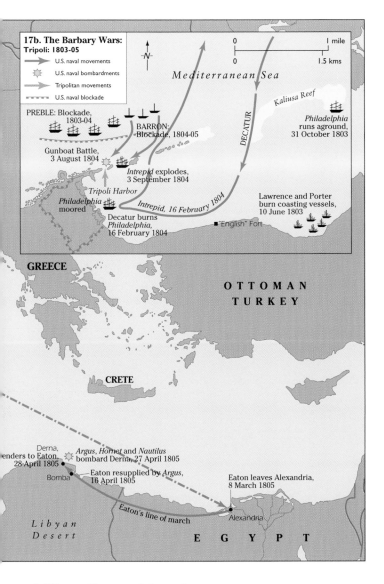

17b. The Barbary Wars:
Tripoli: 1803-05

→ U.S. naval movements
☼ U.S. naval bombardments
→ Tripolitan movements
----- U.S. naval blockade

Mediterranean Sea

Kaliusa Reef

PREBLE: Blockade, 1803-04

BARRON: Blockade, 1804-05

DECATUR

Philadelphia runs aground, 31 October 1803

Gunboat Battle, 3 August 1804

Intrepid explodes, 3 September 1804

Tripoli Harbor

Philadelphia moored

Intrepid, 16 February 1804

Decatur burns *Philadelphia,* 16 February 1804

Lawrence and Porter burn coasting vessels, 10 June 1803

■ "English" Fort

GREECE

OTTOMAN TURKEY

CRETE

Derna, enders to Eaton, 28 April 1805

Argus, Hornet and *Nautilus* bombard Derna, 27 April 1805

Bomba

Eaton resupplied by *Argus,* 16 April 1805

Eaton leaves Alexandria, 8 March 1805

Libyan Desert

Eaton's line of march

Alexandria

E G Y P T

A Three-Pronged Attack

In 1812 the United States launched a three-pronged attack into the American-Canadian frontier across the Detroit River, over the Niagara River, and along the St. Lawrence frontier. The entire campaign ended in failure. In the west, General William Hull surrendered an American army of some 2,000 men at Detroit on 16 August when his British counterpart, General Isaac Brock, threatened Hull with an Indian massacre if he did not capitulate. General James Winchester lost a second army in the west, about 950 men, when he surrendered prematurely at the Battle of Frenchtown on 22 January 1813. On the Niagara frontier, General Stephen Van Rensselaer lost another American army (about 1,000 men) on 13 October in the Battle of Queenston Heights when American militia refused, ostensibly on constitutional grounds, to cross into Canada to reinforce Lieutenant Winfield Scott's regulars. The

only success the United States could claim in this theater was the death of Brock, Britain's best general. On the St. Lawrence front, General Henry Dearborn made little more than a demonstration. After reluctantly marching his army to Canada on the western side of the Richelieu River in mid-November, Dearborn learned that most of his militia, again citing constitutional grounds, would not cross the border. When American forces fired on each other at the first Battle of Lacolle Mill on 19 November, Dearborn gave up the attack and ordered his army into winter quarters.

Success Followed by Losses

In 1813 the United States renewed its three-pronged attack with somewhat greater success, though only in the west. On 10 September, Commodore Oliver H. Perry won a spectacular American naval victory over Robert H. Barclay's British squadron on Lake Erie, thus securing this waterway for the United States. In a memorable message, Perry wrote to General William Henry Harrison: "We have met the enemy and they are ours." The loss of the lake deprived the British of their western supply route and thus forced General Henry Procter to order his army to withdraw from the Detroit River. On 5 October, about fifty miles east of Detroit, American General William Henry Harrison caught up with Procter and defeated his Anglo-Indian force at the Battle of the Thames (Moraviantown). Although Procter himself escaped, about 600 of his men were captured and Britain's most talented and reliable Indian ally, the famed Shawnee Chief Tecumseh, was killed.

Further east, American forces continued to struggle in 1813. On 27 May a combined force nominally under Dearborn's command, but actually commanded by Perry and Scott and covered by Commodore Isaac Chauncey, captured Fort George and forced the British to abandon their positions on the Niagara frontier, but this victory proved ephemeral. American forces were defeated at Stoney Creek at the southeastern end of Lake Ontario on 5 June and at Beaver Dams about ten miles west of Niagara Falls on 24 June. Thereafter, the United States transferred most of its regular troops to the east and the militia left behind had to abandon Fort George on 10 December. Before departing, the Americans burned the town of Newark on the Canadian side of the Niagara River, infuriating the British. After reoccupying Fort George, the British on 18 December sent a force under Colonel John Murray that captured Fort Niagara located on the American side of the border. The British then torched American communities all along the Niagara frontier.

On the St. Lawrence frontier, the United States launched its most ambitious campaign of the war. One army under General James Wilkinson moved down the St. Lawrence from Sackets Harbor to threaten Montreal from the west, while a

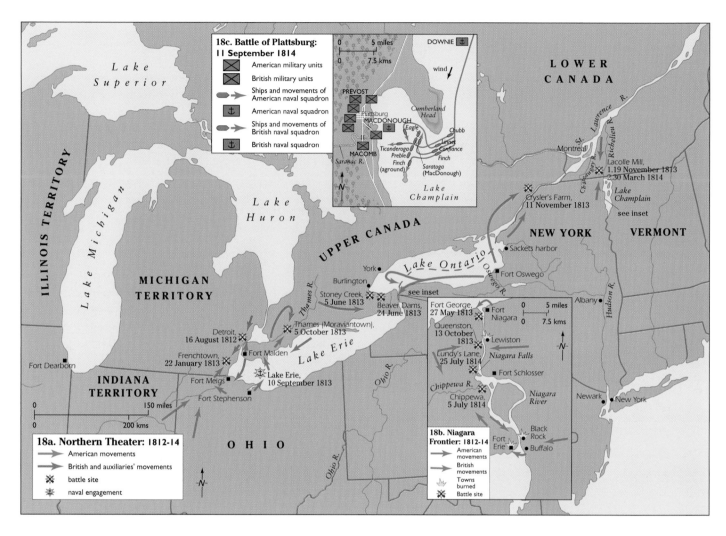

18c. Battle of Plattsburg: 11 September 1814

- American military units
- British military units
- Ships and movements of American naval squadron
- American naval squadron
- Ships and movements of British naval squadron
- British naval squadron

DOWNIE

wind

PREVOST
Plattsburg
MACDONOUGH
Cumberland Head
Chubb
Eagle
Linnet
Confiance
Finch
MACOMB
Ticonderoga
Preble
Finch
(aground)
Saratoga
(MacDonough)
Saranac R.
Lake Champlain

Lake Superior

Lake Michigan

Lake Huron

ILLINOIS TERRITORY

MICHIGAN TERRITORY

Fort Dearborn

INDIANA TERRITORY

Fort Meigs

Fort Stephenson

Detroit, 16 August 1812
Frenchtown, 22 January 1813
Fort Malden
Lake Erie, 10 September 1813

OHIO

Thames R.
Thames (Moraviantown), 5 October 1813

Lake Erie

Ohio R.

UPPER CANADA

York
Burlington
Stoney Creek, 5 June 1813
Beaver Dams, 24 June 1813

Lake Ontario

see inset

Sackets harbor
Fort Oswego
Oswego R.

Crysler's Farm, 11 November 1813

LOWER CANADA

St. Lawrence R.
Montreal
Richelieu R.
Chateaugay R.
Lacolle Mill, 1.19 November 1813 2.30 March 1814
Lake Champlain
see inset

NEW YORK

VERMONT

Albany
Hudson R.

Newark
New York

18b. Niagara Frontier: 1812-14

- American movements
- British movements
- Towns burned
- Battle site

Fort George, 27 May 1813
Fort Niagara
Queenston, 13 October 1813
Lewiston
Niagara Falls
Lundy's Lane, 25 July 1814
Fort Schlosser
Chippewa R.
Chippewa, 5 July 1814
Niagara River
Black Rock
Fort Erie
Buffalo

18a. Northern Theater: 1812-14

- American movements
- British and auxiliaries' movements
- battle site
- naval engagement

0   150 miles
0   200 kms

0   5 miles
0   7.5 kms

0   5 miles
0   7.5 kms

second army under General Wade Hampton moved up the Chateaugay on 26 October. Wilkinson called off his campaign after a detachment of his army, commanded by General John P. Boyd, was defeated on 11 November by a numerically inferior British force under Colonel Joseph Morrison at the Battle of Chrysler's Farm. Wilkinson later renewed his campaign against Canada but withdrew after being rebuffed in the second Battle of Lacolle Mill on 30 March 1814.

After two years of warfare, the United States had little to show for its campaigning. Only in the west, which was too far from the centers of power and population to be strategically important, could the nation claim any success. Even so, since Canada could not be conquered in the west, the conflict was effectively a stalemate.

In the last year of the war, the initiative gradually shifted to the British. Napoleon was defeated and forced into exile in the spring of 1814, thus bringing peace to Europe for the first time in a decade. This enabled the British to transfer military and naval forces to the American theater. With the restoration of

peace in Europe, the movement of men and material to the New World accelerated.

Despite these changes, the United States still took the offensive on the Niagara frontier in the summer of 1814. On 3 July, an American force under General Jacob Brown crossed into Canada, occupied Fort Erie, and then advanced northward. Two bloody battles ensued. On 5 July General Winfield Scott's well-trained army defeated a British force under General Phineas Riall at the Battle of Chippewa. On 25 July, Brown and Scott slugged it out with General Gordon Drummond's army in the war's bloodiest engagement, the Battle of Lundy's Lane, which ended in a draw. The American forces then withdrew to Fort Erie and Drummond took the offensive. On 15 August, Drummond's attack on the fort was foiled when a powder magazine blew up in one of the fort's bastions, killing or wounding many of his men. When Drummond then sought to bombard the fort into submission with an artillery barrage from afar, two American assault forces under Colonel James Miller and General Peter B. Porter launched a bloody and successful nighttime attack on 17 September that knocked the British guns out of commission. With the failure of the artillery bombardment, Drummond called off his offensive. Brown blew up Fort Erie on 5 November, and withdrew to American soil, thus bringing the war on the Niagara frontier to an end.

Elsewhere the British took advantage of their growing strength in America to take the offensive. General George Prevost marched into upper New York state with 10,000 men—the largest army ever to invade the United States—but this force halted at Plattsburgh to await the outcome of an engagement on Lake Champlain. On 11 September, Commodore

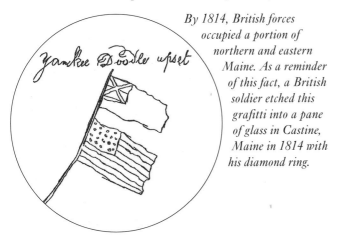

By 1814, British forces occupied a portion of northern and eastern Maine. As a reminder of this fact, a British soldier etched this grafitti into a pane of glass in Castine, Maine in 1814 with his diamond ring.

Thomas Macdonough pounded into submission a British squadron under Commodore George Downie on the lake. The loss of command on Lake Champlain threatened Prevost's supply line, and hence, much to the disgust of his officers, he ordered his army to return to Canada. In another operation that stretched out over the late summer, British amphibious forces successfully occupied about one hundred miles of sparsely populated eastern Maine from Castine to Eastport and retained control of this territory until the end of the war.

A New Series of Operations

The British launched another series of operations in 1814 in the Chesapeake Bay area. Aided by Admiral George Cockburn, General Robert Ross commanded a British army that on 24 August defeated an American force at the Battle of Bladensburg and then occupied Washington, D.C. The British burned most of the public buildings in the capital before withdrawing. Ross then moved his army up the Chesapeake to threaten Baltimore. Although he defeated an American force at the Battle of North Point on 12 September, Ross himself was killed by a sharpshooter. The defenses of Baltimore were formidable and Ross's successor, Colonel Arthur Brooke, was reluctant to hazard an attack without British naval support. The British

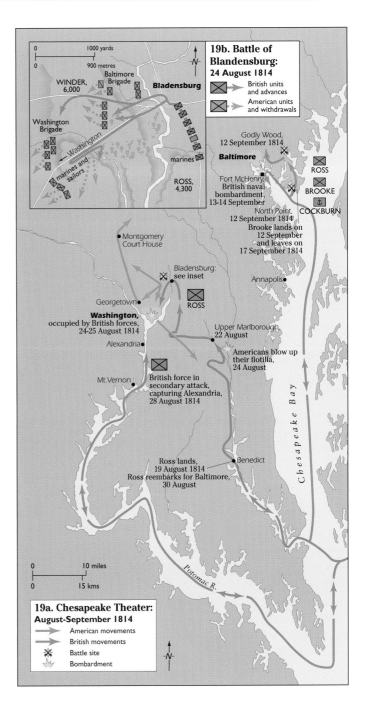

squadron, however, could not get close enough to offer support. Despite a twenty-five-hour bombardment on 13-14 September, Fort McHenry, which blocked the British navy's advance, could not be pounded into submission. After witnessing the unsuccessful bombardment, Francis Scott Key was moved to write "The Star-Spangled Banner," which the U.S. Congress established as the American national anthem in 1931. Meanwhile, Brooke ordered his army to withdraw, giving up the attack on Baltimore.

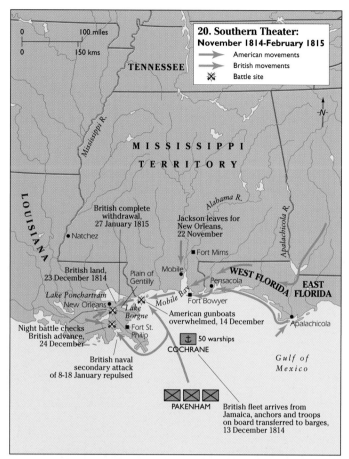

20. Southern Theater:
November 1814-February 1815

→ American movements
→ British movements
✕ Battle site

TENNESSEE

Mississippi R.

MISSISSIPPI

TERRITORY

Alabama R.

Apalachicola R.

LOUISIANA

British complete
withdrawal,
27 January 1815

Natchez

Jackson leaves for
New Orleans,
22 November

Fort Mims

British land,
23 December 1814

Plain of
Gentilly

Mobile

WEST FLORIDA

Pensacola

EAST
FLORIDA

Lake Ponchartrain

New Orleans

Mobile Bay

Fort Bowyer

Lake
Borgne

American gunboats
overwhelmed, 14 December

Apalachicola

Night battle checks
British advance,
24 December

Fort St.
Philip

⚓ 50 warships
COCHRANE

Gulf of
Mexico

British naval
secondary attack
of 8-18 January repulsed

✕✕✕
PAKENHAM

British fleet arrives from
Jamaica, anchors and troops
on board transferred to barges,
13 December 1814

Final Campaign of the War

The British launched their last major campaign of the war on the Gulf Coast. After temporarily occupying Pensacola in Spanish Florida and then threatening Mobile, Alabama, they targeted New Orleans. With a population of 25,000, this was the largest city west of the Mississippi River and the most important outlet for western produce. To get at the city, the British had to break through General Andrew Jackson's defensive lines south of the city. After several preliminary engagements, General Edward Pakenham on 8 January 1815, launched an attack against Jackson's main line on the east side of the Mississippi River and against a secondary line under the command of General David Morgan on the west side. Exposed to devastating artillery, rifle, and musket fire on an open plain on the eastern bank, the British suffered huge losses, about two thousand men, while Jackson's own losses numbered only seventy. This was the last major military operation of the war.

While the war on land went badly for the United States until the Battle of New Orleans, the war at sea was more successful, at least to begin with. By concentrating its small naval force, the United States prevented the British navy stationed at Halifax, Nova Scotia from blockading the American coast in the first six months of the war, thus allowing American ships carrying property worth millions of dollars to get safely back to port. The U.S. Navy also won a series of spectacular duels in the early months of the war. The

The 5,300 British regulars sent to Louisiana in 1814 faced a formidable opponent in Andrew Jackson. With a motley force of only 4,700—U.S. Army regulars, western militiamen, Choctaw Indians, free blacks, and the pirate Jean Lafitte's artillerymen—Jackson (above) defeated the British and laid the base for a political career that catapulted him to the White House.

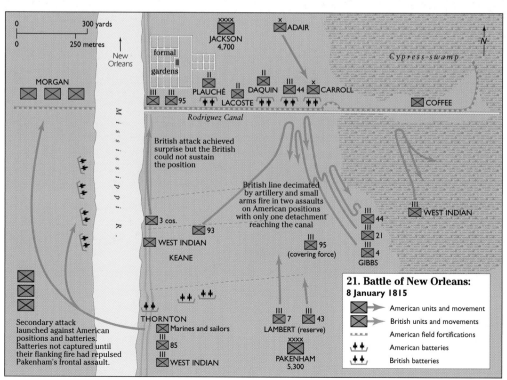

21. Battle of New Orleans:
8 January 1815

⊠→ American units and movement
⊠→ British units and movements
···· American field fortifications
♣♣ American batteries
♣♣ British batteries

New Orleans

formal
gardens

JACKSON
4,700

ADAIR

Cypress-swamp

MORGAN

PLAUCHÉ

DAQUIN

44 CARROLL

95

LACOSTE

COFFEE

Mississippi R.

Rodriguez Canal

British attack achieved
surprise but the British
could not sustain
the position

British line decimated
by artillery and small
arms fire in two assaults
on American positions
with only one detachment
reaching the canal

44

WEST INDIAN

3 cos.

93

95
(covering force)

21

WEST INDIAN

KEANE

4

GIBBS

THORNTON
Marines and sailors

85

WEST INDIAN

Secondary attack
launched against American
positions and batteries.
Batteries not captured until
their flanking fire had repulsed
Pakenham's frontal assault.

7

43

LAMBERT (reserve)

PAKENHAM
5,300

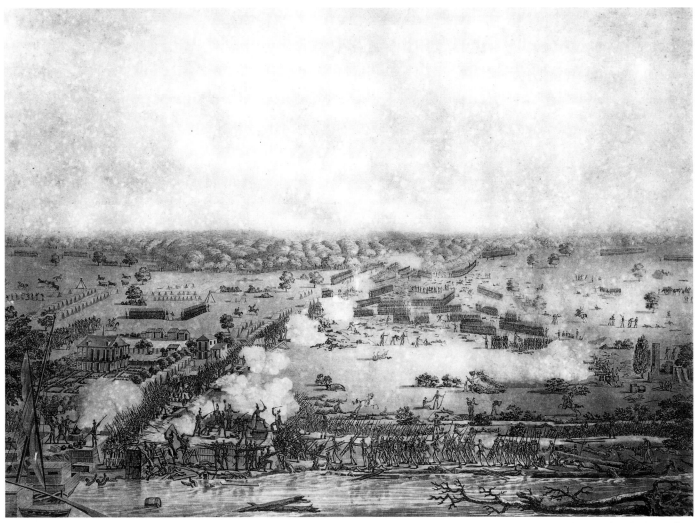

The repulse of the British invasion of New York at the Battle of Plattsburg led the government of Lord Liverpool to seek an end to the War of 1812. Without waiting to learn the outcome of the invasion planned for New Orleans, diplomats signed the Treaty of Ghent on 24 December 1814. On the same day, Andrew Jackson established a line of defense along the Rodriguez Canal outside New Orleans. On the morning of 8 January 1815, General Edward Pakenham, who had not yet learned of the peace treaty, sent his troops to attack the Americans. After several assaults, Pakenham called off the attack. Jackson's artillery and regular troops deserve most of the credit for the victory, but many Americans would credit Jackson's militia with the success and cite their effectiveness at New Orleans to support a policy of maintaining a small regular army and a larger militia. This detailed rendition of the battle was painted by one of Jackson' s engineers, Hyacinthe Laclotte.

U.S.S. *Constitution* defeated H.M.S. *Guerrière* and H.M.S. *Java*, and the U.S.S. *United States* captured H.M.S. *Macedonian*. Thereafter, the British increased their naval forces in the American theater and effectively blockaded the American coast, confining the U.S. Navy to port, and snuffing out American foreign trade. In the last year of the war, the United States had to rely mainly on privateers to carry on the war at sea. American privateers—such as the *Prince-de-Neufchâtel*, the *Governor Tompkins*, the *Harpy*, and the *Chasseur*—took a toll on British merchant shipping and thus drove up British insurance rates, but otherwise, did not directly influence the outcome of the war.

The two sides signed a peace treaty on 24 December 1814. The Treaty of Ghent, also known as the Peace of Christmas Eve did not reach the United States until early February 1815. The war came to an end when the two countries exchanged signed documents on 17 February. Although the war helped solidify the United States as a nation, Canada remained in British hands, and the treaty mentioned none of the maritime aims for which the United States had been contending. Hence, as a matter of policy the war must be considered a failure for the United States.

American Indian Wars: 1790-1859

The decades following the American Revolution brought unexpected challenges for the U.S. Army. Native American people throughout the eastern half of the modern United States continued to assert their autonomy and resist federal attempts to exert control over both their lands and their lives. Much of the initial difficulty arose over land claims in the Ohio Country. The Treaty of Paris of 1787 had transferred political hegemony over the Old Northwest from Britain to the United States. The new American government claimed ownership of the lands there and both land speculators and settlers began to purchase or settle on lands in southern and eastern Ohio. The government envisioned these public land sales as a source of income.

American Indians in the region refuted the American land claim, asserting that they had never relinquished political control or possession of the lands to the British, and that the lands could not be transferred to the United States. Encouraged by the continued British occupation of Detroit and other posts in the region, and buttressed by British arms, ammunition, and promises, the tribes were determined to defend their homelands.

Between 1785 and 1789, as settlers attempted to establish farms in southern Ohio, American agents tried to purchase lands in a series of treaties (Fort McIntosh, 1785; Fort Finney, 1786; Fort Harmar, 1789), but the tribal leaders from the Shawnees, Wyandots, Delawares, and Miamis claimed that the American Indians who had negotiated the agreements had no authority to do so and the treaties were denounced as meaningless. Additionally, the Indians struck back, burning settlements and forcing settlers to flee back to Kentucky.

Conflict in the Northwest

Convinced that military force would intimidate the tribes, in September 1790 General Josiah Harmar led a force of 320 regulars and 1,133 Kentucky and Pennsylvania militia north from Fort Washington (modern Cincinnati) toward Miami, Shawnee, and Wyandot villages along the Maumee Valley in northeastern Indiana and northwestern Ohio. The Indians retreated and Harmar burned several towns, but on 19 October, Colonel John Hardin, thirty regulars, and about 180 Kentucky militia were ambushed by a large war party led by Miami Chief Little Turtle. Most of the militia fled, but the regulars stood their ground and were cut to pieces. In a subsequent firefight two days later, the warriors again defeated Harmar's forces killing over forty regulars including Major John P. Wyllis. Harmar retreated to Fort Washington. A diversionary raid launched from Fort Knox (Vincennes, Indiana) by Colonel John Hamtramck in September against American Indians along the lower Wabash River suffered no casualties, but achieved limited success.

St. Clair's Defeat

During the summer of 1791, when two Kentucky militia raids against American Indian villages in the Wabash Valley accomplished little, Governor Arthur St. Clair led about 2,300 men in another expedition in September 1791 against American Indian villages along the Maumee River. Ill-equipped and poorly trained, about one-third of his force deserted as they marched north through western Ohio. Shortly after dawn on 4 November 1791, their encampment was attacked by a war party of over 1,000 American Indians. Although the surprise attack panicked the militia, the Americans repeatedly attempted to dislodge the Indians from the surrounding forest, but were unsuccessful. After a three-hour battle, the Americans broke through the Indian lines, abandoned their equipment, and ran for their lives. St. Clair's defeat was the greatest American Indian victory over an American military force in history. St. Clair survived the debacle, but 647 of his men were killed and hundreds wounded. Indian losses totaled about 150 warriors.

The Battle of Fallen Timbers

Severely shaken by the defeat, the United States again attempted to negotiate a peace settlement with the American Indians, but when their overtures were rejected, federal officials rebuilt the western army under a new commander. Arriving at Pittsburgh in the summer of 1792, General Anthony

The Miami War Chief, Little Turtle was a formidable defender of the right of the Miami people to keep their land and maintain independence from the U.S. government. At St. Clair's defeat in 1791, he won the greatest American Indian victory over the U.S. military in history.

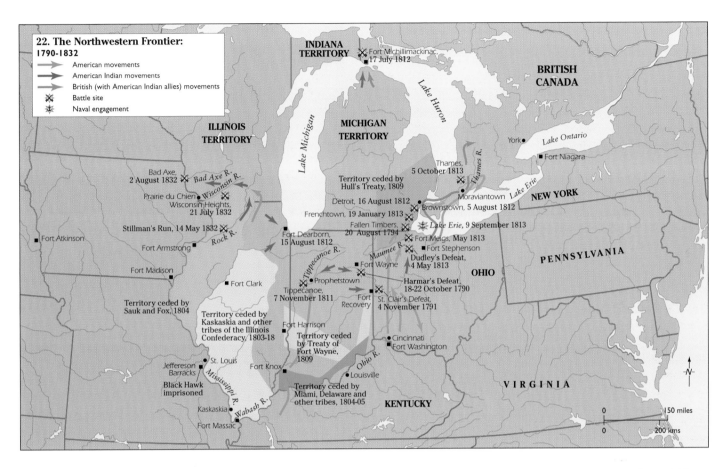

22. The Northwestern Frontier: 1790-1832

- American movements
- American Indian movements
- British (with American Indian allies) movements
- Battle site
- Naval engagement

Wayne recruited and trained a new army of 2,000 men which he called the "Legion of the United States."

Supported by about 1,500 Kentucky volunteers, Wayne marched north from Fort Washington in 1794, constructing a string of supply posts across western Ohio. An unsuccessful Indian attack against Fort Recovery on 30 June split the Indian ranks, and when Wayne reached the Maumee River in mid-August, the tribesmen could muster only about 1,300 warriors. On 20 August, as Wayne advanced down the Maumee, he found the Indians ensconced at Fallen Timbers, protected by a barricade of tangled trees felled by a tornado. Wayne's initial advance was repulsed, but his troops mounted a bayonet charge and the Indians withdrew. The Indians planned to make another stand at Fort Miamis, a newly constructed British fort about four miles downstream, but when the British commander Major William Campbell refused them entry to the fort, the Indians dispersed into the surrounding forests.

Disheartened by Wayne's victory at Fallen Timbers and their abandonment by the British, the American Indian alliance (comprised of the Potawatomis, Ottawas, Chippewas, Wyandots, Delawares, Shawnees, Miamis, Piankashaws, Weas, Eel Rivers, Kickapoos, Kaskaskias, Sacs, and Foxes) signed the Treaty of Greenville in 1795 which opened southern Ohio to American settlement, delineated a boundary line between Indian and American lands in the midwest, and set aside sites for American military posts at Fort Wayne, Fort Dearborn, and other locations.

Battle of Tippecanoe

Yet the Greenville treaty line did not prevent white settlement on tribal lands. In response, the Shawnee Prophet and his brother Tecumseh emerged to forge a new anti-American Indian alliance during the five-year period between 1805 and 1810. Attempting to destroy the Indian coalition, Governor William Henry Harrison of the Indiana Territory led an expedition in October 1811, of 1,000 men from Vincennes against Prophetstown, the center of the Indian coalition, located near the juncture of the Tippecanoe and Wabash rivers. In the pre-dawn darkness on 7 November 1811, the Prophet's followers attacked Harrison's camp and after a three-hour battle, they withdrew and abandoned their village. Both sides suffered casualties of about sixty killed and about 120 wounded, and Harrison destroyed large amounts of Indian food and other supplies. Moreover, Harrison's "victory" at the Battle of Tippecanoe eventually would launch a military and political career that would propel him to the White House in 1840.

For all practical purposes, the Battle of Tippecanoe was the opening engagement of the War of 1812, and in the west much of the warfare was carried out between American Indian and American forces. Commanded by Governor William Hull of Ohio, an American army occupied Detroit in early July 1812, and attempted to invade Canada, but it was forced back to Michigan by British and Indian forces. On July 17, a combined British and Indian force captured Fort Michillimackinac, and Hull's garrison at Detroit was besieged by Tecumseh and his British and American Indian allies. American attempts to break the siege and reestablish ties with American settlements in Ohio were thwarted when American troops were turned back at Brownstown (5 August 1812) and at Monguagon (9 August 1812). Then, on 16 August 1812, Hull surrendered Detroit to American Indian and British forces.

The Offensive Continues

The Indian offensive continued. On 15 August, a large Potawatomi war party attacked and overran the American garrison of Fort Dearborn after it had abandoned the post and was retreating toward Indiana. The Potawatomis killed or mortally wounded fifty-three soldiers and civilians and captured forty-three others. Early in September the Kickapoos unsuccessfully attacked Fort Harrison (near modern Terre Haute) and Potawatomi warriors attacked Fort Wayne. The garrison repulsed the assault, but the fort remained under siege until 13 September, when Harrison relieved the post and a British expedition, sent to support the Indians, turned back toward Canada. Harrison's men then burned several Indian villages in the lower Maumee Valley, while mounted Kentuckians, led by Samuel Hopkins, marched up the Wabash, destroying villages and cutting down cornfields.

During the winter of 1812-13, both sides attempted to regroup and resupply, although an ill-advised American action led by General James Winchester against British and Indian forces in southeastern Michigan resulted in the Battle of Frenchtown (19 January 1813). The Americans were repulsed. Winchester and many of his men surrendered or were captured. Some American prisoners were killed by the Indians. In May 1813, however, a 2,400-strong combined British and Indian army, commanded by Colonel Henry Procter and Tecumseh, surrounded and attacked American forces at Fort Meigs on the Maumee River near modern-day Toledo. Commanded by Harrison, the garrison numbered almost 2,000 men. In addition to being well supplied, the garrison had dug trenches and erected traverses against enemy artillery so that the British bombardment had little effect. On 4 May 1813, however, over 600 Kentucky militiamen led by Lieutenant Colonel William Dudley, proceeding down the Maumee River

to reinforce Harrison's garrison, were killed or captured in a surprise attack by the Indians.

Ironically, many Indian warriors returned to their villages after Dudley's defeat, assuming the Americans had been defeated because the Indians had captured so much American equipment. Because they could not raise Indian reinforcements, Tecumseh and Procter were forced to abandon the siege and return to Canada. Two months later, in mid-July 1813, Tecumseh and Procter mounted another attack on Fort Meigs, but Harrison had reinforced the post and a ruse by Tecumseh failed to lure the Americans outside the walls. Frustrated, on 2 August, Tecumseh and Procter attacked Fort Stephenson, a small American post on the Sandusky River commanded by twenty-one-year-old Major George Croghan. Croghan's force repulsed a frontal assault and killed or severely wounded over one hundred British and Indians. Disheartened, Tecumseh and Procter returned to Canada.

Battle of the Thames

Following Oliver Hazard Perry's victory against the British on Lake Erie on 9 September 1813, the Americans regained the initiative, and on 27 September 1813 American forces invaded Canada. The British and Indians retreated, but on 5 October 1813, 450 British troops commanded by Procter, and about 750 warriors under Tecumseh made a stand at Moraviantown on the Thames River. As Harrison approached with over 3,300 men, including some pro-American Indians, the British troops fired two volleys, then fled. The Indians remained and attempted to repulse the Americans. The ensuing Battle of the

Tecumseh, born in a village on the Mad River in Ohio to a Creek mother and Shawnee father, made an alliance with the British to oppose American expansion into Indian lands. It is believed that Tecumseh was killed by Colonel Richard Mentor Johnson at the Battle of the Thames on 5 October 1813.

Thames effectively ended Indian resistance in the Old Northwest. Tecumseh and about eighty of his followers were killed. American losses were twelve killed and twenty-two wounded.

The Southwest

American forces also periodically encountered pro-British warriors as auxiliaries to larger British military units on the Niagara frontier with Canada, but the other primary focus of Indian-American warfare during the War of 1812 was in the South. Prior to the war, the Creek confederacy had been split by religious and political dissension. The more militant Upper Creeks in northern and central Alabama had fostered the Red Sticks movement which recruited anti-American Creeks throughout the confederacy. In the spring of 1813 Creek warriors attacked isolated settlements in Alabama and Georgia, but on 30 August 1813 an immense war party of Red Sticks led by mixed-blood William Weatherford overran Fort Mims, a poorly fortified stockade on the lower Alabama River, killing all but 36 of the 553 settlers who had taken refuge in the post. In response, Andrew Jackson raised an army of 3,500 Tennessee militia and marched south into Alabama, first attacking the Red Sticks at Tallushatchee, a village on the Coosa River, where Jackson lost only five killed, but killed or mortally wounded over 150 Indians. He then marched to Talledega, where Weatherford and about 1,000 Red Sticks had besieged a village of Lower Creeks friendly to the United States. The Americans were victorious again, inflicting over 300 Creek casualties.

Battle of Horseshoe Bend

Reeling from Jackson's campaign, Weatherford retreated to Tohopeka, a Creek town on the Horseshoe Bend of the Tallapoosa River, fortified by the Red Sticks. In January 1814, an American raiding party was repulsed, but on 27 March 1814 Jackson, pro-American Creeks, and 2,000 militia and volunteers attacked Tohopeka, killing over 500 of the 900 warriors, in addition to hundreds of Indian women and children. Weatherford escaped, but eventually surrendered to Jackson, who allowed him to return to his people. The Battle of Horseshoe Bend, the greatest American Indian battle loss in terms of lives, ended Indian military resistance in the south during the War of 1812 and facilitated the subsequent Treaty of Fort Jackson (9 August 1814) in which the Creeks were forced to cede almost 23 million acres of land. Ironically, most of the land was taken from the Lower Creeks, the pro-American faction which opposed the Red Sticks and supported Jackson.

The Black Hawk War

Although British influence diminished markedly after the War of 1812, American frontiersmen still believed British agents were fomenting hostility among the western tribes. In 1832, for instance, when Black Hawk's Sacs and Foxes attempted to reoccupy their lands in Illinois, they were referred to as the "British Band." In 1804, representatives of the Sacs and Foxes had unwittingly ceded their lands in northern Illinois to the U. S. government, but since American settlement did not approach the region until 1830, they had continued to occupy their land. During the late 1820s, when lead deposits and fertile farmland in northwestern Illinois attracted settlers into the region, American officials convinced most of the tribe, led by the pro-American chief Keokuk, to abandon their village at the mouth of the Rock River and move to Iowa. One band of the tribe, led by Chief Black Hawk, disavowed the treaty of 1804 and determined to remain in their Rock River Valley. After Governor Ninian Edwards mustered the Illinois militia late in the summer of 1831, however, Black Hawk and his band of 1,000 followers fled across the Mississippi River to Iowa.

Short of food, shelter, and blankets, Black Hawk and his followers spent a miserable winter in Iowa. On 3 April 1832, 1,000 Sacs and Foxes, including at least 600 women and children led by their chief, crossed back into Illinois. They planned to join the Winnebagos near Prophetstown, on the Rock River. Black Hawk's return set off a wave of panic in Illinois. Federal troops commanded by General Henry Atkinson were dispatched from Jefferson Barracks in St. Louis to Fort Armstrong (Rock Island, Illinois), while large numbers of Illinois militia and mounted volunteers assembled in southern and central Illinois. The Americans marched north to intercept the "hostiles."

Battle of Stillman's Run

Evidence suggests that Black Hawk only wished to harvest corn his people had abandoned the previous summer and had no hostile intentions. But the 2,000 troops converging on his followers alarmed the old chief, who led his people up the Rock River, away from the Americans. Learning that the Potawatomis and other tribes would not assist him, on 14 May 1832, Black Hawk sent a small party of warriors carrying a white flag and surrender overtures to 350 Illinois volunteers commanded by Major Isaiah Stillman, bivouacked near the Rock River. The Americans seized three of the warriors, then fired upon the others. The Indians fled, pursued by the entire American force toward a small grove of trees where Black Hawk and about two dozen other warriors were awaiting the American response. Convinced that the Americans would not accept their surrender, the Sacs and Foxes held their fire until the Americans came within close range. Then they fired from the shelter of the underbrush. Completely surprised, eleven Americans were shot from their horses. The others fled back to Dixon's Ferry twenty miles away, where they spread

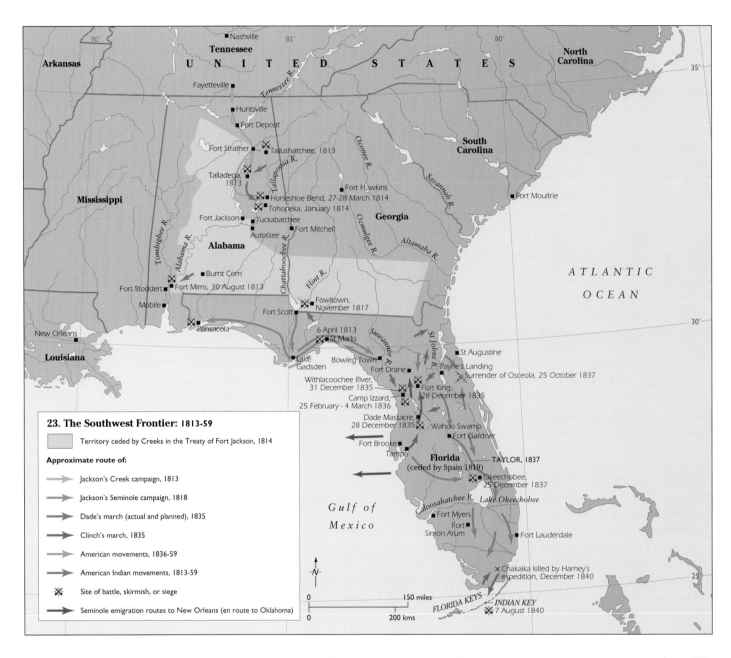

23. The Southwest Frontier: 1813-59

Territory ceded by Creeks in the Treaty of Fort Jackson, 1814

Approximate route of:

Jackson's Creek campaign, 1813

Jackson's Seminole campaign, 1818

Dade's march (actual and planned), 1835

Clinch's march, 1835

American movements, 1836-59

American Indian movements, 1813-59

✕ Site of battle, skirmish, or siege

Seminole emigration routes to New Orleans (en route to Oklahoma)

exaggerated reports that they had been attacked by Black Hawk and 1,000 warriors.

Battle of Wisconsin Heights

Next, Black Hawk led his followers north up the Rock River and then turned west across the rugged "Driftless Area" of southwest Wisconsin. Illinois raised additional militia units and Andrew Jackson ordered General Winfield Scott and eight hundred regulars to Chicago. Scott's force encountered cholera and never joined the campaign. General Atkinson, with troops from St. Louis and Illinois, pursued the Sacs and Foxes up the Rock River into Wisconsin. Skirmishes between

whites and Indian war parties broke out across northern Illinois. On 21 July 1832, Americans troops encountered the fleeing Indians near Sauk City, Wisconsin, as Black Hawk's followers attempted to cross the Wisconsin River. The Battle of Wisconsin Heights resulted in the deaths of about seventy Indians and one American, but the Sacs and Foxes crossed the river and escaped into the forest.

Battle of the Bad Axe

Retreating westward toward the Mississippi River, Black Hawk made repeated attempts to surrender, but they were either misunderstood or ignored. On 2 August 1832, the American army encountered the remaining Sacs and Foxes at the mouth of the Bad Axe River, where the Indians were preparing to cross the Mississippi River back into Iowa. The Indians attempted to flee onto small islands in the river, but they were caught between the troops on the shore and grapeshot fired from the armed steamboat, *The Warrior*, which had come upriver from Prairie du Chien. The Battle of the Bad Axe lasted almost eight hours, and when the firing stopped, over two hundred Indians lay dead. American losses were sixteen killed and eleven wounded. Black Hawk escaped, but later surrendered. He was imprisoned at Jefferson Barracks for eight months and then released. He died in Iowa in 1838.

The First Seminole War

American military action against the Seminoles was more prolonged and expensive than against other tribes. Seminole villages in Spanish Florida had long served as a haven for African-Americans fleeing slavery. Southern slave owners regularly petitioned U. S. Congress for military action against the tribe. In November 1817, Major David Twiggs and 250 men attacked a Seminole village at Fowltown, in southwestern Georgia, killing five Indians. Ambushing a military column and firing upon supply boats on the Apalachicola River, the Seminoles struck back. In response, Andrew Jackson led 500 regulars, 1,000 militia, and about 1,000 Creeks south into Florida in March 1818, where he burned several Seminole and African-American villages, but encountered few Indians. On 6 April 1818, Jackson seized the Spanish fort at St. Marks (just south of modern Tallahassee), and in May he besieged and captured Pensacola. He also captured, tried, and executed two British traders whom he accused of agitating the Indians.

By June, Jackson was back in Georgia and the First Seminole War was over. Jackson's invasion of Florida demonstrated the region's vulnerability to the American military power, and in 1819, the Adams-Onís Treaty was signed in which Spain ceded Florida to the United States. With Florida under American control, the Seminoles retreated to the south, and in 1823, the Treaty of Moultrie Creek was signed, which opened both Florida coastlines to white settlement, while the Seminoles retained lands in the peninsula's interior. Yet trouble continued when American Indians and settlers trespassed on each others' territory. White Southerners clamored for the removal of the Seminoles, who refused to surrender all former slaves living in their villages.

Treaty of Payne's Landing

In 1832, a group of Seminole leaders signed a preliminary removal treaty at Payne's Landing, but the treaty was fraught with controversy. The Seminoles believed the treaty provided for a party of their leaders to travel west to Oklahoma, and if

Seminole leader Osceola opposed the forced removal of his people from their lands in Florida. Until 1837, he led guerilla action against U.S. troops sent to stop the Seminoles. He died in prison in 1838.

the party approved the lands they were to be shown, the Seminoles would be removed to Oklahoma from Florida. The U.S. government, however, claimed that the treaty stipulated that removal of the Indians to the west was mandatory. When the Indian exploratory party returned to Florida dissatisfied, the Seminoles refused to be moved. Federal attempts to force removal on the Indians resulted in the second of the Seminole Wars.

The Second Seminole War

In April 1834, Georgia militia General Wiley Thompson called Seminole leaders to Fort King, near modern Ocala, and informed them they would have to leave for Oklahoma by January 1835. Some Seminole chiefs agreed, but others, led by Osceola and Micanopy, refused. Those opposed were imprisoned and released only after they agreed to sign the removal agreement. But the January removal never took place. Osceola claimed he had signed the treaty only under coercion and disavowed it.

The Seminoles stockpiled arms and ammunition, executed a pro-removal chief, and began to steal livestock from isolated white settlements. When federal troops were dispatched, the raiding Indians fled into the swamps. Supply trains were attacked and plundered, and additional units of Florida militia proved as ineffective as federal troops in catching and defeating the warriors. On 28 December 1835, the U.S. Army suffered twin disasters. Major Francis Dade and 107 officers and men were ambushed north of Tampa near the Wahoo Swamp by the war chiefs Micanopy, Jumper, Alligator, and about 175 Seminoles. Almost half the Americans fell from the first Indian

On the morning of 28 December 1835, reinforcements marching from Tampa Bay to Fort King under the command of Major Francis Dade were surprised by a group of American Indians. Half of the soldiers, most of whom had buttoned their coats over their guns and cartridge boxes to keep them dry, fell when the Indians fired on them from the cover of palmetto trees near the Wahoo Swamp. The Dade Massacre precipitated the Second Seminole War.

volley, but the others held out for two hours. When the firing stopped, all but three Americans, who escaped, were dead. Later in the day, Osceola led a separate attack upon the Indian Agency at Fort King, killing Thompson and six other Americans. The Americans quickly sought retribution. These two incidents effectively started the Second Seminole War.

Battle of Withlacoochee

Following the attacks upon Dade and Fort King, many Seminoles withdrew to the Wahoo Swamp on the Withlacoochee River to celebrate their victories, but they were followed by General Duncan Clinch, 250 regulars, and 460 mounted militiamen. On 31 December 1835, as the regulars crossed the river, they were discovered by Seminole scouts and attacked before reinforcements arrived. After seventy-five minutes of fighting, the Seminoles withdrew and the Americans were exhausted and also retreated.

Two months later, on 25 February 1836, a large war party of 800 Seminoles and 170 ex-slaves attacked General Edmund Gaines, 600 regulars and 500 Louisiana volunteers near modern Citrus Springs. Although superior in numbers, the Americans took refuge at Camp Izzard, a hastily erected log barricade, and were besieged by the Indians. After eight days of fighting, the Seminoles attempted to negotiate a peace, but when their proposals were rejected, they withdrew into the forest.

On 21 January 1836, General Winfield Scott assumed command of all troops in Florida, but his efforts to locate and engage the Indians proved ineffective. Scott's forces trudged through swamps and hammocks, but the Seminoles evaded

them. Meanwhile, Indian war parties besieged a blockhouse on the Withlacoochee River, then launched scattered attacks against the Florida frontier as far north as St. Augustine. In May 1836, Scott was replaced by Governor Richard Call of Florida, who also achieved little success, and in December, Call was succeeded by former Quartermaster General Thomas Sidney Jesup.

Jesup's forces were augmented by pro-American Creeks and additional volunteers from Tennessee. Without sufficient knowledge of Florida's interior, the Americans could not pin down the Seminoles. Yet by early 1837, Jesup had over 8,000 troops in the field. As the Seminoles were finding it difficult to plant crops or replace their stores of supplies and ammunition, in March their leaders agreed to a truce and to assemble at Tampa for removal to Oklahoma. But the arrival of white slave-holders, who attempted to seize both African-Americans and Seminoles, disrupted the proceedings. The Seminoles again retreated into the interior.

Seven hundred mounted militia and almost 1,000 northern American Indians (Kickapoos, Delawares, Shawnees, and a few Peorias, Kaskaskias, Weas, and Piankashows) arrived to augment the government's forces, and during the summer of 1837, the army pursued the Seminoles throughout central Florida. By September, Osceola and other militants indicated they were willing to negotiate an end to the warfare and accept a reservation in southern Florida, but they refused to leave the peninsula. On 25 October 1837, Osceola and other chiefs accepted an offer by Jesup to negotiate, but when they arrived at General Joseph Hernandez's camp to discuss terms, federal troops concealed nearby violated the Seminoles' flag of truce, surrounded and then seized Osceola, seventy-one warriors, six women, and four African-Americans. They were imprisoned at Fort Marion in St. Augustine. Jesup's breach of the laws of war arroused public criticism, which increased in November when Wildcat and eighteen other warriors escaped. The malaria-stricken Osceola, who could not accompany them, was transferred to Fort Moultrie, South Carolina, where he died on 30 January 1838.

Jesup's New Campaign

Following Osceola's imprisonment, Jesup launched another major campaign against the Seminoles. Vastly outnumbered, the Seminoles refused to confront the soldiers. But on 25 December 1837, Wildcat and his fellow warrior Alligator were forced to defend their village near Lake Okeechobee with 400 Seminoles pitted against an American force of 1,100, led by Colonel Zachary Taylor. The Seminoles fought until their women and children could escape and then they dispersed into the swamps. Although twenty-six American troops were killed and eleven were wounded, Taylor had proved that even the most remote Seminole villages were vulnerable to American military expeditions.

Seminole resistance was disintegrating. In the spring of 1838, Jesup captured another 675 Seminoles, promising that he would ask his superiors to let them remain in Florida. When American officials refused, Jesup surrounded the camp before informing the Indians of the negative decision. Under a flag of truce, Micanopy and eighty-one Seminole followers were seized. Other Seminoles surrendered and by June 1838, when Jesup was replaced by Brevet Brigadier General Zachary Taylor, the departing general boasted that he had killed or captured about 2,500 Seminoles.

Taylor still faced approximately 1,000 Seminoles, scattered in small bands in the interior. He managed to capture about 200 of them before March 1839, when he was relieved by Major General Alexander Macomb. Macomb convinced one small band to make peace, but the other Seminoles remained hostile and, in May 1840, Macomb was succeeded by General Walker Keith Armistead. Armistead successfully destroyed several Seminole villages, but captured or killed few Indians. Meanwhile, the warfare spread to the Florida Keys. On 7 August 1840, when Seminoles led by Chakaika attacked Indian Key, thirteen settlers were killed and much of the settlement was destroyed. In response, an expedition led by Lieutenant Colonel William Harney penetrated the Everglades four months later and killed Chakaika and two of his followers. Other Seminoles, starving and destitute, began to surrender in growing numbers. In January 1841, when Armistead was replaced by Colonel Williams Jenkins Worth, fewer than 800 Seminoles remained in Florida.

An End in Sight

Worth continued Armistead's policy of constant harassment. In March 1841, Wildcat was captured and then used his influence to persuade most of his band to surrender. They were shipped to Oklahoma seven months later. Other bands led by Billy Bowlegs, Halleck Tustenuggee, and the Seminole Prophet continued to skirmish with settlers or troops for another year. In July 1842, Worth met with a delegation of Seminole leaders and informed them that President John Tyler desired peace and would offer to remove them to Oklahoma, the option the government preferred, or would allow them to move to a Florida reservation on the Caloosahatchee River, west of Lake Okeechobee.

Although no formal peace treaty was signed with all the scattered bands, for all practical purposes, the Second Seminole War was over. About 600 Seminoles remained in Florida. The Second Seminole War was not the army's finest hour. Unfamiliar with both their enemy and the terrain, the general staff committed an army, which included militia units and friendly Indians that numbered as many as 9,000 men, against no more than 1,300 Seminole warriors and their African-American allies. American military forces and civilians suffered about 1,700 fatal casualties, while inflicting perhaps two-thirds of that number on the Seminoles.

Eventually, the United States removed 4,400 Seminoles to an Oklahoma reservation. The few Seminoles to elude removal rose briefly in a third Seminole War (1855-58), but they were hunted down and sent to join their brethren on the reservation. The cost of warfare with these American Indians was at least twenty million dollars, a staggering sum in the 1840s. Moreover, Jesup's decision to ignore flags of truce in the capture of Osceola and other Seminole leaders was a clear violation of military protocol. Brave men fought valiantly and died on both sides in this conflict; the Seminoles lost most of their homeland, but the victors paid dearly in terms of lives, money, and honor.

The closing of the Second Seminole War marked the end of formal military campaigns against Indians east of the Mississippi River. Acts of violence and armed confrontations marred the peace that followed and wars were fought in the trans-Mississippi West following the American Civil War, but the defeat of the British and the Indians in the Old Northwest during the War of 1812 sealed the fate of the Indians east of the Mississippi River. No longer would they have access to diplomatic and logistical support from European powers against the new American nation. Left on their own, the tribes possessed neither the technology nor the material resources necessary for a prolonged military struggle against a United States that continued to grow stronger in terms of resources and population.

The Growth of the Professional Army: 1815-60

The experience of the War of 1812 convinced the majority of Republican congressmen that an improved standing army was essential to the defense of the United States. Yet, given American politics, the doubling of the nation's land mass between 1821 and 1848, and the relative isolation afforded by the Atlantic and Pacific Oceans, the most significant factor in the growth of the professional army in the United States was the need for a standing force to police the nation's borders and frontiers.

The westward movement of the predominantly white American population led to demands for protection against and the expulsion of American Indians, demands that blunted traditional antagonism towards standing military forces among Jacksonian Democrats, whose national vision and constituency demanded territorial expansion. Though less eager for territorial growth, the Whigs' vision of national cohesion required a climate of stability and order that made them sympathetic to the disciplined hierarchy and bureaucratic system of the regular U.S. Army. Thus, though the authorized strength of the U.S. Army was reduced substantially (by 80 and 40 percent respectively) at the end of the wars with Britain and Mexico in 1815 and 1848, it suffered only one other reduction in strength during this era, leaving a stability and career security that encouraged men to make lifelong commitments to the U.S. Army as an institution and officership as a profession.

Educating an Officer Corps

The average career of the officers on the 1797 U.S. Army Register lasted only ten years, whereas the average service of officers on the 1830 and 1860 registers was more than twice as long. This increased commitment to extended service was fostered and sustained by the aspiring officers' socialization in the ethos of duty, discipline, and service inculcated by Superintendent Sylvanus Thayer's reform of the U.S. Military Academy at West Point, which overcame a period of institutional turmoil to produce all but six of the officers commissioned from 1821 through 1832. Although commissions were later given to some civilians without academy training, the proportion of West Point graduates in the officer corps grew from 18 percent in 1820 to more than 75 percent in 1860, making the U.S. officer corps the most educated in the world (and, on average, substantially more educated than the civilian professions in America, many of whose members did not attend or graduate from colleges or universities).

Though these future lieutenants learned little of strategy or handling large units, they developed a discipline, scientific capability (particularly as engineers), and an ethos of duty, honor (meaning integrity), and country—allegiance to the nation's constitutionally elected representative government, rather than to their own social class, ideology, section, or locality as had been common before 1815. West Point provided the nation's largest source of expert administrators, men who could supply the army, the nation's largest, most far-flung organization, in order to project power over unprecedented distances and maintain peace on the extended borders and frontiers their victories created.

Reduction of Forces and Specialization

After the 1815 reduction of forces, the U.S. Army was left with five battalions of artillery (each the equivalent of what was then considered a regiment, or ten companies of about forty to fifty men each), nine regiments of infantry, and a diminished staff structure. In 1821 this was reduced still further to four regiments of artillery and seven of infantry. Most staff functions (quartermaster, commissary, and ordnance) were returned to the regiments, leaving only a skeleton of the War of 1812 staff structure. The judge advocate generals were abolished, a move that cost far more in uncertainty over military law and the dissension encouraged by the absence of an independent military judiciary than it gained in financial savings.

Yet the need for specialization had finally been accepted, and the staff of the 1820s and 1830s was far larger, more specialized, and more effective than that before 1812. Inspector generals reported annually on unit readiness and quartermasters, subject to military discipline, supplemented and checked up on civilian supply contractors. Men like Quartermaster General Thomas Sidney Jesup (who held that office from 1818 until his death in 1860), Inspector General John Wool (1816-1841), and Adjutant General Roger Jones (1825-1852), veterans whose wartime experiences had taught them the value of standardization and systems, served for decades, providing unprecedented stability in army administration while creating entire systems of specialized regulations and uniform procedures. The result was a far higher standard of fiscal accountability that enabled the U.S. Army to ward off criticism that its expenditures were unnecessary or excessive.

Development of the Junior Officer Corps

Similar trends developed in the junior officer corps, since the "expansible" army plan created by Secretary of War John C. Calhoun and his military advisers in 1820 provided for a disproportionate number of officers in order to maintain the army's institutional infrastructure and prepare for its expansion during future conflicts. Though Calhoun's plan was not fully implemented, and never worked exactly as first envisioned, the limited extent of the 1821 reduction signaled the permanence of the regular standing army and an expert cadre of artillery, ordnance, logistics, and engineer officers. This officer corps was continually enhanced by new West Point graduates, some of whom visited Europe for professional

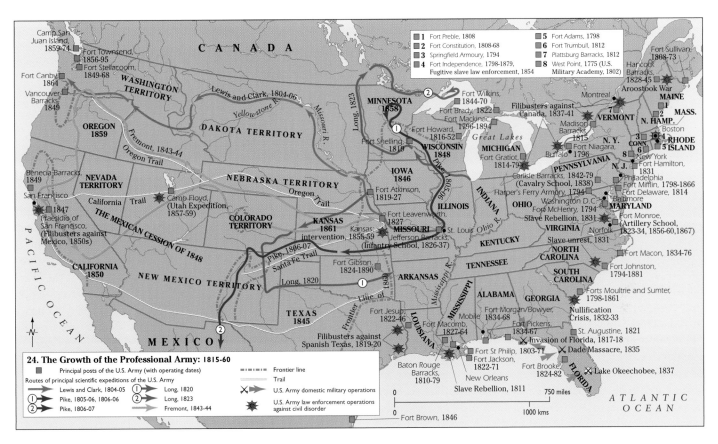

24. The Growth of the Professional Army: 1815-60

development. Some also lent their experience to the mass armies of the Civil War. From 1833 to 1844 these men subscribed to the first professional journals published for (though not by) the military in the United States, the *Military and Naval Magazine* and the *Army and Navy Chronicle*. Directed by senior officers like General Winfield Scott, these officers developed systems of drill (largely translations from France) tested in several "schools of practice" (the Infantry School at Jefferson Barracks in St. Louis, Missouri and the Artillery School at Fortress Monroe near Norfolk, Virginia) when troops were not dispersed on operations, that facilitated discipline and cohesion on the battlefields of Florida, Mexico, and the South.

The Work of the U.S. Army

The U.S. Army of this era served many purposes. It defended the coasts and the Canadian border against Britain, advanced and protected the southern and western frontiers, and tried to keep peace between American Indians and members of the white population. Designing the expensive coastal defense system was charged to the Board of Engineers for Fortifications (composed of U.S. Army and Navy engineers and, for a time, an emigrant French military engineer), the first permanent strategic planning body in U.S. history. Construction was supervised by the Army Corps of Engineers, trained in both

military (fortification) and civil engineering at West Point. Armed with unprecedented but still narrow technical expertise, the Fortification Board came under increasing criticism for seeking ever greater appropriations while making only marginal improvements in construction techniques. And even these improved fortifications later proved powerless against revolutionary new technologies such as steamships and rifled guns. Unable to transcend their commitment to an outmoded technological vision, the engineers pressed on to build a vast coastal defense system that was largely unmanned, unarmed, and obsolete in 1861.

The U.S. Army also performed a variety of tasks to assist the civil government in nation-building. From a national perspective the Corps of Engineers' primary duty was to survey and direct improvements in the civilian transportation infrastructure, ranging from canals to railroads, lighthouses, and harbor improvements. The engineers were aided by a subordinate bureau, and from 1838 to 1863 an independent corps, of army topographical engineers (most famously Major Stephen H. Long and Lieutenant John C. Frémont), who led most of the western exploration conducted by the U.S. Army during this era with some civilian engineers and large numbers of West Point-trained officers who were temporarily detailed from troop duty.

In 1802, West Point, fifty miles up the Hudson River from Manhattan, was chosen as the site of the first U.S. military academy. As its superintendent from 1817 to 1833, Sylvanus Thayer (above) expanded the curriculum, organized the cadets into companies, established the Academic Board to guide curriculum and set graduation requirements, and created the position of commandant. The academy, as it appeared in 1828, is pictured at left.

The Law of 1838

Lucrative opportunities in the booming railroad business and a reluctance to serve in malarial Florida led to the resignation of about 20 percent of the officer corps between 1835 and 1837. Faced with the Seminole Wars (1835-42), forced resettlement of the Cherokees (1838-39), and Canadian border tensions, such as the Maine Boundary Crisis and incursions by American citizens against Canada (1837-42), the U.S. Army was forced to close its schools of infantry and artillery instruction because troops at these schools were needed for the conflicts. The U.S. Congress increased the force by adding a dragoon regiment in 1836, in addition to one created in 1833 for duty on the Great Plains, and an 8th infantry regiment in 1838, while President Martin Van Buren was compelled to commission new officers directly from civilian life, without training or socialization at West Point. The U.S. Congress also outlawed the employment of serving officers on private railroad and canal projects and redirected officers' attention to their military duties, thus deflecting criticism from those civilian contractors who had not benefited from the technical expertise which U.S. Army engineers had provided to the enterprises of some of their competitors. Clearing obstacles to marine navigation from rivers and harbors, and eventually flood control, were duties assigned to the army engineers. These remained their bailiwick, duties they still perform today.

The 1838 law established the structure of the army's staff as it would exist for the rest of the century. It created an autonomous Ordnance Corps and increased the number of staff officers, thus spurring a separation of staff and line (combat arms) functions. These changes were effected, despite the fact that this reorganization aggravated tensions between staff

officers and officers of the line, for in the face of growing demands for military activity along the nation's borders and frontiers, further specialization and efficiency were required.

Peacekeeping Duties

Between 1815 and 1819 several regiments were sent to reoccupy outposts along the northwestern Great Lakes, but the defense of the Canadian border required few troops or fortifications. This was because there was a dramatic movement of the American population into upstate New York and the Great Lakes region during the 1820s and U.S. authorities believed these people could defend themselves in the event of war. The most serious problems the U.S. Army encountered along the northern frontier were unlawful attempts by private U.S. citizens who supported Canadian rebels resisting the authority of the British government in Canada. These Americans threatened to invade Canada, potentially precipitating war between the United States and Britain, a classic example of filibustering. This so-called "Patriot War" of 1837-39 provides the best case study of the complex, politically sensitive duties officers had to perform. They possessed a remarkable ability to mediate among antagonistic local, national, and international forces, born of experience and socialization rather than specialized training. The Patriot War coincided with the Maine Boundary Crisis, which was precipitated by the Aroostook War of 1839 between local authorities in Maine and New Brunswick. Experienced in diplomacy from two trips to Europe and service in Charleston during the Nullification Crisis of 1832-33, when South Carolina's planters tried to nullify federal legislation, General Winfield Scott defused the Aroostook War.

From Detroit to Vermont experienced field grade officers had to balance policing and persuasion with virtually no guidance from Washington. Among these men who took on extraordinary responsibilities were Colonel John Wool, serving his twenty-second year as an inspector general, who had been one of the commissioners sent in 1836 to negotiate a treaty with the Cherokee for their forced removal to the west in 1838; Major Sylvester Churchill, fresh from service in Florida, who took Wool's place when he was promoted and served as inspector general until 1861; Colonel Hugh Brady, who first entered the army in 1792 and commanded the 2nd Infantry Regiment at Detroit from 1815 until his death in 1851; and Colonel William Worth, one of Scott's protégés, for whom Fort Worth is named, who served as commandant of cadets at West Point for more than eight years. They mediated between British commanders, Canadian loyalists, American filibusters, and the local civilian population and authorities (including the militia), who were initially sympathetic to the insurgents. Indeed, U.S. military officers served as the only peacekeeping force on the scene to protect national interests and territory and to avert war with Britain.

Controlling Domestic Unrest

The U.S. Army was sometimes employed to deal with domestic unrest, including the reinforcement of Charleston during the Nullification Crisis, action against filibusters and marauders along the borders with Texas, and plans to intervene, if necessary, to prevent bloodshed in the Dorr War in 1842 between political factions in Rhode Island. Yet the U.S. Army's role in such cases was comparatively limited. Although it was perhaps the ultimate guarantor of slavery, U.S. Army regulars engaged rebel slaves in battle only once, in Louisiana in 1811, and the U.S. Army, so noted for using force against striking workers after 1876, did so on only one occasion, without violence, before the American Civil War. The U.S. Army was never called out to repress the rioting common in the principal cities of the United States during the 1830s-1850s.

Shift to the West

The huge territorial gains of 1848, as a result of the Mexican War, did not fundamentally alter patterns of U.S. Army growth and action. With the exception of the Regiment of Mounted Riflemen, which had been raised to protect the Oregon Trail, none of the regiments raised for the war with Mexico were retained afterward. After 1848, the army's physical center of gravity shifted decisively west, particularly into the Pacific northwest and Texas. Indeed, both the cavalry regiments commanded by Colonel Robert E. Lee, fresh from superintending West Point, and Colonel Albert Sidney Johnston, raised along with the 9th and 10th Infantry in 1855, were sent to Texas, where they campaigned constantly against American Indians and raids by Mexican citizens.

Officers like Brigadier General John Wool, a veteran of the War of 1812, Cherokee removal, the Patriot War, and the war with Mexico in 1848, and Brigadier General Ethan Allen Hitchcock, commandant of cadets at West Point after William Worth, an investigator for the Indian Department, and inspector general for both General Zachary Taylor and General Winfield Scott in Mexico, struggled against filibustering expeditions launched from California against Mexico. General Winfield Scott smoothed over another boundary controversy, his third such experience with Britain, in Vancouver Sound in 1859. Further law enforcement operations were undertaken to suppress Mormon resistance to national sovereignty in Utah (1857-59) and to keep peace between pro- and antislavery forces in Kansas (1855-59). After twenty years' effort Major Robert Anderson, Scott's one-time aide and later the officer in command at Fort Sumter at the outbreak of the Civil War, finally succeeded in establishing a Soldiers' Asylum, the ancestor of today's Veterans' Administration hospitals, to care for old veterans.

The fortification system continued to grow, the Artillery School was reopened in 1856, another wave of official missions was sent to observe military developments in Europe, particularly those in the Crimean War (1854-56), and there was new professional ferment at West Point, but the U.S. Army remained unprepared for the vast scale of combat it would soon face in the second half of the nineteenth century. With their troops dispersed in company-sized garrisons across the vast new western territories, few officers had the opportunity to gain experience commanding formations larger than several hundred men. The absence of a retirement system prior to 1863 meant that aging senior officers remained in the army until they died, while most West Point graduates were still captains or lieutenants after decades of service.

Colonel Phillip St. George Cooke, for example, fought in the Black Hawk (1832) and Mexican wars (1846-48), served in dragoon expeditions across the Great Plains and the Southwest (1829-the 1850s), and directed law enforcement and peacekeeping operations in both Utah and Kansas in the 1850s, but was only promoted to colonel in 1858, after thirty-one years of service. He then published a manual on cavalry tactics, but he was too old to use much of his experience during the American Civil War, despite being promoted to command a corps in the Army of the Potomac.

Yet most West Pointers remained in or quickly returned to service, and their administrative expertise proved crucial to training and supplying the mass volunteer armies of the American Civil War. The professionalism of West Point graduates was recognized by politicians and the public through their dramatic promotion—frequently from captain to general in only a few months—to command the armies that saved the Union.

The Texas Revolution and the U.S.-Mexican War: 1835-48

In 1835 a revolution erupted in Mexico's northern state of Texas. Coalescing behind diverse issues, the revolutionaries opposed authority centralized in Mexico City, supported maintaining the institution of slavery, and wanted more representative government. Included among the revolutionaries were a number of Texans of Hispanic descent, *Tejanos*. Hostilities began in June 1835 when forces, led by William B. Travis, occupied the port of Anáhuac. Armed clashes followed during October and November, culminating in the fall of the Mexican stronghold of San Antonio de Béxar to Texan forces on 9 December 1835. On 2 March 1836 a convention at Washington-on-the-Brazos declared independence from Mexico.

The Battle of the Alamo

Ragtag Texans, many of them adventurers or settlers from the United States, fought uniformed regular Mexican army units in several engagements. Three were crucial. At the Alamo mission, near San Antonio de Béxar, from 23 February to 5 March 1836, about 180 Texans resisted an army of more than 3,000 under General Antonio López de Santa Anna. On 6 March the Mexican army charged to victory, killing all of the Alamo's defenders, including Colonel Travis, Jim Bowie, and David Crockett.

The Struggle for Independence

Wiping out the Alamo's garrison demonstrated Santa Anna's determination to restore national authority, but the battle inspired Texans and others from the United States to rally behind the revolution. After a skirmish with General José Urrea's cavalry at Coleto Creek, eighty miles southwest of the Alamo, Colonel James Fannin surrendered his force of about 400 men nearby at Goliad on 19 March. A few days later the Mexicans executed Fannin and most of his soldiers. General Sam Houston retreated eastward as Santa Anna divided his army trying to trap the rebels; the revolution poised on the edge of failure. Recruiting more volunteers as he retreated, Houston watched for an opening. On 16 April 1836 Houston's force of about 900 launched a surprise attack on Santa Anna's 1,200 men camped along the San Jacinto River (near modern-day Houston), which with the adjoining swamp, blocked the Mexican retreat. Yelling "Remember the Alamo!" and "Remember Goliad!" the Texans carried the day, captured Santa Anna, and forced him to sign a treaty giving Texas independence. Although Mexican forces still outnumbered the Texans, in one stroke Houston had won the revolution.

The Interwar Years

For the next nine years, violence punctuated relations between Mexico and its former province. Mexicans insisted that Texas was still a state in the Mexican Republic. Texans insulted Mexicans by claiming lands they did not control, including Santa Fe, New Mexico, and a disputed zone between the Nueces River and the Rio Grande. The Texan and Mexican

Surrounded today by the city of San Antonio, the Alamo stood among fields in 1836. Its storming has been the subject of numerous romantic depictions. This 1885 painting, considered the most accurate view of the mission and battle, draws on information found in contemporary sources.

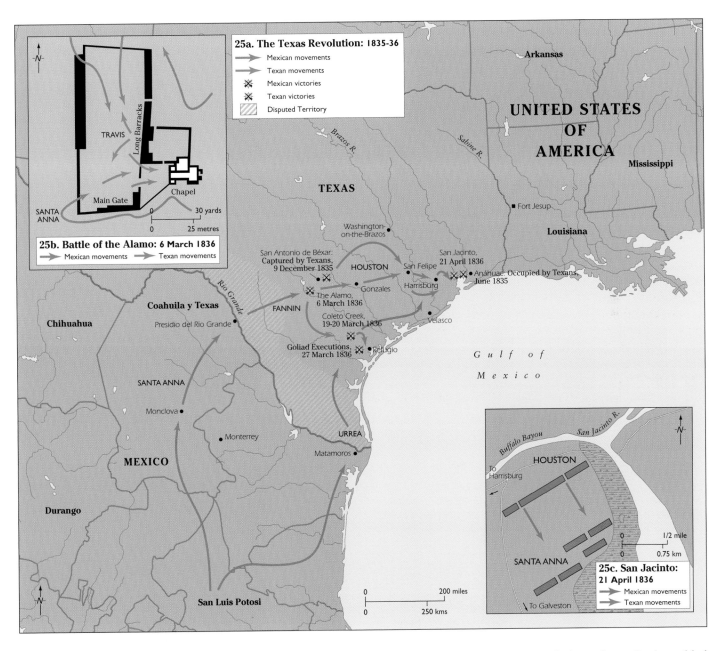

25a. The Texas Revolution: 1835-36

→ Mexican movements
→ Texan movements
✖ Mexican victories
✖ Texan victories
▨ Disputed Territory

25b. Battle of the Alamo: 6 March 1836
→ Mexican movements → Texan movements

TRAVIS
Long Barracks
Chapel
Main Gate
SANTA ANNA
0   30 yards
0   25 metres

Arkansas

UNITED STATES OF AMERICA

Mississippi

Brazos R.

Sabine R.

TEXAS

Fort Jesup

Louisiana

Washington-on-the-Brazos

San Antonio de Béxar:
Captured by Texans,
9 December 1835

HOUSTON

San Felipe

San Jacinto,
21 April 1836

Anáhuac Occupied by Texans,
June 1835

Gonzales

Harrisburg

The Alamo,
6 March 1836

Coahuila y Texas

FANNIN

Coleto Creek,
19-20 March 1836

Velasco

Rio Grande

Chihuahua

Presidio del Rio Grande

Goliad Executions,
27 March 1836   Refugio

Gulf of Mexico

SANTA ANNA

Monclova

Monterrey

URREA

Matamoros

MEXICO

Durango

Buffalo Bayou   San Jacinto R.

HOUSTON

To Harrisburg

SANTA ANNA

0   1/2 mile
0   0.75 km

25c. San Jacinto: 21 April 1836
→ Mexican movements
→ Texan movements

To Galveston

San Luis Potosi

0   200 miles
0   250 kms

military conducted raids across the Rio Grande, heightening tension on both sides. The United States attracted Mexico's hostility in 1845 when the U.S. Congress passed a resolution annexing Texas into the Union.

Meanwhile, a majority of people in the United States favored "Manifest Destiny," the popular notion postulating that God favored the country's expansion across North America. To fulfill Manifest Destiny, President James K. Polk urged Mexican officials to sell their nation's northern provinces, including California and New Mexico, to the United States. Mexico flatly rejected what it regarded as contemptuous overtures. Disputes over old claims for damages and contentions

that U.S. agents had aided Texas independence further added to the bitterness.

War Is Declared

Mexico and the United States declared war against each other in May 1846. In its declaration, the Mexican Congress labeled it a "defensive war," emphasizing U.S. annexation of Texas as the cause of hostilities. In Washington, the U.S. Congress overwhelmingly endorsed Polk's war message by 40 votes to 2 in the U.S. Senate and 174 votes to 14 in the U.S. House of Representatives, vowing to ensure the annexation of Texas and confirm the Rio Grande as the boundary between the two

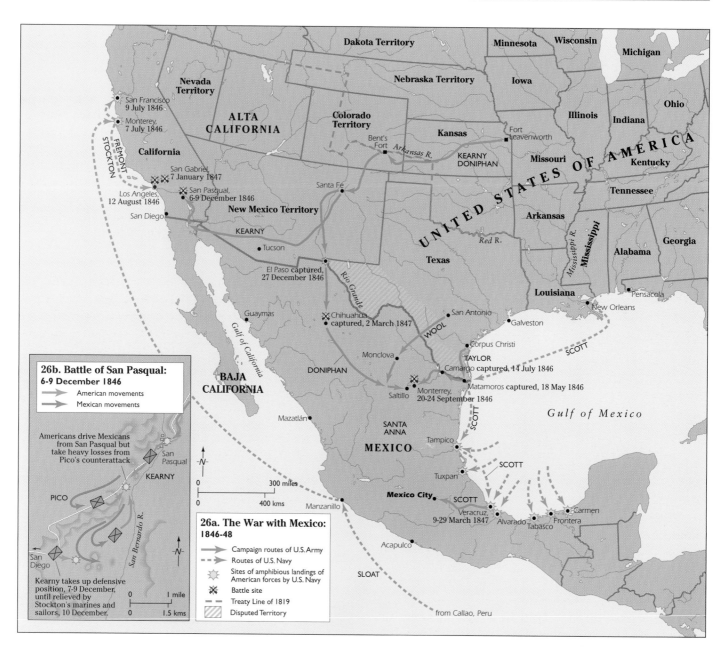

26b. Battle of San Pasqual:
6–9 December 1846

→ American movements
→ Mexican movements

Americans drive Mexicans from San Pasqual but take heavy losses from Pico's counterattack

PICO

KEARNY

San Pasqual

San Bernardo R.

San Diego

Kearny takes up defensive position, 7–9 December, until relieved by Stockton's marines and sailors, 10 December.

0   1 mile
0   1.5 kms

-N-

26a. The War with Mexico:
1846–48

→ Campaign routes of U.S. Army
→ Routes of U.S. Navy
✳ Sites of amphibious landings of American forces by U.S. Navy
✕ Battle site
– – Treaty Line of 1819
▨ Disputed Territory

0   300 miles
0   400 kms

-N-

nations. During the next two years, critics vociferously opposed the war with Mexico including several leaders of the Whig party such as Henry Clay of Kentucky, Abraham Lincoln of Illinois, and Daniel Webster and John Quincy Adams of Massachusetts.

Armed Forces

To wage war, at first the United States relied on its small, but high quality, regular army. Numbering only 7,300 soldiers in 1846, the U.S. Army possessed competent officers and a reliable supply system. Many company officers (captains and lieutenants) were graduates of the U.S. Military Academy at

West Point, New York, where they had acquired skills in weaponry and engineering.

To supplement the regular army, the U.S. Congress authorized a call for 50,000 volunteers. Members of both the Democratic and the Whig parties responded to the call, though the Democrats tended to favor the war more strongly than the Whigs. Before the war was over approximately 70,000 men volunteered, though most were never deployed to a war zone. To lead the troops, President Polk commissioned thirteen volunteer generals, all of them Democrats.

The United States also possessed a small, excellent navy. Manned by well-trained crews and commanded by capable

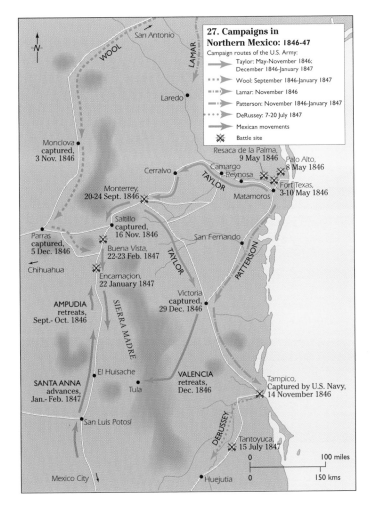

27. Campaigns in Northern Mexico: 1846-47

Campaign routes of the U.S. Army:

→ Taylor: May-November 1846; December 1846-January 1847

⋯▶ Wool: September 1846-January 1847

⋅⋅▶ Lamar: November 1846

⤍▶ Patterson: November 1846-January 1847

⋯▶ DeRussey: 7-20 July 1847

→ Mexican movements

✖ Battle site

Many officers were political appointees who lacked military training or experience.

Strategy

Each side had clear strategic objectives. Mexico intended to defend its territory and hoped to regain all of Texas. Lightly populated, weakly guarded, and distant from their capital, Mexico's northern provinces were difficult to defend against invasion. Polk formulated an ambitious offensive strategy designed to win the war in a few bold strokes. Polk assumed that if U.S. forces occupied the Rio Grande and captured key towns in New Mexico and California, Mexico would have to concede that the United States had won the war.

Initial Campaigns

Even before the declaration of war in the spring of 1846, Polk had ordered General Zachary Taylor with about 2,300 regulars, to establish a defensive perimeter in Texas. A patrol commanded by Captain Seth Thornton skirmished with Mexican troops on 25 April 1846 north of the Rio Grande, on territory

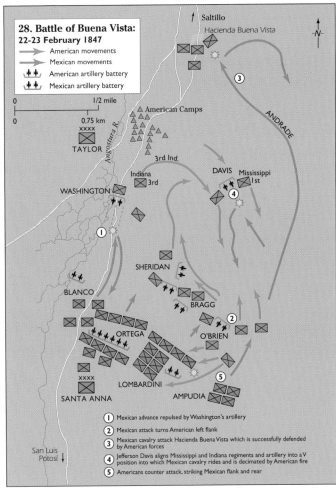

28. Battle of Buena Vista: 22-23 February 1847

→ American movements

→ Mexican movements

✦✦ American artillery battery

✦✦ Mexican artillery battery

① Mexican advance repulsed by Washington's artillery

② Mexican attack turns American left flank

③ Mexican cavalry attack Hacienda Buena Vista which is successfully defended by American forces

④ Jefferson Davis aligns Mississippi and Indiana regiments and artillery into a V position into which Mexican cavalry rides and is decimated by American fire

⑤ Americans counter attack, striking Mexican flank and rear

officers, the frigates, sloops, and steam gunboats of the U.S. Navy blockaded Mexico's ports and coasts from 1846. The U.S. Navy landed forces at Tampico, Tuxpan, Alvarado, Tabasco, Frontera, and Carmen on the Gulf of Mexico, and at Monterey and San Francisco in the Pacific. Furthermore, the U.S. Navy assisted the U.S. Army by guarding convoys and landing troops in a major invasion at Veracruz in March 1847 on the Gulf coast, and by transporting troops from San Francisco to San Diego in the campaign in California.

In several ways Mexico's armed forces contrasted with those of the United States. Mexico's navy played no part in the war. It contained only a handful of vessels; some of those were sold to prevent their capture by the U.S. Navy. Mexico's main defense rested on its large army of approximately 32,000 soldiers, but its numbers masked weaknesses. The numbers of soldiers in some Mexican army units were below reported strengths and the logistical system was unreliable because the Mexican army was unevenly equipped and supplied. Observers rated most Mexican cavalry squadrons as excellent, but infantry units varied in quality, size, and equipment.

claimed by both nations. Taylor took steps to drive Mexican forces south of the Rio Grande. In the initial major battle at Palo Alto (8 May), Taylor's 2,300 troops, including excellent artillery batteries, defeated 6,000 of Mexico's best soldiers under General Mariano Arista. Arista's army retreated to a position at Reseca de la Palma, twenty miles inland from Palo Alto close to the Rio Grande, where 1,700 of Taylor's men defeated 5,700 Mexicans on 9 May. In the weeks to come, state volunteers and Texas Rangers reinforced Taylor's army. It crossed the Rio Grande, captured Matamoros (18 May) and Camargo (14 July), and took Monterrey (20-24 September).

Meanwhile, Polk ordered a contingent of 1,500 soldiers (of whom only 300 were regulars) under Colonel Stephen W. Kearny and Missouri volunteers under Colonel Alexander Doniphan to invade New Mexico, secure Santa Fe, and strike in California. Their march from Fort Leavenworth was harrowing but Mexican forces near Santa Fe provided no resistance, conceding the city on 18 August. Doniphan soon pushed south. With less than 1,000 men, he captured El Paso (modern Juárez) on 27 December and Chihuahua on 2 March 1847, fighting battles outside of each city.

Taking only one hundred regulars, Kearny made another difficult overland march from Santa Fe, reaching California in early December 1846. There he met a few more U.S. Army regulars under John C. Frémont and linked up with two U.S. naval squadrons. One squadron, under Commodore John D. Sloat, had disembarked some U.S. Marines and sailors at Monterey on 7 July 1846, and another under Commodore Robert Stockton had occupied Los Angeles on 12 August. Refusing to capitulate without a fight, the Mexicans rose against the U.S. occupation and fought a sequence of battles, including San Pasqual, near San Diego (6 December 1846), and San Gabriel, below Los Angeles (7 January 1847). The Mexicans were unable to succeed in their efforts, however, and

by the end of January 1847 the United States had effectively conquered California.

Polk's strategic plan was successful but Mexico refused to negotiate, much less surrender. Having learned of U.S. intentions to invade at Veracruz, Mexico's president and senior general, Antonio López de Santa Anna, resolved on a bold strategy: First to defeat Taylor in the north, then to repel the threat from the Gulf. Raising a new army by enrolling 20,000 volunteers, conscripts, and veterans from San Luis Potosí, Santa Anna led his troops on a grueling forced march north, striking Taylor's 5,000-man army at Buena Vista, near Saltillo. In a two-day battle (22-23 February 1847), Santa Anna sent piecemeal assaults into the teeth of U.S. artillery fire. Leading a riposte, Colonel Jefferson Davis' Mississippi Volunteers blunted the Mexicans' attack. Santa Anna retreated to Mexico City and prepared to resist yet another invasion.

The Fall of Veracruz

To end the war, President Polk ordered General Winfield Scott to mount a seaborne campaign leading to the capture of Mexico City. Veracruz was Mexico's biggest seaport and necessary as a supply base for Scott's forces. General Juan Morales commanded strong Mexican defenses designed to meet direct attacks. Morales anchored on the imposing fortress of San Juan de Ulúa where he waited for the enemy attack. Scott, however, located an undefended beach south of the city and, directed by commodores David Conner and Matthew C. Perry, the U.S. Navy landed 14,000 U.S. Army soldiers and 300 U. S. Marines on 9 March 1847, the largest amphibious landing by U.S. forces until World War II. Scott's army put Veracruz under siege and it fell on 29 March.

The Mexico City Campaign

As Mexico City was located 225 miles inland from Veracruz,

This stylized map of the valley of Mexico was published a decade after the outbreak of the U.S.-Mexican War. The route taken by Winfield Scott's army starts on the right side of the map. The army circled south and westward to avoid the defensive positions that had been established east of Mexico City, where the National Road from Veracruz crossed an arm of Lake Texcuco at El Peñon. After defeating General Gabriel Valencia's army at Contreras and Antonio López de Santa Anna's army at Churubusco, Scott camped at Tacabaya and sought to negotiate an end to hostilities. His terms rejected, Scott pressed on to Chapultepec (which has been engulfed by modern-day Mexico City), where the storming of the castle opened the way into Mexico City. American forces entered the Mexican capital the next day and occupied the city until June 1848.

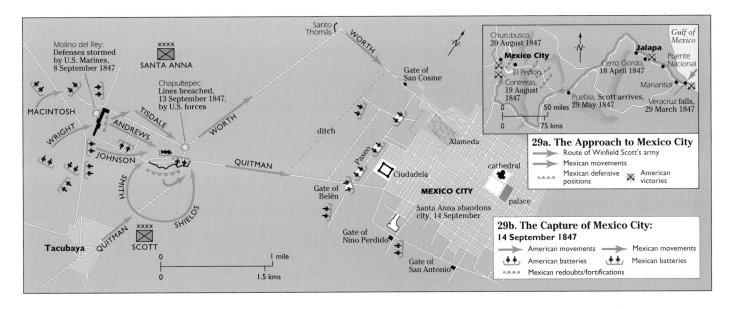

Santa Anna devised a plan to inflict high casualties on Scott's army. He positioned defenses at towns and mountain passes along the way, and also calculated that diseases would further weaken the invaders. Maintaining a supply line to Veracruz, Scott's army moved ahead. Winning a key battle about fifty miles inland from Veracruz at Cerro Gordo (18 April), U.S. soldiers spent a month a few miles west at Jalapa recovering and resupplying before continuing the offensive. Taking a risky step, Scott cut his line to the coast and lived off the land. Reaching Puebla on 29 May, Scott realized that the enlistments of thousands of volunteers were expiring and paused to await reinforcements. Two months later the strength of Scott's army returned to around 10,000 and he resumed the campaign.

In mid-August the fight began for Mexico City. Santa Anna brought together some 20,000 defenders. Strong positions protected the city's eastern approaches. Scott's military engineers gave him information to outflank these defenses. Accordingly, U.S. forces approached the capital from the south, fighting a series of bitter battles at Contreras (19 August) and at Churubusco (20 August). Santa Anna shifted some troops to meet Scott's threat, now pushing in from the west. U.S. Marines and soldiers broke through stout Mexican defenses at Molino del Rey (8 September) and five days later breached lines at Chapultepec and the city gates at Belén and San Cosme (13 September). The next day Santa Anna abandoned the city. Diplomats took several weeks negotiating terms to end the war.

The War's Results

Expending 100 million dollars and losing more than 10,000 military personnel who were killed or died of disease, the United States became a transcontinental power. The Treaty of Guadalupe Hidalgo of 1848 confirmed that the United States possessed Texas with the Rio Grande as the international boundary. The United States gained all of the vast lands Polk had sought to purchase—later to become the states of California, New Mexico, Arizona, Nevada, Colorado, and Utah. Mexico lost half of its land and one percent of its population. The treaty also required the United States to pay Mexico 15 million dollars and assume all claims of U.S. citizens against the Mexican government, which amounted to another 3 million dollars.

Beyond the transfer of land and money, the war produced other important results. The U.S. land and naval forces successfully fought their first major overseas operations and West Point graduates distinguished themselves, thus establishing the professional status of the U.S. Military Academy. Although small numbers of U.S. Marines participated in the campaigns, their exploits garnered favorable publicity and support in the U.S. Congress for the U.S. Marine Corps. President Polk's detailed direction of the war broadened the president's powers as commander-in-chief.

The war also stimulated debate in the U.S. Congress regarding a controversial proposal introduced by the Pennsylvania Democrat Davis Wilmot. The Wilmot Proviso stated that no slavery would be allowed in the territory taken from Mexico. The proposed law passed the U.S. House of Representatives but failed in the U.S. Senate. Disagreements over slavery in the new territories led to the Compromise of 1850. It admitted California as a free state, but allowed slaveowners to bring slaves into the western territories captured from Mexico. Thus, the war that expanded the United States to the Pacific also intensified the debate relating to slavery and led to the American Civil War.

The American Civil War: 1861-65

At 4:20 A.M. on 12 April 1861, a single artillery round arched through the skies over Charleston Harbor. It missed its intended target, the federal post of Fort Sumter. That errant shot, however, signaled the opening of the American Civil War, the nation's single deadliest conflict. Since the birth of the republic, but increasingly since the 1830s, sectional divisions between North and South over such issues as the institution of slavery and its spread to new territories, the proper relationship between the federal government and the territories, the proper relationship between the federal government and that of individual states, and economic programs such as tariffs and internal improvements threatened to rend the whole fabric of the nation. Political and judicial leaders had offered up many potential solutions in the 1840s and 1850s, but all required a degree of compromise that ultimately satisfied no one and resolved nothing. By that April morning in 1861, force of arms replaced political discourse as the way to achieve desired goals.

After the failure of several attempts at political compromise after the election of Republican President Abraham Lincoln, the United States and the new Confederate States of America—comprised of South Carolina, Georgia, Florida, Alabama, Mississippi, Louisiana, and Texas, joined by Virginia, North Carolina, Tennessee, and Arkansas after Fort Sumter—squared off to settle their differences on the field of battle. On paper, it seemed a mismatch from the start.

The Union's Advantage

The Union clearly held many advantages. Its 1860 population numbered 22,339,991. Its government apparatus remained stable, even during a period of political chaos. The secession of the southern states that had begun in December 1860 and Lincoln's ascendancy into office on 4 March 1861 had not interfered with the operations of U.S. Congress or the U.S. Supreme Court. The U.S. Army counted 16,367 officers and

War broke out between the North and South when Confederate General P.G.T. Beauregard opened fire on Union Fort Sumter on 12 April 1861.

men on 1 January 1861. The U.S. Navy possessed about 90 vessels, only 35 ready for immediate duty. The North claimed a respectable industrial base in iron, steel, and other key war materials. Its banking system thrived on substantial investment capital and enjoyed a stable currency. Growing urban centers provided markets for the region's considerable agricultural production of food crops. The recent success of federally funded internal improvement programs had stimulated the growth of a vibrant transportation infrastructure, including roads, canals, and thousands of miles of railroads. No one knew yet the importance of that last commodity in the coming conflict, often tabbed the first "railroad war."

The Challenge of the South

By contrast, the new Confederacy faced multiple challenges. With a population of 9,103,322—3,653,870 being slaves or free blacks—the South felt the disadvantage of inferior numbers from the start. Its political leaders had to create a governmental infrastructure from scratch. Provisional President Jefferson Davis shaped his Cabinet at least in part by naming influential representatives of each state to key posts. The Confederacy possessed no army (except a profusion of militia companies of wildly varying quality) and no navy. The South had no bank-

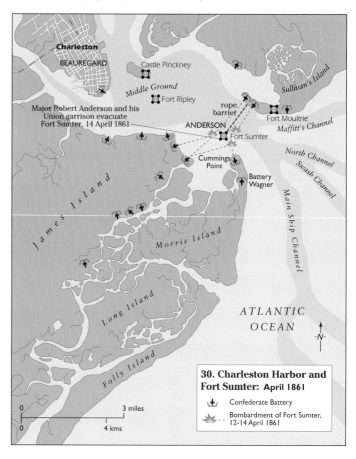

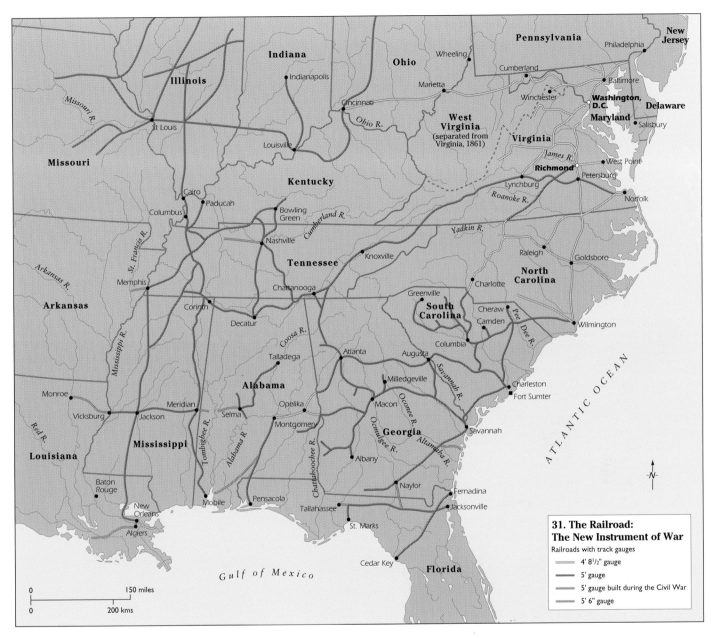

**31. The Railroad:
The New Instrument of War**

Railroads with track gauges

4' 8½" gauge

5' gauge

5' gauge built during the Civil War

5' 6" gauge

ing system, no currency, and no credit rating. Its industrial base remained small and undeveloped; only a few establishments such as Richmond's Tredegar Ironworks were capable of making locomotives, train tracks, or armor plating for ships. The agricultural South produced staple crops such as cotton, rice, and tobacco; food crops and the raising of livestock took a distinct second place in the most intensively farmed regions of the South. The strongly Democratic South had eschewed the internal improvements concept during the antebellum years and, thus, its transportation system remained far more linked to its rivers rather than tied together by rails.

Despite such disparities in numbers and resources, Confed-

erate States put up a stiff resistance for four years. They did so in large part because neither side knew in 1861 what it would take to fight a war on this conflict's scale. Mass armies and large navies had to be recruited, trained, organized, and equipped. Industry had to make a transition from peacetime to wartime production; in the South, entire industries had to be created, including a concentration of activity in the iron country of northern Alabama. But the war lasted four years largely because, at its start, neither North nor South had a clear vision of how to fight, let alone win, the "irrepressible conflict."

Both in Washington and in the new Confederate capital at Richmond, military leaders considered their options for

Jefferson Davis (right) was sworn in as president of the Confederacy on 18 February 1861 in Montgomery, Alabama (far right). An 1828 graduate of West Point, Davis left the army in 1835 and became a cotton planter in Mississippi. During the U.S.-Mexican War (1846-48), he commanded a regiment at the battles of Monterrey and Buena Vista. A senator (1847-51 and 1857-61) and secretary of war (1853-57), Davis considered himself a great strategist and regularly sent his commanders advice, much of which was not welcomed.

winning this war. Planning on the grand scale did not come easily to the leaders on either side. They had little experience in applying the theoretical foundation of the art of war to the reality they now faced.

Planning for War

In Washington, General Winfield Scott, the gouty old Mexican War hero and failed presidential candidate, outlined two objectives that, when accomplished, could force the Confederacy to end its rebellion without excessive bloodshed. First, a naval blockade of Southern ports might throttle the Confederacy's war economy by cutting off the importation of essential supplies from Europe and the exportation of cotton to pay for those goods. Second, control of the Mississippi River and its key tributaries was a move that would divide the new Confederacy and give Union forces the flexibility and security it needed to operate deep within Southern territory. In Scott's mind, neither of these courses of action, while potentially decisive, required the South to suffer excessive loss of life or property. If Confederate political and military leaders realized that they could not win a military showdown, sectional statesmen might yet work out a settlement to undo secession and prevent future hostilities.

Scott's advice seemed militarily sound, given the forces then extant and the level of Confederate military threat to the North. Moreover, it seemed to fit the military principles propounded by Baron Antoine Henri Jomini, a Swiss military theorist who had served on Napoleon's staff, and popularized that great captain's rules for victory. These guidelines included a reliance on the offensive, the application of the mass of one's own force against parts of the enemy, and the destruction of enemy bases, supplies, and communications while protecting one's own. Jomini's theories had become a staple in the

curriculum of the antebellum U.S. Military Academy at West Point, and even if the senior officers in both armies did not always understand their complex nuances, they nonetheless relied upon these ideas for guidance and inspiration.

The Call for Urgent Action

Scott's plan, nonetheless, did not impress impatient Northerners who feared it would take too long. More aggressive action might gain victory more quickly. Indeed, critics soon dubbed Scott's vision the "Anaconda Plan" for its slow strangling approach to killing the rebellion. In Missouri, in western Virginia, and elsewhere in the late spring and early summer of 1861, small Union armies began to contest for control of border areas. But the call, "On to Richmond," became the most pervasive Northern rallying cry of all. But, the ninety-day volunteers that first answered Lincoln's call to arms in mid-April faced discharge in mid-July, and the Confederate Congress planned to convene in Richmond for the first time on 20 July. If Union forces planned to take Richmond before the Confederate congressmen took their seats and before the ninety-day volunteers left for home, active operations had to begin immediately.

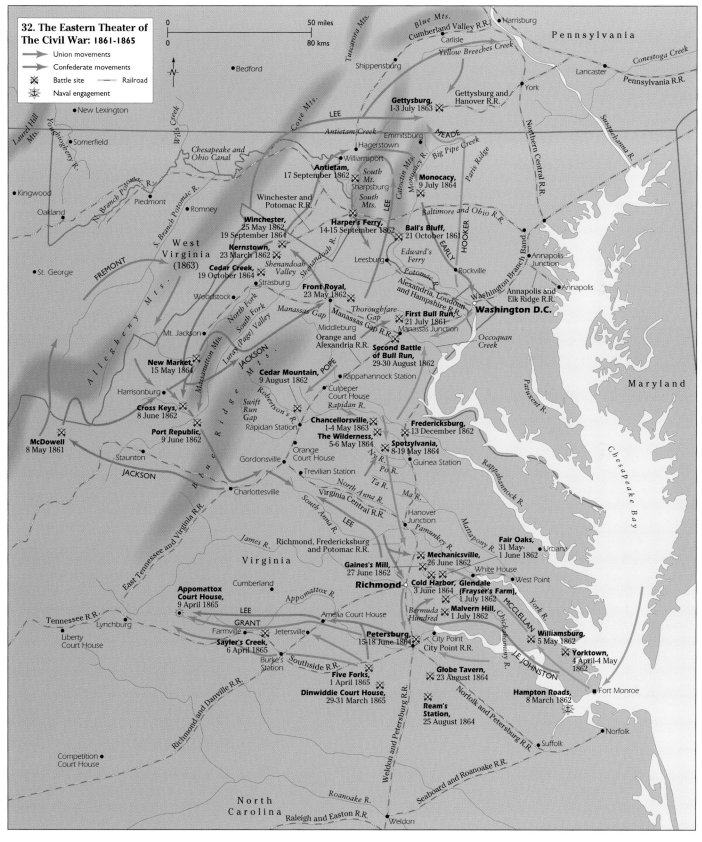

32. The Eastern Theater of The Civil War: 1861-1865

Union movements
Confederate movements
Battle site — Railroad
Naval engagement

0 ——— 50 miles
0 ——— 80 kms
-N-

Pennsylvania

Harrisburg
Blue Mts.
Cumberland Valley R.R.
Carlisle
Yellow Breeches Creek
Tuscarora Mts.
Shippensburg
Lancaster
Conestoga Creek
Pennsylvania R.R.

Bedford

Gettysburg, 1-3 July 1863
Gettysburg and Hanover R.R.
York
Northern Central R.R.
Susquehanna R.

New Lexington

LEE
Antietam Creek
Emmitsburg
MEADE
Hagerstown
Big Pipe Creek
Paris Ridge
Monocacy R.
Catoctin Mts.

Laurel Hill Mts.
Youghiogheny R.
Wills Creek

Somerfield
Chesapeake and Ohio Canal
Williamsport
Antietam, 17 September 1862
South Mt. Sharpsburg
South Mts.
Monocacy, 9 July 1864
EARLY
Baltimore and Ohio R.R.
Annapolis Junction

Kingwood
N. Branch Potomac R.
Piedmont
Romney
Winchester and Potomac R.R.
Winchester, 25 May 1862 19 September 1864
Harper's Ferry, 14-15 September 1862
Ball's Bluff, 21 October 1861
HOOKER
Annapolis

Oakland
S. Branch Potomac R.
West Virginia (1863)
Kernstown, 23 March 1862
Cedar Creek, 19 October 1864
Shenandoah Valley
Leesburg
Edward's Ferry
Rockville
Washington Branch Band
Annapolis and Elk Ridge R.R.
Annapolis

St. George
FREMONT
Allegheny Mts.
Woodstock
Strasburg
North Fork South Fork
Front Royal, 23 May 1862
Shenandoah R.
Alexandria, Loudoun and Hampshire R.R.
Potomac R.
Washington D.C.

Maryland

Mt. Jackson
Massamutten Mts.
North Fork South Fork
Luray (Page) Valley
Manassas Gap
Manassas Gap R.R.
Thoroughfare Gap
Middleburg
First Bull Run, 21 July 1861
Manassas Junction
Occoquan Creek

New Market, 15 May 1864
JACKSON Mts.
Orange and Alexandria R.R.
Second Battle of Bull Run, 29-30 August 1862
Patuxent R.

Harrisonburg
Blue Ridge
Cedar Mountain, 9 August 1862
POPE
Rappahannock Station
Culpeper Court House
Rapidan R.

Cross Keys, 8 June 1862
Swift Run Gap
Roberson's R.
Rapidan Station
Chancellorsville, 1-4 May 1863
Fredericksburg, 13 December 1862
Chesapeake Bay

McDowell 8 May 1861
Port Republic, 9 June 1862
Staunton
The Wilderness, 5-6 May 1864
Spotsylvania, 8-19 May 1864
Rappahannock R.

JACKSON
Gordonsville
Orange Court House
Guinea Station
N. R.
Po R.
Ta R.
Ma R.

Charlottesville
Trevilian Station
North Anna R.
Virginia Central R.R.
Hanover Junction
Pamunkey R.
Mattapony R.

East Tennessee and Virginia R.R.
James R.
South Anna R.
LEE
Richmond, Fredericksburg and Potomac R.R.
Fair Oaks, 31 May-1 June 1862
Urbana

Virginia
Mechanicsville, 26 June 1862
White House
West Point

Appomattox Court House, 9 April 1865
Cumberland
Appomattox R.
LEE
GRANT
Gaines's Mill, 27 June 1862
Richmond
Cold Harbor, 3 June 1864
Glendale (Frayser's Farm), 1 July 1862
MCCLELLAN
York R.

Tennessee R.R.
Lynchburg
Liberty Court House
Farmville
Jetersville
Amelia Court House
Sayler's Creek, 6 April 1865
Burke's Station
Southside R.R.
Petersburg, 15-18 June 1864
Bermuda Hundred
Malvern Hill, 1 July 1862
City Point
City Point R.R.
Williamsburg, 5 May 1862
Chickahominy R.
J.E. JOHNSTON
Yorktown, 4 April-4 May 1862
Fort Monroe

Competition Court House
Richmond and Danville R.R.
Five Forks, 1 April 1865
Dinwiddie Court House, 29-31 March 1865
Globe Tavern, 23 August 1864
Ream's Station, 25 August 1864
Weldon and Petersburg R.R.
Norfolk and Petersburg R.R.
Hampton Roads, 8 March 1862
Suffolk
Norfolk

North Carolina
Roanoke R.
Raleigh and Easton R.R.
Weldon
Seaboard and Roanoke R.R.

Winfield Scott entered the army in 1807, rose to brigadier general during the War of 1812, and won the battles of Chippewa and Lundy's Lane. During the U.S.-Mexican War, his army captured Veracruz and Mexico City. Though Virginia-born, Scott remained loyal to the Union and in 1861 formulated the "Anaconda Plan," the basic strategy executed by Union forces during the Civil War. This photographic portrait dates from the American Civil War.

Brigadier General Irvin McDowell, commander of the Union forces around Washington, opposed such a hasty move. His troops lacked arms, training, transport, and supplies, and they wore a wild variety of different uniforms and flew unfamiliar flags. A mere captain just a few months before, he knew little about the challenges of maneuvering and commanding in battle a force of 35,000 men. His army broke camp and marched out from Washington on 16 July, but they moved only a few miles each day. After a brief skirmish on 18 July at Blackburn's Ford on Bull Run Creek—about 25 miles southwest of Washington—McDowell planned to give battle on 21 July 1861.

Strategy in the South

Well before McDowell's forces crept out of the Washington defenses, Jefferson Davis and his military leaders had made some basic decisions about how they planned to fight this war.

First, the Confederate government decided to remain on the defensive. Although Jomini had promoted the offensive as the stronger form of warfare, too many potential political and diplomatic benefits accrued to the non-aggressor. Additionally, the defensive required fewer troops, an important consideration for a military establishment that did not come into existence until February 1861. Still, not satisfied to remain static in defense of its borders and Richmond, Jefferson Davis and his senior advisors adopted an opportunistic offensive-defensive strategy designed to take advantage of any opening the Union gave them. An elastic defense of small armies posted near the Confederate northern borders provided both territorial defense and troop concentrations around which to build possible offensives.

In Virginia, three small Southern armies attempted to keep Union troops out of the state. Major General George McClellan first made a name for himself in the summer of 1861 by turning back a small Confederate force in western Virginia. Two other Southern armies—General Joseph E. Johnston's at Winchester and General P.G.T. Beauregard's near Manassas Junction, not far from Bull Run Creek—hoped for better fortune. On the approach of McDowell's army toward Beauregard, Johnston faced a dilemma: Should he stay near Winchester to stop any potential threat by a small Union force on his front? Or should he go to Beauregard's aid? Using the Virginia Central Railroad, Johnston began to send his men to Manassas Junction on 20 July.

Union Defeat at Bull Run

Early on 21 July, McDowell's forces began a circuitous march designed to turn Beauregard's left flank along Bull Run Creek. The Southerners saw McDowell coming, however, and Alabamians, Louisianans, Mississippians, and Georgians redeployed to stop him. At first, McDowell's men slowly pushed the Confederate troops back to a strong point on Henry House Hill. Then, about noon, the tide of battle turned. First, a brigade of Virginians under Brigadier General Thomas J. Jackson "stood like a stone wall" and rallied their exhausted brothers-in-arms. Second, the remainder of Johnston's troops arrived from Winchester to strengthen the Confederate left flank and launch a crushing assault against the Union right. This fight between green armies, in which neither side could identify friend from foe by flags or uniforms, ended when McDowell's forces broke for Washington. Under Jefferson Davis's own eye, the Confederates began a slow pursuit, but disorganized in victory, they let their foe go.

Their defeat at First Bull Run stunned the Union. General McClellan, the victor of western Virginia already being touted as the "Little Napoleon," immediately replaced McDowell and soon thereafter took command of the entire Union army

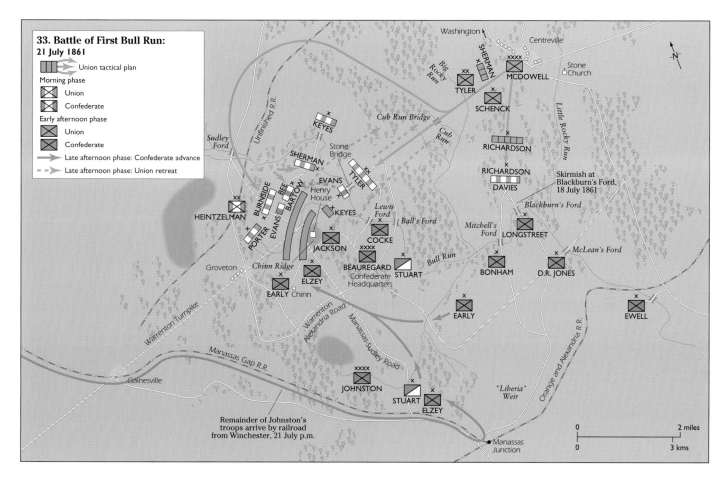

33. Battle of First Bull Run: 21 July 1861

- Union tactical plan

Morning phase
- Union
- Confederate

Early afternoon phase
- Union
- Confederate

→ Late afternoon phase: Confederate advance
⇢ Late afternoon phase: Union retreat

Remainder of Johnston's troops arrive by railroad from Winchester, 21 July p.m.

Skirmish at Blackburn's Ford, 18 July 1861

Confederate Headquarters

from the aging Winfield Scott. McClellan made clear his intent early on: He planned to build an army of "overwhelming" strength to convince the Southern people that resistance was futile and that they should reject their extremist political leaders who created this crisis.

Small Battles Mark the End of 1861

Except for a few relatively insignificant actions, the rest of 1861 passed quietly as both sides built their armies. But even small battles could have significant consequences. The battle at Wilson's Creek on 10 August secured southwest Missouri for the Union. September defeats at Carnifex Ferry and Cheat Mountain forced Jefferson Davis to relieve General Robert E. Lee for his failure to secure western Virginia. A nasty firefight on 21 October at Ball's Bluff along the Potomac induced irate Northern congressmen to organize the Joint Committee on the Conduct of the War, a body in which political partisanship ran amuck and, sooner or later, scrutinized in detail the actions of nearly every senior Union military commander. And, after successes at Cape Hatteras in late August and at Port Royal Sound on 7 November, the Union Navy had set the stage for a true blockade of southern ports.

Continuation of the War in 1862

But all was not well. In the White House, President Abraham Lincoln's impatience had begun to boil over. Although armies rarely conducted winter campaigns, he could not pry from McClellan any substantive plans for action once the weather broke. The general's illness, growing restiveness among his senior subordinates, and Little Mac's poor relationship with his commander-in-chief did not augur well for success. All might have been gloomy in Washington had it not been for good news from the western theater. In early September 1861, to defend the Tennessee border, Confederate forces had advanced into southern Kentucky, ending that state's neutral stance. General Albert Sidney Johnston, the commander of Confederate forces between the Appalachian Mountains and the Mississippi River, then established a thin line of four small armies across southern Kentucky as a "cordon defense" against Union invasion of Tennessee. Small Confederate forces established a presence at the Cumberland Gap; on the Cumberland River at Mill Springs, near Somerset, Kentucky; near a key railroad junction at Bowling Green; and at Columbus, on the Mississippi River.

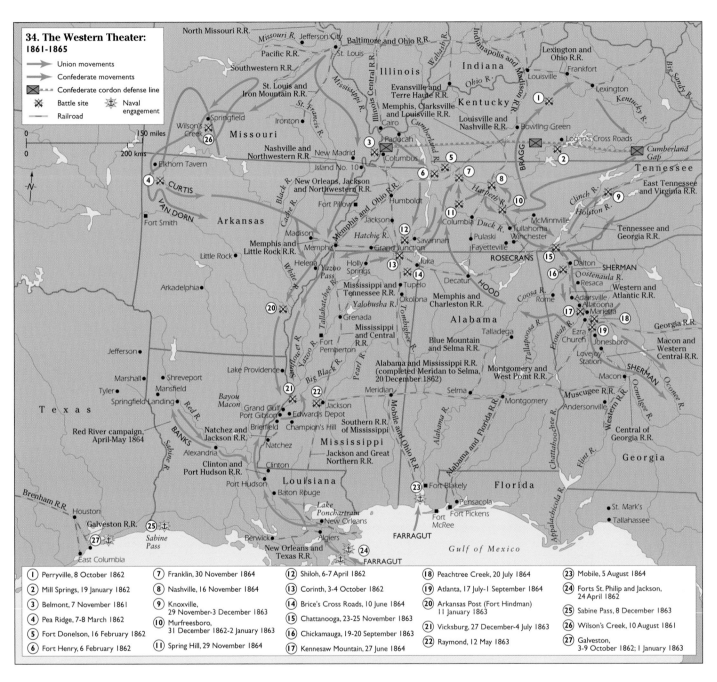

34. The Western Theater:
1861-1865

→ Union movements
→ Confederate movements
⊠┈┈ Confederate cordon defense line
✗ Battle site   ⚓ Naval engagement
— Railroad

0 ——————— 150 miles
0 ——————— 200 kms

① Perryville, 8 October 1862
② Mill Springs, 19 January 1862
③ Belmont, 7 November 1861
④ Pea Ridge, 7-8 March 1862
⑤ Fort Donelson, 16 February 1862
⑥ Fort Henry, 6 February 1862
⑦ Franklin, 30 November 1864
⑧ Nashville, 16 November 1864
⑨ Knoxville, 29 November-3 December 1863
⑩ Murfreesboro, 31 December 1862-2 January 1863
⑪ Spring Hill, 29 November 1864
⑫ Shiloh, 6-7 April 1862
⑬ Corinth, 3-4 October 1862
⑭ Brice's Cross Roads, 10 June 1864
⑮ Chattanooga, 23-25 November 1863
⑯ Chickamauga, 19-20 September 1863
⑰ Kennesaw Mountain, 27 June 1864
⑱ Peachtree Creek, 20 July 1864
⑲ Atlanta, 17 July-1 September 1864
⑳ Arkansas Post (Fort Hindman) 11 January 1863
㉑ Vicksburg, 27 December-4 July 1863
㉒ Raymond, 12 May 1863
㉓ Mobile, 5 August 1864
㉔ Forts St. Philip and Jackson, 24 April 1862
㉕ Sabine Pass, 8 December 1863
㉖ Wilson's Creek, 10 August 1861
㉗ Galveston, 3-9 October 1862; 1 January 1863

The Union army's efforts to break this Confederate line began inauspiciously on 7 November 1861 when Confederate Major General Leonidas Polk turned back Brigadier General Ulysses S. Grant's effort at Belmont, Missouri, designed to test the strength of the Columbus garrison. But, Northern fortunes improved on 19 January, when Brigadier General George H. Thomas's Union force smashed through the Confederates at Mill Springs and killed their commander, Brigadier General Felix K. Zollicoffer. Then, on 30 January, Major General Henry W. Halleck, commander of the Department of the Missouri, unleashed Grant for far more ambitious operations.

Surrender of Fort Henry

In positioning troops at militarily important points along his cordon, General Albert Sidney Johnston had violated the principle of concentration of force. In Virginia the previous summer, General Joseph E. Johnston and General P.G.T. Beauregard had used roads and rails to concentrate their separate armies against McDowell. The much greater area, rough terrain, and the absence of good roads and railroads in the states of Kentucky and Tennessee rendered unlikely a similar result in the west. Additionally, Grant did not attack a Southern strongpoint head on, as McDowell had done at Manassas. Instead, he looked for points of weakness. Leaving Cairo, Illinois, in early February, and in a joint operation with Flag Officer Andrew Foote's gunboats, Grant advanced up the Tennessee River toward partly flooded Fort Henry and the unfinished and undefended Fort Heiman on the Kentucky-Tennessee border. On 6 February, after token resistance, Brigadier General Lloyd Tilghman surrendered Fort Henry's ninety-four soldiers. Union casualties amounted to forty-seven sailors killed, wounded, or missing.

Foote's gunboats returned to the Ohio River in order to move up the Cumberland River, as Grant's force of 15,000 troops slogged overland in the mud to invest Fort Donelson, a far more substantial fortification. Inside and around the Confederate fortress, General Albert Sidney Johnston had gathered 10,000 to 13,500 soldiers—the original garrison, remnants of his Bowling Green detachment forced south by Grant's movement, and reinforcements from Nashville and other posts. On 13 February, Grant probed the newly filled Confederate lines without success. As Grant waited for reinforcements, outstanding Southern gunnery turned back Foote's vessels on 14 February. The Confederates attempted to fight their way out on 15 February, but when they could not breach the Union line, Brigadier General Simon B. Buckner—the third commander of the fort, after two of his superiors chose to escape—asked for terms of surrender. Grant replied, "No terms except unconditional and immediate surrender can be accepted." The phrase, "unconditional surrender," matched the general's initials, caught the North's imagination, and helped make Grant one of the Union's first heroes. Fort Donelson fell on 16 February. Union troops occupied Nashville on 25 February, Johnston's cordon was destroyed, and he pulled his troops back to the northern border of Mississippi and Alabama.

A Larger Offensive

Grant's successes in the west in the spring of 1862, dramatic as they were, remained only part of a much larger offensive effort to reclaim control of the Mississippi River and the land it drained. In the trans-Mississippi, General Samuel Curtis advanced into northern Arkansas, winning a bloody pitched battle over Brigadier General Earl Van Dorn's Confederates at Pea Ridge on 7-8 March. Union naval forces prepared to advance down the Mississippi River itself. In addition, Grant planned to continue advancing up the Tennessee River toward

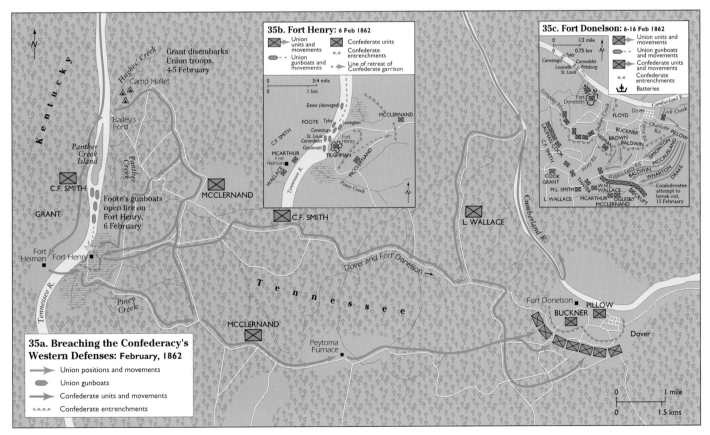

35a. Breaching the Confederacy's Western Defenses: February, 1862

35b. Fort Henry: 6 Feb 1862

35c. Fort Donelson: 6-16 Feb 1862

the key railroad junction at Corinth, Mississippi. Here Albert Sidney Johnston had rebuilt an army to defend the western Confederacy. In late March, Grant's men disembarked from a massive fleet of transports at Pittsburg Landing, from which the road network led to Corinth.

The Battle of Shiloh

Deciding to surprise Grant, Johnston marched north from Corinth to attack. His men talked, straggled, and fired new weapons in the air, all of which should have advertised their nearness to Grant's force. But Grant paid insufficient attention to the security of his army. Nor did he permit his men to dig defenses to protect their camps. Thus, early on 6 April, Johnston's troops screamed out of the woods near Shiloh Church, not far from Pittsburg Landing. They came on in three long, dense lines, each line representing a separate command. This led to confusion as Major General Braxton Bragg's men became entangled with Major General William Hardee's soldiers who had advanced before them. When General Polk's men added their strength, chaos threatened to over-

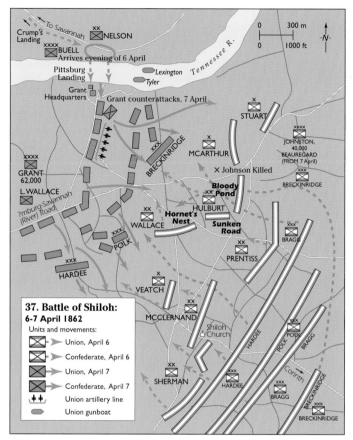

37. Battle of Shiloh:
6-7 April 1862
Units and movements:

⊠→	Union, April 6
⊠→	Confederate, April 6
⊠→	Union, April 7
⊠→	Confederate, April 7
♣♣	Union artillery line
⬭	Union gunboat

take success. The stout resistance by the Union center near the Sunken Road, the Hornet's Nest, and the Bloody Pond, slowed the Confederate advance. While pressing his men forward, Albert Sidney Johnston took a bullet in the leg and soon bled to death. The Union line finally cracked and broke for the landing, but Grant had cobbled together a strong line of artillery to serve as a rallying point for a last stand. That night, Brigadier General William T. Sherman, one of Grant's division commanders, expected orders to retreat. Grant calmly informed him that he intended to stay and win the next day.

With the aid of reinforcements under Major General Don Carlos Buell, Grant proved to be as good as his word. Early on 7 April, Grant counterattacked and by mid-afternoon the tide had turned. The Southern victors of 6 April became the defeated of 7 April, and Beauregard—Johnston's successor— led the bloodied army back to Corinth. The Battle of Shiloh cost the Confederacy 10,694 of the 40,000 men who fought there, plus the loss of General Johnston; the Union lost 13,047 of the 62,000 who ultimately arrived on that field. Shiloh had become the bloodiest battle in North America's history, but it did not hold that distinction for long.

Grant's victory at Shiloh contributed greatly to the real progress the North made in April 1862 toward recapturing

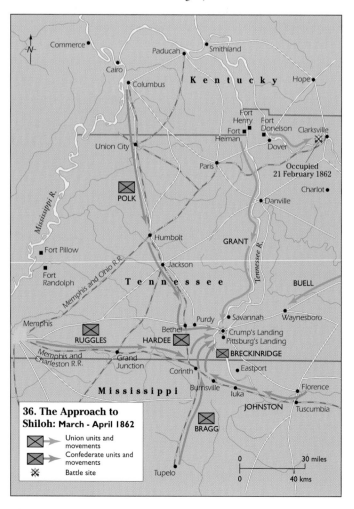

36. The Approach to
Shiloh: March - April 1862

⊠→	Union units and movements
⊠→	Confederate units and movements
✗	Battle site

General Albert Sidney Johnston's Confederates surprised General Ulysses S. Grant's army at Shiloh, Tennessee, on 6 April 1862. Thousands of Union troops fled the battlefield in confusion and made for Pittsburg Landing, as pictured in this contemporary print. Grant rallied his men, and the next day, with reinforcements, counterattacked and forced the Confederates to retreat. The Battle of Shiloh was one of the bloodiest of the entire war.

control of the Mississippi River. On 7 April, the Confederate defenses of Island No. 10 in the Mississippi River, not far from the Kentucky-Tennessee border, fell to Major General John Pope. On 18 April, Flag Officer David Farragut began a six-day bombardment to force a passage between forts Jackson and St. Philip that bracketed the Mississippi nearly fifty miles south of New Orleans; by the end of April, the Crescent City, the South's largest urban center, had fallen into Union hands.

Despite such victories, a disquieting note remained. On 11 April, General Halleck took active command of the combined forces of Grant, Buell, and, soon, Pope. He intended to use that concentrated force to take Corinth. A cautious man spooked by Grant's surprise at Shiloh, however, Halleck moved carefully, stopped frequently, and entrenched every night. On 30 May, Beauregard evacuated his entire army from Corinth without a fight. In so doing, he gave up control of the critically important east-west route of the Memphis and Charleston Railroad and doomed Confederate resistance at Memphis and points north of it along the Mississippi River. Halleck's relatively bloodless victory did little to eliminate the Southern ability to continue the fight in the west, but this did not hurt him. On 11 July, Lincoln called him to Washington and made him general-in-chief of all Union armies.

The Military Situation in Virginia

While Northern forces made progress in the west, McClellan reviewed the military situation in Virginia. Under pressure both to protect Washington and to move on Richmond, he weighed his options carefully. He did not want to repeat McDowell's catastrophic experience of July 1861 by advancing toward strong Confederate defenses at Centreville, near Man-

assas, the direct overland route to Richmond. He determined instead to take advantage of Union naval power to transport his army to a point farther south where he could turn the Centreville position and follow a shorter road to Richmond. That plan, the Urbanna plan, would base his army on the lower Rappahannock River, well south of the Centreville lines. But McClellan's subordinates criticized the plan severely, at least once in Lincoln's presence. McClellan then planned to land his army at Fort Monroe, seventy miles southeast of Richmond at the tip of a peninsula formed by the James and York rivers. But he demanded as a precondition that the Union navy secure command of the waters around Fort Monroe, and the indecisive clash between the U.S.S. *Monitor* and C.S.S. *Virginia* on 9 March, after Confederate successes the previous day, did nothing to calm his fears.

Interference from Washington

Lincoln approved McClellan's peninsula plan, but, always mindful of the need to protect the national capital, he limited the number of troops he gave McClellan to execute his mission. Still believing he required overwhelming strength to force the South's capitulation, McClellan resented the interference of Lincoln and Secretary of War Edwin M. Stanton who, first, reduced his authority over all Union forces on 3 March and later stripped from him great numbers of soldiers he believed he needed for success. The potential strength of Confederate resistance concerned him. His inflated estimates of Southern defenders, based at least in part on information from intelligence chief Allan Pinkerton, reinforced his doubts regularly.

For all his talents as an organizer and trainer of huge armies, McClellan did not know how to use them. He rarely appreciated threats beyond those that complicated his own mission

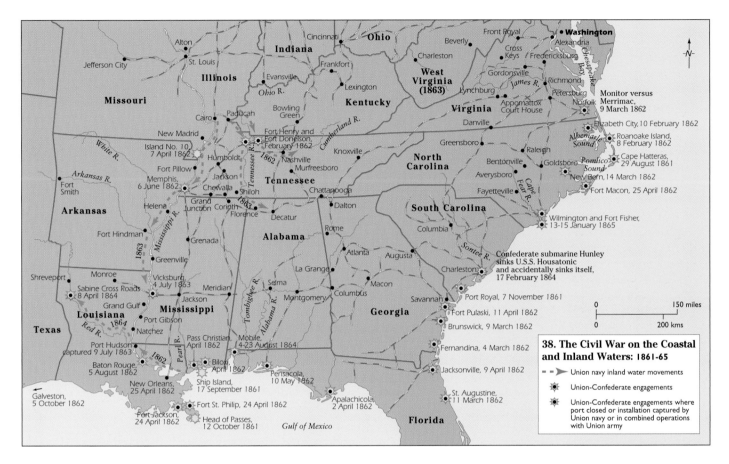

38. The Civil War on the Coastal and Inland Waters: 1861-65

- ▶ Union navy inland water movements
- ✶ Union-Confederate engagements
- ✶ Union-Confederate engagements where port closed or installation captured by Union navy or in combined operations with Union army

planning. While he began the process of transporting his army to Fort Monroe, a potential threat to Washington appeared in the Shenandoah Valley, where Stonewall Jackson's small force began active operation in late March. Although defeated by Brigadier General James Shields at Kernstown on 23 March, Jackson spent April and early May maneuvering until he launched a series of quick marches and hard-hitting attacks, defeating Major General John C. Frémont at McDowell on 8 May, an element of Major General Nathaniel P. Banks's force at Front Royal on 23 May and his main force at Winchester on 25 May, General Shields at Cross Keys on 8 June, and Brigadier General Erastus B. Tyler's force from Shields's command at Port Republic on 9 June.

Road to Richmond

Jackson's actions in the valley stopped Lincoln and Stanton from approving the concentration of force on the peninsula that McClellan demanded. Because he believed he did not possess the strength he needed, Little Mac advanced cautiously. When he arrived at Fort Monroe with 50,000 men in mid-March, he had faced only Major General John B. Magruder's 7,000 troops posted behind a line of strong earthworks along the Warwick River. McClellan's strength grew, but after stiff

repulses at Lee's Mill and Dam No. 1 along the Warwick Line in April, McClellan saw no choice but to lay siege to Yorktown, the key to the Southern defenses. His slowness from the time he left Washington until mid-April bought time for Joseph Johnston to withdraw from the Centreville line and redeploy his men to the peninsula. By the time McClellan approached Yorktown, Confederate strength on the peninsula exceeded 50,000. On 4 May, the very day McClellan intended to start shelling the town, Johnston evacuated Yorktown and the Warwick Line to begin a slow withdrawal toward Richmond. After a sharp rearguard action at Williamsburg on 5 May, McClellan's road to Richmond seemed clear.

Yet he did not take it. While Johnston retreated slowly to a position about five miles east of Richmond, McClellan did not press him, taking time to establish a supply base at White House, near the eastern terminus of the single-tracked Richmond and York River Railroad before moving forward. The peninsula proved so confining that McClellan had to split his forces—now more than 85,000-strong—with the slow-flowing, flood-prone Chickahominy River cutting it in two.

Battle of Fair Oaks

With his army divided, McClellan refused to attack. Thus, on

31 May, Joseph Johnston forced the issue and attacked. Fought over two days, mostly in a blinding rainstorm that raised the Chickahominy out of its banks, the Battle of Fair Oaks decided nothing. Both armies stayed in place, at the cost of a combined total of nearly 11,200 casualties. The single most significant loss, however, was General Johnston himself, hit by a spent bullet and a shell fragment. On 1 June, Jefferson Davis gave

Junior staff officers pose for a photographer at their camp during the Peninsula Campaign. Captain George Armstrong Custer, a June 1861 West Point graduate reclining at right with a dog, joined General George McClellan's staff in June 1862. He was promoted to brigadier general of volunteers a year later, led cavalry with distinction at Gettysburg and in the Virginia campaigns of 1864-65, ending the war at age twenty-five, a major general. Custer became a legend when he was killed with 225 of his men by Sioux Indians at the Battle of Little Big Horn in 1876.

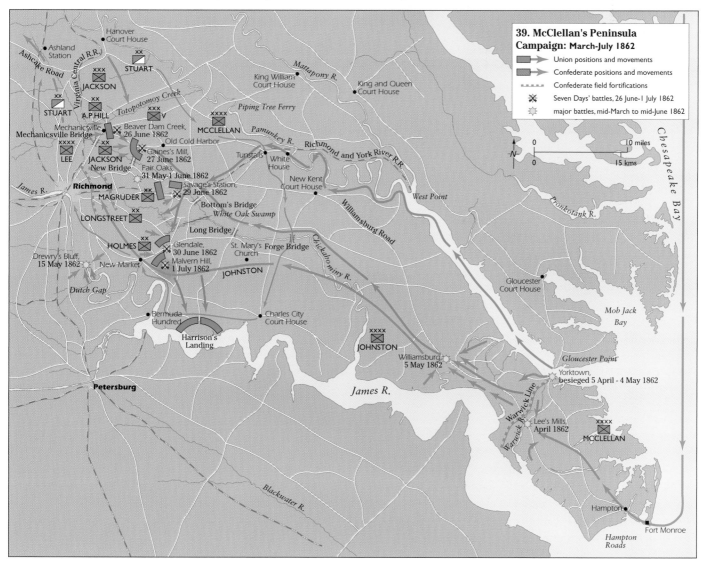

Naval supremacy provided the Union with a strategic flexibility not available to the Confederacy. Sea power made possible attacks on the South's periphery, let Union commanders outflank Confederate defenses in northern Virginia to launch the Peninsula Campaign in 1862, and provided support for operations against Richmond and Petersburg in 1864 and 1865. In this watercolor by Prince de Joinville, a French observer with McClellan's army, Union infantry disembark from paddlewheel transports at Fort Monroe on the tip of the peninsula formed by the James and York rivers.

command of the forces defending Richmond to General Robert E. Lee.

General Lee Takes Charge

Davis's choice did not inspire enthusiasm. At first, Lee seemed to live up to his 1861 nickname "Granny," and he won a new one—"the King of Spades"—as his army built huge earthworks to defend Richmond against McClellan's advance from the east. At the same time, however, he took the measure of his army and its senior leadership to forge the weapon he would lead to many victories: The Army of Northern Virginia.

Determined to attack McClellan rather than await events, Lee sent his cavalry commander, Brigadier General J.E.B. Stuart to reconnoiter the Union lines. After a spectacular ride around McClellan's army with only one combat fatality, Stuart informed Lee that the Union right flank north of the Chickahominy remained weak and unsupported. McClellan, still hoping that Union forces posted near Fredericksburg would join him, had left that space for them to fill. But as long as Jackson remained active in the valley, Lincoln and Stanton expected the Fredericksburg garrison to stop any sudden thrust he might make toward Washington.

Seven Days' Battles

Jackson did plan a bold move to the east, but not toward the Union capital. After meeting with Lee on 23 June, he turned his entire force toward Richmond to help repulse McClellan. With the expectation of Jackson's arrival on the exposed Union right flank Stuart had discovered, Lee proceeded with tactical plans for the rest of his army. The series of clashes that resulted on 26 June through 1 July became known as the Seven

Days' Battles.

On 26 June, Lee planned for the divisions of major generals A.P. Hill, James Longstreet, and D.H. Hill to hit the Union V Corps frontally at Beaver Dam Creek, a sluggish tributary of the Chickahominy near a small crossroads named Mechanicsville. Jackson would attack the right flank simultaneously. But Jackson did not arrive on time, and an impatient A.P. Hill launched his frontal attack unsupported. Union forces held a strong position along the creek, and Hill's men fell in droves as they attempted in vain to penetrate it. The Confederates took nearly 1,500 casualties while inflicting only 361 on the Union defenders. Now aware of his exposed flank, McClellan ordered his V Corps back to high ground near Gaines's Mill that protected the bridges across the Chickahominy that led to the rest of the Union army.

Smelling victory, Lee pursued. Now, with Jackson's men on the field, he ordered for 27 June a more effective execution of the Mechanicsville plan. Once again, however, Jackson contributed less than expected to the outcome of the fight. His flanking column got lost and Lee's own forces carried the bulk of the fighting at Gaines's Mill. Late in the afternoon, in what may have been the biggest frontal assault of the entire war, nearly all the Southern forces on the field advanced to crash through the Union line, sending the Northerners reeling for the bridges across the Chickahominy. McClellan quickly decided that he could not save his White House supply depot on the York River, ordered it emptied or burned, and began a "change of base" to the James River.

It took Lee a day to decipher McClellan's intentions. On 28 June, he probed the Union center near Golding's and Garnett's farms. When McClellan moved south, Lee went in pursuit.

On 29 June, he almost caught up with the Union rearguard near Savage Station, capturing 2,500 Union sick and wounded. The next day at White Oak Swamp, Jackson collapsed exhausted and his men did not attack on the Union right and rear when opportunity presented itself. Thus, the Confederates lost yet another chance to squeeze the retreating army between two forces or even cut it in two when only Longstreet and Hill—without Jackson's assistance—attacked McClellan's forces at nearby Glendale (or Frayser's Farm). On 1 July, a frustrated Lee ordered a frontal assault against McClellan's strong position on Malvern Hill. McClellan's line repulsed with heavy loss a series of Confederate attacks, but Little Mac pulled back his army the next day. Until mid-August, McClellan's army remained at Harrison's Landing, where men died of disease and bad water, while their leader equivocated on whether or not to renew the advance on Richmond.

With aggressiveness and boldness, Lee had saved Richmond, but at a high cost. A week of offensives had drained his ranks of 20,000 men; by comparison, on the defensive, and in retreat, McClellan had suffered 16,000 casualties.

The War Continues in Virginia

Lee could not savor his accomplishment for long. Already, in northern Virginia, General John Pope, commanding the now combined forces that had faced Jackson in the valley and more, had decided to use the axis of the Orange and Alexandria Railroad to advance against Richmond from the north. This required Lee to watch two strong Union forces simultaneously: Pope's Army of Virginia and McClellan's army at Harrison's Landing. Correctly assessing that McClellan would not move, Lee left a small covering force at Richmond and turned the bulk of his army toward Pope. With a rejuvenated Jackson in the lead, the Confederate forces met Pope's advance on 9 August at Cedar Mountain, near Culpeper, and, after a hard fight, sent the Union forces running.

When Lee and Longstreet joined Jackson, Lee planned perhaps his most masterful campaign. Using Longstreet's men to fix Pope's forces along the Rappahannock River line, he sent Jackson's troops on a wide swing to the north and west, where they pushed through the Bull Run Mountains at Thoroughfare Gap and put themselves squarely in the rear of Pope's army. This bold move succeeded handsomely initially. By 28 August, Jackson had captured and burned Pope's primary supply depot at Manassas Junction and took up a defensive position near Groveton to await the arrival of Lee and Longstreet.

Time became the South's enemy now. McClellan's large army already had begun to leave Harrison's Landing for Washington. Major General Ambrose Burnside's IX Corps also returned from its springtime successes in coastal North Carolina. If McClellan, Burnside, and Pope combined their strength, they greatly outnumbered Lee. The Confederates had to force a battle against just one Union force—Pope's—before all the Northern armies concentrated.

Second Battle of Bull Run

Thus, late on 28 August, Jackson attacked Pope's men at

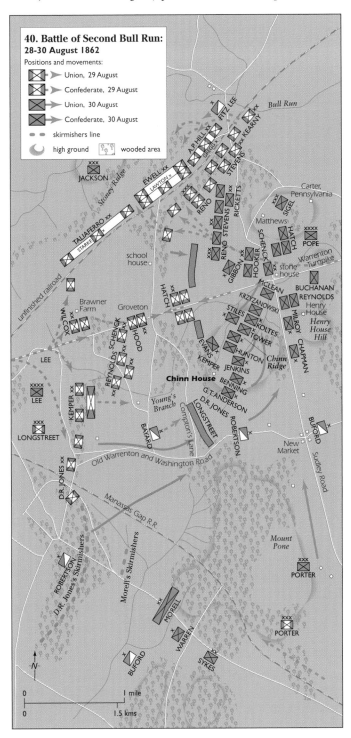

40. Battle of Second Bull Run:
28-30 August 1862
Positions and movements:

Union, 29 August
Confederate, 29 August
Union, 30 August
Confederate, 30 August
skirmishers line
high ground   wooded area

Brawner Farm, just west of Groveton, in a bloody engagement that opened the Second Battle of Bull Run. All day on 29 August, Jackson's men fought from the shelter of an embankment built for the tracks of an unfinished railroad to hurl back repeated frontal assaults of a strengthening Union army. Late that afternoon, Lee and Longstreet arrived and quietly deployed in a line perpendicular to Jackson's position. They had set a trap for Pope—and some of Pope's subordinates told him of Lee and Longstreet's presence on his left flank—but, to Jackson's dismay, they did not spring it until late in the afternoon of 30 August. After yet another day when Jackson's men bore the brunt of furious Union assaults, Longstreet finally launched a crushing attack against the Union left. Despite desperate stands on Chinn Ridge and Henry House Hill, the Union line finally collapsed. Pope withdrew to Centreville, his continued pleas for help from McClellan ignored. A rearguard action at Chantilly the next day in a rainstorm ended the fighting. The Union Army had suffered 16,054 casualties; about 9,200 of Lee's men fell. Lincoln relieved Pope from command on 2 September and restored McClellan to command of all Union forces in Virginia.

Optimism in the South

The sudden reversal of fortune between spring and late summer sparked optimism in the South. Solid victories in the east and the halt of Union progress in the west showed promise for the future. But to secure the potential advantages that might accrue from formal diplomatic recognition by France and England, a goal that seemed quite possible in the fall of 1862, the Confederacy needed its own version of Saratoga. After that crucial American victory during the American Revolution, France had entered the war on the colonists' side, and the Southerners now hoped that crushing wins by Confederate armies in the fall of 1862 might convince the major European powers to take up their cause. Jefferson Davis and his senior military leaders planned a two-pronged offensive into Union territory in the fall of 1862 that—if it brought decisive success—might accomplish that aim.

The Push into Maryland

In the east, Robert E. Lee lost no time moving into Maryland. By 4 September, the vanguard of his forces crossed the Potomac near Leesburg. Each of his five columns marched with its own objective, Lee planning to take Frederick and Harpers Ferry as well as to obtain much needed supplies and recruits. But good fortune no longer followed Lee. Uncounted numbers of soldiers left the ranks before the army crossed the Potomac, claiming a willingness to defend the South but none to invade the North. Worse, Lee's campaign plan fell into Union hands. McClellan now could move on Lee, knowing

fully that his outnumbered foe had divided his already small force. McClellan moved forward with unusual alacrity and attacked elements of Lee's scattered army at South Mountain and Crampton's Gap on 14 September. But Lee knew his plan had been compromised. Allowing Jackson to complete his capture of Harpers Ferry—the post surrendered on 15 September—Lee ordered a reconcentration of his forces near Sharpsburg, Maryland, west of Antietam Creek.

Antietam

On 17 September, the United States witnessed the single bloodiest day in its military history. Rather than take advantage of his numerical superiority to apply the bulk of his army against a single vulnerable point on Lee's thin line, McClellan launched a series of uncoordinated attacks that allowed Lee simply to shift troops to meet each successive crisis. At about 6 A.M., Union I and XII Corps pressed Lee's left flank, advancing through woodlots and a cornfield. General Hood's division

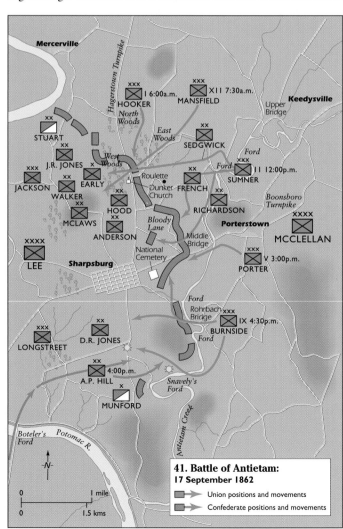

41. Battle of Antietam:
17 September 1862

Union positions and movements

Confederate positions and movements

attacked into the cornfield from the Dunker Church to stabilize the Confederate line. About 9 A.M., a bit farther south, a single unsupported division of the Union II Corps advanced into the West Woods, where Confederates assaulted them from front, left flank, and rear, and inflicted 2,500 casualties in thirty minutes. After a brief lull, the fighting shifted even further south to the natural trench of a sunken farm road that anchored the Confederate center. After two divisions of the Union II Corps took heavy casualties attacking frontally, the Confederate position was flanked, forcing the Southerners to flee. McClellan saw the Confederate center give way and considered a thrust to break the Southern army in two. But his cautious nature won out, and he did nothing.

In the early afternoon, the action moved even further south to the Rohrbach Bridge on the Union left, where troops from General Burnside's IX Corps finally crossed the span and moved forward. Victory still beckoned Union arms. The advance of Burnside's men threatened the road to Boteler's Ford, Lee's only escape route, and, by now, Lee had no forces left to stop them. Then, he spotted flags at the head of a marching column. Fearing at first that the Union army had outflanked him, he soon discovered the Confederate battle flags that marked the head of A.P. Hill's exhausted division, just arriving from Harpers Ferry at the right place at the right time. Hill's men crashed into the left flank of Burnside's advancing troops, halting their advance in sight of Sharpsburg and the roads to the Confederate rear. Night fell. Opportunity evaporated. And in twelve hours of brutal combat at close range, over 23,000 soldiers in the two armies filled the roles of the dead, wounded, or missing. No serious fighting took place on 18 September, although Lee contemplated renewing hostilities. The next day, however, he began withdrawing to Virginia, his expedition into Union territory ended.

Change in the Union's Aims

The end of the Confederate offensive in Maryland set the stage for a significant change in the Union's stated war aims. From the start, Northerners spoke of this conflict as a war to preserve the Union. On 22 September, Abraham Lincoln used the repulse of Lee from Union soil to issue the preliminary Emancipation Proclamation, giving this war a second goal: The eradication of slavery.

The repulse of Lee from Maryland and the Lincoln's pronouncement alone did not crush the optimism with which the South had begun the fall of 1862. On 28 August, while Jackson's men slugged it out at Brawner Farm, General Braxton Bragg led the Confederate Army of Tennessee north into Kentucky, a move intended to secure eastern Tennessee and to force the Union to abandon plans to push on Chattanooga. At the same time, Major General Edmund Kirby Smith uncov-

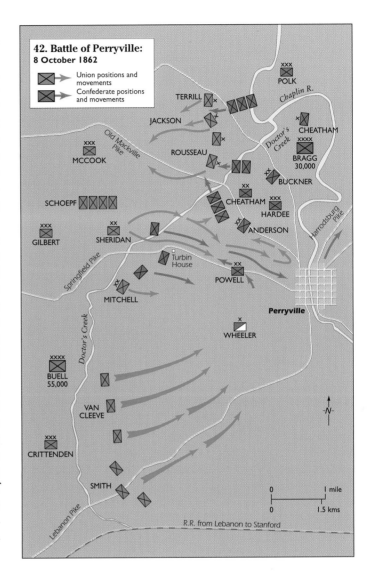

42. Battle of Perryville:
8 October 1862

Union positions and movements

Confederate positions and movements

ered Cumberland Gap on his way into Kentucky; some of his forces marched nearly to the Ohio River before being recalled to join Bragg. By the time Lee fought McClellan at Antietam in mid-September, elements of Bragg's and General Buell's Union forces racing north from the Nashville area began parrying with each other at places such as Henderson and Munfordville, Kentucky. Buell beat Bragg to Louisville on 25 September, but Confederate troops marched through Richmond, Lexington, and Bardstown, and on 4 October, Bragg attended Richard Hawes's inauguration as Confederate governor of Kentucky.

But no serious fighting occurred until 8 October, when, near Perryville, elements of Bragg's force collided in unintended battle with Buell's men, as both armies searched for fresh water. Neither Bragg nor Buell knew about the bloody fighting until late in the day, and, in hard fighting controlled by subordinates, the Battle of Perryville exacted 7,600 casualties, including nearly one-quarter of the 16,000 Confederates who fought there. Bragg decided to return to Tennessee. By 23 October, his army had passed through Cumberland Gap, ultimately taking a position near Murfreesboro, Tennessee. Lincoln relieved Buell on 24 October and replaced him with Major General William S. Rosecrans, as the Union Army, in careful pursuit, returned to Nashville. The Confederate fall offensive had failed.

To add a final blow to Confederate hopes that fall, General Van Dorn's bloody two-day assault on strong Union positions around Corinth on 4-5 October failed badly. He had kept those Union troops from reinforcing Buell's army while Bragg was in Tennessee, but he did not recapture that key railroad junction for the Confederacy or end the Union threat in western Tennessee and northern Mississippi. And he lost 4,233 men to only 2,520 Northern casualties.

Winter Quarters

In the late fall, Civil War armies went into winter quarters usually, but commanders in both armies remained uncharacteristically active in the early winter of 1862. In the east, on 7 November, Lincoln grew tired of McClellan's inactivity after Antietam and relieved him for good. General Burnside replaced him, despite expressing to Lincoln his doubts that he could meet the challenge. At first, Burnside's actions belied his harsh personal assessment. He designed a sound plan to move immediately against Richmond on a direct line from the Fredericksburg area, supported logistically from Aquia Landing and a railroad spur built to link into the Richmond, Fredericksburg, and Potomac Railroad.

Burnside's Command

Burnside quickly sent his army in motion toward Fredericks-

burg. Indeed, he stole a march on Lee, who did not understand what the Union army's quick movements portended. But the destruction of bridges over the fast-flowing and unfordable Rappahannock halted Burnside at Fredericksburg. He requested pontoons from the Engineer Depot in Washington, but two weeks passed before they arrived. By then, Longstreet had arrived at Fredericksburg and established a strong defensive position for infantry and artillery west of town on a ridge of small hills, including Marye's Heights. His pickets occupied the town itself to alert the Confederates to Burnside's movements.

The Battle of Fredericksburg

On 11 December, Burnside began to force a crossing of the Rappahannock. When Confederate pickets picked off his engineers, he used artillery to make them hide and then sent two regiments of infantry across in boats to establish a bridgehead on the town side of the river. Farther south, Union forces established two more crossing points as well. As Burnside's men streamed into Fredericksburg, Lee recalled Jackson from a position farther south along the Rappahannock to extend and protect Longstreet's right flank; a bend in the river protected Lee's left.

On 13 December, the Battle of Fredericksburg developed into a two-part fight. Against Jackson's newly arrived and poorly posted force, the Pennsylvania Reserves pushed through a swamp, hit a gap in the Southern line, and threatened more damage before Confederate reinforcements closed in. But Burnside did not consider his options here. He became obsessed instead by a series of Union frontal attacks against Marye's Heights. Longstreet suggested that with his defenses on those heights and enough ammunition, his troops could have prevented a chicken from making it across those fields alive. At least five separate Union assaults advanced up the

At Fredericksburg, General Lee deployed most of his troops along a low ridge of hills west of town running parallel to the river, the northern portion of which was known as Marye's Heights. Emerging from the cover of buildings in Fredericksburg, attackers had to cross a canal and ascend the Heights' gradual slope. Standing in a sunken road and protected by a stone wall, Confederate troops repulsed repeated Union assaults inflicting heavy casualties.

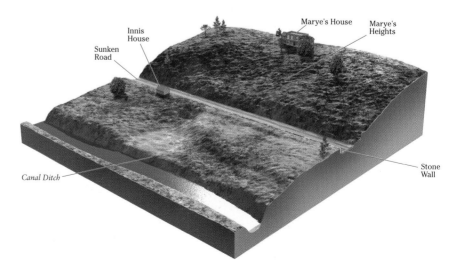

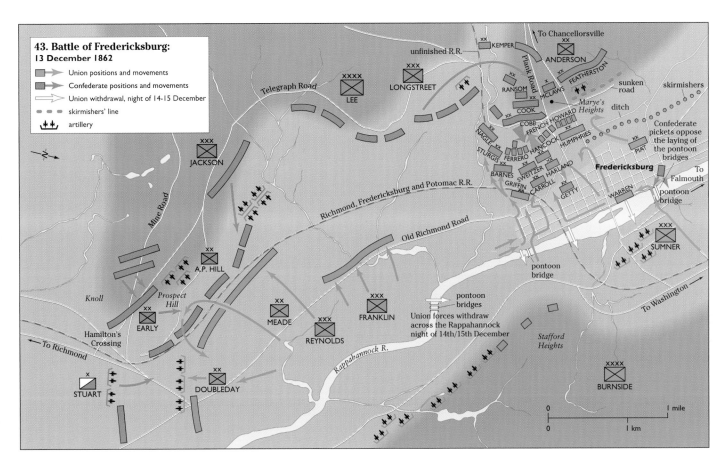

43. Battle of Fredericksburg:
13 December 1862

Union positions and movements

Confederate positions and movements

Union withdrawal, night of 14-15 December

skirmishers' line

artillery

slopes toward the Confederate line, and none got closer than one hundred yards from the sunken stone wall that protected dense lines of Southern infantry. These attacks inspired General Lee to comment, "It is well that war is so terrible, else we become too fond of it." Some Northerners who survived the attacks spent the night of 13 December on a snow-covered field, protected by the coats and the bodies of their slain comrades; Southerners stripped the dead of their coats for warmth. Deciding not to renew the fight on 14 December, Burnside pulled back across the river. Despite its great initial promise, Burnside's plan had cost 12,600 casualties to the Confederacy's 5,300 casualties.

A Tactical Draw

As Burnside's dispirited army went into winter quarters, the year ended on an even bloodier note in the west. On the day after Christmas, Rosecrans advanced from Nashville toward Bragg's position near Murfreesboro, with plans to attack. But Bragg stole the initiative. On 31 December, at dawn, he launched Hardee's Corps on a crushing surprise attack that buckled the Union right flank, forcing Rosecrans to fight with Stone's River to his back in an effort to protect the Murfrees-boro–Nashville Pike, his escape route. As Rosecrans rallied his

men, a cannonball decapitated Colonel Julius Garesche, his chief of staff, spattering the general with brains and blood. Nonetheless, Rosecrans and his senior subordinates, especially Major General George H. Thomas, finally stabilized the line and decided against retreat. Little happened on 1 January 1863, but on 2 January, Bragg shifted the bulk of his force to the other side of Stone's River to attack the Union left flank. After initial success, however, the massed artillery of Union Colonel John Mendenhall smashed the Southern assault. The fighting ended in a tactical draw. Rosecrans pulled back to Nashville in safety and Bragg withdrew to refit his men. This most indecisive end to 1862 exacted over 24,600 casualties from 76,400 combatants, among the war's costliest battles in percentage of combat strength lost.

Substantial Progress in 1863

After nearly two years of fighting, the year 1863 brought the first substantial progress toward stated strategic goals for either side. That progress came at high cost. In January, the rain, snow, and mud quickly ended Burnside's effort to take Lee by surprise by trying his left flank near Fredericksburg. Soldiers quickly dubbed the move the "mud march." Lincoln relieved Burnside on 25 January and replaced him with Major

Flag Officer David G. Farragut's fleet ran past Fort Jackson (lower left) and Fort St. Philip (upper right) below New Orleans and landed there virtually unopposed on 25 April 1862. Believing the forts impassable, the Confederates had stripped the city of defenders, sending them north to counter Grant's invasion of Tennessee. The loss of New Orleans, the South's largest city and busiest port, was a very serious defeat for the Confederacy.

General Joseph Hooker, who, as the president made clear to him, won the spot not because he had made public statements supporting a military dictatorship, but despite them. "Only those generals who gain successes, can set up dictators," Lincoln reminded him, but if Hooker would win victories, Lincoln professed himself willing to risk dictatorship.

Focus on the Mississippi River

As Hooker began to refashion the Army of the Potomac in its winter quarters, all eyes fixed on the Mississippi River as the most active theater for military operations. From the head-quarters of the Army of the Tennessee in Holly Springs, Mississippi, General Grant had begun his efforts to retake control of the full length of the river. For all practical purposes, except for a stretch between Port Hudson, Louisiana, and Vicksburg, Mississippi, the Union controlled the waterway. Grant focused his attention on Vicksburg.

When he began planning his operations in late 1862, Grant could not have foreseen that he would have to wait until 4 July 1863 for the victory he sought. During the Vicksburg campaign, Grant demonstrated patience blended with initiative, imagination, daring, and a bit of frustration. Grant initially planned to advance toward Vicksburg using the Mississippi Central Railroad for logistical support, but he abandoned that notion after General Van Dorn's Confederate cavalry captured 1.5 million dollars of supplies at his advance supply base at Holly Springs on 20 December 1862 and Brigadier General Nathan Bedford Forrest hit other Northern supply depots in western Tennessee about the same time. These events, however, did not disrupt Grant's plan to send General Sherman down

the Mississippi River from Memphis to test Confederate defenses at Chickasaw Bluffs that guarded the northern land approaches to Vicksburg. Right after Christmas, Sherman's men slogged through swamps and bayous, finally attacking the Confederate position on 29 December. Lieutenant General John C. Pemberton's Confederate defenders easily repulsed them, inflicting 1,776 casualties while taking 207 of their own.

Plans to Take Vicksburg

In early 1863, Grant and his subordinates—the latter occasionally operating without Grant's knowledge or approval—explored other options to facilitate taking Vicksburg. On 11 January, Major General John A. McClernand took Arkansas Post on the Arkansas River, an important Mississippi tributary. In early February, the Union ram *Queen of the West* risked the fire of Confederate batteries to disrupt Southern river trade near Vicksburg itself until the ship ran aground in the middle of the month. Union forces launched the Yazoo Pass expedition in February as well, planning to follow the Yazoo, Coldwater, and Tallahatchee rivers into the rear of Vicksburg's defenses. After the Union troops made progress for ninety miles, Major General W.W. Loring turned them back on 16 March at a relatively unimposing earthwork named Fort Pemberton. Several attempts to cut canals near Vicksburg to redirect the flow of the Mississippi River away from the city, rendering it both defenseless and valueless, failed. On 24 March, Sherman gave up yet another effort to find a northern approach into Vicksburg. His failure at Steele's Bayou would be the last such effort before Grant himself decided to take a more active role in operations.

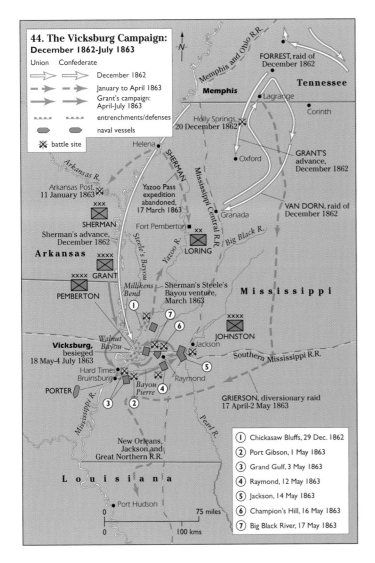

44. The Vicksburg Campaign:
December 1862-July 1863

Union Confederate

⇨ ⇨ December 1862

- - -▶ - -▶ January to April 1863

━━▶ ━━▶ Grant's campaign: April-July 1863

⣿⣿⣿ ⣀⣀⣀ entrenchments/defenses

🛥 naval vessels

✖ battle site

① Chickasaw Bluffs, 29 Dec. 1862

② Port Gibson, 1 May 1863

③ Grand Gulf, 3 May 1863

④ Raymond, 12 May 1863

⑤ Jackson, 14 May 1863

⑥ Champion's Hill, 16 May 1863

⑦ Big Black River, 17 May 1863

there, the Union forces—which brought only necessities to sustain themselves—quickly fanned out to gather up the food and supplies available in a region previously untouched by the hard hand of war. Grant chose not to move north toward Vicksburg's undefended southern approaches. He determined instead to move northeast toward Jackson and the railroad that linked the state capital and Vicksburg. By so doing, he hoped to draw Pemberton's troops out of Vicksburg's defenses and avoid both bloody assaults against earthworks or a lengthy siege.

Jefferson Davis watched Grant's movements with alarm. Despite the president's personal dislike for him, on 9 May Davis named General Joseph Johnston commander of all Confederate troops in Mississippi. Unfortunately, Grant moved too quickly for Johnston to build sufficient force to stop him. After a sharp skirmish at Raymond on 12 May, Grant's men took Jackson on 14 May. With only 12,000 men under his command, Johnston pulled off to the north, ordering Pemberton

This map, showing the siege of Vicksburg, appeared in The New York Herald *on 27 June 1863, a week before the Confederate surrender.*

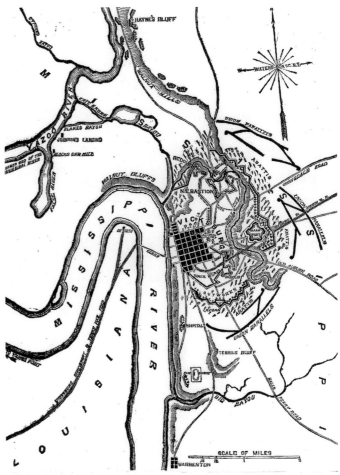

Instead of continuing attempts to take the city from the predictable and well-defended north and northeast directions, Grant now considered approaching from the south or east. In late March, he ordered his infantry to proceed down the western bank of the Mississippi until well south of Vicksburg. On 16 April, Flag Officer David D. Porter ran twelve vessels under Vicksburg's guns, putting in at Hard Times to help transport Grant's infantry across the river to Mississippi soil. A second contingent of ships arrived on 22 April. To distract attention from all these troop movements, Colonel Benjamin Grierson and 1,700 Union cavalrymen set out on 17 April to raid Confederate posts throughout Mississippi and generate consternation in the process.

Grant planned initially to cross at Grand Gulf, Mississippi, but Porter's gunboats could not overwhelm Confederate defenses there. Thus, he moved his men farther south and, on 30 April, Porter's boats began crossing them safely at Bruinsburg. From

to join him. At first, Pemberton refused, but, in response to a second order, he tried on 15 May to join Johnston. Grant ended Pemberton's effort, however, in a sharp fight at Champion's Hill; after taking nearly 3,900 casualties there and losing nearly 1,700 more at the crossings of the Big Black River the next day, Pemberton withdrew the remnant of his force into the safety of Vicksburg's defenses. On 19 May, Grant unsuccessfully assaulted those earthworks, hoping to break through before Pemberton had time to strengthen them. With much greater strength on 22 May, Grant ordered a massed assault against a three-mile segment of Vicksburg's defenses. Some Northern units made temporary breakthroughs, but the day ended in failure. Grant took nearly 3,200 casualties, while fewer than 500 Confederate defenders fell.

The Siege of Vicksburg

Grant reluctantly decided to lay siege to Vicksburg. His tactics appalled Southerners. He refused to allow the civilians to leave the city. He did not stop Union artillerymen from shelling the residential areas, a practice that forced some families to take temporary shelter in old Indian caves. Food supplies dwindled; women in Vicksburg attacked with butcher knives the horses and mules freshly killed by shellfire, seeking meat for dinner.

From 19 May to 4 July 1863, General Ulysses S. Grant laid siege to Vicksburg, the key to control of the Mississippi River. Knowing that the presence of civilians in the bluff-top city would deplete Confederate supplies more rapidly, Grant refused to let them leave during the bombardment. Many of the city's defiant citizens sought safety in caves or burrowed into the ground for shelter (pictured above) and Grant was severely criticized for his inhumane treatment of them.

Newsprint fell into such short supply that the editor of the Vicksburg daily published it on strips of wallpaper taken from shelled-out houses. But all through June, Pemberton held on.

Hooker's Plan

While Grant operated actively but to no decision in Mississippi in May, Northerners and Southerners alike paid serious attention to military operations in Virginia. In revitalizing his dispirited Army of the Potomac, General Hooker, by late April, had amassed a force of over 130,000 men. Morale was high and he had a plan.

Most of Lee's army had remained near Fredericksburg in winter quarters. To distract attention from his main effort, Hooker sent his cavalry on a deep swing behind the Confederate lines toward Richmond. Not wanting to repeat either Burnside's frontal assault against Marye's Heights or his mud march, Hooker planned a broad sweep to the north and west of Fredericksburg with the bulk of his infantry, intending to swing in behind the Confederate defenses. In Hooker's mind, Lee then had only two options: To fight Hooker west of the town where the open and rolling terrain did not favor his small numbers, or, more likely, to withdraw from the Rappahannock line entirely. He did not consider Lee's third option: Stay and fight.

On 28 April, leaving 30,000 troops at Fredericksburg to fix Lee in place, Hooker set his plan into motion. At first, it worked flawlessly. His first infantry corps crossed the Rapidan and Rappahannock rivers at Ely's and U.S. Fords nearly unchallenged, and by 30 April, the advance guard had reached Chancellorsville, a road junction near the eastern edge of a dense second-growth forest known locally as "the Wilderness." Hooker did not expect to fight there. He only intended to use the woods to cover his move and concentrate his strength before advancing into the rolling fields that led to the Confederate rear.

Early on 1 May, Hooker's army began to march east from Chancellorsville along the Orange Turnpike, the Orange Plank Road, and the River Road toward Fredericksburg. Slow at first to gauge Hooker's intentions, Lee now hurried troops into position to counter the Union movements. When Lee stood, and did not flee as Hooker had expected, the Union commander's confidence quickly disappeared, and he ordered his troops to pull back to Chancellorsville.

By nightfall, Hooker had transformed his bold offensive scheme into a plan for defense. His men dug trenches that encircled Chancellorsville from the northeast to the southwest and Major General Oliver O. Howard's XI Corps extended Hooker's right flank further west along the Orange Turnpike into the depths of the Wilderness. Leaving only 10,000 men at Fredericksburg under Brigadier General Jubal Early to watch

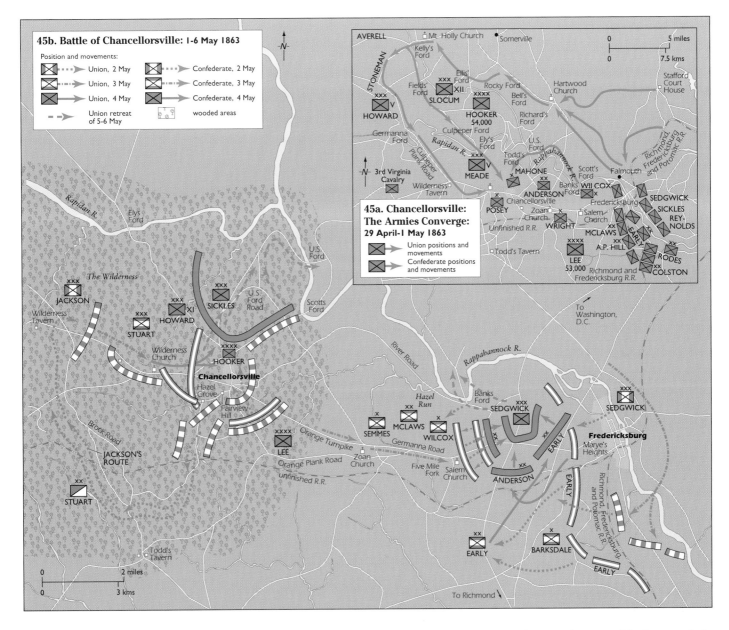

45b. Battle of Chancellorsville: 1-6 May 1863

Position and movements:

Union, 2 May
Union, 3 May
Union, 4 May
Union retreat of 5-6 May

Confederate, 2 May
Confederate, 3 May
Confederate, 4 May
wooded areas

45a. Chancellorsville: The Armies Converge: 29 April-1 May 1863

Union positions and movements
Confederate positions and movements

Union activity there, Lee concentrated the remainder of his small force against Hooker. As he and Jackson made plans for 2 May, they learned that the XI Corps line on the Orange Turnpike remained unguarded. Jackson quickly suggested an attack on that open flank with his entire corps, leaving Lee with only a small force to hold against any Union push west toward Fredericksburg. In short, Jackson had suggested a second division of Lee's already small army. Lee marveled at his subordinate's boldness but accepted the risk and ordered Jackson to march.

Early on 2 May, Jackson's men snaked along a narrow dirt road toward the Union right flank. Union soldiers saw them and Northern gunners even fired shells at the moving column.

When informed of the artillerymen's target, Hooker concluded quite incorrectly that Lee finally had decided to retreat from the field. The Confederates intended no such thing, of course. By 5 P.M., Jackson had amassed over 20,000 troops on Hooker's right flank and attacked.

Many soldiers in Howard's XI Corps had detected activity in the woods to their west all afternoon. Union patrols had reported Confederates massing in the tree line. They had sent word up the chain of command. But when Jackson's men stormed forward, flushing deer and rabbits ahead of them, Howard had deployed only two small regiments and two cannon—about 850 Union soldiers—to face west and meet them head-on. The rest of the XI Corps defenses all paralleled the

Orange Turnpike facing south.

Nothing could stop Jackson's men. The small flank guard crumbled after about ten minutes. A second line facing west, quickly cobbled together near the Wilderness Church, lasted maybe twice that long. A third and final west-facing line put up a good fight for slightly longer. But finally, the XI Corps broke, and from this day forward, critics pointed to the significant numbers of German-born soldiers in the XI Corps, blamed them for the rout, and dubbed them "Howard's cowards." Hooker refused to believe the first reports of the collapse of his right flank. As he arrived at the turnpike, however, the first demoralized soldiers rushed past him. The sight left him speechless.

Jackson's attack finally lost its momentum to confusion and darkness. But Jackson still wanted to press on. After riding forward with his staff to find roads toward the Union rear, nervous soldiers from the 18th North Carolina Infantry fired on the group as it tried to reenter Confederate lines. Stonewall Jackson fell mortally wounded and died on 10 May, his loss to Lee immeasurable.

But Jackson's fall did not end all chance for a stunning Confederate victory. Under the temporary direction of cavalry commander Jeb Stuart, Jackson's infantry—demanding revenge for their fallen leader—crashed in unstoppable waves into the Union line at first light on 3 May. They took prime artillery positions on Hazel Grove and Fairview, and by 9 A.M., trained cannon on Hooker's own headquarters at Chancellorsville. As Hooker watched the fight, a Confederate shell hit the pillar against which he leaned, temporarily paralyzing him. Shortly thereafter, he was evacuated from the scene, and Lee himself—his small force now reunited with Jackson's old command—rode into the Chancellorsville clearing, his men pushing Hooker's forces back to new positions that protected the roads to the Rappahannock fords and safety.

Lee's Skillful Victory

Lee had little time to savor his victory, however. At the same time the Union forces at Chancellorsville accepted defeat, the men Hooker had left under Major General John Sedgwick's command near Fredericksburg had begun to push back Early's small detachment. Indeed, they finally stormed Marye's Heights and pushed west on the Orange Turnpike, becoming a potential threat to the rear of Lee's position at Chancellorsville. Satisfied that Hooker would not counterattack, Lee disengaged several brigades and sent them back toward Fredericksburg to stop Sedgwick. At Salem Church, on a ridge six miles west of Fredericksburg, the Confederates met Sedgwick's vigorous attack with an equally stout defense. Early's counterattack on the Union left flank and rear stopped the advance. The threat to Lee's rear evaporated.

By 6 May, Hooker's army recrossed the Rappahannock. He had lost nearly 17,300 men in defeat. Although Lee had lost Jackson and about 12,800 of his men in a costly victory, he nonetheless had fought one of his most skillful battles, accepting significant risk and employing those few advantages he enjoyed—especially interior lines—to the greatest extent he could.

Lee Moves North

Lee and Davis now gave serious consideration to a second campaign on Union soil. Lee hoped such a move would disrupt Union plans for summer operations in Virginia, take pressure off other active theaters in Virginia and perhaps elsewhere, offer opportunity to obtain supplies, and maybe set the stage for a decisive victory that would end the war. Well before he set his troops into motion, Lee already had taken key steps to support the northward advance of his army. In early 1863, he had ordered pontoon equipment be sent forward from Richmond to facilitate the crossing of the Potomac. His topographical engineers had begun to make maps of Maryland and south-central Pennsylvania toward Harrisburg. On June 3, Lee's army began to move north.

At first, Hooker could not discern Lee's intentions. Union cavalry probing toward the Confederate lines surprised Jeb Stuart's Southern horsemen at Brandy Station on 9 June, but even then, Hooker could not determine with certainty Lee's destination. Adding to Hooker's problems, Stuart's cavalry spread fear and consternation as it rode completely around the Union army yet again. By 22 June, Confederate soldiers had arrived on the free soil of the Keystone State. Pennsylvania Governor Andrew G. Curtin called out 60,000 state militia on 26 June to repulse them, but panicked Pennsylvanians did not respond enthusiastically. Hooker had acted slowly, too, at least partly because of his ongoing squabbles with the War Department over operational control of troops at Harpers Ferry and elsewhere near Washington, troops not formally assigned to the Army of the Potomac. Finally, frustrated by Hooker's inactivity and obstreperous nature, Lincoln relieved him on 27 June and replaced him with Major General George G. Meade. By then, Lee's army stretched in a wide arc from the outskirts of Harrisburg to the Maryland state line.

Lee expected Meade to proceed cautiously and make few mistakes. With Stuart still absent, leaving Lee comparatively blind on enemy soil, the Southern chieftain on 28 June ordered his scattered force to concentrate near Cashtown, Pennsylvania. Eight miles to the east lay the important crossroads town of Gettysburg.

Battle of Gettysburg

On 30 June, Brigadier General John Buford's Union cavalry,

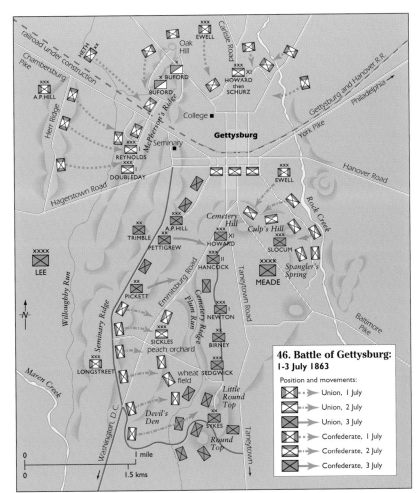

Confederate General Robert E. Lee's (top) reputation as a brilliant commander was tarnished when he met the methodical General George G. Meade (above) at Gettysburg, Pennsylvania.

the advance element of Meade's army, reached Gettysburg and found Lee's forces probing east from Cashtown. Buford quickly determined that the ridges and hills south of Gettysburg offered Meade a strong defensive position if he required one, and he planned to protect it by deploying on rolling ridges north and west of town and trading space for time until Union infantry arrived to take possession. Early on 1 July, a division of Lieutenant General A. P. Hill's new III Corps—organized in the aftermath of Jackson's death—advanced from Cashtown and exchanged shots with Buford's men on School House Ridge, three miles west of Gettysburg. The battle had begun.

Although instructed by Lee not to bring on a fight until the army had concentrated, Hill pressed on against Union forces that initially held their own. Slowly, Buford fell back to McPherson's Ridge, where Union horse artillery stabilized the cavalry line and helped to push back the first substantial Southern infantry assault. At 10 A.M., Hill's men pressed forward again. By now, Major General John Reynolds's I Corps had begun to file onto the battlefield. For fifteen minutes, Reynolds directed the Union defense, and when he fell dead

with a bullet through the head, Major General Abner Doubleday put in one of the most underappreciated defensive performances of the war, holding the line for at least six hours against quickly mounting Confederate numbers. About noon, the lead division of Lieutenant General Richard Ewell's new II Corps—also organized in the aftermath of Jackson's death—deployed on Oak Hill in position to outflank Doubleday's line. But Ewell's initial attacks foundered and the stout Union defenders continued to hold. General Howard's XI Corps had arrived, too, extending the Union line north of Gettysburg.

But about 2 P.M., fortune turned against the Union forces. The XI Corps could not resist a powerful assault that crashed in Howard's right flank at Barlow's Knoll. Its troops withdrew—some fighting a delaying action—to a predetermined rallying point on Cemetery Hill, part of the key ground that Buford already had selected as essential to any Union defensive effort and where Howard had left one of his three divisions to prepare defenses for just this kind of eventuality. By now, Lee himself had arrived on the battlefield. Although he had not sought this fight, about 4 P.M., he ordered a general advance along his whole line. Ewell's men finished off the XI Corps, and now even the stalwart I Corps gave way before the Southern onslaught and retired to Cemetery Hill. One more opportunity remained. Lee sent Ewell discretionary orders to take Cemetery Hill without bringing on a full blown battle. Ewell considered it, and then took no action. He has been second-guessed ever since.

On 1 July, Meade arrived at Gettysburg near midnight. Relying on the judgment of trusted subordinates, and after riding his lines himself, he decided to stand at Gettysburg rather than fall back on his chosen alternative—the Pipe Creek line—several miles south on the Maryland-Pennsylvania border. General Lee also began considering his options for 2 July. He wanted to stay and fight, but his second-in-command, General Longstreet, argued against it, believing that Lee had agreed to conduct an offensive campaign, but should take the tactical defensive if forced to fight. Lee chose to attack.

Lee's Plan

Lee's plan for 2 July called for a coordinated attack against both flanks of Meade's fishhook-shaped line. With two of his own divisions and one from A. P. Hill's Corps, Longstreet would swing south and lead the main effort against the Union left, which Lee believed extended along the Emmitsburg Road. He expected that a Confederate attack up that road could roll up the Union line and expose the rear of the Northern strong point on Cemetery Hill. When Ewell, posted opposite the Union right flank on Cemetery Hill and nearby Culp's Hill, heard Longstreet's artillery, he was supposed to support the main effort with a demonstration or even an attack of his own if opportunity beckoned.

Lee hoped to begin the attack early in the day, but Longstreet's men had to countermarch to screen their movements from the enemy and did not deploy into battlelines until 3:30 P.M. By that time, however, the Union position looked quite different than it had when Lee framed his plans. The main line now extended south from Cemetery Hill along Cemetery Ridge to two rocky hills called the Round Tops. About 2:00 P.M., on his own initiative, Major General Daniel E. Sickles advanced his III Corps westward from low ground on southern Cemetery Ridge to a peach orchard on high ground near the Emmitsburg Road, his right flank extending north along the roadway and his left angling southeastward through a wheat field to a rocky outcropping called Devil's Den. Meade disapproved of Sickles' action, but the III Corps' new position turned Longstreet's flank attack into a frontal assault. Longstreet could not convince Lee to alter his plans to fit changed circumstances, and at 4:00 P.M., the Confederates attacked.

As Longstreet later recalled, the next three hours saw some of the finest fighting the Army of Northern Virginia ever con-

ducted. His own two divisions crashed into Sickles's position, and Meade fed in reinforcements from the II, V, VI, and XII Corps to keep the line from collapsing. Longstreet's men captured Devil's Den first, then cleared blue-clad defenders from the wheat field and cracked Sickles's peach orchard salient and the Union line extending north up the Emmitsburg Road. But, Little Round Top, the anchor of the Union left flank, held. Meade also stabilized his main line on Cemetery Ridge to prevent a breakthrough as Sickles's men withdrew from their advanced position. By 7 P.M., when the attack of the division from A. P. Hill's Corps assigned to cooperate with Longstreet lost momentum, the Confederate main effort ground to a halt, short of its goals. Against the Union right flank, Ewell finally attacked both Cemetery Hill and Culp's Hill with minor success, but he did so too late and with too little strength to accomplish more.

Near midnight, Meade held a council of war with his surviving senior commanders. They ultimately voted on three issues: Should the army stay or leave the field? If they stayed, should they attack or await attack? If they decided to await attack, how long? After some discussion, the generals elected to stay, await attack, and revisit their options after one day. As the meeting broke up, Meade turned to Brigadier General John Gibbon, acting commander of the II Corps, and suggested that if Lee attacked on 3 July, he would attack the Union center on Gibbon's front.

Pickett's Charge

As it turned out, Meade had guessed correctly. But Lee's assault on the Union center known best as "Pickett's Charge" was not initially the Confederate battle plan for 3 July. Indeed, Lee intended to push his advantage on the Union flanks where he had won incomplete victories the previous day. But about 4:30 A.M., on 3 July, soldiers from the Union XII Corps moved to retake positions on lower Culp's Hill that the Confederates had wrested away the night before. Severe fighting swept up and down the slopes of the hill and nearby Spangler's Spring until nearly 11 A.M. The duration and the intensity of that fight convinced Lee that Meade had strengthened his flanks during the night. If Meade had a weakness, it had to be the Union center. Again James Longstreet demurred. Nonetheless, Lee designated a clump of trees on Cemetery Ridge as his army's new goal and named Longstreet tactical commander of the advance. An artillery bombardment would precede the assault, which would be made by Major General George E. Pickett's fresh division of Longstreet's own corps and, from A. P. Hill's Corps, Brigadier General J. Johnston Pettigrew's division and two additional brigades under the temporary leadership of Major General Isaac Trimble.

About 1 P.M., the Confederate artillery bombardment began,

and Union guns returned the fire. For perhaps ninety minutes, the firing continued. When it slowed, the Confederate soldiers advanced in two distinct bodies, Pickett's men separated from Pettigrew's and Trimble's by several hundred yards. Pettigrew's and Trimble's men wavered first, breaking before they reached the Union line. But Pickett's Virginians pressed forward, broke through the Union line near the clump of trees Lee had designated, and absorbed 60 percent casualties while waiting in vain for reinforcements that never came. Pickett's survivors returned to the Confederate lines, where Lee himself met them, proclaiming to anyone who would listen, "It is all my fault."

Gettysburg has been called "the high water mark of the rebellion," but survivors of the two armies that slogged back toward the Potomac—Lee finally recrossed it safely on 13-14 July—did not think of it that way. Gettysburg had lost Meade over 23,000 men and it deprived Lee of more than 29,000 soldiers he would be hard pressed to replace. Nonetheless, at the time, most Southerners viewed Gettysburg less as a crushing defeat and more as an anomaly—a temporary, if costly, setback. Northerners chose to celebrate a rare victory for their eastern army. For truly momentous events, all eyes looked west to events along the Mississippi River.

Union Control of the Mississippi River

On 3 July, finally realizing that no help was coming and no prospects for success remained, General Pemberton—a Pennsylvanian with a Southern-born wife—asked Grant for surrender terms. The Confederate leader had tried to hold out until 4 July, hoping for a generous arrangement, possibly including parole for his troops and assistance for Vicksburg's civilian residents. With the fall of Vicksburg, Grant finally had untangled the biggest knot that had kept the Mississippi River out of Union control. More good news came on 8 July, when Confederate General Franklin Gardner finally requested terms of surrender from Major General Nathaniel P. Banks to complete the capture of Port Hudson, Louisiana, after several months of active operations. The Union now controlled the entire Mississippi River. Grant, Banks, and thousands of Northern soldiers had just accomplished one of General Scott's first strategic goals.

The heady events of July 1863 buoyed Northern spirits, but they had not ended the war. Off Charleston, South Carolina, a joint army-navy effort to recapture Fort Sumter and that key Southern port stalled badly. Both sides learned the answer to one question, though: Black soldiers would and could fight. Although this was not the first time black soldiers fought in combat, the attention given the 54th Massachusetts in its failed attack on Fort Wagner on 18 July won plaudits from those who embraced the cause of emancipation.

In central Tennessee, from June through early September, General Rosecrans executed a masterful maneuver campaign—

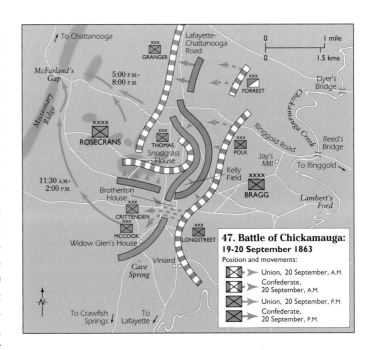

**47. Battle of Chickamauga:
19-20 September 1863**
Position and movements:

Union, 20 September, A.M.	
Confederate, 20 September, A.M.	
Union, 20 September, P.M.	
Confederate, 20 September, P.M.	

the Tullahoma campaign—that, nearly without bloodshed, shoved Bragg's army back into north Georgia. On 9 September, Rosecrans occupied Chattanooga. But for all his successful maneuvering, he had not destroyed his opponent, and Bragg determined to strike back.

Chickamauga Creek

With the addition of two divisions of Longstreet's corps sent from Virginia, Bragg planned to use his Army of Tennessee to hit Rosecrans's force concentrating near Chickamauga Creek just south of Chattanooga. Without knowing Rosecrans's dispositions exactly, on 19 September, Bragg assaulted the Union left flank, making little progress as the fighting extended down the length of both armies' lines. The next day, however, with Longstreet's men now on line, the Confederate troops hit a gap inadvertently opened in the Union center. The Union line bent and nearly broke, but a stout defense by General Thomas, hereafter known as "the rock of Chickamauga," prevented a rout. Rosecrans withdrew to Chattanooga. Bragg followed, taking up positions on the high ground of Lookout Mountain and Missionary Ridge and cutting the Northerners' supply line. Sometimes called the "Gettysburg of the West," Chickamauga exacted a casualty rate of nearly 28 percent of each army.

When it seemed gloomiest in the Union camps of Chattanooga, relief arrived in several forms. Reinforcements arrived from the Army of the Potomac. On 17 October, Lincoln relieved Rosecrans of command of the Army of the Cumberland and replaced him with General Thomas. Even more important, Lincoln named Grant commander of the Military District of the Mississippi and gave him authority over all

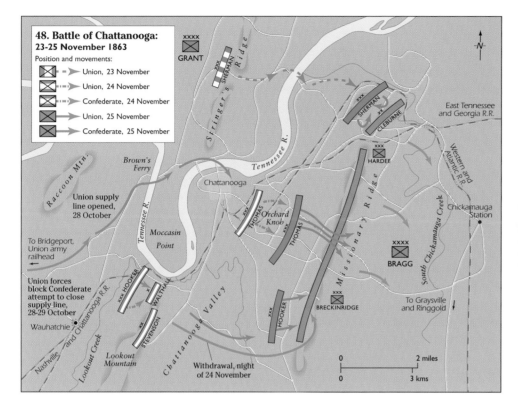

By March 1864, Ulysses S. Grant was asked by President Lincoln to command all the U.S. armies, after an undistinguished early military career.

operations between the Mississippi River and the Appalachian Mountains. Grant arrived in Chattanooga on 23 October. The very next day, he opened the "Cracker line" to improve delivery of food, mail, pay, medicine, and other supplies, and at Wauhatchie on 28 October, he defeated a Confederate attempt to close it down. Then he made plans to break Bragg's stranglehold on Chattanooga.

Battle Above the Clouds

On 23 November, Grant ordered Thomas's men to take Orchard Knob, a Confederate post one mile in advance of Bragg's main line on Missionary Ridge; they did so with light casualties. On 24 November, a revitalized General Hooker sent the XX Corps—the newly arrived veterans from Virginia—on a tough climb up lightly defended Lookout Mountain. Dense clouds of fog made it impossible to determine who had gained advantage until the deep-throated Union "hurrah" proclaimed the victor of the "Battle Above the Clouds." On 25 November, after slow starts to several diversionary efforts, Thomas sent four divisions scrambling up the rocky slopes of Missionary Ridge. Surprised and stunned by the boldness of this unexpected attack, Bragg's men fled back to Chickamauga.

The War Quiets Down

Except for scattered skirmishes, yet another flare-up of naval activity around Charleston, a frustrating Confederate cam-

paign to retake east Tennessee—a horrible affair in which General James Longstreet fared badly against General Ambrose Burnside—and a face-off between Lee and Meade at Mine Run, west of Chancellorsville, military affairs grew quiet. The year 1863 had been the war's bloodiest to date. But it was also the first to show clear progress for one side. The Union had begun to turn the tide.

The Tide Turns: 1864

This critical year, marked by a presidential election in the North, opened quietly. Small-scale Union operations in northern Florida and Sherman's efforts to take Meridian, Mississippi, in February, provided the most notable military news. On 29 February, however, Lincoln approved a congressional act to reinstitute the rank of lieutenant general. On 2 March, the U.S. Senate confirmed the nomination of Ulysses S. Grant to that rank. Lincoln personally handed Grant his new commission on 9 March, and the following day he received official authority to command all the armies of the United States. This move left General Halleck without official responsibility, so he became the army's chief administrator, with the title of chief of staff.

A New Northern Plan

While Grant impressed few Washington politicians, he nonetheless became the agent for at least one major change in military policy designed to bring a quicker end to the war. Scott's Anaconda Plan to squeeze the South into submission worked too slowly and at too high a cost. The time had come to replace the constrictor with a viper that would kill its foe quickly and violently. Rather than continue to focus on geographic targets such as Richmond, Grant agreed with Lincoln that the Southern armies held the key to the Confederacy's ability to resist and determined to make their destruction the primary objective of future Union operations. Additionally—and controversially—anything that helped to sustain enemy armies in the field could become legitimate targets for Union retribution. In actual practice, this included Southern crops, industry, railroads, and even public opinion, through the selective destruction of private property, the ending of prisoner exchanges, and the seizure of contraband.

Grant made a second major decision, too. He would not command from Washington. By 26 March, he had established his official headquarters with the Army of the Potomac. He did so, not from any distrust of its commander, General Meade, but from a hatred of the formalities and the distractions of Washington politics. From his tent in the field, he kept abreast of the news from General Banks's Red River campaign in Louisiana in April and the Fort Pillow "massacre" in Tennessee on 12 April.

The Spring Campaign

Grant also developed his own plans for a spring campaign, a design as exquisite in its simplicity as it was ambitious in scope. In early May, he wanted all Union armies to begin active operations against Confederate forces in their immediate front. By so doing, he hoped to deprive the Confederates of the primary advantage of their interior lines, their ability to shuttle troops from one crisis point to another, just as Longstreet's men had done the previous autumn by coming west from Virginia. Lincoln likened the concept to skinning a mule, noting that Union armies that could not press a fight on the Confederates they faced could at least "hold a leg" by preventing them from going to help another Southern force. A number of Union armies moved out smartly in early May, but, as usual, operations of the main forces in Virginia and, now, Georgia, commanded most attention.

Virginia

In Virginia, Grant functioned as an army group commander, coordinating the operations of Major General Franz Sigel's force in the Shenandoah Valley, Major General Benjamin Butler's Army of the James on the peninsula, and the Army of the Potomac facing Lee. Initial successes in the valley turned sour after Sigel's defeat at New Market on 15 May and Butler slowly made progress toward Richmond, attacking the city's south-

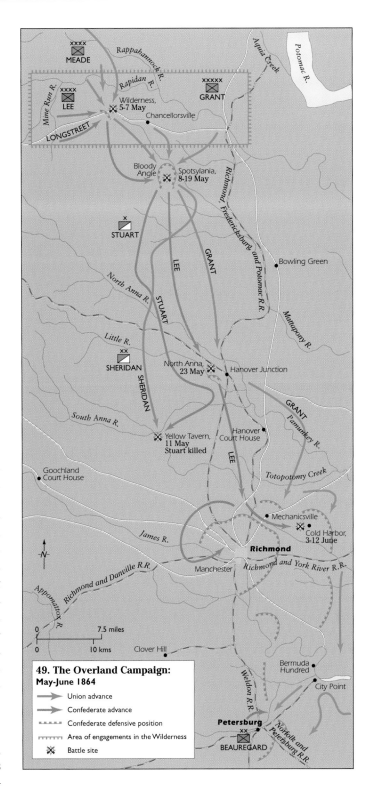

49. The Overland Campaign: May-June 1864
→ Union advance
→ Confederate advance
····· Confederate defensive position
⊓⊓⊓⊓ Area of engagements in the Wilderness
✕ Battle site

eastern defenses near Drewry's Bluff on 16 May. But Grant's immediate attention centered on his first face-off with Lee.

The Army of the Potomac broke camp near Culpeper on 3 May. Grant and Meade wanted to move quickly south, through the Wilderness, and interpose their forces between the Confederate army's winter encampments near Mine Run and Richmond. By so doing, they believed they would give Lee no choice but to attack the strong defenses Union commanders deliberately designed. Lee did not allow the Northern plan to unfold, however. On 5 May, Lee sent his forces east along the Orange Turnpike and Orange Plank Road as he had the previous year at Chancellorsville, this time engaging the Union army in the tangled second-growth of the Wilderness. In one of the most confusing and chaotic clashes of the war, infantrymen rarely saw their enemy for the smoke and vegetation. Officer casualties spiked upward, as the little sunlight penetrating the woods made targets of their brass and braid. Gunpowder sparks ignited fires that incinerated helpless wounded caught between the lines. Grant renewed the fight on 6 May, and Lee's line began to bend. The timely arrival of Longstreet's corps and Lee's personal leadership prevented a fatal break. Shortly thereafter, however, Longstreet fell seriously wounded, depriving Lee of his most trusted subordinate for the next six months.

After two days of furious but indecisive fighting that cost 17,000 Union casualties and the loss of at least 7,000 Southerners, Grant's veterans learned much about their new commander as they approached a key crossroads in the Wilderness. They knew that a march straight ahead or a left turn meant a return to camp; a turn to the right would signify that Grant intended to continue the fight. When the column turned right, Union soldiers signaled their approval with loud cheers. Grant planned to march south quickly to gain the key crossroads at Spotsylvania Court House. Such a move, again, would place his own army between Lee and Richmond and force the Confederates to attack on ground Grant chose. But Union infantry and cavalry clogged the roads south and squabbled over right of way. Moreover, fire prevented some Confederate troops from using their assigned campground near the Wilderness, so they had pushed on toward Spotsylvania. When the first Union cavalry moved up to take possession of the crossroads, Lee's veterans greeted them, already deployed in line of battle.

For the next eleven days—8 to 19 May—these two veteran armies found themselves locked in an unfamiliar kind of combat. Each force now began to dig increasingly elaborate systems of trenches, so close to each other that soldiers learned to live with the near presence of arbitrary death, as sharpshooters found ready targets for their bullets. Tactical success too often required the breaching and capture of those entrenched positions, and a bloody Union repulse at Laurel Hill on 8 May convinced Colonel Emory Upton of the Union II Corps to seek an alternative to using traditional linear tactics to storm broad expanses of earthworks. Upton decided to use a narrow and deep column of Union troops to punch a hole through a restricted portion of the Confederate line instead. On 10 May, with twelve picked regiments arranged in just such a column, Upton successfully breached a particularly weak spot in the Confederate defenses, but he fell back after expected supports failed to arrive.

The Bloody Angle

Grant, however, decided to apply Upton's technique on 12 May, advancing an entire army corps against a prominent and vulnerable Southern salient, nicknamed "the Mule Shoe." About 4:30 A.M., a misty rain silenced the approach of the II Corps, the moisture dampened the Southern infantry's gunpowder, and Confederate artillery had just begun rolling back into position when the Union wave broke over the Confederate line and quickly overwhelmed much of it. Famous Confederate combat units including the vaunted "Stonewall Brigade" evaporated, as many soldiers were captured without firing a shot. When things seemed grimmest, however, Lee counterattacked. The most intense fighting concentrated around the "Bloody Angle," a maze of trenches near the apex of the Mule Shoe where a twenty-two-inch oak tree was toppled, its trunk riddled by rifle bullets. Union artillery reintroduced the field mortar to shower large caliber shells behind Confederate defenses. The Bloody Angle became hell on earth. After the fighting ended, with Lee's men still hanging on to some of the positions they held that morning, loud screams and the stench of death burned into the memories of survivors. Some who drew burial duty a few days later entombed many of the Southerners where they fell, simply by filling in the earthworks of the Bloody Angle on top of the dead who lay there.

Cold Harbor

On 19 May, after more maneuvering to no advantage and 17,500 Union casualties to Lee's approximately 10,000, Grant broke off the fight at Spotsylvania. He again tried to maneuver east and south and headed to the North Anna River, where, again, he hoped to place himself between Lee and Richmond. Again, however, Lee found himself in a race for position—a task made all the more difficult after the death of cavalry chief Jeb Stuart at Yellow Tavern on 11 May. Nonetheless, on 23 May, Lee's weary men established an excellent V-shaped defensive position, its apex anchored on the river itself, allowing Confederate commanders to shuttle troops to any crisis point easily and depriving Grant of the ability to concentrate his army without multiple river crossings. Frustrated once more, Grant maneuvered southward yet again. By 31 May, now east of Richmond, some veterans in both armies redeployed on battlefields they remembered all too well from the Seven Days' battles. Now, some of those already bloodied fields won a new name: Cold Harbor.

For the first two days of June, Grant probed without success for a weak spot in Lee's lines. Finally, on 3 June, in an action he admitted he truly regretted, Grant ordered a frontal assault on Lee's entrenched position. In one month, Lee's men had learned much about the construction of earthworks, and Grant's men charged into a complex network of mutually supporting lines and interlocking fields of fire. Grant lost as many as 7,000 men in thirty minutes; he won only a nickname: "The Butcher."

Petersburg

Despite the heavy losses, Grant made good his numbers, incorporating into his field command the Army of the James that had fought at Drewry's Bluff and even heavy artillerymen from Washington garrisons. He also attempted to return to the maneuver warfare that got him to the outskirts of Richmond. Indeed, while Butcher Grant is most remembered for his frontal assaults that failed, he himself knew that he made his greatest progress through maneuver. He disengaged so slowly and skillfully from Lee's front along the Cold Harbor line that he gave his army a day's head start on its next southward move. On 14 June, the Army of the Potomac began crossing the James River by boat and pontoon bridge. Grant's target was Petersburg, a rail junction twenty-five miles south of Richmond, and the backdoor to the Confederate capital. With speed and luck, Grant might have reached Petersburg before Lee could respond to the threat. General Beauregard, commanding the defenses of the capital region, had only 3,000 men to commit to Petersburg's defense. On 15 June, Grant intended for a force of 16,000 Union troops to sweep in and take Petersburg, but confusing orders, incomplete intelligence and logistical preparation, poor cooperation by Grant's subordinates, and the tenacity of the defenders all contributed to a Union defeat. Grant had lost a golden opportunity. After three days of unsuccessful and bloody assaults, culminating in an extremely costly offensive on 18 June, Grant learned that he now faced Lee's veterans, no longer homeguard. He did not desire to lay siege to Petersburg, but Grant's army now needed a break from six weeks of continuous operations. And Northern Republicans most assuredly needed a break from long casualty lists from Virginia if they hoped Abraham Lincoln would win reelection.

The Georgia Campaign

Loyal Republicans had reason to be concerned. Virginia held no monopoly on the production of long casualty lists. In Georgia, General Sherman's army had begun its advance from Chattanooga toward the key rail center of Atlanta. The terrain of north Georgia favored the defense, and Jefferson Davis had relieved General Bragg in favor of one of the Confederacy's

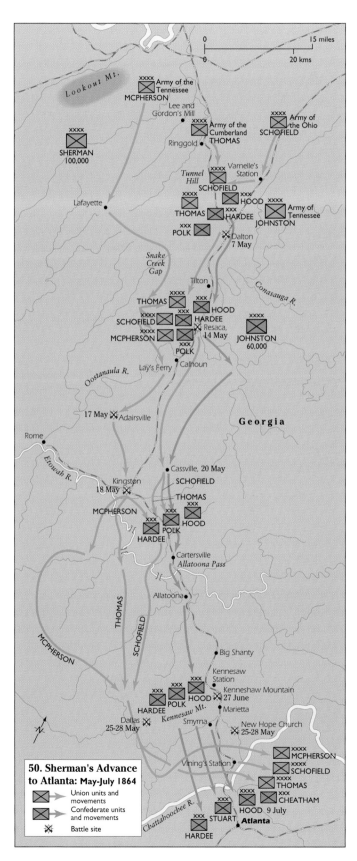

experts on defensive warfare, Joseph E. Johnston, who used the rolling ridges to advantage. Although Sherman had the advantage of numbers (100,000 men to Johnston's 60,000) and talented senior subordinates—Major General George Thomas with the Army of the Cumberland, Major General James McPherson with the Army of the Tennessee, and Major General John Schofield with the Army of the Ohio—Johnston checked him at every turn. On 7-9 May, Johnston stopped Thomas's opening jabs near Dalton, at Rocky Face Ridge and Buzzard's Roost. McPherson attempted a turning movement through Snake Creek Gap that would have put his force in Johnston's rear, but he stopped too soon, allowing Johnston to evacuate his positions around Dalton on 12 May and pull back safely to Resaca the next day. There, he prepared to meet Sherman's entire force, which began a series of probing attacks on his flanks on 14 May. With the Oostenaula River behind him, and fearing that Sherman might turn his position, Johnston withdrew from Resaca during the night of 15 May, first to Adairsville on 17 May, and then to Cassville and Kingston the next day.

Johnston stuck to his pattern of block and parry. Forced back from Cassville and across the Etowah River on 20 May, Johnston set up yet another strong position at Allatoona Pass. Sherman countered by sending his armies toward Dallas, a sweep that took them around the left flank of Johnston's Allatoona line. On 24 May, Johnston guessed Sherman's intent and blocked him at New Hope Church on 25 May, in a severe thunderstorm. The activity of the previous weeks had taken its toll on both armies, and now the appearance of elaborate systems of earthworks suggested that both commanders had decided to change the way they fought.

Until 4 June, Sherman seemed willing merely to probe for openings rather than launch major operations. On that day, Johnston pulled his forces back to prepared positions along Lost, Pine, and Brush mountains near Marietta. For several days, Sherman probed Johnston's new line until the Confederates pulled back even closer to Marietta on 18 June to an even stronger line at Kennesaw Mountain. Now a bit frustrated, Sherman set aside his maneuver tactics in favor of a more traditional frontal assault. On 27 June, Sherman sent the men of Thomas's and McPherson's armies up the slopes of Kennesaw Mountain. In an area of open fields of interlocking fire nicknamed the "Dead Angle," hundreds of Union soldiers and at least two brigade commanders fell dead or mortally wounded. After losing 2,000 men to the defenders's 500, Sherman resorted to maneuver once again. By 2 July, he had forced Johnston to pull back again to a line near the Chattahoochee River, and by 8 July, Schofield's sweep across the river and around Johnston's right flank had rendered that line untenable too. On 9 July, Johnston retreated to the gates of Atlanta. On

17 July, a frustrated Jefferson Davis replaced Johnston with the more aggressive General John Bell Hood.

Battle for Atlanta

Planning to save Atlanta by fighting for it, Hood immediately began a series of mismatched firefights against elements of Sherman's force. At Peachtree Creek, on 20 July, Hood lost nearly 4,800 men in attacking Thomas's column north of Atlanta; Thomas lost fewer than half that number. On 22 July, Hood attacked McPherson's force east of the city, killing McPherson and inflicting 3,800 casualties, but losing perhaps 10,000 of his own men. On 28 July, Hood lost perhaps 5,000 more men in an effort to stop Union forces west of Atlanta at Ezra Church. Hood's aggressiveness accomplished little. By the end of July, Sherman had laid siege to Atlanta.

With Grant encircling Petersburg, Sherman doing the same to Atlanta, and the war dragging on, Lincoln's prospects for a second term seemed dim. Although he won the nomination of his new National Union Party on 8 June, the very existence of that faction revealed the severity of the cracks in his own Republican party. On 31 August, the Democrats nominated George McClellan as their candidate.

Northern Successes

But the military events of late summer and fall 1864 breathed new life into Lincoln's campaign. Victories abounded, and at least two did not exact high cost. On 5 August, Admiral David Farragut led his fleet of eighteen ships into the harbor of Mobile, Alabama, closing one of the two major ports still open to blockade runners. (The other was Wilmington, North Carolina.) The second great victory came in September and October when Major General Philip H. Sheridan finally cleared Confederate armies out of the Shenandoah Valley. Hoping to draw strength away from Grant's army facing Richmond, Lee had detached Major General Jubal Early into the valley and northward. Early crossed into Maryland on 5 July, brushed 6,000 Union soldiers out of his way at Monocacy on 9 July, and threatened Washington itself on 11 July, bringing Lincoln himself under fire at Fort Stevens. But he quickly returned to the security of the valley. From late August, through a major battle at Winchester on 19 September, and then a crushing blow at Cedar Creek on 19 October, Sheridan used reinforcements from Grant's army to hammer Early's small force. He not only went after all armed resistance but also approved the burning of barns and crops in the field, once saying that a crow flying over the valley that winter would have to carry its food on its back.

Lincoln Is Reelected

Just before the November election, a political cartoon showed

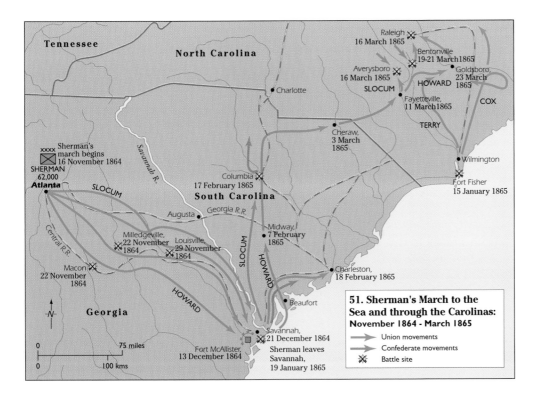

William Tecumseh Sherman proved his maxim that "war is hell" by cutting a swath of destruction through Georgia, from Atlanta to Savannah, in November and December 1864.

Lincoln sitting on a chair set on a table. Two table legs were borne by one of the military heroes of the fall of 1864: The hero of Mobile, Admiral Farragut, Sheridan, Sherman (who finally took Atlanta on 1 September), and Grant, who if he had not won great victories, lost no ground and shortened his casualty lists. On 8 November, Lincoln won reelection.

Nashville

Lincoln's mandate carried over to the battlefield immediately. On 16 November, Sherman's men left Atlanta, cut free from their supply lines, and headed toward the Atlantic coast, the general planning to make Georgia "howl." Sherman's men faced no serious opposition on their march. General Hood had taken the remnants of the Army of Tennessee into Alabama, and on 21 November, he advanced into Tennessee, heading for Nashville. General Schofield failed to parry Hood's move at the Duck River on 27-28 November, but Hood, in turn, failed to trap much of the Union force at Spring Hill on 29 November. At nearby Franklin, on 30 November, a frustrated Hood unleashed massive frontal assaults against the entrenched Union line. At the end of the fighting, Hood had lost six generals killed—including Major General Patrick Cleburne, the so-called "Stonewall of the West"—with 6,300 additional casualties; Union losses amounted to 2,326. Still undaunted, Hood pressed on to Nashville, reaching there on 2 December. Grant ordered Thomas to attack Hood immediately, but Thomas moved so deliberately he nearly lost his command.

When Thomas finally attacked on 15 December, Hood held his own at first, but finally, the next day, nearly cut off from his line of retreat, he could do little more to resist its power. Hood's Army of Tennessee, the mainstay of the Confederacy's western theater, had nearly disappeared.

News of Hood's campaign made the newspapers North and South mainly because Sherman's whereabouts remained

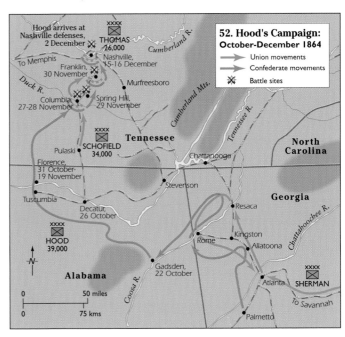

unknown. Grant and Lincoln waited anxiously for word. Finally, on 22 December, good news arrived in a telegram: "I beg to present you, as a Christmas gift, the city of Savannah."

The Winter of 1864-65

The winter of 1864-65 was a harsh one for troops still in the field. The largest concentration of active combatants had been engaged in operations around Petersburg since June. Both sides had made sporadic efforts to break the siege. The most spectacular, by far, became known as the Battle of the Crater, when, on 30 July, Union forces had dug a tunnel under the Confederate lines and attempted to blow open a gap in the defenses, which Southern reinforcements quickly closed. Most efforts, however, centered on Grant's plan to strangle Petersburg by cutting the road and rail links into the city. Lee had stopped Grant at the Weldon Railroad on 22 June. A week of Union probes at Deep Bottom, New Market Road, and other places near Richmond in August, all intended to divert Lee's attention from Grant's plan to take control of the Weldon Railroad, accomplished little. Nonetheless, the railroad fell firmly into Union hands on 18-19 August, despite a short-lived reversal at Reams Station on 25 August. A two-pronged Union offensive on 30 September-1 October brought a Northern victory at Fort Harrison, near Richmond, but forced back a Union attack at Peebles's Farm near Petersburg. A Union effort to take the South Side Railroad failed at Boydton Plank Road on 27 October, and the siege dragged on. When the armies settled down for the winter, Grant had succeeded in extending and thinning the Confederate defenses, but he had not yet broken them.

Final Events of the War

Even before the spring thaw, the final events of the Civil War began to unfold. Several months of futility ended on 15 January when a combined army-navy force under Brigadier General Alfred Terry and Admiral Porter finally captured Fort Fisher, essentially closing Wilmington, North Carolina, the Confederacy's last significant port. On 19 January, Sherman marched north from Savannah. The Union veterans' mood grew dark as they entered the first state to secede, but they faced little armed opposition on their way to Columbia. On 16 February, Union artillerymen shelled the city. Sherman accepted its surrender the next day. That night, the town burned, and controversy still rages about the fire's origins. Southerners blamed Sherman and his men for the conflagration, while Union veterans insisted that retreating Confederates set fire to cotton bales and military supplies and then simply departed, leaving the blazes to grow out of control.

By 7 March, Sherman had entered North Carolina. He faced, in name only, the Army of Tennessee, which was made up of remnants that survived Hood's Tennessee campaign, reinforced by home guards and other detachments, all under the command of General Joseph E. Johnston. At Averysboro on 16 March and at Bentonville on 19-21 March, Johnston proved to Sherman that the Confederacy could still fight, all the while hoping that Lee might break out of Petersburg and come to his aid. Grant, for his part, hoped that Sherman might eliminate Johnston, then come to Petersburg to join him against Lee.

Near Petersburg, in February and March 1865, Union and

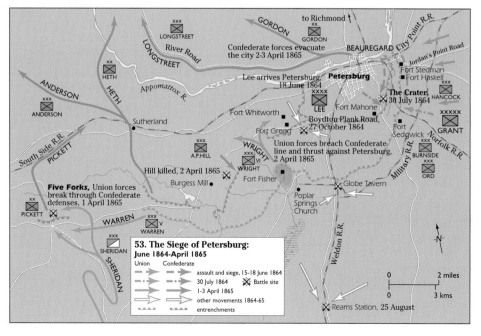

General P.G.T. Beauregard commanded Confederate forces at Fort Sumter and First Bull Run in 1861, directed the defenses of Charleston from 1862 to 1864, and repulsed Union attacks on Petersburg in 1864. He then became commander of the Division of the West until the war's end.

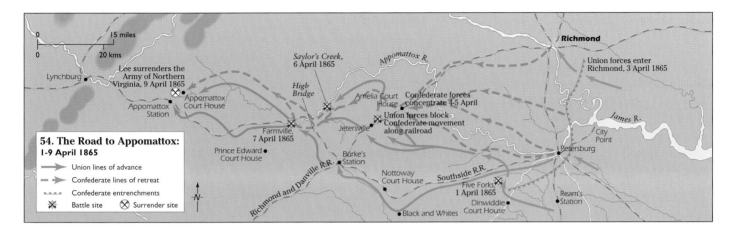

54. The Road to Appomattox:
1-9 April 1865

→ Union lines of advance
⇢ Confederate lines of retreat
⋯⋯ Confederate entrenchments
✗ Battle site   ⊗ Surrender site

Confederate still probed each others' weaknesses. Finally, on 1 April, Union forces broke through the overstretched Confederate defenses at a key crossroads called Five Forks, threatening to cut Lee's potential line of retreat. As news of the fall of Five Forks spread, Lee evacuated his Petersburg line and moved his army westward. Petersburg and its road and rail network had served as the back door to Richmond and now the door opened wide for the Union troops to move on the Confederate capital from the south. Therefore, when Lee's army left the Petersburg front, he also withdrew his forces deployed nearer to the Confederate capital, leaving Richmond an open city. On 2 April, the Confederate government evacuated Richmond. Union troops occupied the city the next day.

Surrender of the South

Lee withdrew westward, hoping to find rations and then break free to join Johnston. An active and skillful Union pursuit thwarted Lee at every turn, however. Union forces swept up much of his rear guard at Saylor's Creek on 6 April. On 8 April, Lee sent the first of several messages through the lines to ask Grant's terms for surrender. On 9 April, at Appomattox Court House, Lee signed the instrument of surrender for the Army of Northern Virginia.

News of Lee's surrender stunned Johnston's men and elated Sherman's forces, but fear and grief replaced those feelings on 14 April when news of Lincoln's assassination swept through both armies. Yet, Johnston did not consider surrender his sole option. While he opened negotiations with Sherman on 17 April, he did not believe his force to be in such dire straits that he could not fight another day. Sherman's terms promised much, including the surrender of not just Johnston's army but all remaining Confederate combatants, and a general amnesty. Johnston agreed to the terms the next day, but when they reached Washington in the aftermath of Lincoln's death, the Radical Republican leadership rejected them as too soft. Johnston could have taken up arms again, but instead he and

Sherman signed more limited terms of capitulation at Bennett Place on 26 April.

For all intents and purposes, Johnston's surrender and the capture of Jefferson Davis on 10 May signaled the end of the rebellion. The word spread slowly, though; the C.S.S. *Shenandoah*, busily attacking the Union whaling fleet in the Bering Sea in the spring, did not furl its flag until 2 August.

Legacy of the War

Historians will never agree on the final tally of the Civil War's death toll, property destruction, disrupted lives, or other collateral damage. The Union armies lost at least 360,222 to death in battle, from disease, or other causes; Confederate military losses approximate 258,000. But numbers tell only a small part of the story.

Since 1865, historians have tried to explain why the Confederacy lost and the Union won. Some have argued that the South's political and economic weaknesses—including its strong commitment to state rights—created an internal fractiousness that doomed the Confederacy to defeat. Others have compared the senior leadership of the two sides, generally finding sparks of genius in Abraham Lincoln that were absent in an embattled and overwhelmed Jefferson Davis. But the Confederacy's last best hopes were dashed when its armies could no longer mount a credible resistance on the field of battle. Union armies, ably led, well supplied, and guided by clear objectives to first, preserve the Union, and second, end slavery, won the war in conventional style: They outlasted their opposing forces and brought them to their knees.

The legacy of the Civil War lives on today in many ways: The national cemetery system, the old soldiers' homes, the income tax, the postwar Reconstruction amendments, the Ku Klux Klan, the Civil Rights Act of 1964, and frequent public debate over the display of the Confederate battle flag nearly 150 years after the surrender. The scars of a civil war are among the deepest and most lasting.

American Indian Wars: 1866-90

Americans have traditionally opposed a large, standing military, and the period following the American Civil War was no exception. The huge armies that had defeated the Confederacy were quickly demobilized and by the early 1870s the effective strength of the regular army had settled at about 22,000 men. About two-thirds of these men were available for duty against the American Indians. In theory, negotiations would prevent armed conflict and pave the way for the removal of American Indians from their traditional lands in exchange for federal annuities and new reservations safe from white intrusion. In practice, the government's patience was short and the Anglo-American thirst for land was almost insatiable; when negotiations collapsed, when new lands became desirable, or when depredations attributed to American Indians increased, the United States was willing to use military force.

American Indian Strengths and Weaknesses

Of the estimated 270,000 American Indians who lived west of the Mississippi River in 1866, about 100,000 belonged to groups that would take up arms against the federal government. Extremely mobile, most tribes sought to avoid pitched battles except under the most favorable of circumstances. On an individual level, the typical American Indian warrior was superior to his regular army counterpart. Some Indians even boasted repeating rifles which they acquired largely through traders, while regulars carried single-shot Springfield carbines. But intertribal feuds prevented American Indians from combining their strengths against the U.S. government. This allowed the army to use the railroads to strip troops from one region and concentrate them against the foe of the moment. It also made it easy for the army to recruit Indian auxiliaries, who almost invariably accompanied successful operations.

Command by Subdivision

The U.S. Army's commanding generals during the period included Ulysses S. Grant (1864-9), William T. Sherman (1869-83), Philip H. Sheridan (1883-88), and John M. Schofield (1888-95). From 1866 to 1876, they partitioned the nation into four divisions—the Atlantic, the South, the Missouri, and the Pacific. Each division was further divided into departments. Following Reconstruction, the South was merged into the Atlantic division. More closely associated with American Indian affairs was the Division of the Pacific, which included Oregon, California, Nevada, and the Washington, Idaho, and Arizona territories. Troops stationed in its three departments—Columbia, California, and Arizona—often saw combat against the Nez Percés, Apaches, Modocs, Bannocks, Utes, and

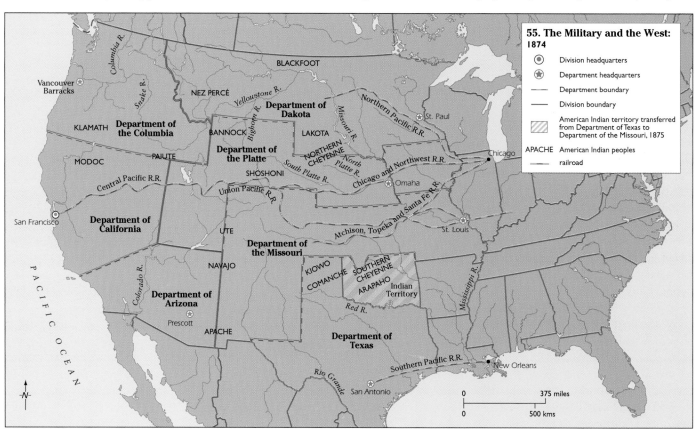

The end of the Civil War led to a sharp increase in westward migration. Troops sent to defend the settlers and those crossing the country from hostile Indians, spent most of their time on routine patrols and protecting communication lines. These infantrymen and their commanding officer (looking out of the coach) were serving as escorts for a United States Express Company stagecoach at Hays City, Kansas, in October 1867.

Paiutes. The largest and most important command was the Division of the Missouri, which encompassed Minnesota, Illinois, Iowa, Kansas, Missouri, Texas, the Indian territory (modern-day Oklahoma) and the territories of Dakota, Montana, Nebraska, Utah, Colorado, and New Mexico. Usually subdivided into the departments of Dakota, the Platte, the Missouri, and Texas, this sprawling command was also home to several powerful American Indian groups, most notably the Comanches, Sioux, Cheyennes, Kiowas, and Arapahos.

Geographic realities, common sense, and personnel issues determined these boundaries. The railroad lines became the main transport routes which cut through the departments. The Santa Fe Trail and the Atchison, Topeka & Santa Fe Railroad cut through the Department of the Missouri. Likewise, the Union Pacific Railroad bisected the Department of the Platte, and the Northern Pacific Railroad eventually spanned the Department of Dakota. Generally speaking, major generals headed divisions and brigadier generals commanded departments. But special arrangements had to be made when the number of commands did not match the number of generals of a particular rank. Divisions and departments were then gerrymandered—as was the case from 1877-80, when the independent Department of West Point was organized to spare Major General Schofield the embarrassment of serving under another major general. As might be expected, personality clashes, competing ambitions, and petty animosities hampered effective cooperation across departments and divisions.

Commonsense Strategies

The U.S. Army developed no formal doctrine for fighting American Indians, instead relying on its superior resources and greater staying power to defeat the tribes. Officers in the field were given enormous discretion. Inexperienced and irresolute officers found that their American Indian foes either caught them by surprise or eluded them completely. Effective commanders, by contrast, pursued their foes regardless of weather, terrain, or time spent in the field. A favorite army stratagem was to converge upon a suspected enemy village from several directions. Such a ploy not only made escape more difficult, but also forced enemy warriors to fight to protect their friends, families, and possessions.

Weather often proved a greater adversary than Indians to troops serving in the West. These members of the Fifth U.S. Infantry wear government-issued buffalo overcoats, fur caps, and mittens to fend off the cold outside their barracks at Fort Keogh, about 1877, the year the fort was built in Sioux country at the fork of the Powder and Yellowstone rivers in Montana Territory.

Campaigns of the 1860s

In spring 1867, General Winfield Scott Hancock launched a major offensive designed to crush American Indian resistance on the Southern Plains. But Hancock could not bring about a decisive engagement. Crusty General Philip Sheridan, newly appointed commander of the Department of the Missouri, initiated a new campaign in 1868-69. Throughout the winter and ensuing spring, columns of soldiers from Colorado, New Mexico, and Kansas swept through the Texas Panhandle and western Oklahoma. Important army victories were won at Washita (27 November 1868), Soldier Springs (24 December 1868), and Summit Springs (11 July 1869).

Ranald Mackenzie directed a series of campaigns against Indians in Texas in the 1870s. In 1873, he crossed the Rio Grande into Mexico to pursue Kickapoo Indians who took refuge there after raids north of the border. His victory at Palo Duro Canyon helped end the Red River War (1874-75). In 1876, Mackenzie led troops from Fort Sill, Oklahoma, to Montana where he fought the Sioux from 1883 to 1884, then returned to Texas.

Defeat of the Southern Plains Indians

The Red River War of 1874-75 finally broke the military power of the Southern Plains Indians. Though hampered by poor interdepartmental cooperation, troops from the departments of Texas and the Missouri moved into action in late summer and continued their campaigns through the following spring. Ranald Mackenzie scored the biggest victory. At Palo Duro Canyon (28 September 1874), he crippled a group of Kiowas, Comanches, and Cheyennes by destroying most of their winter stores and capturing or killing nearly 1,400 ponies. In the end, however, exhaustion, not defeat in battle, forced the tribes to accept reservation life.

The Northern Challenge

To the north, the Lakota (Teton) Sioux, and their Northern Cheyenne allies posed an even more formidable challenge. Captain William J. Fetterman's eighty-one-man detachment

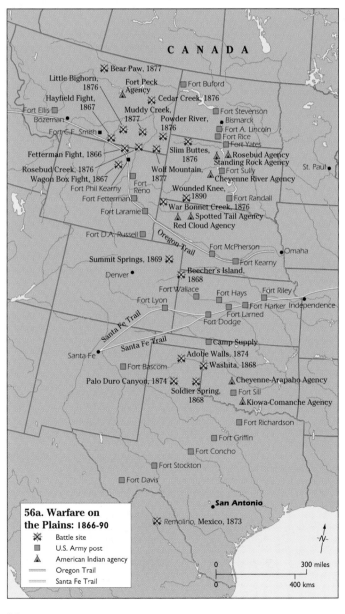

56a. Warfare on the Plains: 1866-90
- ✗ Battle site
- ◼ U.S. Army post
- ▲ American Indian agency
- Oregon Trail
- Santa Fe Trail

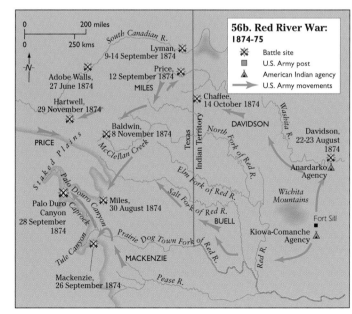

56b. Red River War: 1874-75
- ✗ Battle site
- ◼ U.S. Army post
- ▲ American Indian agency
- → U.S. Army movements

was annihilated just outside Fort Phil Kearny, Wyoming (21 December 1866). Under Red Cloud, associated forces soon closed the Bozeman Trail, a victory consummated when the U. S. Army withdrew its garrisons the following year. As sporadic violence continued, Sheridan, now commanding the Division of the Missouri, organized what he hoped would prove a crushing blow in early 1876, but when frigid weather stalled operations, more concerted efforts did not follow until

This map of the Battle of Little Big Horn traces Major Marcus Reno's advance down the river and his retreat (bottom), and depicts Custer's approach, repulse, and the spots where units of his command were destroyed (top). Sitting Bull approved the map before its publication in The New York Herald *on 16 November 1877.*

Short of field artillerymen in the West, the army pressed infantrymen into service. Five members of the 20th Infantry pose with their 1-inch Gatling gun at Fort McKean, Dakota Territory, after their service in the 1876 Little Big Horn Campaign. Many officers considered Gatling guns too unwieldy for use in campaigns against Indians, believing that operating in the field with artillery of any kind restricted movement over rugged terrain and slowed cavalry.

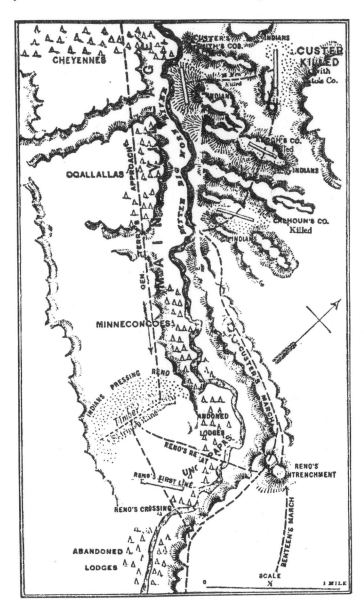

the summer. With only vague information about where the others might be, George Crook, George A. Custer, and John Gibbon pushed into the Black Hills from the departments of the Platte and Dakota. Unknown to the U.S. Army, the Hunkpapa Sioux leader, Sitting Bull, had forged an unusually cohesive alliance. Looking for an encounter with their enemy, the American Indians dealt Crook a stinging reverse at Rosebud Creek (17 June 1876). Eight days later, Custer found signs of their large village along the banks of the Little Bighorn. Custer promptly assaulted, dividing his forces in hopes of surprising his enemies and preventing their flight by converging from different points. Unaware that the village contained more than 4,000 inhabitants, Custer's troops were soon stopped. The five companies remaining with Custer were annihilated; detachments under the command of Major Marcus A. Reno and Captain Frederick W. Benteen barely escaped a similar fate.

Custer's defeat shocked the nation and has remained one of the most controversial engagements in the long history of Indian/non-Indian warfare in North America. Reinforcements were quickly dispatched to avenge the loss. As summer turned to fall, the U.S. Army's superior resources allowed it to continue the campaign. Colonel Nelson A. Miles defeated Sitting Bull near Cedar Creek (21-22 October 1876). Defying Montana's bitterly cold weather, Miles kept his troops in the field and eventually was victorious against Crazy Horse at Wolf Mountain (8 January 1877). Meanwhile, Mackenzie destroyed Dull Knife's Northern Cheyenne encampment in the Powder River

Valley (25 November 1876). American Indian resistance crumbled the following spring, although the defiant Sitting Bull would not be defeated ultimately for four more years.

The Nez Percés Revolt

Just as the Sioux and Northern Cheyenne conflicts were winding down, another major confrontation was developing in the Department of the Columbia. In June 1877, Nez Percés followers of Chief Joseph took up arms rather than leave their homelands. During a campaign that extended over 1,700 miles, the Nez Percés killed thirty-four of the attacking soldiers at White Bird Canyon (17 June 1877) at a cost of only three Indian wounded, they escaped what could have been a decisive setback at the Clearwater River (11-12 July 1877), and through surprise at Big Hole River (9 August 1877), they inflicted heavy casualties, killing thirty and wounding thirty-eight. Reinforcements from the Department of Dakota, led by the redoubtable Miles, surrounded the Nez Percés at Bear Paw Mountain and forced Chief Joseph to surrender on 5 October.

Other Conflicts

Fighting was not limited to the Great Plains. In Oregon, Crook had forced the Paiutes to resettle in reservations after a year and a half struggle in 1867-68. From 1872 through mid-1874, troops in southern Oregon and northern California fought the Modocs, a conflict highlighted by the assassination of General Edward R. S. Canby—the only regular army general killed

during the Indian wars—during aborted peace talks. About seven hundred Bannocks and Paiutes broke from their reservations in Idaho and Oregon in early June 1878. After a six-week chase, the main party was stopped just south of Fort Walla Walla, Washington. The following year, Ute Indians at Colorado's White River Agency won the Battle of Milk Creek (29 September-5 October 1879). Further violence was avoided when the Utes gave up their remaining captives and eventually agreed to move.

Guerrilla-Style Tactics

The southwest, where various groups of Apaches carried out a spirited resistance against reservation life, was the scene of almost continual conflict. The guerrilla-style methods employed by war leaders like Cochise, Juh, Victorio, Nana, and Geronimo, whose more mobile followers gave battle only when the tactical situation was in their favor, bedeviled the much larger, but more cumbersome, U.S. Army columns. Only through exhausting pursuits, assisted by swarms of hired American Indian auxiliaries, did the army eventually prevail. On several occasions the U.S. Army crossed the border into Mexico (often without permission from the Mexican government), most notably during Mackenzie's strike against Kickapoo villages at Remolino (18 May 1873).

The Final Conflicts

The final conflicts erupted in the winter of 1890-91, with the

As a youth, Geronimo (left), one of the most resourceful American Indian leaders, joined Cochise and other Chiricahua leaders in raids on Mexican, American, and Indian settlements. Though not born into the tribe, he soon assumed a leadership role. In 1875, Geronimo rejected orders to move to a reservation and eluded capture until 1878. Never reconciled to reservation life, he fled to Mexico (1881-83 and 1885-87). After Geronimo's third surrender, on 4 September 1887, the army sent him to Fort Pickens at Pensacola, Florida, where he was held with fellow Chiricahuas, Nachise (center) and Magnus (right). Transferred to Fort Sill, Oklahoma in 1893, Geronimo tried several times to return to Arizona, but finally accepted his fate, took up farming and stock-raising, and even converted to Christianity. In his sixties, he became something of a celebrity with people paying to see him at the Omaha Exposition (1898), Buffalo Exposition (1901), and St. Louis World's Fair (1904). In 1905, he rode in Theodore Roosevelt's inaugural procession.

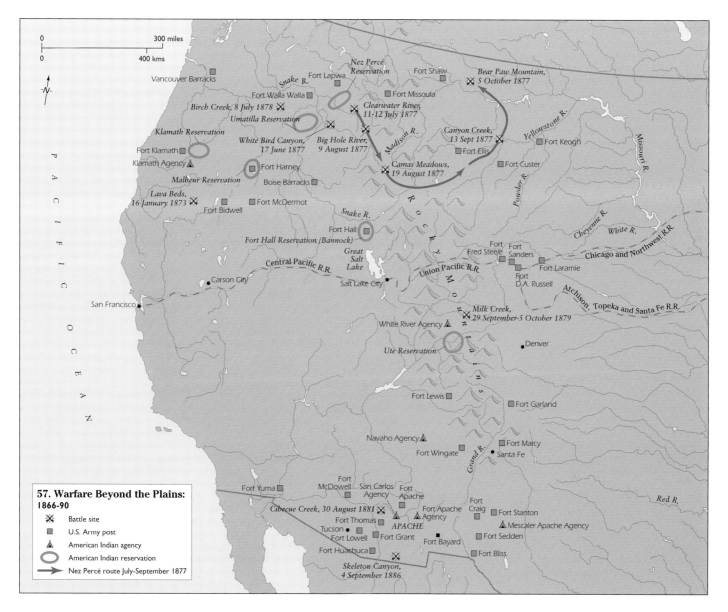

57. Warfare Beyond the Plains:
1866-90

✕ Battle site

▪ U.S. Army post

▲ American Indian agency

⬭ American Indian reservation

➜ Nez Percé route July-September 1877

Sioux and Northern Cheyenne. Fired by abominable living conditions and the spread of the Ghost Dance, a movement that blended Christianity, American Indian tradition, and the promise of a millennium free of whites, reservations in the Dakotas reached a state of near anarchy. Frightened by the growing numbers of army troops assembling in the region, several American Indian groups bolted from their reservations. The tense situation exploded at Wounded Knee (29 December 1890), when Colonel James W. Forsyth badly mismanaged an effort to disarm the followers of Big Foot, leaving over 150 American Indians and 25 soldiers dead. Several sharp skirmishes followed, but by February 1891 the American Indian wars had ended.

In the end, superior United States resources, an aggressive

policy of land acquisition, and divisions between the various tribes had combined to defeat the American Indians. The U.S. Army's command system and strategies had been tailored more for convenience than frontier effectiveness, but the regulars' grueling campaigns after the American Civil War finally forced the American Indians to adopt reservation life. Within the U.S. Army, the wars against the American Indians meant that many soldiers would enter the new century with combat experience, but the wars resulted in few changes in doctrine or policy. As historian Robert Utley has noted, most regulars viewed the American Indian wars as "a fleeting bother," and failed to recognize that the lessons they had learned fighting these unconventional foes might be applicable as the United States faced a new century.

The Spanish-American War: 1898

The United States went to war with Spain and its empire in Cuba, Puerto Rico, and the Philippines in 1898 for strategic and humanitarian reasons. The trigger was Spain's unsuccessful effort to defeat a nationalist rebellion in Cuba which affronted American interests and sensibilities in a time of heightened national pride and expansionist sentiment. From the rebellion's beginning in 1895, presidents Grover Cleveland and William McKinley tried without success to secure a compromise peace between Spain and the Cuban insurgents. On 15 February 1898, the battleship U.S.S. *Maine*, while on a "show-the-flag" mission to Cuba, exploded in Havana harbor. This disaster, the real cause of which remains a mystery, coincided with the failure of a Spanish autonomy offer to the Cubans and struck the final blow to peace.

Preparations for War

Early in March, President McKinley secured fifty million dollars from the U.S. Congress to begin war preparations. On 11 April, after the Spanish government rejected McKinley's

Contemporary newspapers (below) blamed the loss of the U.S.S. Maine on a mine. Navy investigations in 1898 and 1911 agreed that an external explosion sunk the ship, but a 1977 study concluded that spontaneous combustion in a coal bunker set off stored ammunition.

demand that Madrid agree to Cuban independence as the only remaining way to avert war, McKinley asked the U.S. Congress for authority to use the American armed forces "to secure a full and final termination of hostilities between the government of Spain and the people of Cuba." After the U.S. Congress granted his request on 21 April and added a demand that Spain immediately withdraw from Cuba, McKinley ordered the U.S. Navy to blockade Havana and other Spanish-held, Cuban ports. An exchange of war declarations followed within days.

American War Resources

At the outbreak of war with Spain, the U.S. Navy, which had been undergoing reform and modernization since the early 1880s, possessed a small but powerful fleet of five steel-armored battleships, two armored cruisers, thirteen other relatively new steel warships, and six torpedo boats, as well as an assortment of older vessels. Secretary of the U.S. Navy John D. Long and his assistant, Theodore Roosevelt, used the U.S. Navy's share of the fifty million dollar appropriation to secure supplies, ammunition, and auxiliary vessels needed to ready the fleet for active operations. Influenced by the same reform currents, the U.S. Army had adopted new coastal and field artillery weapons and infantry small arms, and established postgraduate schools for its officers, among other improvements. However, its standing regular force numbered only 25,000 officers and men. Until war was declared, the U.S. Army had no legislative authority to expand from its peacetime strength or to mobilize the 125,000 ill-trained and poorly equipped state troops of the National Guard for overseas service. After much political wrangling, the U.S. War Department, late in April, secured authority to enlarge the regular U.S. Army to 60,000 men and to raise a temporary volunteer force that eventually totaled almost 250,000 men, built around the regiments of the National Guard. While the U.S. War Department struggled to assemble, train, and equip the volunteers, at the outset only the 25,000 peacetime regulars were available for operations.

Spain's Force

Whatever the deficiencies of America's forces, those of Spain were in far worse condition. The Spanish navy included one obsolescent battleship and five relatively modern armored cruisers, plus numerous torpedo boats, and an assortment of older, smaller vessels. On paper, Spain's armored vessels were a match for those of the United States in speed and gun power. Poor dockyard maintenance, deficiencies in guns and equipment, and unskilled crews reduced their performance, however, to well below their estimated levels. Spain had sent more than 150,000 troops to Cuba to suppress the rebellion, and

President McKinley's call for volunteers in 1898 provided for three regiments "of frontiersmen possessing special qualifications as horsemen and marksmen." Assistant Secretary of the Navy Theodore Roosevelt turned down command of one of the units saying that he lacked military experience and asked instead to serve under Leonard Wood. Granted his wish, Roosevelt left the navy and joined the First U.S. Volunteer Cavalry Regiment, nicknamed "The Rough Riders." After the battle at Las Guásimas, Wood was promoted and left the unit. Roosevelt assumed command in time to lead the Rough Riders up Kettle Hill, part of the Spanish defenses along the San Juan Heights outside Santiago (where he posed with his men, above). Roosevelt's wartime fame propelled him to the governorship of New York in 1898 and the vice presidency in 1901.

substantial garrisons held Puerto Rico and the Philippines. Although well armed with Mauser rifles, the Spanish soldiers were woefully short of modern field artillery and machine guns, not to mention supplies and land transportation. Tropical diseases ravaged their ranks. The large army in Cuba, dispersed to fight the 35,000 Cuban insurgents, consisted of isolated garrisons incapable of mutual support or reinforcement and facing starvation by the American naval blockade. Among Spain's colonial cities, only Havana, the Cuban capital, had fortifications and artillery capable of resisting a conventional army and fleet.

War Begins

The opening moves of both sides reflected the state of their forces. Following prewar, U.S. Navy contingency plans, President McKinley dispatched the principal American naval squadron, under Rear Admiral William T. Sampson, to blockade Havana and other ports in western Cuba. A second force, the Flying Squadron, under Commodore Winfield S. Schley, with two battleships and an armored cruiser, remained in Hampton Roads, at the mouth of Chesapeake Bay, to guard the Atlantic coast against the unlikely event of a Spanish naval raid. The United States also launched a Pacific diversion. On 27 April, the Asiatic Squadron, under Commodore George

58. Spanish-American War:
The Caribbean Theater, 1898

- - - → U.S. Navy movements
— → U.S. Army movements
— → Spanish movements
✹ U.S. naval bombardments

101

Dewey, sailed from Hong Kong to attack Spanish warships in the Philippines and blockade Manila. Meanwhile, the U.S. Army concentrated its regulars at New Orleans, Mobile, and Tampa and began assembling the volunteers at Chickamauga Park, Tennessee, Washington, D.C., San Antonio, Texas, San Francisco, California, and other points. At the outset, the army was to conduct only limited incursions into Cuba to probe Spanish defenses and bring weapons and supplies to the Cubans. When enough volunteers were ready for action, a larger U.S. Army expedition against Havana would follow if the blockade and increased activity by the insurgents did not induce Spain to yield.

Spain's opening was much simpler. In Cuba, the Spanish garrisons stood fast, hoping that stubborn defense, combined with disease, would defeat any American invasion. In the Philippines, the Spaniards concentrated their weak naval squadron at Manila to meet Dewey's attack. As its only offensive gesture, the Madrid government sent Admiral Pascual Cervera y Topete, in command of its four best armored cruisers and three torpedo boat destroyers, to the Caribbean with the general mission of defending Spain's island possessions against the Americans. With his vessels in poor repair (one cruiser sailed without its main guns and with no bases or coaling stations in the Caribbean to support him), Cervera warned his superiors that his voyage could end only in disaster. Nevertheless, on 29 April, his force left its anchorage in the Cape

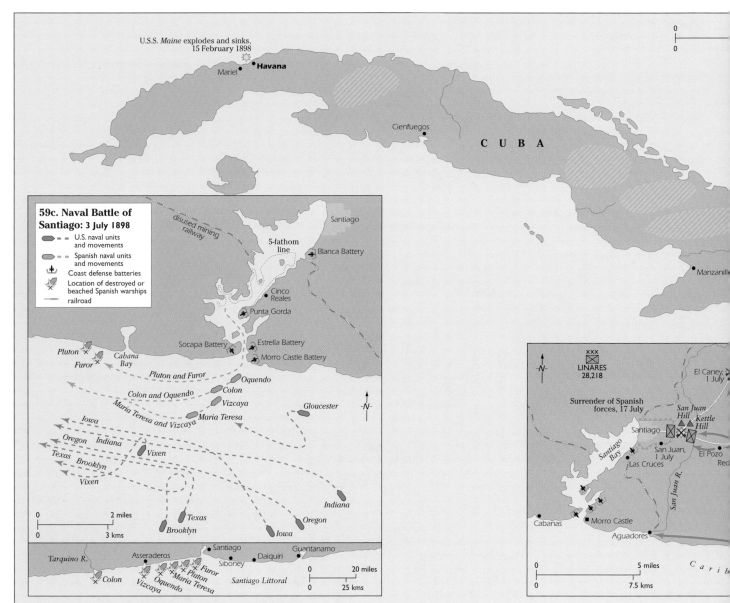

59c. Naval Battle of Santiago: 3 July 1898

- ◗ - - - U.S. naval units and movements
- ◗ - - - Spanish naval units and movements
- ⚓ Coast defense batteries
- ⚔ Location of destroyed or beached Spanish warships
- ╫ railroad

Verde Islands and steamed slowly westward.

An Early Success

Commodore Dewey struck the first blow. On the night of 30 April, his six vessels steamed into Manila Bay, easily running past the Spanish batteries to the harbor entrance. Early in the morning of 1 May the Americans sighted the seven warships of Rear Admiral Patricio Montojo, drawn up for battle off the Cavite naval base. Although neither squadron possessed any first-line armored ships, Dewey's vessels were newer and in better condition than Montojo's, they carried heavier artillery, and American gunnery and ship-handling were decisively superior. By midday, the Americans, at the cost of nine men

wounded and only minor damage to their vessels, had sunk or set on fire every Spanish ship and inflicted 371 Spanish casualties. The victory left Dewey in control of Manila Bay and Cavite. The Philippine capital and its 10,000-man garrison lay helpless under American guns.

Changes in Strategy

Dewey's victory, by demonstrating Spain's naval weakness, caused convulsive changes in American strategy. During the first days of May 1898, to take advantage of the momentum Dewey had established, President McKinley directed the U.S. Army, then in the earliest throes of mobilization, to launch two expeditions as rapidly as they could be prepared. The first, which ultimately numbered about 20,000 troops concentrated at San Francisco, was to occupy Manila. The second, to include all the regulars assembled on the Gulf coast, was to embark at Tampa and occupy the small port of Mariel in western Cuba as a base for an early assault on Havana. Assembly of both forces began at once, amid much haste and confusion, especially at Tampa. The Philippine expedition embarked in three contingents on 24 May, 15 June, and 17-29 June; but before the regulars at Tampa could board ship, plans for Cuba changed yet again.

After Cervera's squadron left the Cape Verdes, the U.S. Navy lost track of its movements. On the chance that Cervera might be heading for Puerto Rico, Admiral Sampson took a squadron to San Juan, where he bombarded the city's fortifications on 12 May, but found no Spanish vessels. Sampson then headed back to his base at Key West. Meanwhile, Cervera

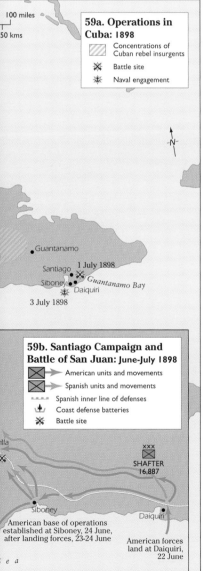

59a. Operations in Cuba: 1898

⬚ Concentrations of Cuban rebel insurgents

✳ Battle site

✳ Naval engagement

Guantanamo

Santiago 1 July 1898
Siboney ✳ Guantanamo Bay
Daiquiri
3 July 1898

59b. Santiago Campaign and Battle of San Juan: June-July 1898

⊠→ American units and movements

⊠→ Spanish units and movements

Spanish inner line of defenses

⚓ Coast defense batteries

✳ Battle site

villa

SHAFTER
16,887

Siboney   Daiquiri

American base of operations established at Siboney, 24 June, after landing forces, 23-24 June

American forces land at Daiquiri, 22 June

Sea

Rear Admiral William T. Sampson (above). Fifth Army Corps embarking for Cuba at Tampa (below).

entered the Caribbean on 13 May. After futile attempts to secure coal at neutral Martinique and Curaçao, he found refuge on 19 May in the harbor of Santiago de Cuba, on that island's southeast coast. There, anchored in an almost land-locked bay with a narrow entrance guarded by forts and mines, Cervera was secure from attack from the sea. From various sources, the American authorities learned of Cervera's presence at Santiago on the day of his arrival. After some delay and confusion, Commodore Schley's Flying Squadron blockaded Santiago on 29 May. Sampson arrived with his force from Puerto Rico on 1 June, completing a concentration of all the U.S. armored vessels against Cervera.

To assist the navy in rooting out the Spanish squadron, McKinley and his advisers changed their plan for land operations in the Caribbean. Instead of attacking Mariel, they directed the regulars assembling at Tampa to move against Santiago, capture the city—Cuba's third largest—and help the fleet eliminate Cervera's squadron. They planned to follow up this operation with an invasion of Puerto Rico, using troops from Santiago, reinforced by regiments of volunteers from the training camps in the United States. The assault on Havana, for which the U.S. Army was not ready at any event, would be postponed until autumn.

The Santiago Expedition

Although hastily improvised, plagued by logistical difficulties, and punctuated by U.S. Army–U.S. Navy disputes over tactics, the Santiago expedition accomplished its objectives. Commanded by Major General William R. Shafter, a corpulent but aggressive American Civil War and American Indian Wars

campaign veteran, the 17,000-man force left Tampa on 14 June. It was composed primarily of regulars from the peace-time standing U.S. Army but also included three volunteer regiments, among them the 1st U.S. Volunteer Cavalry, Theodore Roosevelt's Rough Riders. With U.S. Navy assistance and that of the local Cuban insurgent forces, U.S. Marines occupied Guantanamo Bay on 10 June and U.S. Army troops landed between 22 and 24 June at Daiquiri and Siboney, small ports southeast of Santiago, and marched toward Santiago. The Spaniards, who had offered no resistance to the landings, retreated toward Santiago.

On 24 June, Shafter's troops fought a brief engagement with a Spanish rear guard at Las Guásimas. On 1 July, in the war's only major land battle, the Americans stormed Santiago's outer defenses at San Juan Hill and El Caney. The confused engagement, won by hard fighting rather than tactical finesse, cost the Americans about 1,200 killed and wounded. The Spanish losses were less with only 593 casualties.

On 3 July, with the city closely invested and certain to fall, Admiral Cervera attempted to run his squadron out of the harbor and escape. As at Manila, superior American ships and crews decided the issue. In a running fight, Sampson's warships destroyed all the Spanish vessels. One American and 323 Spaniards died in the one-sided gunnery duel. After a two-week siege and much negotiation, Santiago's 12,000 defenders surrendered on 17 July, as did the garrisons of six smaller posts which depended on Santiago for supplies and reinforcements. Besides eliminating Spain's only significant naval force, the campaign left the United States in control of the entire eastern end of Cuba.

While approaching Spanish defenses on the San Juan Heights, the 71st New York Volunteers were scattered by enemy fire, took refuge in the heavy jungle across a field from the base of San Juan Hill, and played no part in the battle. Once the heights were stormed and their Spanish defenders were forced to retreat by other regiments of General William Shafter's V Corps and by Cuban insurgents commanded by Calixto García, men of the 71st moved into trenches on San Juan Hill, where they were photographed (right) on 1 July 1898. Shaken by the chaos of the battle, by the casualties suffered, and by supply problems, Shafter, who had not been present during the engagement, considered ordering a withdrawal from the heights to reorganize his army. Ordered to remain in position, Shafter held out until reinforcements began arriving on 10 July. A week later, General José Toral surrendered the city of Santiago.

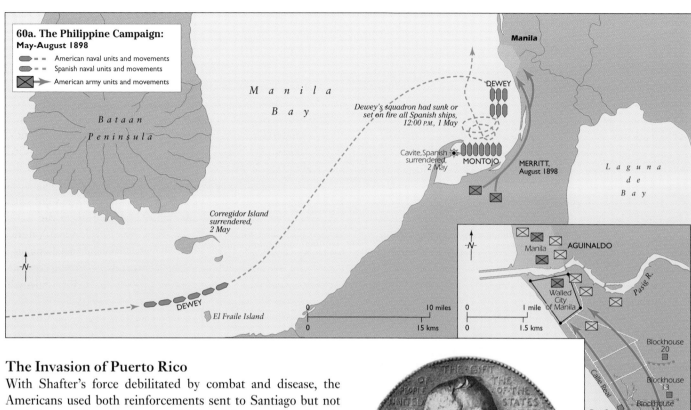

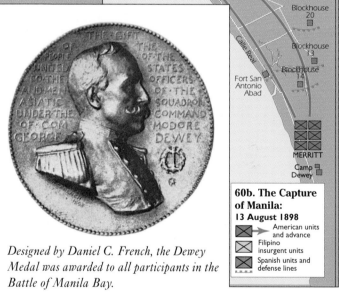

The Invasion of Puerto Rico

With Shafter's force debilitated by combat and disease, the Americans used both reinforcements sent to Santiago but not used there, and regiments from U.S. training camps to invade Puerto Rico. To avoid strong Spanish defenses around San Juan, the capital, Major General Nelson A. Miles landed his force at Guanica, Ponce, and Arroyo on Puerto Rico's south coast. Between 24 July and 9 August, he built up his army, which eventually totaled about 17,000 men, almost all state volunteers. Then he sent four columns driving toward San Juan. Outflanking and enveloping the 8,000 Spanish defenders, the Americans quickly overran most of Puerto Rico, losing four men killed and about forty wounded in the campaign's few skirmishes. By 12 August, when an armistice ended the fighting, Miles's troops were closing in on San Juan.

Designed by Daniel C. French, the Dewey Medal was awarded to all participants in the Battle of Manila Bay.

Battle for Manila

The war's last act was played out at Manila in the Philippines. By early August, about 10,000 U.S. troops under Major General Wesley Merritt had reached the city and established Camp Dewey on the bay shore between Manila and Cavite. They operated in uneasy alliance with the Filipino insurgent army of General Emilio Aguinaldo. On 13 August, Merritt's troops attacked Manila in a battle designed to give the Spanish governor, who had been negotiating with Merritt and Dewey, justification for surrendering to the Americans. Nevertheless, some fighting occurred in which five Americans died and forty-four were wounded. The day ended with the American army occupying Manila, which was surrounded by Aguinaldo's forces.

Due to slow communications, the battle of Manila occurred after the United States and Spain concluded an armistice and peace protocol. Negotiations had begun on 18 July, after the fall of Santiago, and the agreement was signed on 12 August. Spain renounced sovereignty over Cuba and withdrew her forces from Cuba and Puerto Rico. She ceded the city and bay of Manila to American occupation pending the negotiation of a definitive peace treaty. The treaty, signed in Paris in December, gave the United States possession of the Philippines, Guam, and Puerto Rico. With a de facto protectorate over Cuba and colonies in the Caribbean and the Pacific, the United States had joined the ranks of the great powers.

America's Rise to World Power: 1867-1917

In the decades following the American Civil War, most Americans expressed little interest in foreign affairs. With their attention focused on the rise of cities and industry in the North, on settling the West, and on reconstructing the South, the vast majority of Americans ignored both Prussia's assault on the traditional balance of power system and the European scramble for colonies in Africa and Asia. American leaders with an eye on international affairs generally believed that the Atlantic Ocean and the preoccupation of European nations with their continental rivals insulated the United States from foreign threats.

The U.S. Military After the American Civil War

Soon after Lee's surrender at Appomattox signaled an end to the American Civil War, America returned to its traditional defense policy. Reduced by 1876 to approximately 27,500 men, the U.S. Army stationed only skeleton forces in coastal defense fortifications, the bulk of its men being divided between protecting the new settlers and pacifying the American Indians in the West and enforcing congressional plans for Reconstruction in the South. Reduced from 700 ships and 57,000 men at the end of the war to only a tenth of those numbers less than a

decade later, the U.S. Navy reestablished its prewar squadrons. Charged as before the American Civil War with protection of American citizens and their property, the European, North and South Pacific, North and South Atlantic, and Asiatic Squadrons each consisted of only a few vessels. By showing the flag and standing ready to send sailors and marines ashore whenever American interests were threatened, the U.S. Navy demanded and exacted respect for the United States.

U.S. Expansionism

In the five years immediately following the American Civil War, Secretary of State William H. Seward pressed for expansion of U.S. territory in the Western Hemisphere. In rapid succession he negotiated treaties to purchase Alaska (1867) and part of the Danish Virgin Islands (1867) and took steps to annex the Dominican Republic (1869) and the Midway Islands (1867). The U.S. Congress, reflecting public opinion, blocked his moves in the Caribbean as well as his attempt to purchase the Hawaiian Islands.

Just over a decade later, during the 1880s, attitudes had started to change. Influenced by the ideas of social Darwinism that stressed competition among nations and the survival of

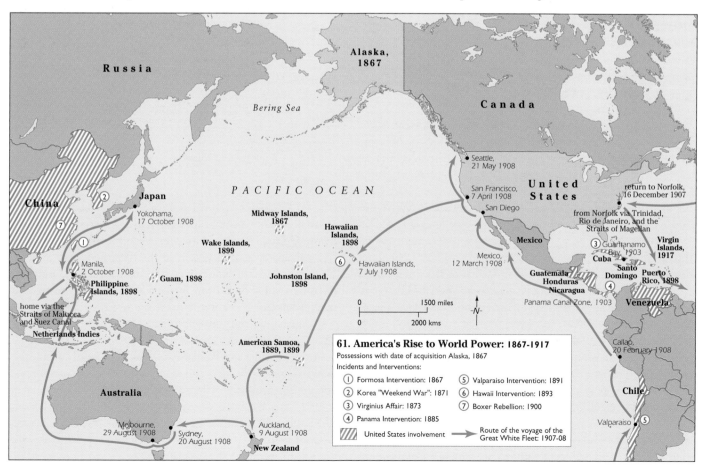

61. America's Rise to World Power: 1867-1917

Possessions with date of acquisition Alaska, 1867

Incidents and Interventions:
① Formosa Intervention: 1867
② Korea "Weekend War": 1871
③ Virginius Affair: 1873
④ Panama Intervention: 1885
⑤ Valparaiso Intervention: 1891
⑥ Hawaii Intervention: 1893
⑦ Boxer Rebellion: 1900

United States involvement

Route of the voyage of the Great White Fleet: 1907-08

the fittest by economists who believed that American industry must seek markets abroad, and by Christians who considered it a duty to spread their faith, American opinion leaders began "looking outward." That term came from an essay by Captain Alfred Thayer Mahan, a U.S. naval officer who wrote a series of books and articles on the role of sea power in the competition among nations for wealth and power and on the future of the United States. Mahan's writings provided an intellectual basis for American expansionism.

During this same era American naval officers were preparing themselves to play a leading role in American expansion by establishing the U.S. Naval Institute (1873), the Office of Naval Intelligence (1882), and the Naval War College (1884). Construction of the Indiana-class of battleships during the 1890s gave the U.S. Navy the ability to engage foreign navies outside the Western Hemisphere and to project American power far beyond its shores.

Transformation into a World Power

The Spanish-American War of 1898 set in train a series of events that would in less than ten years transform the United States into a world power. The conflict began when the U.S.S. *Maine* was destroyed by a mysterious explosion while visiting Havana, Cuba on a typical mission to protect American lives and property in an area of instability. For the first time in its history, the assistance of foreign people for humanitarian reasons played an important role in the formation of American foreign policy. Victory in the Spanish-American War brought with it ownership of the Philippine Islands and Guam, the first acquisition by the United States of territory outside the Western Hemisphere. In rapid succession the Hawaiian Islands, Johnston Island, the Wake Islands, and American Samoa were added to the American empire in the Pacific.

In 1900, the United States joined forces with European nations and Japan to restore order in Beijing in China by subduing the Boxer Rebellion. Stating plainly that it sought no territorial concessions in China, the U.S. government issued the Open Door Notes (1900-01). In what became a basic tenet of American foreign policy, these notes committed the nation to the "preserv[ation of] Chinese territorial and administrative entity [and to] safeguard[ing] for the world the principle of equal and impartial trade with all parts of the Chinese Empire." It was a bold statement that served notice that the United States was expanding beyond its traditional sphere of influence in North America and the Caribbean. President Theodore Roosevelt punctuated that statement when he acted as mediator to end the Russo-Japanese War (1905).

The Panama Canal

Closer to home, in 1903, Roosevelt assisted Panamanians in their revolt against Columbia and secured from the new nation a hundred-year lease for a Canal Zone and the right to construct in it a canal to link the Atlantic and Pacific Oceans. A year later, the assertive Roosevelt issued his corollary that transformed the Monroe Doctrine from one of nonintervention in the Western Hemisphere by European powers to one of intervention by the United States.

Support for an Aggressive Foreign Policy

To support his aggressive foreign policy, Roosevelt launched a naval building program designed to give the United States a fleet second in size and strength only to the Royal Navy of Great Britain. For the remainder of Roosevelt's administration, and for much of that of his successor, William H. Taft, naval expansion was limited not by funding but by the capacity of dockyards to build new ships. Following the precepts of Alfred Thayer Mahan, Roosevelt also reorganized the U.S. Navy by deploying all battleships into a single fleet stationed in the Atlantic.

When tensions with Japan led residents of the west coast to question the ability of the U.S. Navy to defend them should war erupt, Roosevelt dispatched the Great White Fleet around South America to demonstrate the ability of the navy to cruise long distances and arrive ready for combat. Once the fleet reached California, Roosevelt ordered it to continue around the globe to impress foreign nations. The entire voyage lasted fourteen months, covered 46,000 miles, captivated public opinion, and increased support for additional naval expansion. In 1914 when war erupted in Europe and soon spread around the world, President Woodrow Wilson was determined to keep the United States neutral in the conflict. As a precautionary measure, however, he called upon the U.S. Congress to build "a navy second to none" in 1916.

World War I

Work had hardly begun on this massive construction program before German intrigue with Mexico and interference with the free passage of neutral vessels in the Atlantic Ocean drew the United States into World War I. In half a century, American attention had shifted from internal developments to fighting, in Wilson's phrase, "a war to make the world safe for democracy." There would be no turning back. Irrevocably the United States had become a world power. For another quarter century it would resist permanent overseas commitments, but it could never return to being simply a power in the Western Hemisphere. World War I shattered the state system that traced its roots to the Treaty of Westphalia of 1648 and a restructuring of world order began. The role played by the United States would make the 1900s, in the phrase of Henry Luce, founder of *Time* magazine, "The American Century."

Rise of the United States as an Asian Power: 1899-1922

Emerging victorious from the Spanish-American War of 1898 and its subsequent acquisition of the Philippine Islands, the United States became a power in eastern Asia. For over a century there had been an American presence in the region. American merchants, seamen, and missionaries had participated in the western penetration of the region from the beginning of the U.S. republic. The first U.S. consulate opened in China in 1786 and the East India Squadron, a naval squadron assigned to the Pacific, was established in 1835. In 1854, U.S. Navy Commodore Matthew C. Perry negotiated a most favored nation treaty of amity and commerce with Japan, ending that country's isolation. For the most part, however, American involvement in eastern Asia was limited almost exclusively to trade and was largely incidental.

This was to change after the Spanish-American War. The U.S. Navy's destruction of the Spanish squadron at Manila Bay in May 1898 was followed by the dispatch of 11,000 American troops to the Spanish colony of the Philippines. Arriving in late July 1898, its commander, Major General Wesley Merritt, formed an uneasy alliance with the Filipino nationalist leader, Emilio Aguinaldo and laid siege to the Spanish in Manila City. On 13 August 1898, one day after the signing of the Peace Protocol in Paris ending the war, American troops took Manila.

President William McKinley decided to retain the Philippines for the United States for various reasons, including a wish to avert a possible scramble for possession of the islands by other powers, a motivation strengthened by America's own expansionist impulses. The Philippines were 7,100 miles from San Francisco, but a mere 700 miles from southern China, a position which could serve as a springboard into the mythical Chinese market. Before they could fulfill such visions, the Philippines had to be occupied. The size of the Philippines—over 500,000 square miles divided among over 7,000 islands extending from Luzon in the north to the Sulu grouping in the south—coupled with its distance from the American mainland were factors which operated against U.S. forces sent to extend U.S. control over the archipelago.

Although the U.S. Navy controlled the sea lanes connecting the islands, Aguinaldo's troops surrounded the American units in Manila. Aguinaldo claimed that American officials had assured him of independence for the Philippines, which the U.S. denied. The Americans insisted that the Filipinos "must recognize the military occupation and authority of the United States" before there could be any discussions concerning the future of the islands.

As tensions rose, scattered clashes around the Manila perimeter turned into a full-scale battle on 4 February 1899. Fighting for control of Manila continued until 23 February, when U.S. troops finally secured the city. Through the rest of the year, the Americans mounted several successful offensives against the insurgents. By January 1900, American forces had largely won the war against the Filipinos on Luzon, and moreover, the American command had extended its authority throughout the archipelago. Facing defeat in conventional battle, the insurgents reverted to guerrilla warfare.

The Boxer Rebellion

At this juncture, the Boxer Rebellion erupted in China. Since the end of the Sino-Japanese War of 1894-95, foreign powers had carved out several "spheres of influence" in China, while paying lip service to its sovereignty. In 1899, the United States issued its first Open Door Notes to allow equal commercial opportunity in China for all nations. Although most of the nations addressed in the notes responded evasively, U.S. Secretary of State John Hay announced in May 1900 that the powers had agreed to the Open Door policy.

By this time, China was in the throes of the Boxer Crisis. As imperial authorities stood by, the nationalist rebels known as the Boxers, because of their dedication to ritual forms of combat imbued with a fanatical hatred of the foreign presence in China, had attacked Christian missionaries and other foreign citizens. In March 1900, in response to the Boxer threat, foreign naval fleets gathered off Taku, the fortified harbor of the city of Tientsin at the mouth of the Pei Ho River. On

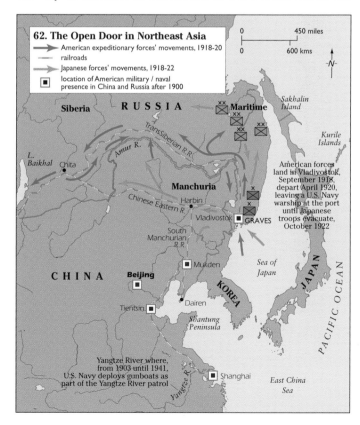

62. The Open Door in Northeast Asia

Men of the 6th U.S. Cavalry at Tientsin, part of the 2,500-man force led by Major General Adna R. Chaffee, guard Chinese Boxer prisoners who had attacked foreign citizens in 1900.

30 May, fifty U.S. Marines joined about 350 troops in Beijing. On 17 June, the foreign fleets offshore forced the surrender of the Taku forts after a ground expedition to open the railroad link to Beijing failed. There, in the Chinese capital, Boxers reinforced by imperial troops surrounded the international legation area. On 20 June, with the murder of the German minister, the "55-day siege" of the legations began. Further south, in Tientsin, later in the month, a U.S. Marine battalion reinforced by English and Russian troops secured the foreign settlement. In two days of bloody fighting in mid-July, the Allies captured the entire city.

In August, the Allies decided to relieve Beijing with a force of 14,000 men which included 2,500 Americans. Although a German general was in charge, there was no unified command. Basic decisions were made unanimously or not at all. Arriving on 14 August, the allied troops relieved the besieged legations and then entered the Forbidden City. Two weeks later, the Allies held their victory parade. For the Americans, this largely ended their participation.

Fearful of the aims of many of its erstwhile allies, the United States issued the second of its Open Door Notes that summer, prior to the relief of the legations. In this reiteration, Secretary Hay asserted an international guarantee of the "territorial and administrative integrity of China." Support for the Open Door policy would form the basis of U.S. policy in China for forty years.

After some excursions without the participation of American troops against Chinese forces outside Beijing, the Allies and the Chinese were ready to come to terms. In September 1901, the powers forced the Chinese to accept the Boxer Protocols, which laid a heavy monetary indemnity upon the Chinese government and forced the Chinese to accept provisions that allowed the foreign powers to maintain legation guards in Beijing and elsewhere. The only thing that saved China from partition at this point was the suspicion of the powers of one another. Russia kept significant forces in Manchuria, while Japan and Great Britain signed a treaty of alliance in 1902.

Even the United States made its demands upon the hapless Chinese government. Worried about the vulnerability of the Philippines, U.S. Navy strategists wanted an advance base in China for its Asiatic Fleet. Their first recommendation was the Chusan archipelago, but they also considered three other sites on Sansa Inlet, Nankwan Bay, and Bullock Harbor in China. With the U.S. State Department opting for the Open Door policy and the U.S. Congress reluctant to spend money outside the continental United States, plans for the advance bases in

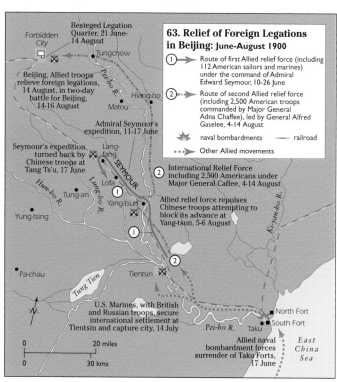

U.S. Army troops guarded the American legation in Beijing from 1900 until marines replaced them in 1905. This marine was photographed on sentry duty in 1915. U.S. Marines served in China until 28 November 1941 when the last member of the 4th Marines sailed from Shanghai to Subic Bay in the Philippines.

China, like naval plans for construction of facilities at Subic Bay in Luzon in the Philippines, would remain paper projects.

After the signing of the Boxer Protocols, the U.S. Army presence in China largely was relegated to a few army troops guarding the U.S. legation in Beijing. In 1903, the U.S. Navy deployed several gunboats as part of the international Yangtze River patrol along this main economic artery. Two years later, a U.S. Marine detachment relieved the army guard detachment of its legation security duties.

War in the Philippines

In the Philippines, despite the Boxer diversion, the American forces waged a successful counterguerrilla war against the Filipino insurgents from 1899 to 1902. Handicapped by the harsh terrain and unfamiliarity with the culture, the Americans still enjoyed some advantages. With the assistance of U.S. Navy gunboats, the U.S. Army used the numerous waterways to isolate the guerrilla strongholds. More importantly, the U.S. Army had developed a coherent, although unstated, pacification policy that balanced conciliation with harsh retribution. By the middle of 1901, the Americans had established in power a civilian commission, headed by William Howard Taft, and had begun a progressive program of civil works and education, and the building of an effective intelligence network.

Moreover, the American effort was abetted by the shortcomings of the rebels. Aguinaldo's political support lay mostly among the local, large landowners, who often exploited the peasants. Unable to obtain local allegiance, many of the guerrilla groups collapsed. In March 1901, American Colonel Frederick Funston captured Aguinaldo in a daring raid. Acting on intercepted correspondence that disclosed the location of Aguinaldo's headquarters, Funston and a group of soldiers pretended to be prisoners of Philippine scouts loyal to the United States. The bogus guards took Funston and his men to Aguinaldo's headquarters where they seized the leader and took him to Manila. Despite Aguinaldo's capture, the guerrilla war was not over.

The most notorious incident of the entire war occurred just south of Luzon on the small jungle-covered island of Samar. On 28 September 1901, Filipino insurgents there "massacred" a U.S. Army company. Brigadier General Jacob H. Smith dispatched units of his 6th Separate Brigade and a battalion of U.S. Marines under Major Littleton W. T. Waller to Samar. The marines burned several villages and killed at least

Almost half the U.S. troops in the Philippines in 1899 were members of state volunteer regiments. They were expected to return home when a peace treaty was signed, but the outbreak of hostilities with the Philippine Republican Army led the U.S. government to extend their service. For the next six months, most of the operations in the Philippines were conducted by state volunteer forces, including the First Regiment Nebraska Volunteers, one of the most distinguished of these units, whose members are shown here embarking for passage home on 23 June 1899.

64. The Philippines War: 1899-1902

→ Principal movements of American forces

▨ Areas of greatest Filipino guerrilla activity

thirty rebels. In December, after an ill-fated reconnaissance march across the southern end of the island, Waller ordered the summary execution of eleven Filipinos. When Smith and Waller received court martials, Waller stated that Smith had ordered him to turn Samar into "a howling wilderness." Smith denied this charge but was forced into retirement. Waller was acquitted on technical grounds. Historians still argue about the facts of the campaign and its unfortunate symbolism. Nevertheless, most of the armed resistance by the time of Samar was petering out. On 4 July 1902, President Theodore Roosevelt declared the U.S. pacification campaign completed.

With the Philippine War, the imperialist experiment of the United States began to die. A large, vocal, domestic opposition arose to the war while the hopes of access to the Chinese market proved a delusion. The desire of the U.S. Navy to build Subic Bay in the Philippines as its major base became a bone of contention between the U.S. Navy and Army, whose leaders wanted to center all defenses around Manila Bay. By the end of 1907, the government abandoned all plans to build a major naval base in the Philippines. Even Theodore Roosevelt declared the Philippines, "the heel of Achilles" for the United States. In 1916, the U.S. Congress provided the islands with limited self-government and a promise of eventual independence.

Tensions With Japan

The vulnerability of the Philippines and the overwhelming victory of Japan in the Russo-Japanese War of 1904-05 provided much of the impetus to U.S. national policy. As a result of the U.S.-mediated Portsmouth Peace Treaty of 1905, Japan had become the dominant power in eastern Asia. In July 1905, William Howard Taft, then the U.S. Secretary of War, signed

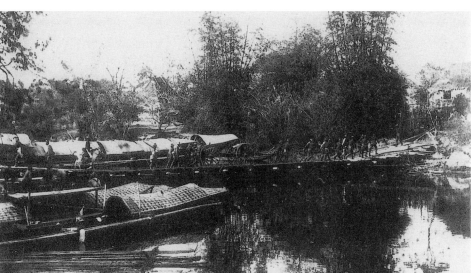

After U.S. forces captured Maloso (right), many Filipinos fought as guerrillas, led by men like Miguel Malvar (above).

The American "Great White Fleet" was photographed in 1908 anchored off Yokohama, Japan, along with the grey ships of the Japanese fleet. Traditionally, U.S. battleships were painted grey to make them more difficult to spot in combat. But, to emphasize the pacific character of its round the world voyage, the Navy Department left the "Great White Fleet" white.

a secret memorandum with the Japanese Prime Minister Katsuro Taro recognizing Japanese authority in Korea and that of the United States in the Philippines. This marked the first of several attempts by U.S. leaders to negotiate its differences with Japan. This was complicated, however, by American racism, especially in San Francisco. In an informal agreement with Japan in 1907, the United States promised not to discriminate against Japanese children in American schools. The United States asserted its right to restrict immigration and the Japanese promised in turn to limit the number of its citizens it would allow to emigrate to the United States.

While willing to negotiate with Japan, Roosevelt, in a demonstration of American strength, sent the entire U.S. battle fleet, in December 1907, on a tour around the world including Japan. The Japanese warmly welcomed the American "Great White Fleet" and appeared to signal a warming in relations. In November 1908, Secretary of State Elihu Root negotiated with the Japanese Ambassador, the Root-Takhira Agreement. Papering over their differences, the two governments agreed to support the Open Door policy in China while at the same time recognizing the "existing status quo" in the Pacific.

President Roosevelt's successor, William Howard Taft, and Secretary of State Philander Knox modified the Open Door policy with "Dollar Diplomacy," a policy of government support for American enterprises abroad and the use of American investment to support U.S. foreign policy objectives. The new administration supported an attempt to purchase the South Manchurian Railroad, which would run from Manchuria south through China and compete with the railroads planned by Russia to funnel trade to Vladivostok and another by Japan that would terminate in Japanese-dominated Korea. This only

succeeded in antagonizing both Japan and Russia. After the Chinese Revolution in 1911-12 forced the abdication of the last Chinese dynasty, the United States sent an army regiment to Tientsin in 1912 to protect American property. The incoming President Woodrow Wilson considered the presence of American forces in Tientsin an infringement on Chinese sovereignty and a violation of the Open Door policy, although the American regiment remained in Tientsin until 1938.

Woodrow Wilson faced another potential crisis with Japan at the start of his administration as a result of a racist California law denying citizenship to Japanese residents. Like Roosevelt, he used diplomacy to defuse the situation, but unlike Roosevelt, he avoided any bellicose deployment of U.S. military force despite dissent from military leaders. With the outbreak of World War I in 1914, U.S. policy makers focused upon Europe, but the weakness of the new Chinese republic and continuing Japanese aggressiveness still were causes of concern. At the outset of the hostilities in Europe in 1914, the Japanese joined with the Allies and immediately seized Germany's holdings in the Mariana, Caroline, and Marshall islands and on Shantung Peninsula. In January 1915, the Japanese made their "Twenty-One Demands" upon China which would have greatly expanded Japanese economic influence in China and undermined Chinese administrative sovereignty. At that point the Wilson administration protested and the Japanese abandoned or modified their most blatant conditions. The United States slightly expanded its Yangtze navy patrol in China but also indicated that it was not prepared vigorously to enforce its Open Door policy.

Although not aimed exclusively at Japan, the United States in the 1916 Naval Appropriation Act started its determination to construct a "navy second to none." The entry of the United States into World War I in 1917 on the side of the Allies only partially allayed tensions with Japan. In September 1917, the two nations once more tried to settle their differences over China. In the Lansing-Ishii Treaty, negotiated by U.S. Secretary of State Robert Lansing and Japanese Viscount Ishii Kikujiro, the two nations evaded the basic issues. The Japanese agreed once more to adhere to the Open Door policy in China, while the United States recognized that Japan had special interests in China because of territorial propinquity.

Intervention in Siberia

The closest the United States and Japan came into open conflict occurred not in China, but in Russian Siberia. After Russia's withdrawal from World War I in December 1917, Great Britain, France, the United States, and Japan sent forces to Vladivostok in Siberia and to northern Russia. Ostensibly there to protect the Trans-Siberian Railroad and to assist in the evacuation of a Czech legion that had fought with the Russians, Allied troops often engaged in combat with Russian Bolshevik troops, especially in northern Russia.

By mid-1919, the American contingent had departed from northern Russia, but the situation remained tense in Siberia. Suspicious that the Japanese, who had landed a large force at Vladivostok might be thinking of annexing the Russian maritime province, in September 1918 the United States sent two reinforced infantry regiments under the command of Major General William S. Graves to that port city. President Wilson resisted calls by Britain and France to intervene directly in the Russian civil war (1917-22), but he ordered U.S. troops to provide guards for the railroad line used by the British to send supplies to anti-Bolshevik forces. While occasionally skirmishing with rival Russian groups, the American and Japanese forces kept correct but wary relations with one another. With the eventual evacuation of the Czech legion and the advance of Russian Communist troops, the U.S. ground forces under Graves departed Vladivostok in April 1920. The Japanese remained for two more years, but because of international diplomatic pressure, they finally left. A U.S. Navy warship remained at Vladivostok until the last Japanese soldier boarded his transport.

With the end of World War I, the United States continued to see Japan as a likely antagonist in eastern Asia. While Japan had been stifled somewhat in its attempt to turn large parts of China into virtual dependencies as a result of the Versailles Treaty of 1918, it had obtained Germany's former island possessions in the Pacific. Japan still posed a threat to the United State's hold on the Philippines and continued to place pressure on the weakened Chinese republic, ravaged by regionalism and local warlords. In the Washington Peace Conference

of 1921-22, the leading nations of the world agreed to the Seven Power Pact endorsing the principles of the Open Door Notes; the Four Power Pact committing the United States, France, Britain, and Japan to respect each other's possessions in the Pacific; and to the Five Power Pact which limited naval armaments and bases and included a moratorium on naval construction. In the aftermath of these agreements, the Japanese withdrew many of their demands upon China. This postponed for a few years the clash of interest between the United States and Japan.

While U.S. leaders remained uneasy about America's strategic position in the Far East, the general public did not share their concerns. The 1920s were marked by a wish to return to "normalcy" and a peace movement determined to outlaw war. In such an atmosphere, the U.S. Congress was in no mood to appropriate funds for construction of defenses in the Pacific or to bring the navy up to "treaty strength," the size allowed by the Five Power Pact. The Great Depression of the 1930s focused government spending on relief at home, and the determination of Americans to stay out of foreign conflicts led to passage of a series of neutrality acts designed to prevent a reoccurrence of conditions which many believed had led the United States into World War I. Thus, when rival Japanese-American interests led to a diplomatic impasse, and Japan sought a military solution by attacking Pearl Harbor, the U.S. armed forces were ill-prepared to defend the nation's interest in the Far East. The result was a long and bloody war.

When Russia withdrew from World War I, the Allies intervened. On 29 June 1918, marines from the U.S.S. Brooklyn *landed at Vladivostok to protect the U.S. consulate. They remained until relieved by two infantry regiments on 15 August. Elements of those regiments and sailors from the ships that accompanied them are shown marching through Vladivostok prior to the 1 September arrival of an additional 5,000 U.S. troops. The last American troops left Vladivostok in April 1920.*

Intervention in Central America and the Caribbean: 1903–35

The highly successful and nationally invigorating Spanish–American War of 1898 ushered in new vistas of expansion for the United States. By 1900, the dawn of what historians and political scientists came to call "The American Century," a new focus of foreign intervention by the United States emerged. In no part of the world was this new manifestation of American missionary and economic zeal so prevalent as in Central America and the Caribbean. From the time that Spain surrendered in 1898, until the advent of Franklin D. Roosevelt's "Good Neighbor" policy of nonintervention more than three decades later, a variety of U.S. forces imposed America's will on the region. These ventures were usually clothed in altruist terms and sustained by strong public support.

Panama

The first intervention by American military forces occurred in Colombia's province of Panama in 1903. For generations, the United States had considered the security of the cross-isthmian railway, that ran from Colón on the Caribbean side to Panama City on the Pacific shore, to be a vital link in its overseas trade. The United States intervened with naval forces

When unrest threatened American lives and property in Panama in 1903, U.S. sailors and marines went ashore at Boca del Toro for a week in April, then again in September. Sailors from the U.S.S. Cincinnati, manning a rapid-fire gun mounted on a railcar (below), landed at Colón on 17 September and stayed until order was restored in November.

whenever free transit of the route appeared to be threatened, the most sizeable incursion taking place in 1885. During the late nineteenth century a French company had begun, but by 1903 abandoned plans to construct a canal across Panama. The forced voyage of the battleship *Oregon* around South America during the Spanish–American War made manifest the strategic imperative of such a canal to the United States. Thus, in 1903, the United States negotiated a treaty with Colombia for a 100-year lease to build and operate such a waterway. Colombian officials later balked at the rental price that the United States had agreed to pay.

When a revolution by Panamanian nationalists broke out on 2 November 1903, President Theodore Roosevelt immediately supported the uprising. Naval parties were sent ashore from American ships to prevent Colombian troops from suppressing the rebellion. Additional U.S. Marines were dispatched from barracks at home until the deployment to Panama reached brigade-size by early 1904. The size of the force was later reduced, but a battalion of U.S. Marines remained in Panama until 1914 to protect workers constructing the canal and to ensure the stability of the new government.

Cuba

After expelling Spain from Cuba in 1898, the United States insisted on the right of intervention in the island's affairs as part of the treaty ending hostilities. A clause in the Cuban constitution—the Platt Amendment—inserted at the behest of the United States in 1902, allowed for American intervention to maintain stability on the island or to preserve Cuban independence. Less than a decade after the guns fell silent, U.S. Marines returned to Cuban soil. In 1906, election irregularities fomented a rebellion among Cuba's black population. Concluding that the upheaval threatened U.S. lives and properties, President Theodore Roosevelt ordered naval forces in the region to send landing parties ashore. The subsequent arrival of U.S. Army troops brought the total U.S. force, called the Army of Cuban Pacification, to 5,600, the last of which were not withdrawn from the island until early in 1909.

Mexico

Of all the nations in the Caribbean, U.S. relations with Mexico remained the most contentious. The apparent decay of democratic processes during the first decade of the twentieth century in Mexico, America's southernmost neighbor, drew criticism from the Roosevelt and Taft administrations, but provoked a more assertive diplomatic and military response from Woodrow Wilson during his presidency. In September 1913, bluejackets and U.S. Marines from the Pacific Fleet landed at Ciaris Estero on the Gulf of California to escort Americans and foreigners away from the political unrest in the

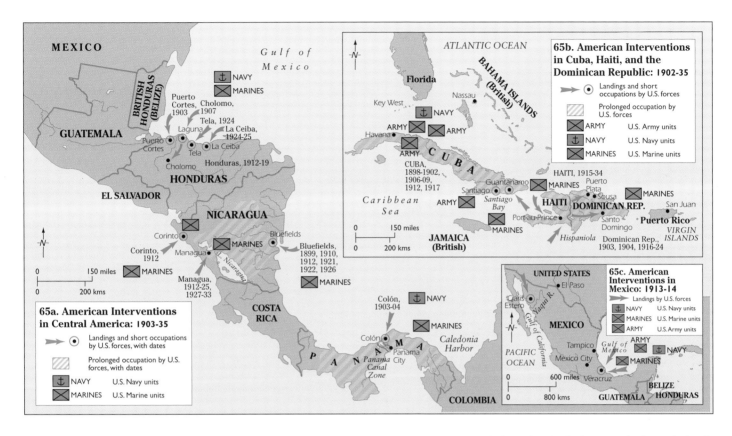

65a. American Interventions in Central America: 1903-35

→ ⊙ Landings and short occupations by U.S. forces, with dates

▨ Prolonged occupation by U.S. forces, with dates

⚓ NAVY   U.S. Navy units

☒ MARINES   U.S. Marine units

65b. American Interventions in Cuba, Haiti, and the Dominican Republic: 1902-35

→ ⊙ Landings and short occupations by U.S. forces

▨ Prolonged occupation by U.S. forces

☒ ARMY   U.S. Army units

⚓ NAVY   U.S. Navy units

☒ MARINES   U.S. Marine units

65c. American Interventions in Mexico: 1913-14

→ Landings by U.S. forces

⚓ NAVY   U.S. Navy units

☒ MARINES   U.S. Marine units

☒ ARMY   U.S. Army units

Yaqui River Valley.

Less than a year later the incident that resulted in the most significant American naval intervention in Mexico occurred on the other side of the country beginning at Tampico in April 1914. The stage was set by the refusal of the Wilson administration to recognize the government headed by the usurper Victoriano Huerta. Back in 1911, Francisco Madero and Huerta had conspired in the overthrow of President Porfirio Díaz; then Huerta's henchmen assassinated Madero. When Huerta assumed the presidency, President Wilson ordered the deployment of a sizeable naval force to the Caribbean and declared an arms embargo of Mexico. Tensions increased; when Mexican troops detained a party of American sailors at Tampico in April 1914, the U.S. demanded an apology and a twenty-one-gun salute. The Huerta government tendered the apology, but refused to render the salute.

Meanwhile, word reached Washington that a German freighter was approaching Veracruz with a cargo of small arms and ammunition for Huerta's government. To prevent the munitions from reaching that illegitimate government, Wilson ordered the commander of U.S. naval forces off Veracruz to intercept the cargo. In an unopposed landing, bluejackets and Leathernecks streamed ashore, receiving only a fusillade of small-arms fire from tiny pockets of resistance within the city. Eventually, an entire brigade of U.S. Marines landed at Veracruz and was reinforced quickly by an U.S. Army brigade that remained in the city until November 1914. By then the damage was done: U.S.-Mexican relations were poisoned for a generation to such a degree that Mexico briefly considered entering World War I on the side of Germany.

Mexico's political instability continued, and in March 1916 the violence spilled over into the United States when forces loyal to a revolutionary leader, Francisco "Pancho" Villa, crossed the border and attacked the town of Columbus, New Mexico. In response, the United States ordered a punitive expedition into northern Mexico to seek out the elusive Villa. More than 10,000 American soldiers under Brigadier General John J. Pershing deployed across the border in a wide swath as far as the southern end of the state of Chihuahua. Mexican President Venustiano Carranza initially approved the Punitive Expedition, but his acceptance of U.S. troops on Mexican soil evaporated quickly following skirmishes, of which the most notable was at Carrizal, ninety miles south of the U.S. border, between Pershing's cavalrymen and forces of the Mexican army. Pershing never caught up with Villa, and the American expedition withdrew in February 1917.

A Curious Interpretation of Law

Except for the case of Mexico, U.S. interventions in the Caribbean were all conducted by naval forces. Jurists advising

By 1914, Pancho Villa (above), was the strongest of the regional leaders in rebellion against a succession of Mexican governments. Villa became a popular hero when he evaded U.S. troops sent to punish him for a raid he led on Columbus, New Mexico, on 9 March 1916. After several months of pursuit, Brigadier General John J. Pershing (below) and his troops returned home in February 1917, without even sighting Villa.

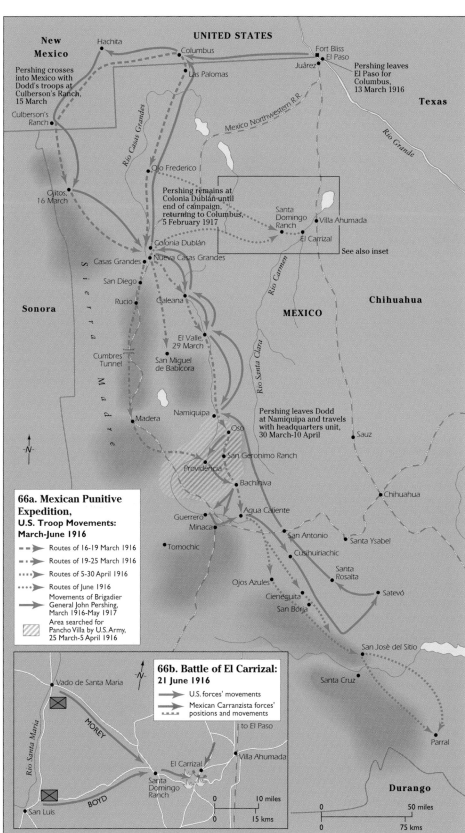

New Mexico

Hachita
Columbus
UNITED STATES
Fort Bliss
El Paso
Juárez

Pershing crosses into Mexico with Dodd's troops at Culberson's Ranch, 15 March

Las Palomas

Pershing leaves El Paso for Columbus, 13 March 1916

Texas

Rio Grande

Culberson's Ranch

Mexico Northwestern R.R.

Ojo Frederico

Rio Casas Grandes

Ojitos, 16 March

Pershing remains at Colonia Dublán until end of campaign, returning to Columbus, 5 February 1917

Santa Domingo Ranch

Villa Ahumada

El Carrizal

See also inset

Colonia Dublán
Casas Grandes
Nueva Casas Grandes

San Diego

Rio Carmen

Rucio
Galeana

Sierra Madre

Sonora

El Valle, 29 March
San Miguel de Babicora

Chihuahua

MEXICO

Rio Santa Clara

Cumbres Tunnel

Madera
Namiquipa

Pershing leaves Dodd at Namiquipa and travels with headquarters unit, 30 March-10 April

Oso

Sauz

San Geronimo Ranch

Providencia

Bachiniva

Chihuahua

66a. Mexican Punitive Expedition,
U.S. Troop Movements:
March-June 1916

Agua Caliente

Guerrero
Minaca

San Antonio
Santa Ysabel

Tomochic

Cusihuiriachic

Santa Rosalta

- - ▶ Routes of 16-19 March 1916
- - ▶ Routes of 19-25 March 1916
···· ▶ Routes of 5-30 April 1916
···· ▶ Routes of June 1916
──▶ Movements of Brigadier General John Pershing, March 1916-May 1917
▨ Area searched for Pancho Villa by U.S. Army, 25 March-5 April 1916

Ojos Azules
Cieneguita
San Borja

Satevó

San José del Sitio

Vado de Santa Maria

66b. Battle of El Carrizal:
21 June 1916

Santa Cruz

MOREY

──▶ U.S. forces' movements
──▶ Mexican Carranzista forces' positions and movements

to El Paso

Parral

Rio Santa Maria

El Carrizal
Villa Ahumada

Santa Domingo Ranch

San Luis
BOYD

0   10 miles
0   15 kms

0   50 miles
0   75 kms

Durango

successive presidential administrations asserted that the deployment of army troops ashore constituted an act of war while a similar dispatch by naval forces did not. This curious interpretation of international law was rendered to President William Howard Taft by his Secretary of State and to President Calvin Coolidge by his Secretary of the Navy. While these successive naval interventions were intended to be temporary in nature, they lasted sometimes for years; indeed, one continued for almost two decades.

Hispaniola

Between 1908 and 1915, Haiti, the troubled nation on western Hispaniola, had no fewer than eight chief executives, the last of whom was literally torn to pieces by an angry mob. Fearing for the safety of American citizens and their property, and to counter the possibility of foreign intervention, Rear Admiral William B. Caperton deployed a large landing force ashore at Port au Prince. Those U.S. sailors and marines were soon replaced by marines from barracks in the United States. The Leathernecks organized and trained a local constabulary, the Gendarmerie d'Haiti, to restore order to the countryside, but the American forces remained until 1934. Results remained mixed: Haiti continued its slide into abysmal poverty as the poorest nation in the region, and the revolutionary unrest, so deplored by a succession of American presidents, repeated itself often.

The Dominican Republic, on the eastern half of Hispaniola, became the scene of unrest not unlike that in Haiti. In May 1916, rebels overthrew an elected government and at the request of the ousted leaders, U.S. Marines entered the Dominican Republic from Haiti, and with others deployed from the U.S. fleet, forced an uneasy peace on the nation. In a pattern similar to the U.S. occupation of Haiti, U.S. Marines were sent from the United States to relieve those from the U.S. fleet. Rebel officials withdrew to the city of Santiago. U.S. Marines launched a campaign against that city followed by a counterinsurgency campaign that lasted three months. Next, as in Haiti, they organized and trained a native constabulary to bring order to a countryside beset with banditry. Only a measure of stability was achieved before the last marines were withdrawn in 1924.

Nicaragua

In Nicaragua, situated between Panama and Mexico, similar unrest led to the U.S. interventions at Bluefields, the nation's principal port on the Caribbean, in 1899, 1910, 1912, 1921, early 1922, and 1926, and at Corinto on the Pacific in 1912. For over a decade after 1912, a large legation guard was stationed in Nicaragua as a sign of American interest in the nation. President Calvin Coolidge withdrew the U.S. Marines

of that guard in 1925, but the following year U.S. Marines were again ordered into the country, this time to remain until 1933. While there, the Leathernecks patrolled the countryside and kept the rival Liberals and Conservatives from each other's throats. In the process, the U.S. Marines supervised and led a native constabulary patterned after similar organizations established in Haiti and the Dominican Republic, but the entire U.S. naval intervention in Nicaragua proved less successful than those into other countries in the region. Once the U.S. Marines had departed, long, festering, internecine squabbles among competing political factions began to surface anew.

On a number of other occasions, commanders of U.S. ships and squadrons responded to unrest by sending parties of U.S. sailors and marines ashore to protect American property and lives. All these deployments—in Honduras at Puerto Cortes in 1903, at Laguna from which troops moved inland as far as Choloma in 1907, at Tela in 1924, and at La Ceiba in 1924 and 1925; in the Dominican Republic at Santo Domingo in 1903, and around Sosua and Puerto Plata the following year; in Cuba at Guantanamo Bay in 1912 and in Oriente Province, the region around Santiago, in 1917—were of short duration and were not reinforced by marines sent from the United States.

Good Neighbor Policy

By the late 1920s the American policy of intervention in nations bordering the Caribbean began to change. A new, "Good Neighbor Policy," which had begun in theoretical terms in the administration of President Calvin Coolidge and grown in Herbert Hoover's renunciation of the Roosevelt Corollary to the Monroe Doctrine in his inaugural address, reached fruition under President Franklin D. Roosevelt. Based on principles of equality and friendship rather than benevolent intervention by the United States, the policy was tested when Gerardo Machado y Morales, the dictatorial leader of Cuba was overthrown in August 1933. Roosevelt ordered warships to Cuban waters, but did not send military forces ashore, and the ships were withdrawn in early 1934.

The adoption of the Good Neighbor Policy and the withdrawal of the U.S. Marines from their lonely outposts throughout the Caribbean seemed to bring to an end an era of American intervention. Ostensibly stable governments populated the region, at least temporarily. American economic interests seemed secure in the region, opposition grew within the United States to continue occupations, and the attention of U.S. policy makers shifted ever more to focus on the growing estrangement with Japan as the forces of Nippon encroached further into China. The military implications of the increasing strength of fascist governments in Germany and Italy grew worrisome, further forestalling any penchant for U.S. naval intervention in the Caribbean.

The United States in World War I: 1917–18

The United States entered World War I most reluctantly in 1917, abandoning its traditional policy of neutrality. After his reelection in 1916, President Woodrow Wilson made a secret attempt to mediate the conflict with the belligerents, with the ultimate objective of establishing a postwar world order underpinned by an institutional system of collective security. This mediation, however, was rejected by both sides. Furthermore, in February 1917, despite pleas from Wilson, Germany resumed unrestricted submarine warfare against the shipping of the United States and other neutral powers, thus inflaming U.S. public opinion and forcing the president's hand. The combination of his failure to restrain German submarine activity and his desire to impose his plan for peace caused Wilson to intervene in the war on the Allied side on 6 April 1917 in the belief that such intervention would assure an Allied victory and thus the success of his peace program.

Unprepared for a Land War

The United States was unprepared to fight a land war in Europe. During 1916, the U.S. Congress enacted legislation providing for the construction of "a navy second to none" and a modern army, but these measures were taken too late to permit immediate dispatch of U.S. forces to Europe in sufficient numbers to influence the outcome. A 1917 decision, to create an army capable of fighting under its own flag, with its own commanders and staffs, in its own sector of the western front, and supported by its own supply services, added to the delay. A year or more passed before units could be trained, equipped, and transported to France and sufficiently prepared to fight as an independent army.

Operations of the U.S. Navy

The U.S. Navy was significantly better off than the army in 1917. It was capable of making an early and useful contribution to the containment of the German submarine offensive that had been designed to interdict the maritime supply lines of the Allies. Germany's attempt to win the war with a submarine offensive against Allied merchant shipping before the United States could deploy significant land forces in Europe

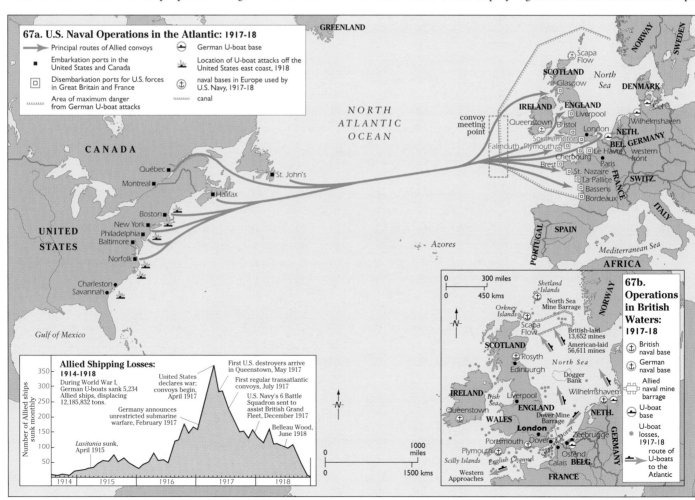

67a. U.S. Naval Operations in the Atlantic: 1917-18

- Principal routes of Allied convoys
- Embarkation ports in the United States and Canada
- Disembarkation ports for U.S. forces in Great Britain and France
- Area of maximum danger from German U-boat attacks
- German U-boat base
- Location of U-boat attacks off the United States east coast, 1918
- naval bases in Europe used by U.S. Navy, 1917-18
- canal

Allied Shipping Losses: 1914-1918

During World War I, German U-boats sank 5,234 Allied ships, displacing 12,185,832 tons.

- *Lusitania* sunk, April 1915
- Germany announces unrestricted submarine warfare, February 1917
- United States declares war; convoys begin, April 1917
- First U.S. destroyers arrive in Queenstown, May 1917
- First regular transatlantic convoys, July 1917
- U.S. Navy's 6 Battle Squadron sent to assist British Grand Fleet, December 1917
- Belleau Wood, June 1918

67b. Operations in British Waters: 1917-18

- British naval base
- German naval base
- Allied naval mine barrage
- U-boat base
- U-boat losses, 1917-18
- route of U-boats to the Atlantic

North Sea Mine Barrage
British-laid 13,652 mines
American-laid 56,611 mines
Dover Mine Barrage

By the time the United States entered the war in 1917, Germany's submarines, not her battle fleet, posed the greater threat to the allies. To counter the threat, the U.S. Navy sent 121 wooden-hulled, 120-foot submarine chasers to Europe. Early models were armed with one 6-pound gun, and either two machine guns or two 3-inch guns. When photographed at Spalato on the Adriatic Sea in 1918, these subchasers had exchanged one of the smaller guns for a depth-charge projector.

determined the role of the U.S. Navy, which was soon focused on conducting antisubmarine warfare in cooperation with Britain's Royal Navy. Shortly after the United States declared war, the British Admiralty adopted the convoy system as the principal means of dealing with German U-boats. Armed ships of war would rendezvous with merchant ships southwest of the British Isles and escort them through areas where submarines lay in wait. The most efficient escorts were destroyers, although other types of warships and auxiliaries, such as armed yachts and cruisers, were used when necessary.

Admiral William S. Sims was sent to London in March 1917 to coordinate U.S. naval activities with those of the Allies. He became a strong supporter of the convoy system, urging the U.S. Navy to concentrate on antisubmarine warfare. This approach meant postponement of America's 1916 naval construction plan that envisioned building battleships and cruisers along with destroyers and other vessels. Construction of destroyers and merchant ships was given priority and continued throughout the war, but work ceased on creation of a comprehensive battle fleet capable of establishing command of the sea.

Antisubmarine Tactics

In May 1917, American destroyers were sent to the Irish port of Queenstown where they were placed under the command of the British Vice Admiral Sir Lewis Bayly. Later in the war, other U.S. vessels were based at the French port of Brest, especially during 1918 when protection of troop transports carrying the American Expeditionary Forces (A.E.F.) to French ports en route to the western front became a priority.

German submarines exited the North Sea into the Atlantic Ocean through the passage between Norway and Scotland or through the Straits of Dover, where Great Britain established a barrage of mines, patrol vessels, and other protective mea-

sures. The U.S. Navy wanted to create a similar system across the northern passage, and in 1918, with the help of the British, the North Sea Mine Barrage was constructed between the Norwegian coast and the Orkney Islands. Though fully operational only in the last four months of the war, and thus not thoroughly tested, it probably sank six or seven submarines and seriously complicated the passage of others by war's end.

Although the principal contribution of the U.S. Navy was to support the convoy system, it also lent assistance to the British Grand Fleet stationed at Scapa Flow, in the Orkney Islands, to counter the German High Seas Fleet. In December 1917, the U.S. Navy sent Admiral Hugh Rodman and five coal-burning battleships to assist the Grand Fleet. Designated the 6th Battle Squadron, this force enhanced the British advantage in battleships. It was also one of the reasons why the German fleet did not undertake an operation during 1918 like the one that culminated in the Battle of Jutland in 1916, in which the German fleet seriously damaged a number of British vessels, but broke off the engagement and returned to German waters.

Half of the two million U.S. troops sent to Europe during World War I traveled there in ships like the U.S. Hancock, *protected by the U.S. Navy; the other half were transported in Allied ships.*

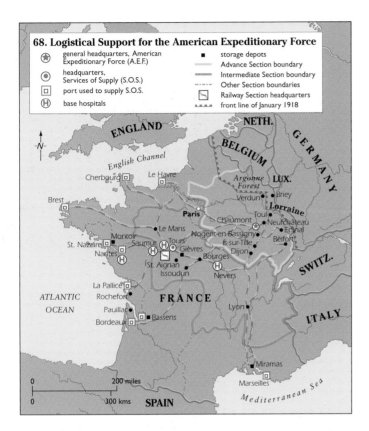

68. Logistical Support for the American Expeditionary Force

- ⊛ general headquarters, American Expeditionary Force (A.E.F.)
- ◉ headquarters, Services of Supply (S.O.S.)
- ▢ port used to supply S.O.S.
- Ⓗ base hospitals
- ■ storage depots
- ── Advance Section boundary
- ═══ Intermediate Section boundary
- ─·─ Other Section boundaries
- ▨ Railway Section headquarters
- ▪▪▪ front line of January 1918

In 1917-18 the United States considered the possibility that Germany might send U-boats to the western Atlantic. Because of the time and effort required to reach U.S. waters, the officials in Washington agreed with Admiral Sims that Germany would not undertake an extensive transatlantic submarine campaign, because supporting the operations of one U-boat in American waters would eat up the same resources as operating three or four submarines near Europe. No submarines approached the American coast in 1917, but in 1918 six U-boats appeared in positions ranging from New England to South Carolina. Their objective was to divert Allied antisubmarine forces from European waters and to weaken the convoy system. The Germans sank only ninety ships, totaling about 170,000 gross tons, but had little or no effect on the Allied convoy system.

Build up in France

While U.S. naval forces helped counter German operations at sea, the U.S. Army prepared for entering the war on the Western Front. In June 1917, General John J. Pershing was ordered to France to lead the American Expeditionary Forces (A.E.F.). He selected the right end of the active front, in Lorraine, as the sector the A.E.F. would eventually take over, and began planning operations. Pershing believed that the capture of the city of Metz in northeast Lorraine, close to the German bor-

der, would strike a decisive blow because it would interdict German lines of supply to forces farther west and force a withdrawal to the east.

To provide lines of communication from ports on the French coast to the Lorraine sector, Pershing established an agency called Services of Supply (S.O.S.) to maintain the troops required to operate independently against Metz. Bordeaux, Brest, Cherbourg, La Pallice, le Havre, and St. Nazaire on the Bay of Biscay, and Marseilles on the Mediterranean were designated to serve the A.E.F. Headquarters for the S.O.S. were established at Tours in central France.

During 1917, only five American divisions were shipped to France, a total of fewer than two hundred thousand troops. During 1918 their numbers were constantly augmented, but the need for additional training in France and the desire to preserve the divisions so that they could become part of an independent force limited the combat role of these American divisions until the summer of 1918.

Meanwhile, the German High Command launched a series of offensives on the western front intended to force a decision before the A. E. F. gave the Allies sufficient manpower to win the war. The United States made only minor contributions to the beleaguered French and British armies when German attacks pushed Allied lines back forty miles during the Somme Offensive (21 March-4 April) and ten miles during the Lys

When it arrived in France, the U.S. Army was poorly equipped for combat. To provide it with a mobile artillery piece, the army modified a French, 37-mm gun (shown below in the Argonne Forest), so it could fire either high explosive shells against fortifications or shrapnel canisters containing thirty-two lead balls against personnel.

artillery barrage, U.S. infantry advanced behind borrowed French tanks, overran the surprised German defenders, then repulsed counterattacks. It was a modest action costing the United States only 1,800 casualties, but it bolstered Allied morale and demonstrated the value of American reinforcements.

A more significant U.S. contribution also came during the third German attack, the Aisne Offensive (27 May–4 June). The American 2nd Division, which included the 4th Brigade of the U.S. Marines, entered the lines as part of the French Sixth Army. From 6–26 June, they fought to clear Belleau Wood near Château-Thierry in the west of the Marne Valley. Massed formations of American troops engaged well-entrenched German troops in extremely difficult terrain that greatly benefited the defenders. In the initial attacks on 6 June, U.S. Marines suffered 1,087 casualties, the greatest U.S. Marine losses in a single day prior to the battle for Tarawa in November 1943. Critics of American tactics argued that the wood should have been bypassed or bombarded and cut off from supply lines. Small unit struggles in the wood continued for almost three weeks until the German defenders were finally forced to abandon the site. The 2nd Division suffered casualties of 170 officers and 8,793 enlisted men during the campaign, including over a thousand fatalities.

Posters, like this one, issued by the U.S. government, were used extensively by both sides to rally support for the war. In Allied posters, Germans were often depicted as "evil and barbaric Huns," who violated innocent women and children. Neutral Belgium, invaded by Germany at the start of the war, was often symbolized as a helpless young woman.

Offensive (9–27 April). When the third German offensive crossed the River Aisne on 27 May and advanced twenty miles in a single day, the U.S. 2nd and 3rd Divisions were moved forward to support the French forces that blocked the German advance at the River Marne, less than fifty miles from Paris. Following six weeks of fighting, the 2nd Division was withdrawn from the front lines after suffering 7,900 casualties.

U.S. Offensives at Cantigny and Belleau Wood

On 28 May 1918, the 28th Infantry Regiment of the American 1st Division executed the A.E.F.'s first offensive of the war. The carefully planned and executed attack was launched at Cantigny, a small town three miles west of Montdidier. After an

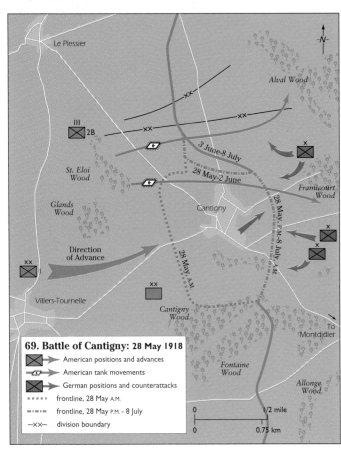

69. Battle of Cantigny: 28 May 1918

- American positions and advances
- American tank movements
- German positions and counterattacks
- ••••• frontline, 28 May A.M.
- –•–•– frontline, 28 May P.M. - 8 July
- –××– division boundary

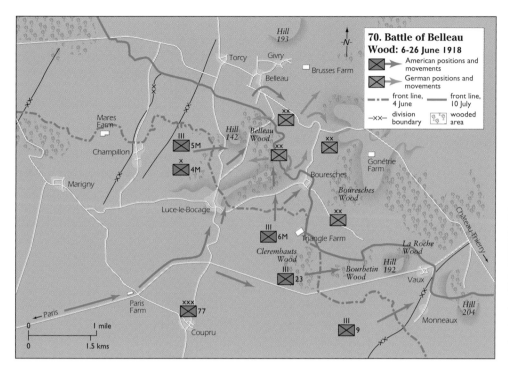

Stretcher-bearers (above) carry away casualties following the capture of Vaux, France, in the Marne Valley, by the U.S. 2nd Division, 1 July 1918.

A.E.F. Under British and French Command

By mid-1918, seven of the twenty-five U.S. divisions in France had seen action, many of them shoring up British and French units attacked during Germany's Noyon-Montdidier Offensive (9-13 June), during which the 1st Division fought near Cantigny, and in the Marne Offensive (15-17 July), during which the 3rd, 26th, 28th, 42nd, and 91st divisions fought under French commanders in the defense of the Allied line on the southeastern side of the Marne salient. Other U.S. divisions were attached to British and French units for training during the spring and summer of 1918 in quiet sectors.

As soon as the last German offensive was contained in July 1918, French General Ferdinand Foch, Allied Commanding General of all French, British, Belgian, and American units on the western front, began a series of limited counteroffensives designed to eliminate German salients and improve lateral communications. These operations, intended to prepare for more extensive attacks later on, brought several American divisions into extensive combat service, again while serving under Allied commanders. General Pershing approved this use of U.S. troops, though he hoped to limit the number of such engagements in order to preserve his troops for independent service later on in the war.

The British held the left side of the Allied lines in a sector that stretched from Belgium at the northwest to the Vosges Mountains at the southeast, to a point south of the River Somme. Following the repulse of the German attacks that

U.S. troops first saw combat in Europe in October 1917, when General Pershing sent a single battalion at a time from each regiment, to serve alongside a French division at the front. These U.S. troops, trying to move mules hauling an ammunition wagon, head for the front through terrain scarred by German shelling.

ended in July 1918, the British Expeditionary Force launched two limited offensives.

In the first of these offensives, ordered by Foch against the salient which German attacks had created at Amiens the previous March, two American units, the 33rd Division and the 80th Division, broke through the German fortifications and regained critical rail communications. During another offensive, on the Ypres-Lys front in August and September, the American 27th and 30th Divisions helped British forces recover control of additional rail communications and placed Marshal Foch's forces in the north in a position to participate in a general offensive.

Southeast of the British sector, the French launched a nearly simultaneous attack designed to regain control of the Marne salient between Soissons and Reims. The first phase of this Aisne-Marne Offensive engaged by far the largest number of American units yet committed to battle in the war. Four regular U.S. Army divisions (the 1st, 2nd, 3rd, and 4th) and four National Guard units (the 26th, 28th, 32nd, and the 42nd divisions) fought as part of the French XX Corps pushing the surprised Germans back over three miles. Then U.S. divisions

pressed the attack as German resistance stiffened. The 1st Division suffered 6,900 casualties and the 2nd Division suffered 4,300 while erasing any lingering doubts that the Americans would not accept losses to gain their objectives.

A renewal of these thrusts in August, designated the Oise-Aisne Offensive, engaged three American divisions, the 28th and 32nd, both National Guard units, and one from the conscripted national U.S. Army, the 80th Division. These units of the American III Corps, commanded by Major General Robert Bullard, joined the French in occupying a large area north of the River Vesle to the River Aisne while pressing the Germans to abandon the region.

Confident that the Germans were greatly weakened following the failure of their offensives, Marshal Foch decided the time was right for the Allies to turn the tables on their enemy. Thus, in September, Foch launched a general counteroffensive, intended to drive the German army out of France. Several American divisions participated under Allied command. A renewed offensive in the Ypres-Lys sector included the American 27th, 30th, and 91st divisions. Serving as part of the Flanders group of armies, these units helped drive the German

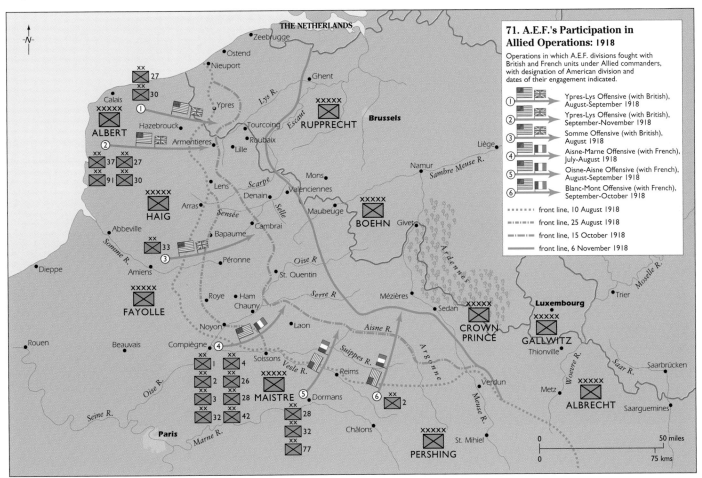

71. A.E.F.'s Participation in Allied Operations: 1918

Operations in which A.E.F. divisions fought with British and French units under Allied commanders, with designation of American division and dates of their engagement indicated.

① Ypres-Lys Offensive (with British), August-September 1918
② Ypres-Lys Offensive (with British), September-November 1918
③ Somme Offensive (with British), August 1918
④ Aisne-Marne Offensive (with French), July-August 1918
⑤ Oisne-Aisne Offensive (with French), August-September 1918
⑥ Blanc-Mont Offensive (with French), September-October 1918

· · · · · · · · front line, 10 August 1918
· — · — · — front line, 25 August 1918
— · · — · · — front line, 15 October 1918
———————— front line, 6 November 1918

defenders eastward to the vicinity of Ghent and Brussels, pushing the Germans out of territory they had occupied for over three years. Meanwhile, on 3–4 October, the American 2nd Division, attached to the French Fourth Army, attacked and captured a key German strong point on Blanc–Mont Ridge, in an area just to the west of the Meuse–Argonne sector. The experienced unit then held its position until the U.S. 36th Division relieved it. A week later the 2nd Division participated in the advance of the French to the River Aisne (10–18 October).

The St. Mihiel Campaign

While these units fought in conjunction with French and British forces, Pershing was organizing for independent action under American leadership. On 24 July, General Foch had approved establishment of the American First Army and on 10 August, Pershing began organizing a headquarters staff and planning an offensive near St. Mihiel in what was designated the American sector. By September, Pershing committed the American First Army to battle.

Foch agreed that the Americans were ready for independent

action and assigned to them the last limited offensive of the summer: The reduction of another German salient just south of Verdun. The triangular-shaped area was twenty-five miles wide at the base and extended sixteen miles into Allied lines. With barbed-wire entanglements, concrete shelters, and over 500,000 defenders, it was considered a fortress.

The American First Army plan of operations envisioned strong attacks on the south and west face of the salient. Converging attacks to the north by the American I and IV Corps and to the east by the American V Corps were intended to push the German Composite Army C out of the salient. The French II Colonial Corps, attached to the American First Army for the operation, launched holding attacks against the point of the salient to prevent the enemy from reinforcing its units facing the principal American thrusts. Some fifteen hundred Allied aircraft, of which almost half were American, were assembled under the command of Brigadier General Billy Mitchell of the U.S. Army Air Service, to support ground operations and penetrate German airfields. This was the largest concentration of aircraft employed by either side during the war. Americans manned 144 of the almost 400 tanks,

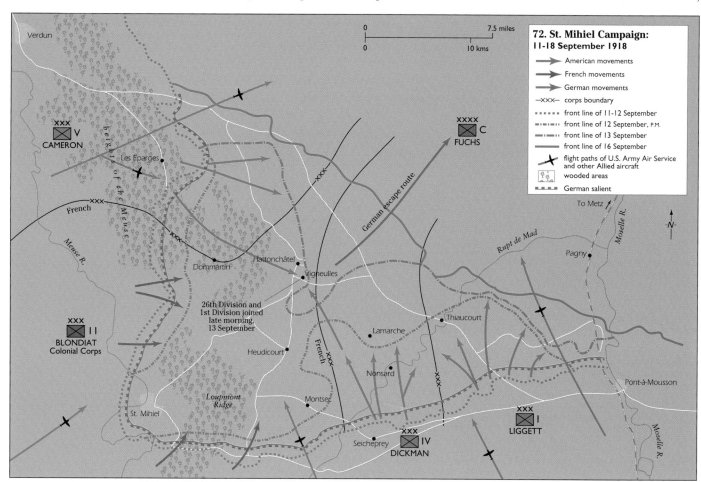

Major General John LeJeune (above) led the U.S. 2nd Division in France and became commandant of the U.S. Marine Corps after the war. At Meuse, France, Second Lieutenant Valentine Browning (right) demonstrates the machine gun his father developed.

mostly of French manufacture, which led the assaults.

German composite Army C had anticipated an attack and wished to resist it, but instead, the German High Command decided to evacuate the salient, which the German General Ludendorff termed "a tactical abortion." Accordingly, a plan for evacuation, called the Loki Movement, was developed. On 11 September, some German equipment was taken out, but no troops were withdrawn. The American attack, on 12 September, came sooner than the Germans expected and it accelerated and confused the German withdrawal. The American attacks converged on Vigneulles, but the junction of the two attacking elements there did not occur until a large number of German troops managed to escape. By 16 September, the Germans had established a defensive position at the base of the salient, and the U.S. First Army called a halt to the attack.

In total, the U.S. First Army had taken nearly 16,000 prisoners, seized stockpiles of German weapons and ammunition, and regained 200 square miles of French territory. It suffered 7,000 casualties in the 12-14 September attacks and 3,000 more as it consolidated its control of the salient during the period of 13-16 September. Some American commanders wanted to continue the assault, but the First Army was assigned an important role in forthcoming operations to the north and west. The success at St. Mihiel obscured numerous command and staff failures which reflected a lack of experience in the conduct of large unit operations. These difficulties became evident in later engagements.

The Meuse-Argonne Campaign

After concluding the limited counteroffensives of the summer,

Marshal Foch launched a general counteroffensive designed to seize the section of the lateral railroad between Aulnoy and Mézières which supplied the German army. To prevent the enemy from moving troops to this area, Foch decided on four coordinated attacks in active areas of the western front from Flanders at the northwest end, to Lorraine on the southeast end of the front. The Flanders group of armies, which included British, French, and Belgian units, attacked toward Ghent in Belgium. The British First and Third Armies moved toward Cambrai. The British Fourth Army and the French Tenth Army struck toward Busigny, between Peronne and La Fere. The French Fourth Army and the American First Army drove toward Sedan and Mézières.

The American First Army front stretched for twenty miles between the River Meuse and the western side of the Argonne Forest. The heights of the Meuse, east of the fordless river, provided excellent positions for German artillery. Elevations of Montfauçon, Cunel, and Romagne formed a hogback west of the Meuse that forced the Americans to attack through the defiles to the east and west of the high ground. The Argonne Forest provided cover for skillful German machine gun and artillery fire. Four distinct lines of fortifications provided strong defensive locations that allowed observation of American movements against them. Pershing's plan of operations called for a powerful, sustained push that would carry through the third and strongest line of fortifications, the Kriemhilde Stellung, an extension of the Hindenburg Line between Romagne and Brieulles, and open the way toward Sedan and the railroad that passed through it. He had only ten days after the end of the St. Mihiel campaign to relocate his forces to the

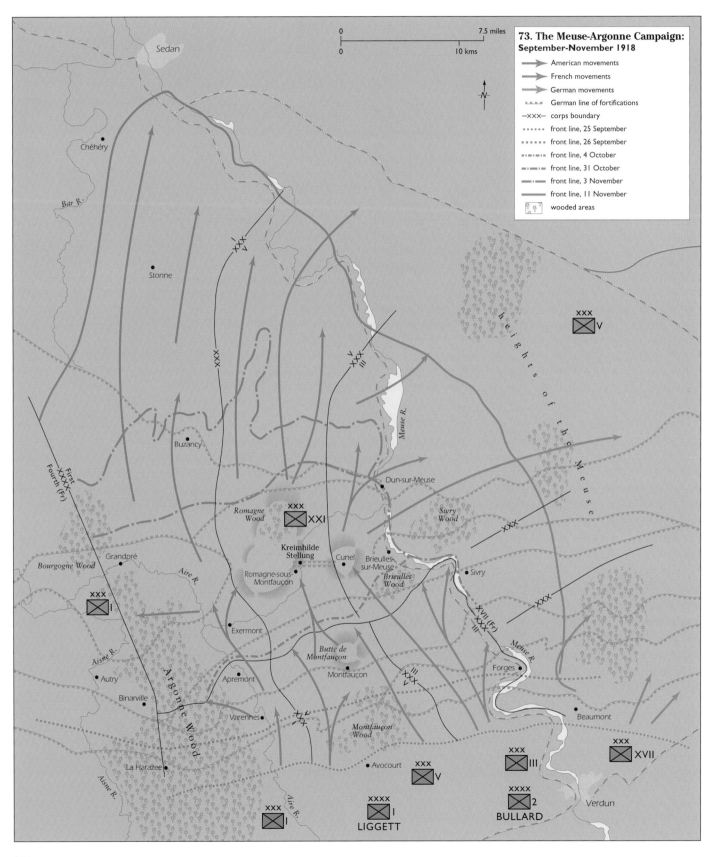

Sedan

0   7.5 miles
0   10 kms

**73. The Meuse-Argonne Campaign:
September-November 1918**

American movements
French movements
German movements
German line of fortifications
—XXX— corps boundary
front line, 25 September
front line, 26 September
front line, 4 October
front line, 31 October
front line, 3 November
front line, 11 November
wooded areas

-N-

Chéhéry

Bar R.

Stonne

heights of the Meuse

XXX V

XXX

XXX III

Meuse R.

First
Fourth (Fr)

Buzancy

Dun-sur-Meuse

Siwry
Wood

XXX

Romagne
Wood

XXX XXI

Kreimhilde
Stellung

Cunel

Brieulles-
sur-Meuse

Grandpré

Bourgogne Wood

Aire R.

Romagne-sous-
Montfauçon

Brieulles
Wood

Sivry

XXX I

Exermont

Butte de
Montfauçon

XVII (Fr)
III

Meuse R.

Aisne R.

Argonne Wood

Autry

Apremont

Montfauçon

Forges

III

Binarville

Varennes

Montfauçon
Wood

Beaumont

La Harazée

XXX I

Aire R.

Avocourt

XXX V

XXXX I

LIGGETT

XXX III

XXXX 2

BULLARD

XXX XVII

Verdun

Aisne R.

Meuse-Argonne sector. Only a few of Pershing's more experienced units were available for the initial attack, which depended for success on superior manpower and surprise tactics. Three American corps were to move forward on 26 September: I Corps (77th, 28th, and 35th divisions) down the valley of the River Aire on the left; V Corps (91st and 79th divisions) in the center; and III Corps (4th, 80th, and 33rd divisions) along the eastern side of Montfauçon Hill. Only two reasonably passable roads were available for reinforcement, resupply of the assault troops, and forward displacement of artillery.

The assault, launched at 5:30 A.M. on 26 September, did not meet expectations. Taking full advantage of the difficult terrain, the German defenders poured heavy machine gun and artillery fire on the advancing Americans who became disorientated in the morning fog. Montfauçon Hill, the first of three ridges fortified in depth by the Germans, was captured at midday on 27 September. A traffic jam paralyzed the supply system. By 30 September, the U.S. First Army occupied positions just short of the Kriemhilde Stellung, the second German line of defense where it was forced to dig in, having advanced about eight miles. At this point veteran units, including the U.S. 1st, 2nd, and 3rd divisions, relieved exhausted troops, and preparations began to resume the attack. On 16 October, the Kriemhilde Stellung, the objective of the first day's attack, finally fell to the Americans.

During October, the U.S. First Army conducted a series of offensives designed to break through the German defenses. Stubborn German resistance led to many American casualties and limited gains. To compensate for his losses, Pershing was forced to reclaim divisions attached to the French and British armies and to break up newly arrived divisions for use as replacements. Major General Hunter Liggett, the most competent and experienced corps commander of the A.E.F., had been elevated to the command of the U.S. First Army. When the U.S. Second Army was organized with General Bullard at its head, Pershing assumed command of the American group of armies. Liggett took advantage of the last two weeks of October to institute training in the tactics that the Allied armies had perfected which emphasized cooperation between armor, artillery, and infantry.

Despite the stubborn German defense on the right of the Allied lines, British forces to the northwest of Picardy broke through the massive German fortifications, an achievement that led to the resignation of German General Ludendorff and the initiation of peace negotiations. By 1 November, Foch was prepared to launch another general attack along the entire western front to drive the enemy out of France and to end the war. The U.S. First Army played an important role in that offensive. By 3 November, the U.S. III Corps had forced the

Members of the American "Colored Regiments" were attached to the Fourth French Army. Troops of the 368th infantry are shown here wearing French helmets and fighting in the Argonne Forest.

Germans to abandon artillery positions in the heights east of the River Meuse and on the next day began crossing the Meuse. U.S. railroad batteries, mounting 14-inch naval guns, quickly began shelling the rail communications vital to the maintenance of the German army. By 11 November, Allied forces achieved Foch's principal objective by sweeping across those rail lines and were preparing for a massive attack scheduled for 14 November.

The War Ends

That offensive was not needed. On 11 November, at the eleventh hour, an armistice negotiated by Marshal Foch went into effect, and the exhausting struggle in the Meuse-Argonne sector came to an end. In the last six weeks of the war, U.S. forces suffered 117,000 casualties while inflicting 100,000 casualties on the Germans and capturing another 26,000 men. Although the U.S. First Army did not make geographical gains comparable to those of the French and British, its sustained operations drew German reinforcements to its sector and inflicted severe casualties against the German defenders. American forces made an honorable contribution to the inter-Allied operations that brought victory to the Allied and associated powers after four years of warfare. The A.E.F.'s over 2 million troops that served overseas during the war, with 1.39 million stationed in France, and 50,475 killed and 205,600 wounded, did not make the decisive combat contribution to the victory that Pershing had planned, but at war's end, American arms had helped to place President Woodrow Wilson in a position to gain acceptance of the nation's diplomatic and political objectives at the peace conference at Versailles.

The United States in World War II in the Pacific: 1941-45

The hesitant aspirations of the United States as a colonial power in the Pacific were not given full expression until well into the second half of the nineteenth century. The purchase of Alaska and the Aleutians from Russia in 1867 brought America thousands of miles of additional coastline on the Pacific, while the acquisition of the islands of Midway and Samoa propelled her influence out to the west and south. By the end of the century the United States had annexed Hawaii, the Philippines, and Guam, and the completion of the Panama Canal in 1914 set the seal on America's claims to be a two-ocean power.

Even though the old colonial powers Britain, France, and the Netherlands had already established themselves in the Far East, it was not their hostility that confronted the United States' westward expansion. The principal reaction came from Japan, a nation which was emerging towards the end of the nineteenth century from two hundred years of self-imposed isolation. Growing steadily as a modern military and industrial power, Japan looked acquisitively at the territory of her neighbors and especially at China.

By the 1930s Japan saw her principal opponents as Great Britain, China, France, the Netherlands, Russia, and the United States. In July 1937, Japan began an all-out, though undeclared, war on China. Her armed forces also clashed with the Red Army on the Manchurian and Korean borders as they attempted to gain territory at the expense of Russia. Encouraged by German victories over the French, Dutch, and British in Europe, Japan pressed for concessions in Indochina. But the critical factor for the Japanese was how to achieve their desired conquests in the south while still avoiding war with the United States. In September 1940, in what was an overt signal to the United States to remain neutral, Japan concluded a defensive alliance with Germany and Italy through the Tripartite Pact. A non-aggression pact with Russia in April 1941, and the German execution of Operation Barbarossa, Hitler's invasion of Russia in June, gave Japan greater strategic freedom to exploit her aims in the south.

Japan's Decision for War

America's response to Japan's military policies centered upon the attempt to restrict the development of her economic and military power by sanctions, and to provide aid to her opponents such as Chiang Kai-shek and the Chinese Nationalists. In June 1940, the United States began to limit the export of aviation gasoline, lubricating oils, and iron and steel scrap, and two months later, banned export of all types of iron and steel scrap. The American Volunteer Group, organized by U.S. aviator Claire Chennault and known as the Flying Tigers, began to train in their fighter aircraft in Burma in the spring of 1941 in order to assist the Chinese against the invading Japanese forces. Lend-Lease supplies were pushed through to the Chinese along the Burma Road and Lieutenant General Joseph Stilwell became the senior American soldier in the China theater. On 26 July 1941 President Franklin Delano

Although Admiral Husband Kimmel (above), Commander-in-Chief of the U.S. fleet, took steps to protect his fleet from sabotage and submarine attack and raised it to battle efficiency by December 1941, neither he nor his colleagues based in Hawaii on 7 December could have anticipated the chaos the Japanese delivered from the air at Pearl Harbor (right), in only two-hours' time, as seen in this photograph taken several hours after the attack.

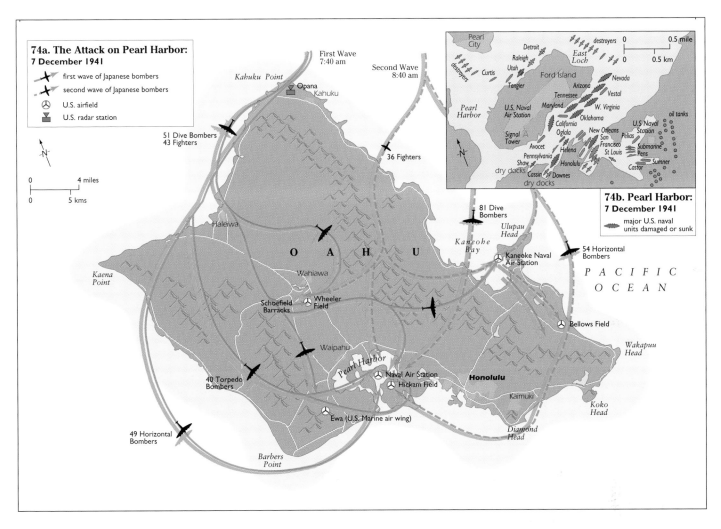

**74a. The Attack on Pearl Harbor:
7 December 1941**

first wave of Japanese bombers

second wave of Japanese bombers

U.S. airfield

U.S. radar station

First Wave
7:40 am

Second Wave
8:40 am

Kahuku Point

Opana
Kahuku

51 Dive Bombers
43 Fighters

36 Fighters

81 Dive
Bombers

*Ulupau
Head*

*Kaneohe
Bay*

Kaneoke Naval
Air Station

54 Horizontal
Bombers

0   4 miles

0   5 kms

Haleiwa

O   A   H   U

*Kaena
Point*

Wahiawa

Schoefield
Barracks

Wheeler
Field

*P A C I F I C
O C E A N*

Bellows Field

*Wakapuu
Head*

Waipahu

40 Torpedo
Bombers

Pearl Harbor

Naval Air Station
Hickam Field

Honolulu

Kaimuki

*Koko
Head*

Ewa (U.S. Marine air wing)

49 Horizontal
Bombers

*Barbers
Point*

*Diamond
Head*

Pearl
City

destroyers   0   0.5 mile

0   0.5 km

Detroit

*East
Loch*

Raleigh

destroyers

Curtis

Utah

Nevada

Tangier

Ford Island

Arizona

Tennessee

Vestal

*Pearl
Harbor*

U.S. Naval
Air Station

Maryland

Oklahoma

W. Virginia

oil tanks

Signal
Tower

California

New Orleans
San
Francisco

Pelias

U.S Naval
Station

Oglala

Avocet

Helena

St Louis

Submarine
Pens

Sumner

Pennsylvania

Honolulu

Castor

Shaw

Cassin

Downes

dry docks

dry docks

**74b. Pearl Harbor:
7 December 1941**

major U.S. naval
units damaged or sunk

Roosevelt froze all Japanese funds in the United States, closed the Panama Canal to Japan, and laid an embargo on all oil. When the British and Dutch adopted America's policy, Japan was faced by an almost total embargo on strategic imports.

Pearl Harbor

The decision to go to war was taken in Tokyo on 1 December 1941. Within a week, on Sunday, 7 December (Hawaiian time; 8 December Tokyo time), many of the most powerful warships in the U.S. Pacific Fleet lay in ruins on the seabed in Pearl Harbor in Hawaii. They had been blasted to destruction by an aerial armada of Japanese fighters, bombers, and torpedo planes that had launched a surprise attack on them and the adjoining air bases with ruthless precision.

From the autumn of 1940, President Roosevelt and his immediate circle of advisers were kept informed of Japan's progress towards war through the decrypts of the Japanese diplomatic code, known as "Purple." With access to Purple the Americans could read signals between Tokyo and the Japanese

embassies in Berlin and Washington. Roosevelt thus knew that Tokyo's timetable for war was gathering speed dramatically, but the strategic analysis he received assumed that the Japanese threat was focused on the Philippines and on British and Dutch possessions in Southeast Asia, rather than on Pearl Harbor. The immediate danger to the Pacific Fleet's anchorage was identified as action by enemy saboteurs or submarines. Lieutenant General Walter C. Short, commanding the army units in Hawaii, and Admiral Husband Kimmel, commander-in-chief of the U.S. Fleet and Pacific Fleet, took measures designed to counter these specific dangers and not against air attack. Even the early radar location of the Japanese squadrons as they approached Hawaii on the morning of 7 December, was explained away as the approach of friendly aircraft.

As the Japanese began their bombing and torpedo runs over Pearl Harbor, ninety-four American warships and auxiliary vessels lay at their mercy in the harbor. Included were the battleships *Arizona*, *California*, *Maryland*, *Nevada*, *Oklahoma*, *Pennsylvania*, *Tennessee*, and *West Virginia*, two heavy and six

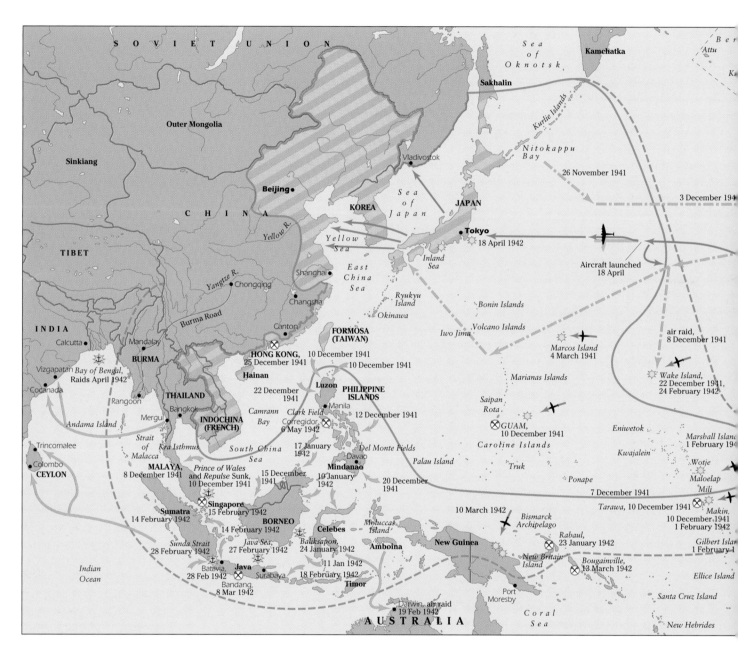

light cruisers, twenty-nine destroyers, and five submarines. Within the space of two hours, eighteen ships—eight battleships, three light cruisers, three destroyers, and four auxiliary vessels—had been sunk, had capsized, or were badly damaged. Eighty naval aircraft and a number of small ships and transports had also been lost, together with seventy-seven U.S. Army aircraft of all types destroyed, and another 128 planes damaged. Civilian and service casualties amounted to 2,403 dead and 1,178 wounded. The Japanese lost twenty-nine planes, one submarine, and five midget submarines during the attack.

Even so, the Japanese were robbed of one major prize, the four carriers *Enterprise*, *Hornet*, *Lexington*, and *Yorktown*, which they believed were based at Pearl Harbor. In fact, the *Hornet* and the *Yorktown* were on duty in the Atlantic and the *Saratoga* did not reach Hawaii from San Diego until a week after the attack. Almost as critical for the Japanese was the fact that in failing to launch a second strike while Pearl Harbor was virtually defenseless, they allowed the U.S. Pacific Fleet's invaluable infrastructure—its fuel and ammunition reserves, repairs shops, dry docks, and submarine pens—to survive to fight another day. Thus, on the day of a great tactical victory the seeds of Japan's strategic defeat were left intact. The tragedy had not eradicated the Pacific Fleet's strike power—

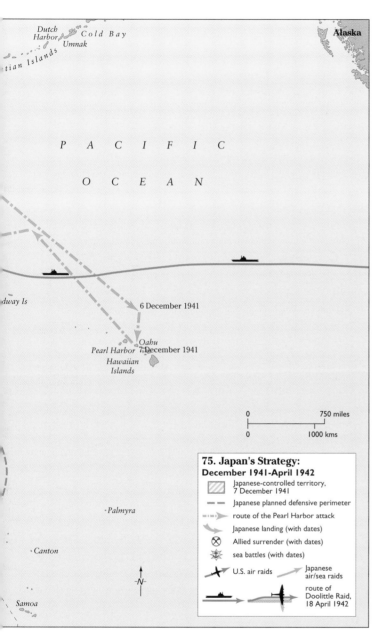

7 December 1941 assaults were launched against the Philippines, Hong Kong, and Malaya. Japanese planes bombed the islands of Guam and Wake, and on 10 December, troops of the Japanese South Seas Detachment stormed ashore on Guam and crushed the garrison of U.S. Marines and native police with overwhelming force. The next day a Japanese force of 500 naval landing troops, accompanied by cruisers and destroyers, attempted to do the same to the garrison on Wake Island. They were in for a bloody surprise. Wake's defenders from the 1st U.S. Marine Defense Battalion and a U.S. Marine fighter squadron, VMF-211, fought the Japanese invasion force to a standstill, sinking or damaging three cruisers, five destroyers, and two transports. Thereafter, the Japanese bombed Wake Island unmercifully. When a relief expedition was not pushed forward to Wake Island with sufficient energy, the island finally fell to the Japanese on 23 December. Isolated American garrisons in Shanghai, Tientsin, and Beijing were also forced to surrender.

The period from Pearl Harbor to the Battle of the Coral Sea (7 December 1941-7 May 1942) was, in territorial terms, one of almost unremitting defeat for the United States and her allies. The Japanese crushed resistance in British Borneo, Burma, Malaya, and Hong Kong, the Philippines, the Dutch East Indies, and numerous islands across the west and south Pacific. Yet at the same time it became clear that Japan had outrun its strategic capabilities and that America's enormous industrial and military strength would eventually deliver victory in the Pacific.

The Philippines

The Philippines were central to America's prewar plans for the conduct of operations against Japan, Plan Orange. For Orange to have any chance of success, the Philippines (or at least the approaches to Manila Bay) had to be held until the Pacific Fleet could leapfrog from island base to island base across the 5,000 miles of the Pacific Ocean to destroy Japan's naval strength in fleet combat. In 1941, the plight of the British Commonwealth, in its stand against the full weight of the Axis powers and the recognition that Great Britain's survival was crucial to U.S. interests, led to the replacement of Orange by another plan known as Rainbow-5. By according priority to the war against Germany and Italy, Rainbow-5 meant the abandonment of an early offensive in the Pacific and the isolation of the Philippines once war with Japan had broken out. The Philippines' only hope was a massive reinforcement of its garrison before hostilities occurred.

In July 1941, Lieutenant General Douglas MacArthur was recalled from retirement to organize the defense of the Philippines under Rainbow-5. MacArthur was given command of both the Philippine Army and U.S. troops in the Far East.

within six months its carriers began to roll back Japan's conquest—and the surprise attack, before a declaration of war had been delivered, gave Tokyo the character of a flagrant aggressor in the eyes of the world. The attack on Pearl Harbor united the American people in a deadly determination to destroy Japan's ability to make war. The declaration of war upon the United States by Japan's allies, Germany and Italy, four days after the Pearl Harbor attack, only served to add insult to injury.

Beginning of Japan's War Campaign

Although of crucial importance to the Japanese, the attack on Pearl Harbor was only the beginning of their campaign. On

Not about to go down in history as the commander of an unsuccessful garrison, he bombarded Washington with requests for aircraft, men, equipment, and supplies. Within two months of MacArthur's appointment, reinforcements and equipment were heading for the Philippines as quickly as the available shipping would allow. By December 1941, MacArthur had over 30,000 U.S. Army troops under command together with thirty-five B-17 bombers, over one hundred Curtiss P-40 Warhawk fighters, and the support of three U.S. Navy cruisers, thirteen destroyers, six motor torpedo boats, twenty-nine submarines, and the men of the 4th U.S. Marine Regiment. Although poorly equipped and only partly trained, the island's ten Philippine divisions could put about 110,000 soldiers into action.

The first Japanese air attack on the Philippines was delivered about nine hours after news of the attack on Pearl Harbor had reached MacArthur, but it still managed to achieve tactical surprise. The reasons for the slowness of the American response in the Philippines are still obscure. What is clear is that a U.S. Army Air Corps bomber strike of B-17s against Japanese airbases in Formosa was postponed and then suddenly scheduled again. While the B-17s, the only real American strike force in the area, were refueling, they were destroyed on the ground at Clark Field. Clark Field and other U.S. airfields were destroyed causing American fighter strength to be devastated in the Philippines. Without air cover, the major units of the U.S. Asiatic Fleet, with the exception of its submarines, headed south—out of range of the Japanese aircraft based on Formosa. The Japanese were stunned by their good fortune, for in two days and with only light losses, they had crippled U.S. air power in the Philippines and the Far East.

The main invasion of the Philippines was undertaken by Japanese Lieutenant General Masaharu Homma's two divisions—the 16th and 48th at Lingayen Gulf, 120 miles to the north of Manila, on 22 December 1941. On 24 December, MacArthur activated Plan Orange, declared Manila an open city, and withdrew his headquarters to the fortress of Corregidor at the mouth of Manila Bay. MacArthur also ordered a general retreat to the Bataan Peninsula, and the U.S. and Philippine defenders began a two-week fighting withdrawal, during which they bought time by temporarily stopping the Japanese at a succession of defensive positions. Nevertheless, the Japanese Fourteenth Army took Manila on 2 January 1942, but were denied use of the port by MacArthur's defense of Corregidor and Bataan. American and Philippine troops also continued to resist on Bohol, Cebu, Leyte, Mindanao, Panay, and other islands. The Japanese believed that only a simple campaign to mop up the last vestiges of resistance lay before them, but instead they ran into an American defense line running across the Peninsula, from Mauban in the west to Mabat-

ing on Manila Bay. Nearly 90,000 troops defended Bataan under the command of U.S. Major General Jonathan Wainwright in the west and under U.S. Major General George Parker in the east.

The defenders outnumbered the attackers, but their physical condition (many were wracked by beriberi, dysentery, and malaria) was already poor, and they lacked material vital for the proper fortification of their field positions. Gradually, hope waned among the defenders as it became clear that they could not be reinforced adequately from outside. Notwithstanding their dismal position, the U.S. and Philippine troops held out for six days against the main Japanese attack delivered on 9 January, until the enemy threatened to outflank them. On 24 January, MacArthur ordered his exhausted troops to fall back to a second defense line, eight miles to the south. Worn down by heavy casualties incurred during a series of frontal assaults, the Japanese were forced to call a halt until reinforcements arrived. During the next two months, from 8 February to 3 April 1942, the Japanese laid siege to Bataan. Not until the beginning of April did a heavily reinforced Japanese command feel confident enough to mount an all out assault. The defenders, now pitiably reduced in numbers and physique, were forced to surrender on 9 April. MacArthur did not witness the end as he had obeyed President Roosevelt's order, made on the recommendation of the Joint Chiefs of Staff, who did not want MacArthur to risk being captured by the Japanese. MacArthur was ordered to leave the Philippines for Australia. He left on 11 March, vowing to return one day.

Although they now controlled all of Luzon, the Japanese were still denied the use of Manila Harbor by the garrison of Corregidor and its outlying forts in the entrance to the bay. Corregidor's strength as a fortress lay in its seaward defenses, but for almost four weeks, from 9 April to 6 May, its 10,000 defenders resisted a punishing level of bombardment. Conditions for the garrison deteriorated as supplies of water, food, and ammunition were depleted. By May 1942, the defenders held out little hope of resisting a direct Japanese assault and, although they fought with tenacity and courage, they were forced to surrender along with the remaining U.S. and Philippine garrisons on 6 May. Rather than become prisoners of the Japanese, many Filipino and some U.S. troops took to the mountains to wage guerrilla war against their conquerors.

During their campaign in the Philippines, the Japanese suffered some 12,000 casualties, U.S. and Philippine units lost approximately 16,000 men, and 84,000 were taken as prisoners of war. It was a bitter defeat for the United States—the largest U.S. Army in American history to surrender—and made worse by the inhumane treatment of their prisoners by the Japanese. Yet the Japanese could take little comfort from such a dearly bought victory. The defenders of Bataan and Corregi-

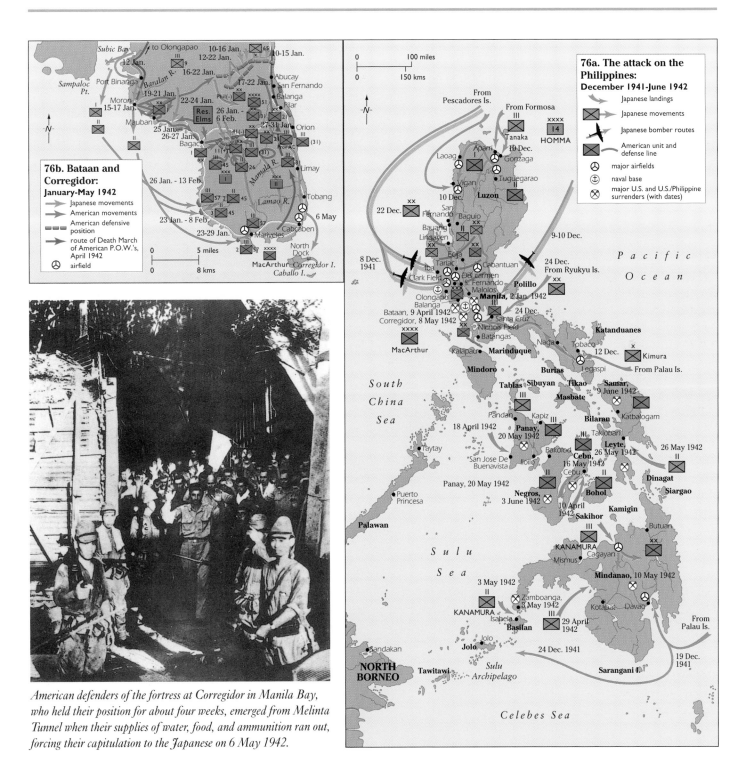

American defenders of the fortress at Corregidor in Manila Bay, who held their position for about four weeks, emerged from Melinta Tunnel when their supplies of water, food, and ammunition ran out, forcing their capitulation to the Japanese on 6 May 1942.

dor made the Japanese pay for every inch of gain and their troops were chastened by the experience. MacArthur's defense of the Philippines was riddled with tactical flaws and his leadership was not of the highest order. His actions compromised a successful, long term defense and led to great suffering among his troops who fought the enemy while handicapped by severe shortages of ammunition, food, and medical supplies. Yet it was MacArthur who became a national hero. General Homma, although eventually successful, was relieved of his command.

Allied Changes

During the struggle for the Philippines, fundamental changes had been implemented in the command and control structures of the Allied forces in the Pacific and Far East. At the Arcadia summit conference between President Franklin D. Roosevelt, British Prime Minister Winston S. Churchill and their military staffs in Washington (22 December 1941-14 January 1942), the president reorganized the Joint Army-Navy Board as the Joint Chiefs of Staff. When the Joint Chiefs sat in conference with their British counterparts, the Chiefs of Staff Committee, they were collectively called the Combined Chiefs of Staff. The new Commander-in-Chief of the Pacific Fleet was Admiral Chester W. Nimitz, formerly chief of the U.S. Bureau of Navigation. Admiral Ernest J. King was appointed Commander-in-Chief of the U.S. Fleet and Chief of Naval Operations and General George C. Marshall continued as the Chief of Staff of the U.S. Army until 1945. In the Far East, a new command structure was formed on 15 January 1942 to embrace the Allied forces—American, British, Dutch, and Australian—opposing the Japanese. Known as ABDACOM, it was commanded by a distinguished British Army officer, General Sir Archibald Wavell, but it proved to be a problematic command given the limited resources it was assigned to fulfill a myriad of responsibilities over so vast a geographical area.

Admiral Thomas C. Hart, briefly commanded ABDA-COM's British, Dutch, and U.S. naval forces (known as ABDAFLOAT) from Surabaya in western Java, which had to cover the Philippines, Malaya, and Borneo while holding open the sea lanes between Hawaii, Australia, and New Zealand. Hart, however, was a fighting admiral and he made several attempts to catch Japanese forces in the midst of an amphibious landing. At Balikpapan Bay in Borneo, he succeeded and his cruiser/destroyer attack force sank a number of enemy ships without loss of Allied lives. ABDAFLOAT's next mission was very much less successful. Dutch Rear Admiral Karel Doorman sought to destroy the troop convoys of the Japanese Eastern Invasion Force as it headed for Java, but in the process, his five cruisers and nine destroyers clashed with the Japanese defensive force of four cruisers and fourteen destroyers during the afternoon of 27 February. A running battle ensued and accurate Japanese gunfire and sustained torpedo attacks took a mounting toll of Allied ships. During the next twenty-four hours, Doorman lost the 8-inch cruiser H.M.S. *Exeter*, the Dutch 6-inch cruisers *De Ruyter* and *Java*, and the cruisers U.S.S. *Houston* and H.M.A.S. *Perth*, as well as a number of Allied destroyers. Only four American destroyers under Doorman's command survived the Battle of the Java Sea. ABDACOM's forces were inadequate for the tasks to which they had been assigned and their record was unimpressive. Yet, despite the enormous difficulties under which ABDACOM attempted to halt the progress of Japan's offensives, it proved that the goal of close Allied cooperation was no chimera and

in that, at least, it provided an essential model for the future.

A Division of Responsibilities

The end of ABDACOM brought about a reorganization of the Allied war effort in the Pacific and a division of responsibilities between Great Britain and the United States. From April 1942, Britain assumed strategic control of operations for the defense of India, the Indian Ocean, and Sumatra, while the United States undertook responsibility for the entire Pacific, including China, Australia, and New Zealand. General MacArthur took command of the southwest Pacific Area, which consisted of Australia, the Solomon Islands, the Bismarck Archipelago, New Guinea, the Philippines, Borneo, and the Dutch East Indies, except for Sumatra. Admiral Chester Nimitz took control of the Pacific Ocean Area, which comprised the remainder of the Pacific, except for the approaches to the Panama Canal and the west coast of South America, and designated as the Southeast Pacific Area. The Pacific Ocean Area was subdivided into three further command areas—North, Central, and South—with Nimitz in command of the first two and Vice Admiral Robert Ghormley, the third. MacArthur's and Nimitz's orders instructed them to defend vital military areas, to stop the Japanese advance, and to mount attacks on enemy forces whenever feasible.

Bombing Raid on Tokyo

Nimitz employed his three intact fleet carriers *Enterprise*, *Lexington*, and *Yorktown* as aggressively as possible, and struck the Gilbert and Marshall Islands, Lae and Salamaua on the north coast of New Guinea, Rabaul, Wake Island, and Marcus Island in February and March of 1942. A strike against Japan itself was also very much in American minds, and on 13 April 1942, two carriers set sail for a position about 450 miles off Tokyo. Their objective was a hit and run raid on the Japanese capital delivered by sixteen B-25 Mitchell bombers loaded aboard the newly commissioned U.S.S. *Hornet*. The crews from the 17th U.S. Bombardment Group commanded by Lieutenant Colonel James Doolittle had to cover about 1,500 miles to reach landing grounds in China after completing the raid. Amid great secrecy, the *Hornet*, accompanied by a second carrier, the U.S.S. *Enterprise*, with two cruisers, four destroyers, and a tanker, closed to within 700 miles of the Japanese coast before they were located by an enemy picket boat. The commander of the strike fleet, Vice Admiral William F. Halsey Jr., launched Doolittle's bombers immediately, even though this extended the distance they had to cover. At 12.15 P.M. (Tokyo time) on 18 April the first planes released their bombs over Tokyo. The damage to the city was insubstantial but the shock to Japanese morale was significant. The Japanese armed forces had patently failed to prevent a threat to the emperor's safety and

The raid on Tokyo led by Lieutenant Colonel James Doolittle, commanding members of the 17th U.S. Bombardment Group, provided a great boost to American morale in early 1942. One of his sixteen B-25 Mitchell bombers is shown departing from the flight deck of the U.S.S. Hornet *on 18 April 1942. The success of the raid led strategists to make Midway, as opposed to the Indian Ocean or a more southern drive eastward into the Pacific, the focus of Japan's next major operation.*

their loss of face was considerable. Moreover, Halsey's task force reached Pearl Harbor without loss and not one of Doolittle's bombers was shot down, although several crewmen were captured by the Japanese when their planes crash-landed in China.

The Battle of Coral Sea

Tactical victories provided welcome boosts to morale in the United States, but they did not stop the Japanese strategic offensive. Only a serious reverse at sea or the defeat of an important land campaign would cause the Japanese to reassess their strategic priorities. Such a possibility arose in the South Pacific in April 1942. U.S. intelligence intercepts of the Japanese naval code JN25 revealed that the enemy planned to advance on Tulagi in the Solomons, and Port Moresby on the south coast of Papua New Guinea, both garrisoned by Australian forces. The U.S. plan was to use the carriers *Yorktown* and *Lexington*, together with an Australian cruiser squadron, to intercept and destroy the Japanese units sailing for Port Moresby.

Rear Admiral Frank J. Fletcher, commanding from the *Yorktown*, attempted to intercept a Japanese Fleet landing force at Tulagi on 4 May, but he missed the main enemy covering force, and pressed on towards the Jomard Passage between the eastern tip of New Guinea and the Louisiade Archipelago in search of the Japanese carriers. The light carrier *Shoho* escorted the invasion fleet, but a second task force of two fleet carriers, the *Zuikaku* and *Shokaku*, and two heavy cruisers, commanded by Rear Admiral Takagi, entered the Coral Sea on

5 May and was only about seventy miles behind the American task force. Fletcher's planes sank the *Shoho* on 7 May, and the following morning, his reconnaissance aircraft sighted the main Japanese task force. Air strikes were launched from the *Yorktown* and *Lexington*. Only the *Shokaku* was hit by SDB Dauntless dive bombers. Unable to launch aircraft, the Japanese carrier withdrew from the battle.

Meanwhile, Japanese strike aircraft located Fletcher's carriers and they scored a bomb and two torpedo hits on the *Lexington* and a bomb hit on the *Yorktown*. The *Lexington*'s wounds were serious and soon fires raged out of control. During the afternoon of 8 May, her crew abandoned ship and a destroyer sent the *Lexington* to the bottom with torpedoes. Both sides now withdrew their remaining carriers from the Coral Sea, and the Japanese postponed their planned landing at Port Moresby. Coral Sea was the first battle in naval history to be fought entirely by carrier aircraft from fleets which never sighted each other, and it led to the first strategic defeat of the Japanese during World War II.

In the first six months of the war in the Pacific, Japan achieved nearly all of her initial strategic aims. These centered upon the acquisition of territory that would provide the steady supply of raw materials needed by the armed forces and bases from which to repulse the inevitable riposte by the United States. Having reached this position, the problem for the Japanese High Command was what to do next. Should they wait passively until the enemy struck at a time and place of its own choosing, or should they try to preempt the Americans by launching their own strategic offensives? The question was

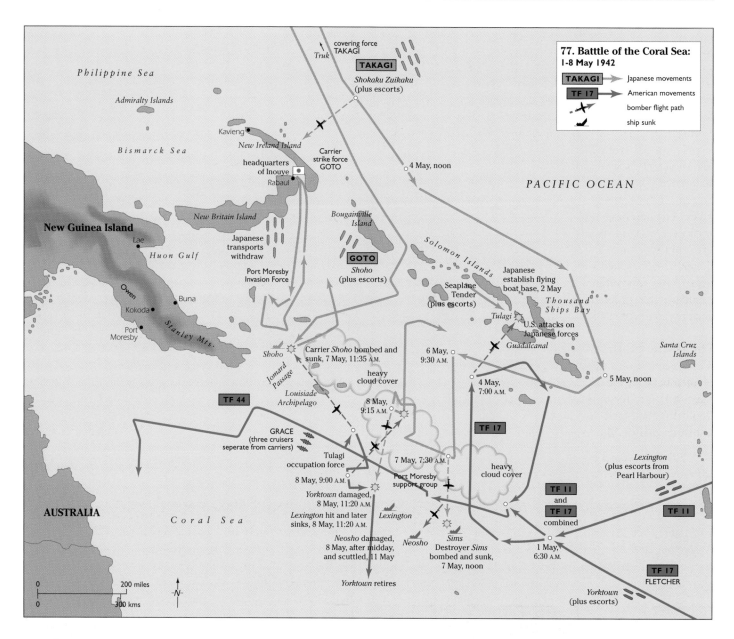

The map shows:

77. Batttle of the Coral Sea: 1-8 May 1942

- TAKAGI → Japanese movements
- TF 17 → American movements
- bomber flight path
- ship sunk

Philippine Sea

Admiralty Islands

covering force TAKAGI
Truk
TAKAGI
Shokaku Zuikaku (plus escorts)

Kavieng
New Ireland Island
Bismarck Sea
Carrier strike force GOTO
headquarters of Inouye
Rabaul
4 May, noon

PACIFIC OCEAN

New Guinea Island
Lae
New Britain Island
Bougainville Island
Japanese transports withdraw
Port Moresby Invasion Force
GOTO
Shoho (plus escorts)
Solomon Islands
Japanese establish flying boat base, 2 May
Seaplane Tender (plus escorts)
Thousand Ships Bay

Huon Gulf
Buna
Owen
Kokoda
Port Moresby
Stanley Mts.
Shoho
Carrier *Shoho* bombed and sunk, 7 May, 11:35 A.M.
Tulagi
U.S. attacks on Japanese forces
Guadalcanal
Santa Cruz Islands
6 May, 9:30 A.M.
heavy cloud cover
4 May, 7:00 A.M.
5 May, noon

Jomard Passage
Louisiade Archipelago
TF 44
8 May, 9:15 A.M.
TF 17
Lexington (plus escorts from Pearl Harbour)

GRACE (three cruisers seperate from carriers)
Tulagi occupation force
8 May, 9:00 A.M.
7 May, 7:30 A.M.
Port Moresby support group
heavy cloud cover
TF 11 and TF 17 combined
TF 11

AUSTRALIA
Coral Sea
Yorktown damaged, 8 May, 11:20 A.M.
Lexington hit and later sinks, 8 May, 11:20 A.M.
Lexington
Neosho damaged, 8 May, after midday, and scuttled, 11 May
Neosho
Sims Destroyer *Sims* bombed and sunk, 7 May, noon
1 May, 6:30 A.M.
TF 17 FLETCHER

0 200 miles
0 300 kms
-N-

Yorktown retires
Yorktown (plus escorts)

complicated by the Japanese navy's wish to strike at the Americans or the British, and the Japanese army's desire to attack the Russians. The Japanese planners' aims stopped far short of an outright defeat of the United States because this goal was seen as clearly unattainable, but they believed that something more than the mere consolidation of past gains might be achieved with careful targeting. Spurred by the ease of their early victories, the Japanese decided to attack.

The strategic options before the Japanese ranged from strikes westwards against India and Ceylon, southwards against Australia, southeastwards from Rabaul to cut communications between the United States and Australia, or eastwards against Hawaii. To move to the west could lead to the elimination of Britain's Eastern Fleet, the conquest of Ceylon, and the reduction of British air power in the Indian Ocean. A move southeastwards would disrupt fatally the Allies' vital supply lines from the United States to Australia and, if followed by an invasion of Australia, could deny the Allies bases on that continent for use as staging ports for a campaign against Japanese conquests in the East Indies. Allied leaders understood this threat and, despite the established policy of Germany first, the United States sent infantry and supporting troops to Australia. The Allies also reinforced garrisons on American Samoa, New Caledonia, Espiritu Santo, Fiji, and other islands that were vital to protecting communications across the Pacific.

Australia's importance to the Allies was obvious to the Japanese, and they rightly feared that unless action was taken, the subcontinent would become the springboard for the U.S. assault on their southern defensive perimeter. Thus, the Japanese navy launched over 200 aircraft against Darwin on 19 February 1942. Joined by planes from the 21st Japanese Air Flotilla at Kendari on Celebes, Admiral Nagumo's four fleet carriers sortied from Palau, crossed the Banda Sea at night, and launched their aircraft in the Timor Sea. The attackers sank eleven ships in Darwin harbor, destroyed twenty-three aircraft on the ground, and inflicted over 500 casualties on the Allies. The bombing of Darwin and subsequent raids on other northwest ports in Australia did not provide, however, a long term solution, and a number of officers on the Japanese Navy General Staff argued that Japan must invade and occupy key areas of the subcontinent. The Japanese army moved quickly to squash this proposal and stated bluntly that the ten divisions required for such an enterprise were simply not available.

The Battle of Midway

With rejection of a campaign southward, strategic discussion by members of the General Staff of the Imperial Japanese Navy shifted to focus on the Indian Ocean and Central Pacific. Doolittle's Raid on Tokyo settled the debate in favor of a strike eastwards against Midway Atoll, with a diversionary attack on

the western Aleutians. The occupation of Midway could achieve three desirable results. It would bring the U.S. carriers to battle and possibly destruction, provide an advance base for Japanese forces, and interdict U.S. communications in the central Pacific. On 5 May 1942, Admiral Osami Nagano, Chief of the Japanese Navy General Staff, directed Admiral Yamamoto to carry out the operations against Midway and the Aleutians.

The United States knew that the Japanese were planning a large strategic operation. U.S. Navy intelligence teams were able to decipher much, but not all, of the Japanese navy's code JN25. When the combat intelligence group, led by Commander Joseph Rochefort in Hawaii, decided that Midway was the next Japanese objective, Admiral Nimitz ordered the U.S. Navy's fleet carriers, under the command of Rear Admiral Frank J. Fletcher, to defend Midway. Task Force 16, composed of the *Enterprise* and *Hornet*, five cruisers, and nine destroyers sailed from Hawaii on 28 May, followed the next day by Task Force 17, composed of the *Yorktown*, two cruisers, and six destroyers. American plans for defending Midway were simple compared with the Japanese plans for the assault. Over 200 Japanese fleet units, including eleven battleships, eight carriers, twenty-two cruisers, sixty-five destroyers, and twenty-one submarines, were to sail in five separate geographically dispersed commands: Main Force (Admiral Yamamoto), First Carrier Striking Force, Midway Invasion Force, Northern

The TBD-1 Devastator torpedo bombers, obsolete by the start of World War II, were easy targets for the Japanese Zeros, but the United States had nothing better when these Devastators were photographed on the flight deck of the U.S.S. Enterprise, *just before the Battle of Midway.*

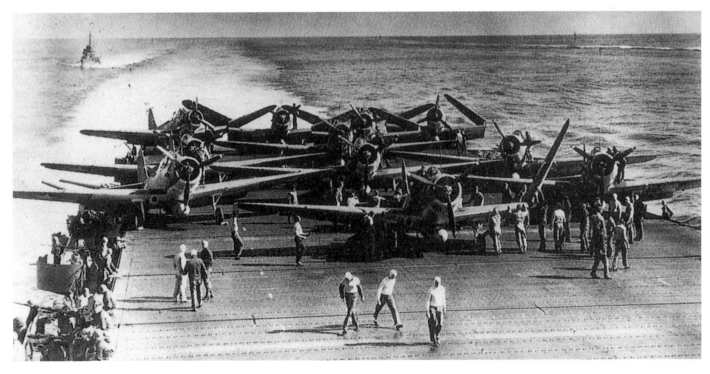

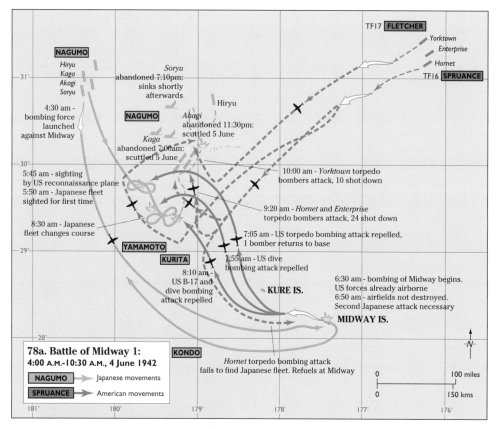

TF17 **FLETCHER**
Yorktown
Enterprise
Hornet
TF16 **SPRUANCE**

NAGUMO
Hiryu
Kaga
Akagi
Soryu

Soryu
abandoned 7:10pm:
sinks shortly
afterwards

Hiryu

4:30 am -
bombing force
launched
against Midway

NAGUMO

Akagi
abandoned 11:30pm:
scuttled 5 June

Kaga
abandoned 7:00am:
scuttled 5 June

5:45 am - sighting
by US reconnaissance plane
5:50 am - Japanese fleet
sighted for first time

10:00 am - Yorktown torpedo
bombers attack, 10 shot down

8:30 am - Japanese
fleet changes course

9:20 am - Hornet and Enterprise
torpedo bombers attack, 24 shot down

YAMAMOTO

7:05 am - US torpedo bombing attack repelled,
1 bomber returns to base

KURITA

7:55 am - US dive
bombing attack repelled

8:10 am -
US B-17 and
dive bombing
attack repelled

KURE IS.

6:30 am - bombing of Midway begins.
US forces already airborne
6:50 am - airfields not destroyed.
Second Japanese attack necessary

MIDWAY IS.

78a. Battle of Midway 1:
4:00 A.M.-10:30 A.M., 4 June 1942

| **NAGUMO** | Japanese movements |
| **SPRUANCE** | American movements |

KONDO

Hornet torpedo bombing attack
fails to find Japanese fleet. Refuels at Midway

0   100 miles
0   150 kms

Admiral Chester Nimitz, commander in chief of the U.S. Pacific Fleet, was ready for the carefully planned Japanese attack on the Midway Atoll in early June, because American cryptographers had intercepted and read the basic plans for the attack gathered from Japanese radio signals. Still, an element of luck helped the Americans, as they caught Japan's carriers unprepared and set off munitions strewn on the enemy's decks. At Midway, Nimitz won one of the decisive battles in history.

Fleet Admiral Isoruku Yamamoto commanded Japanese attacks on Pearl Harbor and Midway. He had mixed success in the Solomon Islands, before radio intercepts allowed U.S. fighters to sight and shoot down his airplane as it approached Bougainville, killing him.

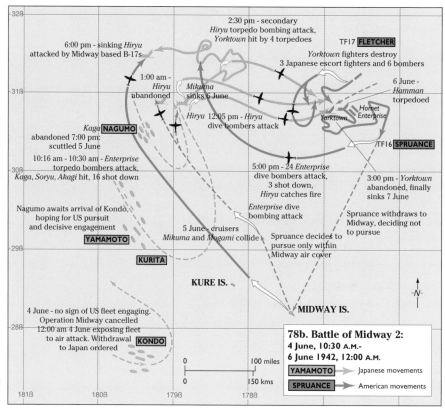

2:30 pm - secondary
Hiryu torpedo bombing attack,
Yorktown hit by 4 torpedoes

TF17 **FLETCHER**

6:00 pm - sinking Hiryu
attacked by Midway based B-17s

Yorktown fighters destroy
3 Japanese escort fighters and 6 bombers

1:00 am -
Hiryu
abandoned

Mikuma
sinks 6 June

6 June -
Hamman
torpedoed

Hiryu 12:05 pm - Hiryu
dive bombers attack

Yorktown
Hornet
Enterprise

Kaga **NAGUMO**
abandoned 7:00 pm:
scuttled 5 June

SPRUANCE TF16

10:16 am - 10:30 am - Enterprise
torpedo bombers attack,
Kaga, Soryu, Akagi hit, 16 shot down

5:00 pm - 24 Enterprise
dive bombers attack,
3 shot down,
Hiryu catches fire

3:00 pm - Yorktown
abandoned, finally
sinks 7 June

Enterprise dive
bombing attack

Nagumo awaits arrival of Kondo,
hoping for US pursuit
and decisive engagement

5 June - cruisers
Mikuma and Mogami collide

Spruance decides to
pursue only within
Midway air cover

Spruance withdraws to
Midway, deciding not
to pursue

YAMAMOTO

KURITA

KURE IS.

4 June - no sign of US fleet engaging.
Operation Midway cancelled
12:00 am 4 June exposing fleet
to air attack. Withdrawal
to Japan ordered

KONDO

MIDWAY IS.

78b. Battle of Midway 2:
4 June, 10:30 A.M.-
6 June 1942, 12:00 A.M.

| **YAMAMOTO** | Japanese movements |
| **SPRUANCE** | American movements |

0   100 miles
0   150 kms

Aleutians Force, and the Advance Submarine Force.

Japan began the overall campaign on 3 June, with an attack on the Aleutians and planned to land on Midway on 7 June. It was hoped that the Aleutians raid would act as a huge diversion and draw American forces northward, away from Midway. The islands of Attu and Kiska were occupied and air attacks were launched against U.S. installations at Dutch Harbor. Aware of the forthcoming assault on Midway, Nimitz sent only a token force of five cruisers, fourteen destroyers, and six submarines to the Aleutians, and reserved all his carriers and most of his other ships for defensive operations to the south.

With Nagumo's four carriers, *Akagi*, *Hiryu*, *Kaga*, and *Soryu* closing in on their objective, the Japanese remained ignorant of the location of Task Forces 16 and 17, and completely unaware of the reception the Americans were planning for them. Admiral Fletcher was intent upon air action against the Japanese carriers, rather than a slugging match between major fleet units, and he maneuvered to strike Nagumo's carriers from the north in a flank attack as they struck at Midway. Just before dawn on 4 June 1942, Nagumo launched his aircraft against Midway while patrol search planes flew a number of search patterns in an attempt to locate any U.S. ships in the area. But it was U.S. scout planes which found the Japanese carriers and bombing strikes were launched from Midway. When a Japanese search plane reported the presence of a U.S. surface fleet only 240 miles to the north, the Japanese were thrown into confusion. They had not anticipated a U.S. riposte so soon in the battle and their carrier aircraft were at that moment being armed with fragmentation bombs for use against the installations on Midway. To attack Fletcher's carriers they had to be rearmed with armor-piercing ordnance and torpedoes. At 7:45 A.M., the order was given to rearm the bombers and this single directive sealed the fate of Nagumo's carriers.

To the northeast, Fletcher was determined to attack the Japanese carriers without any delay and at 8 A.M. he ordered the thirty-three SBD Dauntless dive bombers from the *Enterprise*, which were already airborne, to head for the Japanese carriers without fighter cover. Dive bombers and fighters from the *Hornet* took off next, quickly followed by the remaining SBDs and Wildcats from the *Enterprise*. The U.S. attack badly misfired. The dive bombers and fighters from the *Hornet* failed to locate the Japanese carriers which had turned north to deal with Fletcher and the other squadrons, which did find Nagumo, but fell prey to Japanese fighters. Not a single enemy ship was hit. Yet just as Nagumo was ready to launch his rearmed strike aircraft, thirty-three SDB dive bombers from the *Enterprise*, led by Lieutenant Commander Wade McClusky, dropped out of the cloud base and tore down on the Japanese carriers. The Japanese Zeros, which had just

destroyed the American torpedo bombers, were still almost at sea level and could not climb quickly enough to meet this unexpected attack. As McClusky's bombers swept in, they were joined by those of Lieutenant Commander Maxwell Leslie from the *Yorktown*. Within minutes the carriers *Kaga*, *Akagi*, and *Soryu* were turned into a maelstrom of exploding bombs, wrecked aircraft, and burning fuel. Amid this inferno, the Japanese aircrews were incinerated as they sat in their planes.

As the victorious American aircraft headed back to Fletcher's carriers, they were followed by bombers and fighters from the surviving Japanese carrier, the *Hiryu*. These aircraft fought their way through the *Yorktown*'s fighter screen and hit the carrier with three bombs and two torpedoes that inflicted such damage that the *Yorktown* crew had to abandon ship. *Yorktown* remained afloat for another forty-eight hours and was eventually taken under tow by the U.S.S. *Vireo*, only to be sunk by four torpedoes from the Japanese Submarine I-168. Revenge was taken on the *Hiryu* during the afternoon of 4 June, when American bombers inflicted such heavy damage that she had to be sunk by torpedoes from Japanese destroyers. Attempts by the remainder of the Japanese fleet to engage with Task Forces 16 and 17 were frustrated by evasive action by Fletcher, and, on 5 June 1942, Japan abandoned the operation against Midway and began a general retirement to the west. Preparing for a final strike against Midway, Japanese Cruiser Division 7 (*Kumano*, *Mikuma*, *Mogami*, and *Suzuya*) was maneuvering into position to bombard Midway when a lookout sighted an American submarine. As the four heavy cruisers began to zigzag, the *Mikuma* and *Mogami* collided at twenty-eight knots. A day later, aircraft from the *Enterprise* and *Hornet* found the damaged cruisers, sank the *Mikuma*, and badly damaged the *Mogami*.

The Battle of Midway was a signal victory for the United States. It cost the Japanese four carriers and literally hundreds of its most skillful and experienced aircrews. Neither could be replaced. It was a defining moment of the war in the Pacific. The strategic initiative now shifted to the United States.

The Solomons

Although their plans had been frustrated at Midway, the Japanese were still intent upon taking Port Moresby on the southern coast of New Guinea and upon consolidating their position in the Solomons. At the same time, the Americans decided on a step-by-step strategy for their own offensive in the southwest Pacific, but while their plans were being developed, the Japanese landed troops on the north coast of New Guinea on 21 July 1942. Their plan to take Port Moresby by amphibious assault had been frustrated at the Battle of the Coral Sea. The Japanese now attempted to secure their

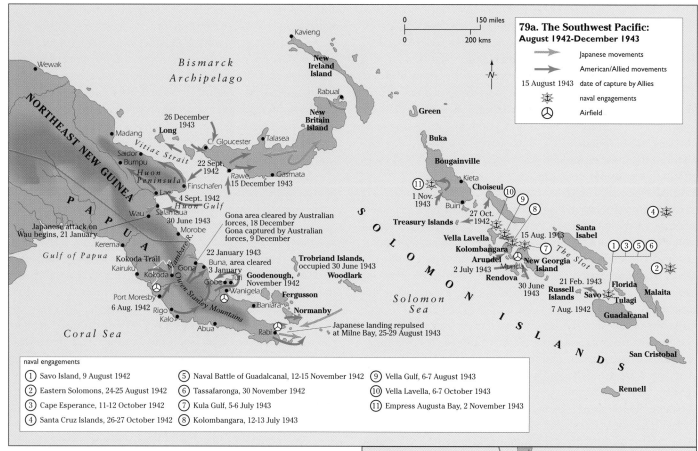

79a. The Southwest Pacific:
August 1942–December 1943

→ Japanese movements

→ American/Allied movements

15 August 1943 date of capture by Allies

⚔ naval engagements

✈ Airfield

naval engagements

① Savo Island, 9 August 1942

② Eastern Solomons, 24-25 August 1942

③ Cape Esperance, 11-12 October 1942

④ Santa Cruz Islands, 26-27 October 1942

⑤ Naval Battle of Guadalcanal, 12-15 November 1942

⑥ Tassafaronga, 30 November 1942

⑦ Kula Gulf, 5-6 July 1943

⑧ Kolombangara, 12-13 July 1943

⑨ Vella Gulf, 6-7 August 1943

⑩ Vella Lavella, 6-7 October 1943

⑪ Empress Augusta Bay, 2 November 1943

objective by following an overland route along a precipitous jungle track which wound through the foothills of the Owen Stanley Ranges, known as the Kokoda Trail.

General MacArthur rushed Australian reinforcements to New Guinea, but the tactical situation was complicated by a Japanese landing at Milne Bay, on the eastern tip of Papua, which threatened the Allied forward airbase recently established there. The combined Australian-American garrison, supported by fighter aircraft of the Royal Australian Air Force, crushed this enemy bridgehead in bloody, close-range combat and achieved the distinction of being the first Allied force to destroy a Japanese beachhead and to throw the attackers back into the sea. News of this decisive victory raised the morale of Allied troops throughout the Far East and the Pacific.

Countering the Japanese on the Kokoda Trail took longer. Wracked by malaria and dysentery, the Australians were outnumbered at the front by almost five to one. The Japanese also suffered. Close to starvation, they began a fighting withdrawal on 26 September. The Australians reoccupied Kokoda before American reinforcements could come into action. The American and Australian troops then went forward together against the Japanese enclaves at Gona, Buna, and Sanananda. Casual-

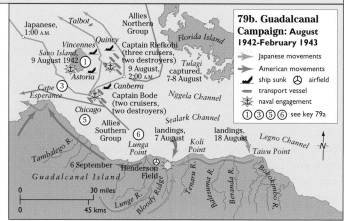

79b. Guadalcanal Campaign: August 1942–February 1943

→ Japanese movements

→ American movements

⚓ ship sunk ✈ airfield

⬡ transport vessel

⚔ naval engagement

①③⑤⑥ see key 79a

ties were heavy, but by 22 January 1943, after six months of some of the most difficult campaigning of World War II, the Japanese forces in Papua had been destroyed.

During this same period, U.S. Marines were fighting in the Solomon Islands and making progress toward Rabaul. On 7 August 1942, the first stage of the offensive began with amphibious landings by the 1st U.S. Marine Division on Guadalcanal and Tulagi. The Japanese garrison and the construction troops, building the airstrip that was to become known as Henderson Field, were taken completely by surprise. As Rear Admiral Fletcher's task force opened fire, the enemy fled into the jungle. The initial Japanese response to the U.S. landing came from the air with bombing attacks on the task force and the airfield once it was captured by the Americans. Japanese commanders also sent a surface force under Vice Admiral Gunichi Mikawa to counter the U.S. invasion.

To reach the transports of the amphibious force supporting the landing on Guadalcanal, the Japanese warships had to sail through the passage, known as the Slot, between the Solomons group of islands. Before entering Iron Bottom Sound, between Guadalcanal and Tulagi, where the American transports were congregated, the Japanese had to swing to the north or south of Savo Island, which lay across the southern end of the Slot. The possible routes were patrolled by Allied ships: The cruisers H.M.A.S. *Canberra* and U.S.S. *Chicago* with two U.S. destroyers were patrolling to the south of Savo Island and the cruisers U.S.S. *Astoria*, *Quincy*, and *Vincennes*, also with two destroyers, to the north.

As the Japanese approached Savo Island they slipped past the advance radar picket and took the southern group of Allied warships by surprise in the early hours of 9 August. At 1:36 A.M., on 9 August, Mikawa launched torpedoes and opened a deadly barrage of gunfire against the Allied cruisers. The Japanese had trained assiduously in the problems of night action between surface fleets, and their 23-inch oxygen torpedoes, which could deliver 770 pounds of explosive to a range of nine miles at a speed of 45 knots, were weapons that American cruisers, generally not equipped with torpedo tubes, simply could not match. The *Canberra* was struck by two torpedoes and battered into a flaming wreck by gunfire, while the *Chicago* was damaged, though not seriously, by a single torpedo. The second group of Allied cruisers, which still did not realize that the enemy was upon it, was shattered by another concentrated salvo of gunfire and torpedoes. Within moments the *Astoria*, *Quincy*, and *Vincennes* were reduced to exploding hulks. Fortunately for the Americans, the Japanese, content with their night's work, turned back before they reached the American troop transports and supply ships. The greater prize was spared.

Fearing for the safety of his carriers, Fletcher withdrew his covering force, including the battleship *North Carolina*, six cruisers, and sixteen destroyers, to a position southwest of Guadalcanal. Though left without protection, Rear Admiral Richmond Kelly Turner pressed on with the unloading of the U.S. Marines's supplies and equipment, and only withdrew his amphibious force on 9 August. For the next fourteen days, the 17,000 U.S. Marines on Guadalcanal and Tulagi remained virtually isolated. During this time they blocked further attempts by the Japanese to land troops. Admiral Fletcher,

now back on patrol off the Solomons, sank a carrier supporting a Japanese reinforcement convoy and suffered damage only to the *Enterprise* in return. The Japanese went to enormous lengths to push reinforcements and supplies into the battle for the Solomons. Japanese destroyers and cruisers timed their passage down the Slot so that they arrived off Gaudalcanal in darkness. Once their cargoes had been landed, the Japanese paused to shell the U.S. Marines's positions and Henderson Field, and then steamed through the Slot at high speed. So regular and well timed were these missions that the marines nicknamed the Japanese ships the "Tokyo Express."

Both sides continued to feed new troops into the battle as quickly as their resources would allow, and the Americans paid a heavy cost to maintain their naval presence off Guadalcanal. By the middle of September 1942, the Americans had lost the *Wasp* to enemy torpedoes, and the carrier *Saratoga*, the battleship *North Carolina*, and the destroyer *O'Brien* were damaged and forced to make for harbor.

On Guadalcanal, the Japanese suffered appalling casualties in piecemeal frontal attacks against U.S. Marine positions. There were also losses for the Japanese at sea, when the ships of the Tokyo Express were intercepted by American warships guarding the Slot. The Americans' trump card was Henderson Field which had been flying operational sorties since 20 August. No matter how successful the Japanese navy might be at night, daylight saw U.S. fighters and bombers dominating the air over Guadalcanal and American control of the waters around the island was reasserted. Events reached fever pitch in the middle of October as the 20,000 Japanese troops on Guadalcanal launched an all out offensive against Henderson Field. The U.S. Marines were waiting and the Japanese attacks were turned back with heavy casualties. At sea, the Japanese fared better, and on 26 October, they sank the *Hornet* and damaged the *Enterprise*, the *South Dakota*, and the cruiser, *San Juan*, while suffering bomb damage to two of their carriers.

Further desperate night actions between U.S. and Japanese warships took place along the Slot and especially in Iron Bottom Sound, including the night action of 14 November, one of the few battleship-to-battleship actions of the war. But by the end of that month, the Allies finally and irrevocably gained control of the seas around the southern Solomons. As the Japanese troops on Guadalcanal reached the point of starvation, the American XIV Corps, commanded by Lieutenant General Alexander Patch, set out to drive the Japanese into the sea once and for all. But the Japanese, recognizing painful signs of final defeat, withdrew the 13,000 starving, disease-ridden survivors of the Japanese garrison by sea without the Americans being aware of what was happening. Guadalcanal was now safely in Allied hands, but the cost of the six-month battle was high for both sides. For the Allies, the threat to

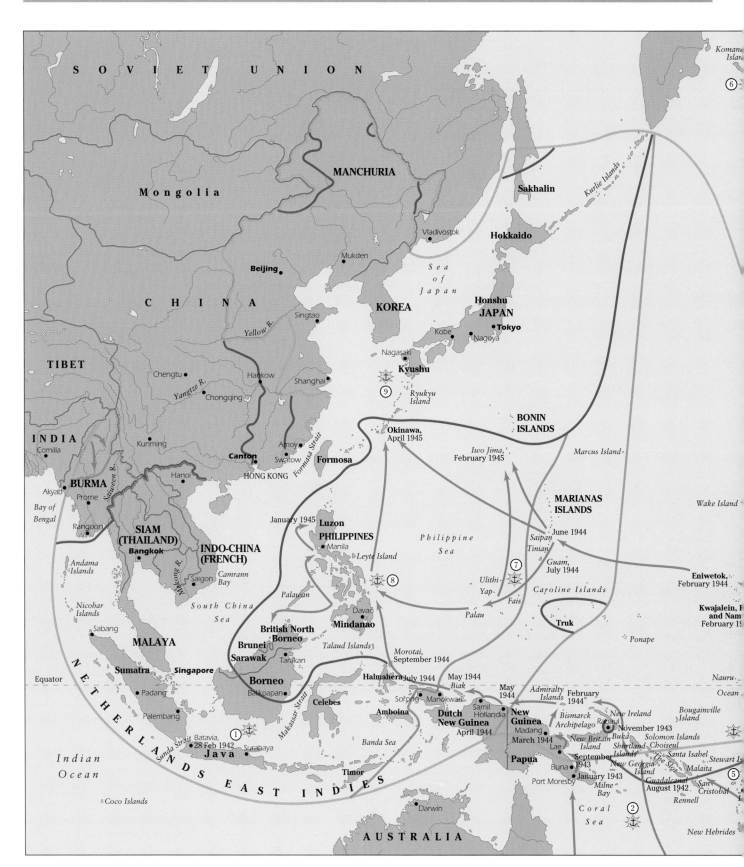

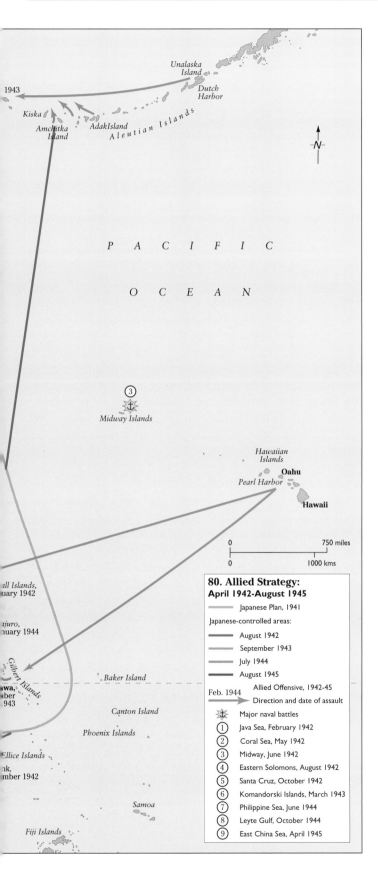

**80. Allied Strategy:
April 1942-August 1945**

Japanese Plan, 1941

Japanese-controlled areas:

August 1942

September 1943

July 1944

August 1945

Feb. 1944   Allied Offensive, 1942-45

Direction and date of assault

⚓   Major naval battles

①   Java Sea, February 1942

②   Coral Sea, May 1942

③   Midway, June 1942

④   Eastern Solomons, August 1942

⑤   Santa Cruz, October 1942

⑥   Komandorski Islands, March 1943

⑦   Philippine Sea, June 1944

⑧   Leyte Gulf, October 1944

⑨   East China Sea, April 1945

Australia and the lines of communication had been lifted and the Japanese were now strategically firmly on the defensive. Perhaps more importantly, the aura of Japanese invincibility was shattered in New Guinea and on Guadalcanal.

For 1943, the Joint Chiefs decided upon three main operations in the Pacific. In the south, U.S. forces would advance on Rabaul; in the center, they would capture the Gilbert Islands; and in the north, they would evict the Japanese from the Aleutians. The Japanese had been able to land some reinforcements on the Aleutians, but as American sea power in the north Pacific increased, the Japanese garrison was effectively cut off from significant support. On 11 May 1943, a U.S. task force, including an escort carrier and three battleships, landed troops of the 7th Division, under Major General Albert Brown, on Attu. The landing was not opposed, but the Japanese, who had withdrawn their troops to the mountains, fought to the death before the island was finally cleared on 29 May. Kiska was heavily bombed, and on 15 August, 30,000 American troops and 5,000 Canadians went ashore to find that the garrison of 6,000 men had been secretly evacuated to Japan two weeks earlier.

While events were unfolding in the north Pacific, operations in the south had begun at the end of June with MacArthur's troops fighting their way up the New Guinea coast, striking some Japanese garrisons, and bypassing others. Salamaua fell to the Australian 29th Infantry Brigade, and Lae was also captured by Australian troops. Finschafen was taken by amphibious assault on 2 October, and with the fall of Sattelberg, it was clear that the Allies were winning the battle for the Huon Peninsula. But the Japanese defense seldom slackened. Garrisons had to be destroyed in bitter fighting, and gradually there was a change in Allied strategy by which U.S. troops assumed the operational role of Australian units in New Guinea. The Australians were used increasingly to relieve U.S. divisions that had occupied island bases during the advance, but which had not cleared the enemy from the interior. The Australians suffered considerably in MacArthur's hands and of the 24,000 casualties among his ground troops in 1943, 17,000 were Australian.

While the assault on the Huon Peninsula was in progress, the offensive in the central Solomons was breaking over New Georgia. The fighting was undertaken by a task force commanded by Admiral Halsey and by the 43rd U.S. Division in cooperation with U.S. Marine Raiders and Fijian commandos. Rendova was taken against only fitful opposition, but from the beginning the main campaign on New Georgia went badly, as the 43rd U.S. Division suffered heavy casualties in the swamps, hills, and jungles of the island. It was not until the end of August that the whole of New Georgia was occupied. As the battle for New Georgia raged, Admiral Halsey worked

New Georgia Island, the Japanese stronghold in the Solomon Islands northwest of Guadalcanal, contained an airfield at Munda Point, and when U.S. Marines and army troops landed on the island in July 1943, Japan rushed in reinforcements to protect the vital facility. These are some of the U.S. casualties being moved out on stretchers.

out his strategy for dealing with the remaining Japanese-held islands in the group: Arundel, Kolombangara, and Vella Lavella. Assault landings were carried out on Arundel and Vella Lavella, but Halsey bypassed the 11,000-strong garrison on Kolombangara. With Arundel and Vella Lavella occupied by U.S. and New Zealand troops, the Japanese evacuated Kolombangara and Halsey was able to concentrate on his next step, the invasion of Bougainville. Kolombangara was the first example of a planned leapfrogging strategy being put into action, and it rapidly became the normal policy in the Pacific theater.

Plans were already being drawn up for an offensive by U.S. amphibious forces in Micronesia, a collection of some 1,000 tiny islands dispersed in four main groups that had been occupied by the Japanese during the first month of hostilities. Moving from east to west, amphibious task forces invaded the Gilbert Islands, then the Marshall Islands, before reaching the 550 islands of the Caroline group, which spread across about

2,000 miles of the Pacific. The ultimate prize was the Marianas Islands, reaching 400 miles from Guam to a point only about 500 miles from Iwo Jima. With Micronesia in their hands, the Allies would control the strategic route between the United States and the Philippines and dominate a crucial sector of the Japanese defense perimeter. The offensive was conceived as a step-by-step, fighting approach by the Pacific Fleet with individual islands providing the stepping stones.

Although the conquest of New Guinea and the Solomons would prove to be important, the key to final victory was the central Pacific, much as Plan Orange had envisaged. MacArthur disagreed, believing instead that an advance to the Philippines via the south Pacific along the northern coast of New Guinea and Mindanao would be shorter and quicker. The Quadrant Conference in Quebec, on 14 August 1943, authorized a central Pacific strategy that projected Allied power from the Gilbert Islands to the Marianas. This ambitious offensive also took in the islands of Ponape, Truk, Palau, Yap, and Guam. Concurrently, the advance in the southwest Pacific continued with operations in New Guinea that led to the capture of the Vogelkop Peninsula at the northwest tip of the island, and via the neutralization of the Admiralty Islands, the Bismarck Archipelago, and Rabaul. The twin advances through the central and southwest Pacific campaigns were mutually supporting, but the central drive took overriding priority.

The China-Burma-India Theater

In the China-Burma-India theater (CBI), the United States' interests were controlled by Lieutenant General Joseph Stilwell (a fluent Chinese speaker) who served as chief of staff to the supreme commander of the China theater, Generalissimo Chiang Kai-shek. As the senior United States officer, Stilwell effectively commanded all American and Chinese forces in the CBI from the spring of 1942 to the autumn of 1944. Amid a web of political tension, strategic intrigue, and outright confusion, Stilwell attempted to improve the fighting capabilities of China's armies and the efficacy of America's military aid. He led his Chinese troops in the battle to recapture northern Burma, where they were supported by the three battalions of Merrill's Marauders, and also served as deputy supreme allied commander in Southeast Asia Command. The China Air Task Force (later Tenth Air Force), commanded by Major General Claire Chennault, fought under Stilwell. It ferried supplies from India over the Himalayas to China and launched bombing raids on Japanese forces in China and Formosa with B-24s and B-29s that were based on vulnerable air fields in southeast China. The strategic importance of Stilwell's command to the United States was gradually undermined, however, by the success of the island-hopping campaign across the Pacific.

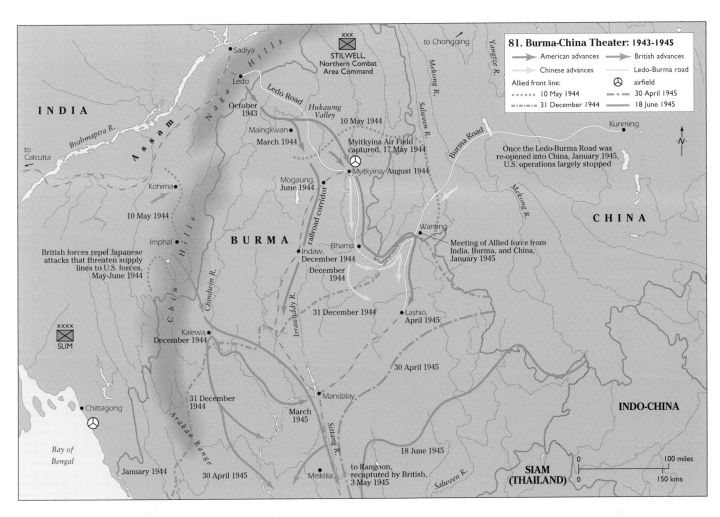

81. Burma-China Theater: 1943-1945

American advances → British advances →
Chinese advances → Ledo-Burma road
Allied front line: airfield
10 May 1944 · · · · 30 April 1945
31 December 1944 · — · 18 June 1945

to Chongqing

INDIA

Brahmaptra R.

to Calcutta

Sadiya

Naga Hills

STILWELL, Northern Combat Area Command

Ledo

Ledo Road

October 1943

Hukawng Valley

10 May 1944

Maingkwan March 1944

Myitkyina Air Field captured, 17 May 1944

Myitkyina August 1944

Mekong R.

Salween R.

Burma Road

Kunming

Once the Ledo-Burma Road was re-opened into China, January 1945, U.S. operations largely stopped

Kohima

10 May 1944

Mogaung, June 1944

railroad corridor

CHINA

Imphal

British forces repel Japanese attacks that threaten supply lines to U.S. forces, May-June 1944

BURMA

Chindwin R.

Bhamo

Indaw, December 1944

December 1944

Wanting

Mekong R.

Meeting of Allied force from India, Burma, and China, January 1945

Chin Hills

31 December 1944

Lashio, April 1945

Kalewa, December 1944

SLIM

Irrawaddy R.

30 April 1945

INDO-CHINA

Chittagong

Arakan Range

31 December 1944

Mandalay

March 1945

Sittang R.

Bay of Bengal

January 1944

30 April 1945

Meiktila

18 June 1945

to Rangoon, recaptured by British, 3 May 1945

Salween R.

SIAM (THAILAND)

0   100 miles
0   150 kms

N

Dual Advance

In the south Pacific, the Cartwheel offensives were going forward under Halsey and MacArthur's command. The 40,000 Japanese troops on Bougainville were initially leapfrogged in favor of an assault on the Treasury Islands by the 8th New Zealand Brigade. When landings were made on Bougainville, nearly 40,000 Japanese troops were cut off to be mopped up by Australian militia brigades in a costly and largely pointless campaign.

Although the principal aim of Cartwheel had been the destruction of the Japanese garrison in Rabaul, it was decided while the campaign was underway to bypass this objective rather than capture it. With Allied air power within range of Rabaul, the harbor, airfields, and installations were neutralized by fighter and bomber attack, and an amphibious or land assault was considered unnecessary. From February 1944, the Japanese base at Rabaul remained intact, but in a strategic limbo, until the end of the war. Rabaul was part of an offensive pattern that was to become paramount in Allied operations in the Pacific. An assault against a strongly fortified island or base

would be declined, whenever possible, if its target was a Japanese garrison that was strategically unimportant. The coordinated application of land, sea, and air power under a single, unified command became the essential process leading to victory.

An obvious factor in Allied policy in the Pacific was how to achieve the defeat of Japan in the quickest time and with the fewest possible casualties. There appeared to be three options: Invade the Japanese home islands; blockade the home islands by sea and air; or attempt to bomb the Japanese into submission. The Allies believed that Japan would not surrender until its armed forces were destroyed at home and abroad. A combination of bombing and blockade offered the Allies the hope that Japan's ability to prosecute the war would be curtailed to the point at which an invasion, while costly, would not be disastrous in terms of casualties. Bases on Formosa and in eastern China would be required to carry out an effective bombing campaign. The prime objective in the Far East, therefore, became the seizure of strategic bases from which a sustained bomber offensive could be conducted against Japan. To

145

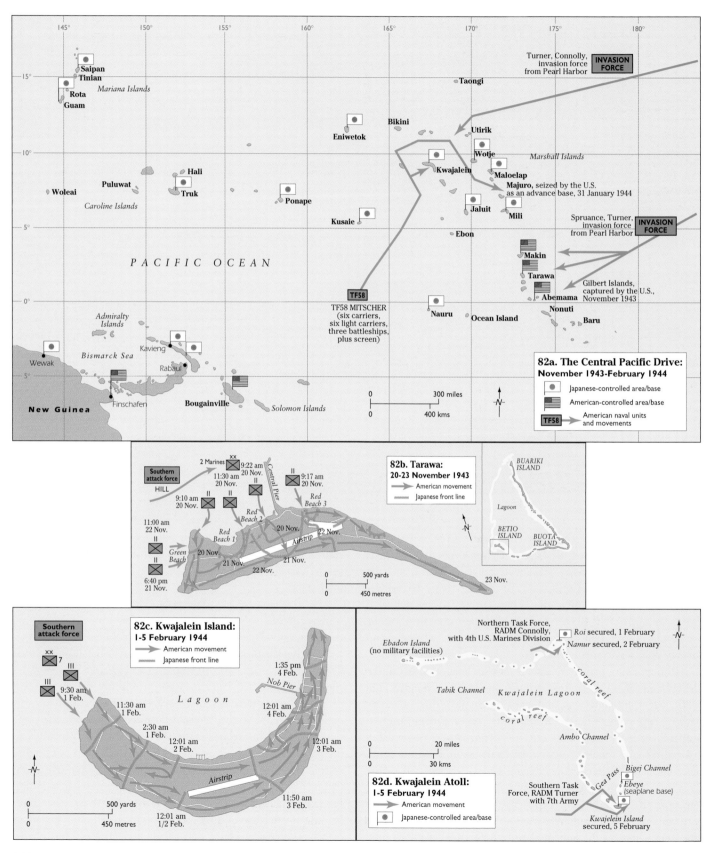

82a. The Central Pacific Drive:
November 1943–February 1944

- Japanese-controlled area/base
- American-controlled area/base
- **TF58** American naval units and movements

TF58 MITSCHER
(six carriers,
six light carriers,
three battleships,
plus screen)

Turner, Connolly,
invasion force
from Pearl Harbor — **INVASION FORCE**

Spruance, Turner,
invasion force
from Pearl Harbor — **INVASION FORCE**

Majuro, seized by the U.S.
as an advance base, 31 January 1944

Gilbert Islands,
captured by the U.S.,
November 1943

PACIFIC OCEAN

Mariana Islands — Saipan, Tinian, Rota, Guam

Caroline Islands — Woleai, Puluwat, Hali, Truk, Ponape, Kusaie

Marshall Islands — Taongi, Bikini, Utirik, Wotje, Kwajalein, Maloelap, Eniwetok, Jaluit, Mili, Ebon

Makin, Tarawa, Abemama, Nonuti, Baru

Nauru, Ocean Island

Admiralty Islands, Kavieng, Rabaul, Wewak, Bismarck Sea, Finschafen, Bougainville, Solomon Islands, New Guinea

300 miles / 400 kms

82b. Tarawa:
20–23 November 1943

→ American movement
— Japanese front line

Southern attack force
HILL
2 Marines
9:22 am 20 Nov.
11:30 am 20 Nov.
9:10 am 20 Nov.
9:17 am 20 Nov.
Central Pier
Red Beach 2
Red Beach 3
Red Beach 1
Green Beach
Airstrip
11:00 am 22 Nov.
20 Nov.
21 Nov.
22 Nov.
21 Nov.
6:40 pm 21 Nov.
23 Nov.

BUARIKI ISLAND
Lagoon
BETIO ISLAND
BUOTA ISLAND

500 yards / 450 metres

82c. Kwajalein Island:
1–5 February 1944

→ American movement
— Japanese front line

Southern attack force
7
9:30 am 1 Feb.
Lagoon
11:30 am 1 Feb.
2:30 am 1 Feb.
12:01 am 2 Feb.
1:35 pm 4 Feb.
Nob Pier
12:01 am 4 Feb.
12:01 am 3 Feb.
11:50 am 3 Feb.
12:01 am 1/2 Feb.
Airstrip

500 yards / 450 metres

82d. Kwajalein Atoll:
1–5 February 1944

→ American movement
- Japanese-controlled area/base

Northern Task Force,
RADM Connolly,
with 4th U.S. Marines Division
Roi secured, 1 February
Namur secured, 2 February

Ebadon Island
(no military facilities)

Tabik Channel
Kwajalein Lagoon
coral reef
Ambo Channel
Bigej Channel
Gea Pass
Ebeye
(seaplane base)

Southern Task
Force, RADM Turner
with 7th Army

Kwajalein Island
secured, 5 February

20 miles / 30 kms

Between 20 and 29 November 1943, U.S. forces initiated the Central Pacific Campaign by occupying six atolls of the Gilbert Islands. The heaviest fighting occurred when U.S. Marines assaulted Betio Island in the Tarawa Atoll and when Army troops, shown above wading ashore on Butaritari Island, north of Tarawa, took Makin Atoll.

acquire the sites for these bases, the southwest and central Pacific offensives were given priority in order to secure the Philippines-Formosa–east China triangle. Also with the new B-29s in mind (with an operational range of 1,500 miles), and given the almost certain logistical problems of operating squadrons from China, the seizure of the Marianas Islands was seen as urgent. The strategic directive for Admiral Nimitz in 1944 stressed the need to take the Marshall Islands, Ponape, Truk, and the Marianas.

Central Pacific Drive

The first assault in the central Pacific struck the Gilbert Islands in November 1943 in overwhelming strength. The Fifth Fleet, under Vice Admiral Raymond Spruance, could call upon some nineteen aircraft carriers, twelve battleships, and a complementary range of cruisers and escort vessels. The administrative and logistical support to the Fifth Fleet at sea over an extended period was a crucial problem, and the answer was found in a floating supply train. This provided oil tankers, ammunition ships, repair ships, tugs, hospital ships, and supply vessels which together formed a floating base that followed the fleet wherever the fighting led it.

In a tactical scenario that was to be repeated many times in locations across the central Pacific, the amphibious assault by the 27th Division at Butaritari in the Makin Atoll on 20 November was preceded by air strikes on the defenses, by a two-hour bombardment by warships of the fire support group, and by rocket and machine gun strafing. The assault on Betio, the main island in the Tarawa Atoll, one hundred miles to the south, encountered in-depth fortifications that stretched from the surrounding reef across the beach, and on 20 November, the U.S. Marines of the 2nd Division found themselves involved in one of the most difficult amphibious assaults in history. The epithet "Bloody Tarawa" was cruelly earned.

The assault on Kwajalein Atoll, the command center of the Marshalls, on 1 February 1944, was so successful that Nimitz quickly pressed on with a landing on Eniwetok on 17 February, nearly six weeks ahead of schedule. Despite heavy fighting, within five days the Marshalls were effectively in American hands. The unexpected speed of these successes meant that the planned timetable for the Pacific in 1944 could be advanced and Nimitz suggested to the Joint Chiefs of Staff that the landings in the Marianas be brought forward to 15 June 1944, and that Truk, in the Carolina Islands, should be neutralized rather than occupied. A mighty war machine had arrived in the Pacific: The fast carrier task force and the all-arms amphibious assault underpinned by the most powerful industrial nation the world had ever seen.

As MacArthur advanced towards the Philippines, Nimitz pushed to the northwest towards Japan itself and southwest towards Leyte Gulf. But the Marianas were crucial, since the larger islands of the group—Guam, Saipan, and Tinian—would provide bases from which B-29s could reach Japan. No less important was the fact that this island group stood across Japan's communications with the territories it had occupied in

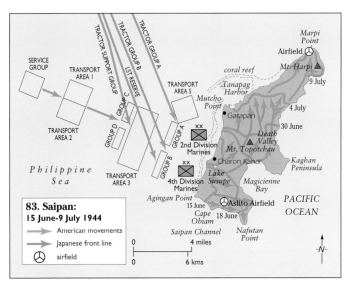

On 15 June 1944, U.S. troops began landing on Saipan, the largest of and the most strongly defended of the Marianas Islands, and a part of Japan's inner defensive perimeter. U.S. Marines, shown here, picked their way through Garapan, the largest town on Saipan. Loss of the pre-war possession led to the downfall of Prime Minister Hideki Tojo's government and gave the Americans airbases within range of Japan's home islands.

Malaya and the Dutch East Indies. This strategic weight brought together on the U.S. side a Fifth Fleet stronger than any force in any previous assault landing in the Pacific. Vice Admiral Mark Mitscher's Fast Carrier Force alone included fifteen fleet carriers, nearly a thousand aircraft, seven battleships, twenty-one cruisers, and sixty-nine destroyers. A screen

of twenty-eight submarines sailed ahead of the main fleet and the aircraft of eleven escort carriers provided close-in cover and ground support. The landing force, under Turner, totaled 127,000 men mainly from the 2nd and 4th U.S. Marine Divisions and the U.S. Army's 27th Infantry Division. The first landing was on Saipan with subsequent assaults against Guam and Tinian.

As the U.S. Marines stormed ashore on Saipan, Vice Admiral Jisaburo Ozawa, with the Japanese Mobile Fleet of nine carriers, five battleships, and thirteen cruisers, sortied from Tawi Tawi to intercept Mitscher. The Battle of the Philippine Sea began in earnest on 19 June, when the American submarine *Albacore* torpedoed Ozawa's flagship, the carrier *Taiho*, which blew up that afternoon. The main fleet action opened with a Japanese strike of 326 aircraft against the task forces. The U.S. fighter defense tore the heart out of the attacks, and the antiaircraft fire of Spruance's battleships destroyed most of the aircraft that eluded the fighters. The Japanese scored only one bomb hit, while losing 240 aircraft. The Japanese lost so many aircraft so quickly, that the air engagement was christened "the Marianas Turkey Shoot." In return, American aircraft from the Fast Carrier Force sank the carrier *Hiyo*, and badly damaged the battleship *Haruna* and the carriers *Chiyoda* and *Zuikaku*. Ozawa decided that retreat was the order of the day, and the Mobile Fleet turned for home. The Battle of the Philippine Sea virtually destroyed the air arm of the Japanese

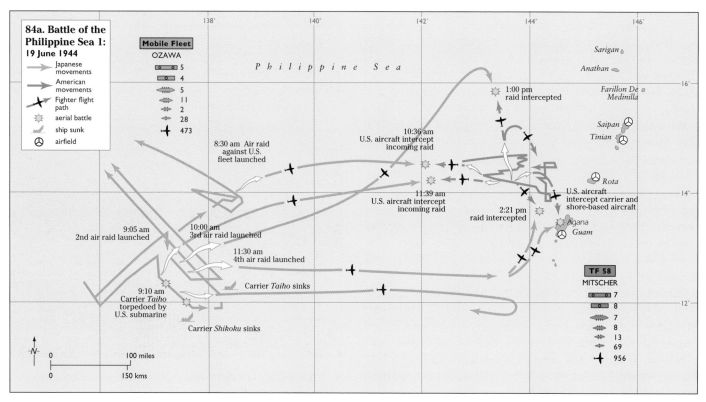

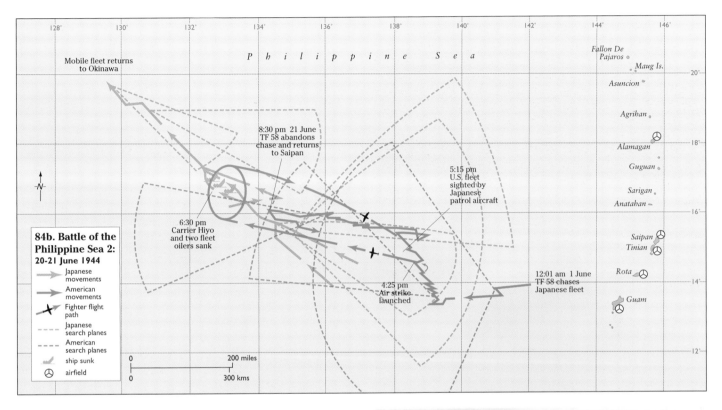

84b. Battle of the
Philippine Sea 2:
20-21 June 1944

- Japanese movements
- American movements
- Fighter flight path
- Japanese search planes
- American search planes
- ship sunk
- airfield

0   200 miles
0   300 kms

Philippine Sea

Mobile fleet returns
to Okinawa

8:30 pm 21 June
TF 58 abandons
chase and returns
to Saipan

5:15 pm
U.S. fleet
sighted by
Japanese
patrol aircraft

6:30 pm
Carrier Hiyo
and two fleet
oilers sank

4:25 pm
Air strike
launched

12:01 am 1 June
TF 58 chases
Japanese fleet

*Fallon De
Pajaros*

Maug Is.

Asuncion

Agrihan

Alamagan

Guguan

Sarigan

Anatahan

Saipan

Tinian

Rota

Guam

navy, rendering it impotent for the rest of the war.

On the islands, the Japanese defenders dissipated their strength in suicidal *banzai* charges, although not without inflicting heavy casualties on the attackers. Crushing bombardments by American battleships and cruisers destroyed the visible enemy defenses on Guam, but those concealed in caves survived to cause the U.S. Marines endless problems. Sniping continued until the end of the war and the last Japanese soldier on Guam surrendered in 1972.

With Nimitz advancing in the central Pacific, the U.S. Seventh Fleet, together with the VII Amphibious Force, carried out assault landings in New Guinea beginning in April 1944. From there they pressed on to Morotai and Peleliu, midway between New Guinea and the Philippines. MacArthur's springboard for his return to the Philippines was in place by October 1944, but the strategy of fighting for the Philippines was not widely supported especially in the U.S. Navy. President Roosevelt's express authority launched MacArthur's invasion of the Philippines but only four of the 7,000 islands comprising the Philippine Archipelago were considered militarily significant enough to merit capture. These were Mindanao in the south, Leyte and Mindoro in the center, and Luzon in the north. When reconnaissance flights over Mindanao reported few aircraft stationed there, the Joint Chiefs ordered MacArthur to bypass the island and to attack Leyte on 20 October 1944 and Luzon on 20 December.

In July 1944, six U.S battleships, including the New Mexico
(above), covered U.S. landings on Guam, a prewar U.S. possession.

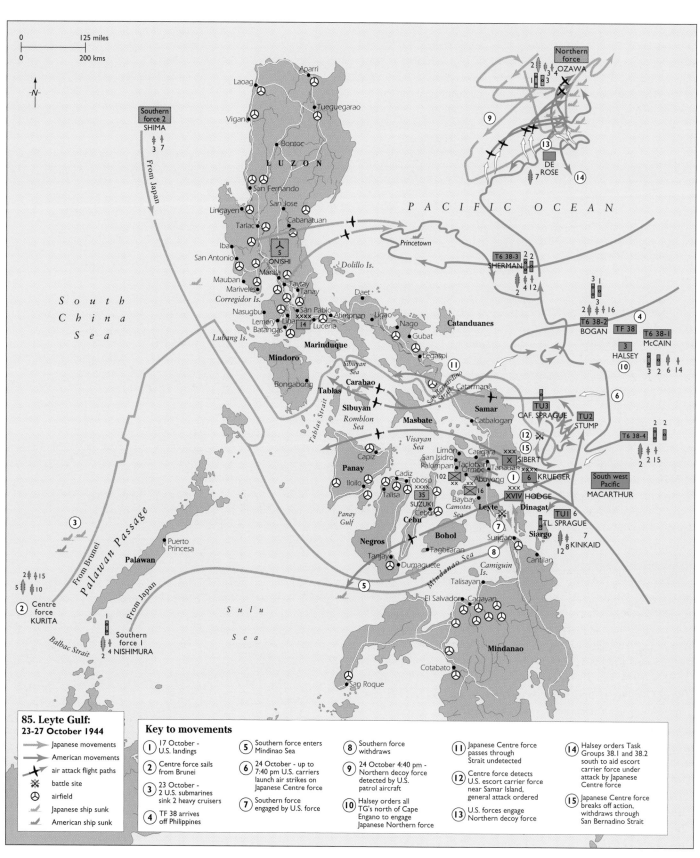

85. Leyte Gulf:
23-27 October 1944

→ Japanese movements
→ American movements
✕ air attack flight paths
✕ battle site
⊗ airfield
⚓ Japanese ship sunk
⚓ American ship sunk

Key to movements

① 17 October - U.S. landings

② Centre force sails from Brunei

③ 23 October - 2 U.S. submarines sink 2 heavy cruisers

④ TF 38 arrives off Philippines

⑤ Southern force enters Mindinao Sea

⑥ 24 October - up to 7:40 pm U.S. carriers launch air strikes on Japanese Centre force

⑦ Southern force engaged by U.S. force

⑧ Southern force withdraws

⑨ 24 October 4:40 pm - Northern decoy force detected by U.S. patrol aircraft

⑩ Halsey orders all TG's north of Cape Engano to engage Japanese Northern force

⑪ Japanese Centre force passes through Strait undetected

⑫ Centre force detects U.S. escort carrier force near Samar Island, general attack ordered

⑬ U.S. forces engage Northern decoy force

⑭ Halsey orders Task Groups 38.1 and 38.2 south to aid escort carrier force under attack by Japanese Centre force

⑮ Japanese Centre force breaks off action, withdraws through San Bernadino Strait

Battle of Leyte Gulf

Naval leaders were reluctant to invade the Philippines, preferring instead to bypass the islands and attack Formosa, but they abandoned opposition to invading the Philippines when they concluded that Japan would have to commit the remainder of its navy to defense of the former American possession. When patrol planes from Admiral Halsey's fleet reported few Japanese aircraft in the southern Philippines, Leyte, in the center of the islands, became the focus of an amphibious assault mounted by 200,000 men of the Sixth U.S. Army and 500 ships. By noon on 20 October, General MacArthur, following in the wake of the U.S. X and XXIV Corps, waded ashore to achieve a dramatic return to the Philippines for the world's newsreels. The U.S. landings brought the desired naval response from the Japanese in the form of a complex, three-pronged attack. Despite a number of anxious moments for the Americans as Japanese warships came close to gaining a telling advantage, the Battle of Leyte Gulf ended as a stunning American victory. Among the many triumphs in the course of the battle, aircraft of the U.S. Third Fleet accounted for all four of Ozawa's carriers. Ominously, the Battle of Leyte Gulf also witnessed the first example of what was to become a deadly tactic of the war in the Pacific, when Japanese suicide planes targeted American carriers in *kamikaze* attacks.

The defense of Leyte, ruthlessly and bloodily prosecuted, destroyed five Japanese divisions, a significant number of aircraft, and thousands of tons of shipping, all to little purpose except to delay the inevitable. The battle for Luzon, during which MacArthur directed an amphibious landing at the southern end of the gulf, followed by the construction of airfields, an advance into the Central Plain, and the seizure of Manila, began in earnest on 9 January 1945 as troops of the

Sixth U.S. Army, under General Walter Krueger, stormed ashore at Lingayen Gulf from the ships of the Seventh U.S. Fleet under Admiral Thomas Kinkaid. The Japanese slowly

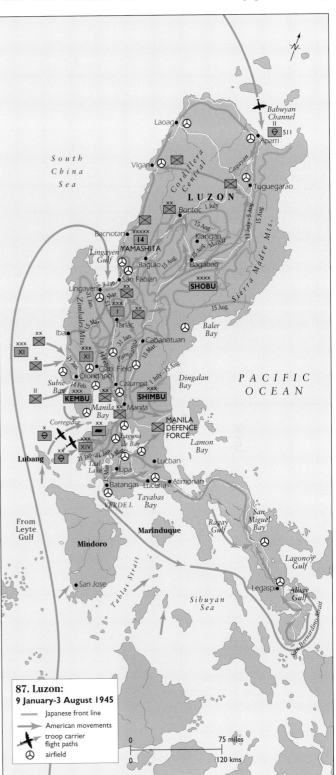

87. Luzon: 9 January-3 August 1945
- Japanese front line
- American movements
- troop carrier flight paths
- airfield

0   75 miles
0   120 kms

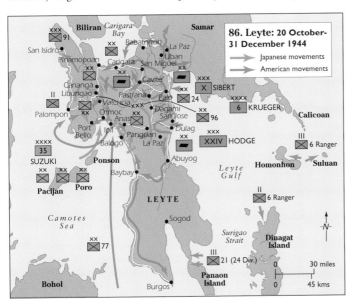

86. Leyte: 20 October-31 December 1944
- Japanese movements
- American movements

0   30 miles
0   45 kms

could be escorted all the way to their targets by P-51 Mustangs and P-47 Thunderbolts. The eight-square mile island was heavily defended by some 21,000 men, with the advantage of a formidable position in depth. The Japanese fought a largely static battle anchored on Mount Suribachi, and the initial landings on the beaches were not opposed. Instead, Suribachi and the plateau between airfields 2 and 3 were crisscrossed with over 600 gun emplacements and pillboxes, as well as a complex system of cave defenses and deep shelters.

An extended battering of the island was carried out by the 7th U.S.A.F. from the Marianas and by U.S. Navy bombardment before the Fifth U.S. Amphibious Corps, comprising the 3rd, 4th, and 5th U.S. Marine Divisions, went ashore. Even so, the 4th and 5th Divisions found themselves pinned down by accurate fire which was being directed by observers on Suribachi. Despite bitter fighting, the U.S. Marines scaled Suribachi on 23 February, but Iwo Jima was not secured until 26

Japan first employed suicide attacks against U.S. ships out of desperation during the Battle of Leyte Gulf, when kamikazes *sank one carrier and damaged five others, also damaging one cruiser and several destroyers. The U.S.S.* Saratoga *(above) was hit by a* kamikaze *attack on 21 February 1945 off Iwo Jima. Despite terrible damage, the carrier was able to leave the area using its own power to get to safety. Three months later at Bikini atoll, the* Saratoga *was sunk in atomic bomb tests. During the Okinawa campaign Japanese suicide pilots sank 30 ships, damaged 368, and killed an estimated 5,000 U.S. Navy men.*

withdrew before the American troops into three mountain strongholds located around Baguio, in the Cabusilian Mountains, and in the mountains to the east of Manila. After bloody fighting against 16,000 naval personnel in the streets of Manila, the capital was taken on 4 March. The island of Corregidor fell to a combined airborne and amphibious assault and thereafter the American troops fought against dogged resistance in their efforts to eliminate the surviving Japanese pockets of resistance. When the enemy garrison finally surrendered on 15 August 1945, it still had 50,000 troops under arms.

Iwo Jima

While the battle for the Philippines wore on, the strategically situated island of Iwo Jima, one of the Bonin Islands, became the focus of an extremely difficult and bloody campaign. Located approximately halfway between Tokyo and Saipan, Iwo Jima had two operational airfields, while a third was under construction. These airfields were only 660 miles, or three hours flying time, from Tokyo as opposed to the 2,800 miles of the return trip from the Marianas. B-29s flying from Iwo Jima

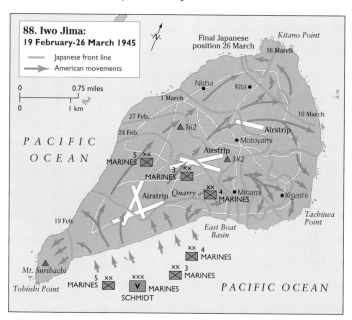

March 1945. Its capture led to 25,000 U.S. casualties, but during the remainder of the war 2,251 B-29s made emergency landings on the island, thereby saving thousands of airmen.

Okinawa

With Iwo Jima in American hands and an invasion of Formosa dismissed as unnecessary, orders for a landing upon Okinawa, in the Ryukyu Islands, were issued. Okinawa was only 350 miles from Kyushu, the most southerly island of Japan, and it was eminently suitable for airfield construction and a fleet anchorage. But the island was defended by 100,000 men of the Japanese Thirty-Second Army, and Nimitz would have his work cut out to get his forces ashore. A gigantic armada, and a

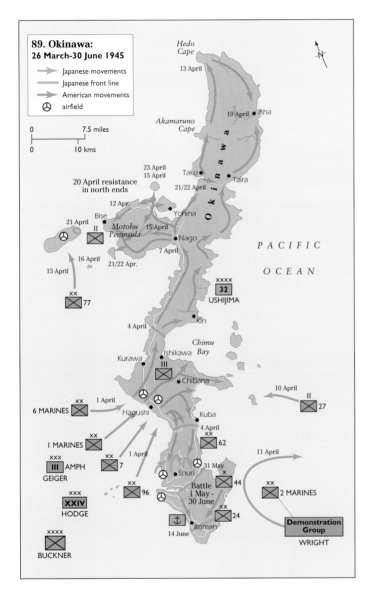

89. Okinawa:
26 March–30 June 1945

→ Japanese movements
— Japanese front line
→ American movements
Ⓐ airfield

Okinawa had been high, with 110,000 Japanese killed, and 37,000 Americans wounded and 12,500 killed. At sea, thirty-six American ships were sunk and nearly 400 damaged. In what proved to be the final American amphibious invasion of the war, the Allies gained a priceless base for the assault on the home islands if it proved necessary.

Major General Curtis LeMay, who commanded 21st Bomber Command, was able, once the air support of operations on Iwo Jima was completed, to mount a sustained bombing campaign against Japan from March to August 1945. Precisely targeted raids against individual military objectives produced poor results, but incendiary raids on fifty-eight urban areas were terrifyingly effective. Over two million buildings were destroyed, nearly 700,000 people were killed or injured, and a further nine million made homeless. Vital supplies of food and raw materials were also seriously affected by a close blockade of Japanese waters. In addition to the successful operations by the Pacific Fleet's submarines, 21st Bomber Command began long distance mine laying. In March 1945, the Fast Carrier Force carried out raids against shipping in harbors and at sea off the home islands, while bombardment groups destroyed industrial

Pre-invasion aerial and naval bombardment had little effect on Okinawa's well dug-in defenders. The rugged volcanic island was riddled with natural caves that the Japanese linked by tunnels. The 6th U.S. Marines landed on Okinawa's western coast on 1 April 1945, and inched their way northward, using satchel charges and flame-throwers to kill Japanese defenders or to seal them inside their caves. The machine gun crew pictured here, is cautiously working its way around a cliff to cover the mouth of a Japanese-occupied cave.

logistical nightmare, comprising 290,000 Allied troops and 1,500 ships, was assembled for an assault landing on 1 April 1945. In the event, the landings were not contested, but the U.S. Marines encountered fanatical opposition as they attempted to take the Kakazu Ridge. On 4 May, the Japanese commander, Lieutenant General Mitsuru Ushijima, launched a counterattack at a cost of 5,000 casualties. The counterattack by U.S. forces progressed slowly in the face of a defense in depth, especially on Sugar Loaf and Conical Hills. The critical moment of the campaign came in the second half of May when the 96th U.S. Division took Conical Hill, forcing the Japanese to withdraw to the Yaeju Dake Escarpment. By 14 June, the U.S. divisions had begun to crack open this position and, within a week, Japanese resistance was reduced to the point where all that remained was mopping up. The cost of taking

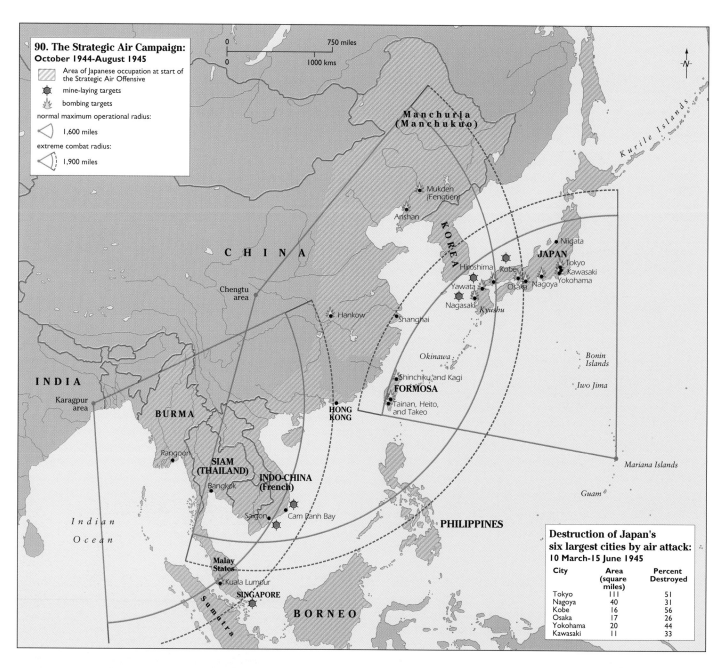

90. The Strategic Air Campaign:
October 1944–August 1945

Area of Japanese occupation at start of the Strategic Air Offensive

mine-laying targets

bombing targets

normal maximum operational radius:

1,600 miles

extreme combat radius:

1,900 miles

City	Area (square miles)	Percent Destroyed
Tokyo	111	51
Nagoya	40	31
Kobe	16	56
Osaka	17	26
Yokohama	20	44
Kawasaki	11	33

Destruction of Japan's six largest cities by air attack:
10 March–15 June 1945

installations with shell fire. Three months later, U.S. submarines entered the Sea of Japan for the first time and by July, the U.S. Navy and Army air force were confident that they could prevent the transfer of Japanese forces to the home islands. Still, plans went ahead to mount an invasion of Kyushu in November 1945, and Honshu in March 1946.

The probability that an invasion of the home islands would lead to a collective act of national suicide, carried out through attacks on the Allied invasion force, was a nightmare that occupied both Allied commanders and statesmen. At whatever cost, it was felt that this scenario must be avoided, if at all pos-

sible. The solution came in a chilling demonstration of what might await the world in the nuclear age. Faced with the harsh reality of the consequences of an invasion, President Truman and his advisers considered the possibility of dropping one or more atomic bombs on Japan. The Potsdam Declaration of 25 July 1945 had warned the Japanese Government that the failure to surrender would lead to the "prompt and utter destruction of their country."

Shortly after 8 A.M., on 6 August 1945, three B-29s from the 509th Composite Group arrived over Hiroshima, a Japanese city of 343,000 people. One B-29, *Enola Gay*, piloted by

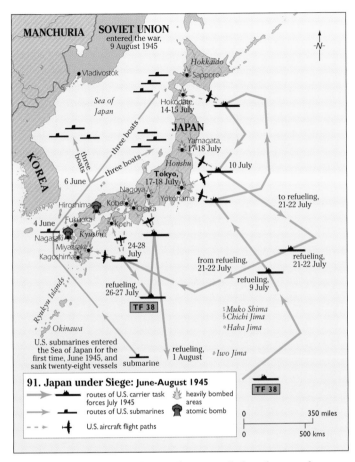

The U.S. Army Information Branch produced weekly news maps during World War II. Each 47 x 35-inch sheet contained text, maps, and illustrations covering all theaters of operation. This map (below) depicts operations in east Asia near the end of World War II. The bomb symbols identify major railroad junctions and ports that the Japanese could use to transport troops from the mainland to the Japanese home islands for a final stand against Allied invasion. The Japanese finally surrendered (above) on 2 September 1945, on the deck of the battleship Missouri *after the intervention of Emperor Hirohito who stepped in to persuade the Japanese military to quit the war.*

Colonel Paul Tibbets, dropped an atomic bomb over the center of the city. An estimated 78,000 people were killed and a further 51,000 injured. The dropping of a second atomic bomb on Nagasaki on 9 August, as a result of which a further 66,000 people were killed or injured, served to emphasize the very real prospect of the complete destruction of Japan's cities. The atomic bomb and the Russian declaration of war on Japan provided the opportunity for the Japanese emperor to persuade his Supreme War Council that surrender was the only option. On 14 August 1945, Japan agreed to surrender unconditionally and hostilities came to an end on 15 August, except in North China, Manchuria, and the Kuriles, where the Soviet Union was pursuing separate territorial objectives.

The war in the Pacific claimed the lives of roughly 90,000 American servicemen and of about 40,000 Filipinos serving under U.S. command. Japan lost 1,140,000 servicemen killed and 295,000 wounded. Japanese civilian casualties approached 700,000. In broad terms the Allies won because of their stronger industrial base, their advanced logistical skill, their reserves of manpower, and the ultimate superiority of their technology and battle plans. In the stark confrontations on the battlefield, both sides produced soldiers of courage, endurance, and professionalism.

The United States in World War II in Europe: 1941-45

America's involvement in World War II in Europe did not begin with a single overt act, as it did at Pearl Harbor in the Pacific. Instead, it began incrementally as the United States abandoned the Neutrality Acts of 1935-39, designed to keep it out of war, and in a series of steps, almost drifted into the conflict. When Britain and France responded to Adolf Hitler's invasion of Poland in 1939 by declaring war on Germany, President Franklin D. Roosevelt reacted by warning belligerents not to conduct military operations within 300 miles of the Western Hemisphere, south of the U.S. bor-

der with Canada. He followed this 5 September 1939 declaration with a message to the U.S. Congress asking it to amend the Neutrality Acts to allow the purchase of arms and munitions by warring nations on a "cash-and-carry" basis. This measure was hardly neutral, for it was designed to assist Britain and France, since they controlled the Atlantic and thus could deny its benefits to the German enemy.

Until the fall of France in June 1940, most Americans were confident the Allies would win the war without additional assistance. After Germany took possession of France's ports

The invasion of French North Africa by the Allies, known as Operation Torch, began on 8 November 1942, with the largest amphibious, military operation ever undertaken. British troops were not involved in the initial landing for fear that the Vichy French, theoretically neutral in the war, would remember the Royal Navy's bombardment of the French navy at Mers-el-Kébir and oppose a British operation. In fact, the French resisted landings by U.S. troops far more strongly than they fought German troops when they entered Tunisia.

on the Atlantic, however, its war against Allied shipping entered a dangerous stage. From June 1940 through the end of 1941, dubbed "The Happy Time" by German submariners, Germany threatened to cut Britain off from overseas assistance. On 2 September 1940, the United States promised to deliver fifty destroyers to Britain in return for ninety-nine-year leases on British bases in the Western Hemisphere. Two months later, as Britain neared a point at which it could no longer purchase war goods, Roosevelt announced that the United States would provide friendly nations with the tools of war as a way to insure that America would not have to enter the war. His announcement was the genesis of the Lend–Lease Act, eventually signed into law by the U.S. Congress on 11 March 1941. In June 1941, the United States occupied Greenland and Iceland and began escorting its supply convoys halfway across the Atlantic. In November, Roosevelt extended those escorts so they provided cover all the way to "friendly ports." The U.S. Navy was engaged in what amounted to an undeclared naval war against Germany.

Ironically, it was not events in the Atlantic that ultimately drew the United States into war, but Japan's attack on Pearl Harbor half a world away that led Germany to declare war on the United States on 11 December 1941. Allied with Britain and the Soviet Union, the United States entered a worldwide struggle against exceedingly aggressive and operationally formidable Axis foes. It would take the Allied powers more than three-and-a-half years to defeat Germany, Italy, and Japan in the twentieth century's bloodiest conflict.

During the first six months of 1942, the Allies struggled to survive. At first, they suffered seemingly endless setbacks in the Pacific and Southeast Asia, lost merchant ship after ship when Germany shifted its U-boat operations to America's Atlantic coast, and witnessed a hard-pressed Soviet Union bear the brunt of the fighting on land. By mid-year, the balance began to shift in favor of the Allies in both the Pacific and

the Atlantic. The Allies believed they had the resource base and the determination eventually to stem the tide. But, to do this, they had to develop a strategy for allocating resources and coordinating their operations.

Strategic Priorities

Strategic planning had actually begun before the United States entered the war. During staff talks, ABC-1, in Washington (January–March 1941), U.S. and British military leaders agreed that if America entered the war, the United States would focus on defeating Germany first before turning Allied attention and resources to defeating the Japanese.

Although the desperate situation in the Pacific meant that President Franklin Roosevelt and his Joint Chiefs of Staff had to delegate at least a portion of America's resources and effort to that theater in 1942, it did not deflect the Anglo-Americans from their original thinking. Roosevelt in particular wished to get U.S. forces into combat across the Atlantic for political as well as for strategic reasons. As a result, in July 1942, he rejected the advice of his service chiefs, who wanted to establish a second front in France to help relieve the Soviets, and opted instead for a northwest African operation code-named "Torch." Prime Minister Winston Churchill and his Chiefs of Staff were obviously pleased with Roosevelt's decision to participate in the first joint Allied offensive operation of the war.

Invasion of North Africa

On 8 November 1942, the plan went forward. There were three main assaults planned for Operation Torch. In the vicinity of Casablanca, 35,000 troops under U.S. General George Patton landed along Morocco's Atlantic coast. American Major General Lloyd Fredendall commanded 22,000 soldiers coming ashore near Oran in Algeria on the Mediterranean, and General William Ryder's 10,000-soldier contingent attacked farther east near Algiers, with the British providing follow-on forces.

The Allied landings were accomplished against Vichy French units, which offered only scattered resistance and not against German troops of Adolf Hitler's Third Reich. The Americans and British were further assisted when Vichy officials in the area ordered their troops to observe a cease-fire.

Though tactically surprised, the Germans reacted quickly by beginning to move army and air force units into Tunisia on 9 November. After taking over the major ports of Morocco and Algeria, the Allies had difficulty organizing themselves, and in the face of overextended supply lines and winter rains, they suffered serious losses to Wehrmacht troops in late November and early December. Although the Allies advanced to within twenty miles of Tunis, the original objective, they were stopped, and U.S. General Dwight D. Eisenhower, the overall commander, decided to reorganize his forces before attempting another offensive.

The Casablanca Conference

In the midst of the North African fighting, the British and Americans decided that a strategy conference was needed. The Soviet leader, Joseph Stalin, declined to take part, presumably because of pressing military matters on his western front. But Roosevelt and Churchill and their military staffs, called the Combined Chiefs of Staff, decided to meet because, in Churchill's words, "the tide had turned." Not only had Operation Torch succeeded, though incompletely, but British and Commonwealth forces had, after their victory at El Alamein in November 1942, assumed the initiative in Egypt and Libya, and the Red Army had achieved a triumph of great, long-term significance at Stalingrad in southern Russia that same month.

In this brightening atmosphere, between 14 and 24 January 1943, the Casablanca Conference took place. It was a highly productive meeting, for the Allies adopted a military strategy that would see them through the course of the war. To succeed against the Axis, the British and Americans decided it would be necessary to defeat Italy, Germany, and Japan, and in that order, though maintaining that agenda resulted subsequently in many heated exchanges.

At Casablanca, the Allies also decided for the first time that the means for defeating the Axis would consist of eight elements: 1) winning the naval Battle of the Atlantic; 2) pursuing a Combined Bomber Offensive; 3) undertaking additional Mediterranean operations; 4) preparing for the invasion of western Europe; 5) continuing to support the Soviets, though not with troops; 6) advancing toward Japan through the Pacific; 7) assuming the offensive in the China-Burma-India theater; and 8) developing and using the atomic bomb. These eight elements formed the core of Anglo-American strategy. Only one other element was added subsequently—an assault

against southern France—but as in the case of resolving which of the Axis opponents to take on first, the British and Americans had to decide in which order and to what extent they would pursue each objective. Reaching these decisions also led to intense debates between the two partners. Yet, they were able to overcome their differences and carry out what had now become a comprehensive, combined military strategy. Much to their detriment, the Axis powers never achieved such a unity in planning.

Battle of the Atlantic

The most immediate concern of the Allies was the defeat of Germany's submarine force in the Atlantic. This long battle had begun in late 1940. Allied merchant shipping losses peaked in 1942 with the destruction of 8.3 million tons. By the time Churchill and Roosevelt met in Casablanca in January 1943, the Germans had 180 U-boats in North Atlantic waters—enough to have a decisive effect. By this time the Americans, British, and Canadians also had increased their defensive capabilities so that they could cope with the German navy.

At first, however, it seemed like the Germans were in control. During the first twenty days of March 1943, the Allies lost their ability to read Germany's coded transmissions to its U-boats, which the Allies called "Ultra." Enemy wolfpacks of eight-to-twenty boats took advantage of the information blackout to score numerous successes against the Allied convoys. One especially devastating attack took place between 16 and 20 March, during which the U-boats, suffering no losses, sank twenty-one of ninety merchant ships in two convoys.

During the next two months, however, the battle changed dramatically in the Allies' favor. Between 20 March and the

The crew of U.S. Coast Guard cutter Spencer, *which sank German U-boat 175 on 17 April 1943, watches depth charges explode as their convoy continues on its trip across the Atlantic.*

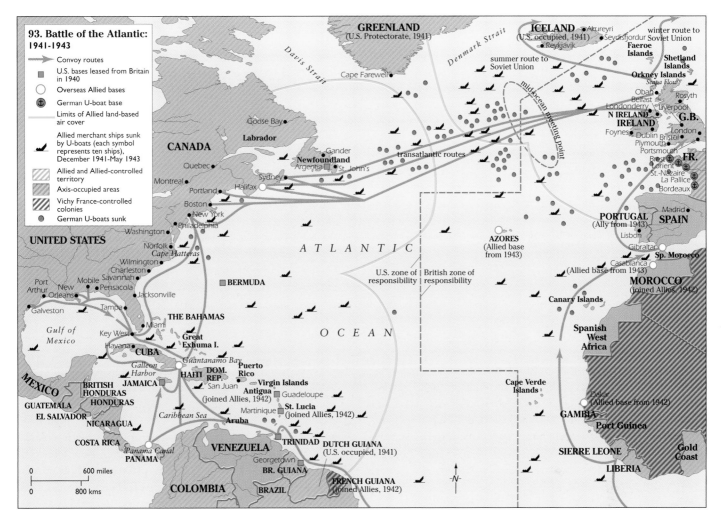

93. Battle of the Atlantic: 1941-1943

→ Convoy routes

■ U.S. bases leased from Britain in 1940

○ Overseas Allied bases

⊕ German U-boat base

Limits of Allied land-based air cover

Allied merchant ships sunk by U-boats (each symbol represents ten ships), December 1941-May 1943

Allied and Allied-controlled territory

Axis-occupied areas

Vichy France-controlled colonies

● German U-boats sunk

end of the month, operating conditions improved, in large part, because the Allies had again broken the German ciphers. During April, to counter increasingly effective Allied defensive measures, German naval headquarters ordered its submarines to resurface during daylight hours to recharge their batteries, necessary for underwater propulsion. This method of operating proved disastrous for the U-boats, despite their 37-mm deck guns, which were no match for undetected B-24 Liberator aircraft. During May, the Allies gained the upper hand. By 24 May, the Germans had lost thirty-six U-boats. These losses were prohibitive, and U-Boat Command alerted its wolfpacks that attacks in the North Atlantic would have to cease. Although the German navy hoped to renew the battle at a future date, Germany's naval war in the Atlantic was irretrievably lost.

The heroes in the Allied victory were not admirals and air generals, but little known sailors and airmen who took advantage of a combination of factors that eventually spelled success. Besides Ultra intelligence, pilots began flying planes equipped

with 10-cm radar, which the German submarines could not detect. Naval personnel had placed high-frequency, direction-finding radar (Huff-Duff) on their escorts, which allowed them to locate U-boats nearby. Hedgehogs—mortars which fired twenty-four projectiles through the air ahead of the vessel and only detonated on contact with a target so that the sonar tracking of the target was not interrupted—were used successfully. Moreover, by 1943 the number of naval support groups had increased, as had the number of escort carriers and long-range aircraft, flying from bases in Labrador, Northern Ireland, and Iceland, which helped provide continuous coverage across the Atlantic. Another factor was the Allied shipyards, which as early as the autumn of 1942, were producing more ship tonnage than was being lost in combat. The Allies' tonnage advantage continued to increase during the ensuing months. The combination of ship construction and antisubmarine measures helped the Allies win the Battle of the Atlantic. With the Atlantic shipping lanes no longer in jeopardy, other aspects of the Allies' strategy, such as the invasion

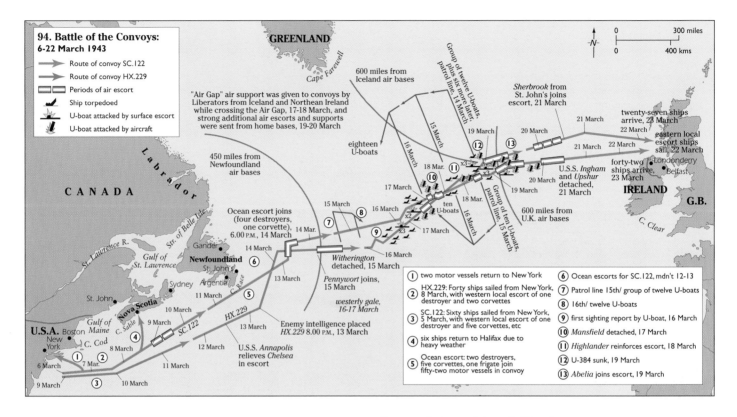

94. Battle of the Convoys:
6-22 March 1943

→ Route of convoy SC.122
→ Route of convoy HX.229
▭▭ Periods of air escort
⚓ Ship torpedoed
⚓ U-boat attacked by surface escort
⚓ U-boat attacked by aircraft

GREENLAND

Cape Farewell

600 miles from
Iceland air bases

Group of twelve U-boats,
plus six more later,
patrol line, 14 March

Sherbrook from
St. John's joins
escort, 21 March

twenty-seven ships
arrive, 23 March

"Air Gap" air support was given to convoys by
Liberators from Iceland and Northean Ireland
while crossing the Air Gap, 17-18 March, and
strong additional air escorts and supports
were sent from home bases, 19-20 March

eighteen
U-boats

21 March

22 March

eastern local
escort ships
sail, 22 March

Labrador

450 miles from
Newfoundland
air bases

15 March

16 March

19 March

20 March

21 March

22 March

forty-two
ships arrive,
23 March

Londonderry
Belfast

CANADA

18 Mar.

17 March

U.S.S. Ingham
and Upshur
detached,
21 March

IRELAND

G.B.

Ocean escort joins
(four destroyers,
one corvette),
6.00 P.M., 14 March

15 March

16 March

Group of ten U-boats,
patrol line, 15 March

19 March

20 March

600 miles from
U.K. air bases

C. Clear

St. Lawrence R.

Gulf of
St. Lawrence

Gander

Newfoundland

14 March

14 Mar.

Witherington
detached, 15 March

16 March

17 March

ten
U-boats

18 Mar.

16 March

Str. of Belle Isle

St. John's

Argentia

C. Race

13 March

Pennywort joins,
15 March

Sydney

11 March

westerly gale,
16-17 March

St. John

Nova Scotia

10 March

9 March

C. Sable

Gulf of
Maine

13 March

Enemy intelligence placed
HX.229 8.00 P.M., 13 March

U.S.A.

Boston

New
York

C. Cod

8 March

12 March

13 March

U.S.S. Annapolis
relieves Chelsea
in escort

6 March

7 Mar.

11 March

9 March

10 March

① two motor vessels return to New York

② HX.229: Forty ships sailed from New York,
8 March, with western local escort of one
destroyer and two corvettes

③ SC.122: Sixty ships sailed from New York,
5 March, with western local escort of one
destroyer and five corvettes, etc

④ six ships return to Halifax due to
heavy weather

⑤ Ocean escort: two destroyers,
five corvettes, one frigate join
fifty-two motor vessels in convoy

⑥ Ocean escorts for SC.122, mdn't 12-13

⑦ Patrol line 15th/ group of twelve U-boats

⑧ 16th/ twelve U-boats

⑨ first sighting report by U-boat, 16 March

⑩ Mansfield detached, 17 March

⑪ Highlander reinforces escort, 18 March

⑫ U-384 sunk, 19 March

⑬ Abelia joins escort, 19 March

0 — 300 miles
0 — 400 kms

of western Europe and the Combined Bomber Offensive, could now proceed without fear of interruption because of supply and personnel shortages.

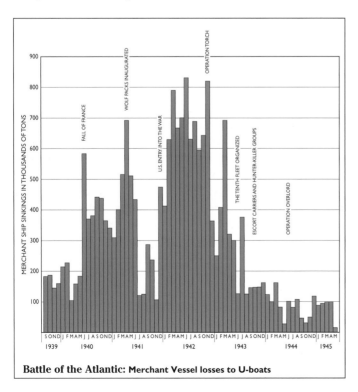

Battle of the Atlantic: Merchant Vessel losses to U-boats

Strategic Bombing Offensive

Even more drawn out than the Battle of the Atlantic was the Allies' strategic bombing campaign. Britain's Bomber Command had started bombing targets in western Europe and Germany sporadically in 1940. Its raids had continued, though with limited effect, for the next two years. By 1943, the U.S. Eighth Air Force was ready to contribute to the strategic effort. The British acknowledged this fact at the Casablanca meeting and the Combined Bombing Offensive started in earnest in June, with British Bomber Command attacking at night and the U.S. Eighth Air Force during the day to keep up a "round the clock" bombing campaign.

Britain's primarily Lancaster bombers and America's B–17s and B–24s took heavy losses throughout 1943. German radar, antiaircraft fire, and fighter aircraft proved effective and caused the Allies significant damage. A particularly disastrous raid was flown against Schweinfurt in south–central Germany on 14 October, during which the U.S. Eighth Air Force suffered a loss rate of 26 percent (77 out of 291 bombers that were sent out). The Americans also lost 642 crew members during the raid.

But a solution was at hand. The Americans and the British began using P-51 Mustangs as long-range bomber escorts, and the Mustang, upgraded with a Rolls-Royce Merlin engine, changed the course of the bomber offensive. It had a range of over 600 miles with a top speed of over 400 miles per hour.

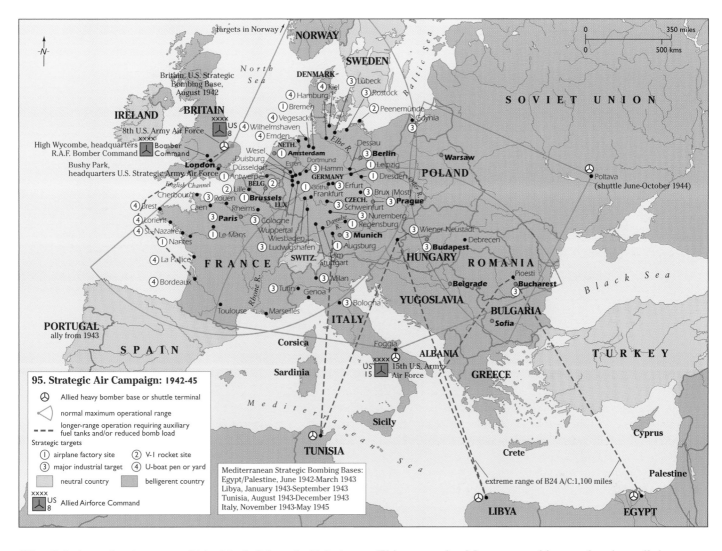

-N-

Targets in Norway

NORWAY

North Sea

SWEDEN

DENMARK

Britain, U.S. Strategic
Bombing Base,
August 1942

④ Kiel   ③ Lübeck
④ Hamburg   ③ Rostock
① Bremen   ② Peenemünde
④ Vegesack   ③ Gdynia
④ Wilhelmshaven
④ Emden

Baltic Sea

SOVIET UNION

IRELAND   **BRITAIN**

8th U.S. Army Air Force

High Wycombe, headquarters
R.A.F. Bomber Command

Bushy Park,
headquarters U.S. Strategic Army Air Force

English Channel

Cherbourg
④ Brest
④ Lorient
④ St. Nazaire
① Nantes
④ La Pallice
④ Bordeaux

PORTUGAL
ally from 1943

SPAIN

US
8
US
8
Bomber
Command

London
Antwerp
NETH.
Amsterdam
Wesel
Duisburg
Düsseldorf
Essen   Dortmund
① Hamm   ③ **Berlin**
Dessau
① Leipzig
① Dresden
Brux (Most)
POLAND
Warsaw

Elbe R.
Oder R.

Poltava
(shuttle June-October 1944)

BELG.   ② Lille
② Rouen
Brussels
LUX.
Caen
Rheims
③ Cologne
Wuppertal
Wiesbaden
③ Ludwigshafen
GERMANY
① Frankfurt
③ Erfurt
③ Schweinfurt
③ Nuremberg
③ Regensburg
CZECH.
③ **Prague**

Danube R.

③ Wiener Neustadt

③ Paris
① Le Mans

FRANCE

Rhône R.

③ Turin
Genoa
③ Milan

SWITZ.
Ulm
Stuttgart
③ **Munich**
① Augsburg

ITALY

③ Bologna

Corsica

Sardinia

Toulouse
Marseilles

Foggia

Mediterranean Sea

HUNGARY
Budapest

ROMANIA

Debrecen

Pioesti
Bucharest

Black Sea

YUGOSLAVIA
Belgrade

BULGARIA
Sofia

ALBANIA

GREECE

US
15
15th U.S. Army
Air Force

TURKEY

Sicily

Cyprus

Crete

Palestine

extreme range of B24 A/C:1,100 miles

TUNISIA

LIBYA

EGYPT

0 —— 350 miles
0 —— 500 kms

95. Strategic Air Campaign: 1942-45

⊕ Allied heavy bomber base or shuttle terminal

◁ normal maximum operational range

- - - longer-range operation requiring auxiliary
fuel tanks and/or reduced bomb load

Strategic targets
① airplane factory site   ② V-1 rocket site
③ major industrial target   ④ U-boat pen or yard

☐ neutral country   ☐ belligerent country

xxxx
US
8   Allied Airforce Command

Mediterranean Strategic Bombing Bases:
Egypt/Palestine, June 1942-March 1943
Libya, January 1943-September 1943
Tunisia, August 1943-December 1943
Italy, November 1943-May 1945

When Britain sought a long-range, high-altitude fighter, the United States produced the P-51 Mustang in eight months. American Mustang fliers like this group were escorting bombers on daylight raids over Germany and downed more German planes than any other fighter during the war.

This meant that Mustangs could escort bombers all the way to the target and back, and their speed and maneuverability proved effective against the German fighters. By May 1944, the Allies gained air superiority over western and southern Europe, and by the end of the year, they achieved undisputed superiority over Germany as well.

During the last year of the war, Britain's Bomber Command and America's Eighth and Fifteenth air forces destroyed German oil production, dislocated the transportation and communications systems, and caused untold damage everywhere. Photographs of the bombed-out German cities of Wesel, Nuremberg, and Berlin give evidence of how destructive aerial bombing had become. In addition, countering the Allied bombing campaign devoured scarce German resources. Air power came of age during World War II.

Allied Victory in North Africa

Although aerial and naval warfare made great strides during

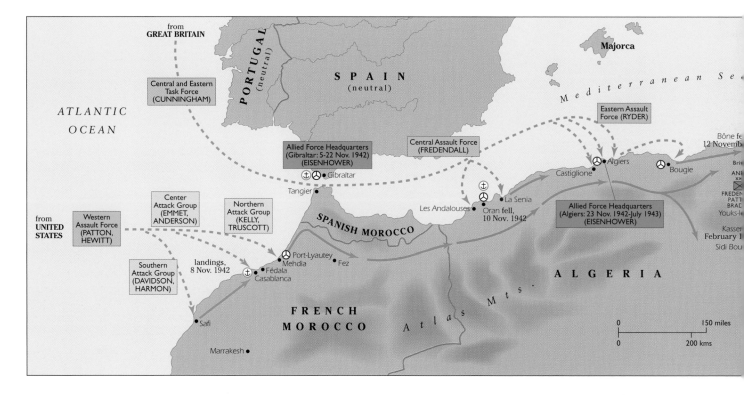

the war, the Allies still had to rely on land warfare as the decisive component. At the time of the Casablanca Conference, the Germans had stopped the Allies, short of taking North Africa, and British and American leaders realized they had to defeat the Germans and Italian formations in the region before additional Mediterranean operations could ensue. By March 1943, American, British, Commonwealth, and Free French forces were closing in on German units in Tunisia. However, they faced a formidable opponent in Germany's master operational commander, Field Marshal Erwin Rommel, who proceeded to deal the Americans a tactical setback at the Kasserine Pass, southwest of Tunis, in February. General Eisenhower responded by replacing his II Corps commander, General Lloyd Fredendall, with General George Patton, who rejuvenated the U.S. divisions.

During March, the Allied troops, led by British General Bernard Montgomery's Eighth Army and by Patton's II Corps, gained the upper hand. Besides the ground forces, Allied tactical aircraft dominated the skies over the battle area, and the fighters and bombers also waged an effective campaign against Axis shipping in the Mediterranean. General Patton did not participate in the final stages. General Omar Bradley replaced him in April 1943, so that Patton could return to his army in Morocco to participate in planning and continue preparations for the next Mediterranean undertaking, the invasion of Sicily. But the Allies kept up the pressure and finally forced the Axis to capitulate on 13 May. As an added

bonus, the Allies took 275,000 prisoners.

Invasion of Sicily

The amphibious assault against Sicily, preceded by days of heavy air bombardment, took place on 10 July. A huge operation, it included airborne drops as well as seaborne landings. The first wave of invasion troops struck at seven different beaches on the southeastern portion of the island, with Montgomery's Eighth Army on the right, and Patton's Seventh Army on the left. Supporting the approximately 160,000 ground troops were 2,600 ships and landing craft, and 3,500 aircraft. The Axis had eight divisions, 435 aircraft, and portions of the Italian fleet to defend the island.

The first several days of the operation went relatively smoothly, but then Montgomery's forces ran into stiff resistance on the Catania plain. In the meantime, Patton's army fanned out and quickly liberated Palermo and the western portion of the island. However, as the Americans turned and drove east toward Messina on the northeastern tip, the jumping-off place to the Italian mainland, they also found their momentum slowing as the Germans tenaciously held on to their defensive positions.

In the midst of the July fighting, two events of overriding strategic importance occurred. One was the overthrow and arrest of the Italian dictator, Benito Mussolini, on 25 July, by the Fascist Grand Council and his replacement by Field Marshal Pietro Badoglio. Both the Allies and the Germans were

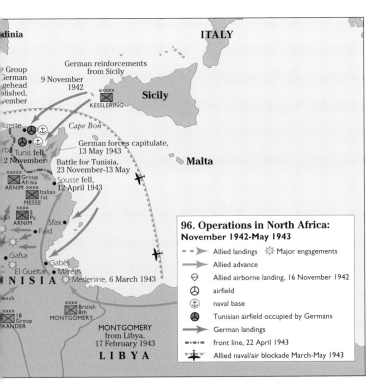

well aware that Mussolini's ouster would lead to Italy exiting from the war. One day later, Theater Commander Eisenhower received orders from the Combined Chiefs to invade the Italian peninsula as soon as it was practical. This decision meant that the Allies were to continue to try to force Italy to surrender, and it also signified an ongoing Allied commitment in the Mediterranean until Germany was defeated in the European theater.

On 1 August, the Allies were positioned for a final push on Messina, but by the time they captured it on 17 August, 135,000 German and Italian soldiers had managed to get away. The Germans made such an effective use of their anti-aircraft positions on both sides of the Straits of Messina that they had prevented Allied aircraft from stopping the evacuation. In August, General Patton was replaced by General Omar Bradley. During the Sicilian campaign, Patton had wrongly slapped two soldiers for what he considered cowardice while they were hospitalized for battle fatigue. The slapping incident led Eisenhower to make this change; but he refused to end the career of the man he considered his top operational commander because he realized that Patton could well be of use later on in the war.

In Sicily, Lieutenant General George Patton twice slapped soldiers suffering from the stress of combat. He said that he tried to shock the men out of their dazed condition so they could return to duty, but his actions were interpreted as abuse, and led to demands for his removal from command. General Dwight Eisenhower refused to replace Patton and ordered him to apologize to his troops. Patton is shown delivering his apology to men of the 1st Infantry Division on 27 August 1943.

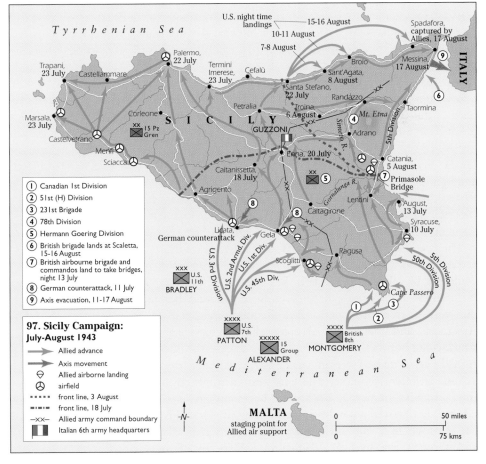

Operations in Italy

Without pausing to assimilate the lessons of the Sicilian campaign, on 3 September, British and Canadian units crossed the Straits of Messina, landed on the Italian mainland, and began moving northward. On 8 September, the new Italian government announced an armistice with the Allies, taking Italy out of the war. The next day, portions of U.S. General Mark Clark's Fifth Army made the attempt to outflank the Germans, who were rapidly occupying the peninsula, by undertaking an amphibious attack at Salerno Bay, 170 land miles north of the British landing. The American and British troops at Salerno withstood with difficulty a determined Wehrmacht counterattack. Only on 16 September did the Germans give way and start to withdraw. That same evening Americans on the beachhead contacted British soldiers coming up from the south, and Anglo-American units began moving toward Naples, capturing it on 2 October. By 6 October, they had reached the Volturno River about twenty-five miles north of the city.

On the other side of the peninsula, a British division landed at Taranto on 9 September, took the port of Bari, and seized Foggia, with its precious airfields nearby, by the end of the month. Thus, by early October, three excellent harbors—Naples, Taranto, and Bari—and two airfield complexes near Naples and Foggia were in Allied hands, and Clark's Fifth and Montgomery's Eighth armies, supported by tactical air units, were in position to move northward.

But during the autumn of 1943, the Allied attempt to push quickly up the peninsula floundered. Bad weather and a stubborn, formidable enemy figured prominently in the slow down. One German defensive barrier after another gave way, but Allied progress was painstakingly slow. Finally, along the Gustav line—an effective mix of field defenses, artillery guns, and natural fortifications which stretched from the Garigliano River in the west through Cassino to north of the Sangro River on the east coast—the Germans held fast. The first winter of discontent in Italy began.

The two other main European objectives set forth at Casablanca—a western invasion and support of the Soviets—could not be achieved in 1943. In Britain, the Allies engaged primarily in preparations for the assault in the west, but by mid-year, given the situation in the Mediterranean, both the Americans and the British accepted that a cross-Channel attack could not take place until 1944. In the east, the Soviets turned back a major German assault at Kursk and started to assume an offensive on several of its western fronts. By this time, supplies from the Allies were beginning to have an effect. They arrived not only in the north by convoy and from the south via Iran, but also through Siberia by way of Alaska and through the port of Vladivostok. While the Soviets received some tanks and artillery pieces, they were even more pleased to receive a variety of sturdy trucks, jeeps, and also large supplies of Spam. Despite Soviet reluctance during the Cold War to admit the extent of Anglo-American assistance, it was considerable.

Toward the end of 1943, at Teheran, the Big Three—Roosevelt, Churchill, and Stalin—and their military advisors met for the first time. The outcome of their discussions set the agenda for the next few years. The plan fashioned at Casablanca was fine-tuned at Teheran. Details were established such as the timing of and the amount of effort to be expended for each of the Allies' remaining objectives. The Allied leaders understood that the war had turned decisively in their favor, but they also realized that a misstep could be costly. In the European fronts, they decided to coordinate a series of concentric attacks on the Continent from the south, east, and west in 1944. The goal was to keep up the pressure on all sides and to allow Germany no respite.

In Italy, the stalemate continued throughout the winter and spring. On 12 January 1944, the Allies started an offensive on the western portion of the front. One of the battles, an attempt to cross the Rapido River, south of Monte Cassino, proved particularly bloody, with the decimation of the U.S. 36th Infantry division. The entire operation was designed to break through the Gustav Line and to advance up the Liri River Valley, while American and British soldiers under the U.S. VI Corps executed an amphibious end run at Anzio, thirty-five miles south of Rome, to outflank German defenses. The assault on 22 January achieved tactical surprise, but the Allies did not seize the high ground beyond the beachhead to prevent German divisions from being rushed to the area. When the Allies were ready to advance eight days later, the Germans could not be dislodged from around Anzio, and their forces even undertook several counteroffensives. One of them almost

General Henry Harley "Hap" Arnold (left), spent most of the war in Washington as a member of the Joint Chiefs of Staff, but he toured every American front to inspect units and to gauge the success of the strategic air campaign. He was photographed with U.S. Fifth Army Commander Mark Clark.

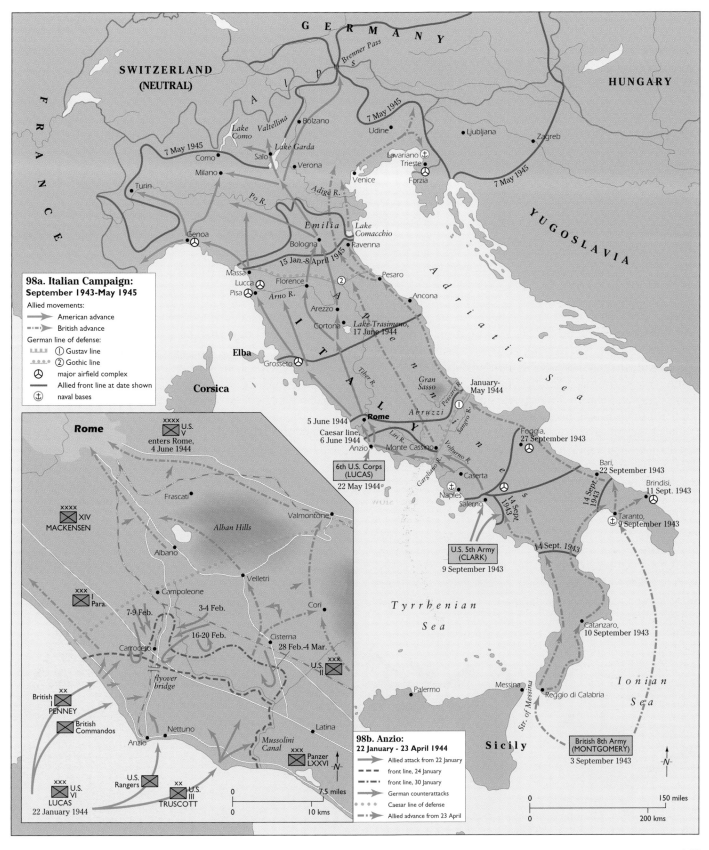

98a. Italian Campaign:
September 1943-May 1945

Allied movements:

→ American advance

⇢ British advance

German line of defense:

⊥⊥⊥⊥ ① Gustav line

••••• ② Gothic line

Ⓜ major airfield complex

— Allied front line at date shown

⊕ naval bases

Rome

xxxx U.S. V — enters Rome, 4 June 1944

xxxx XIV — MACKENSEN

xxx I Para.

xxx U.S. II

7-9 Feb.   3-4 Feb.

16-20 Feb.

28 Feb.-4 Mar.

Carroceto

flyover bridge

British I PENNEY — xx

British Commandos

Anzio   Nettuno

Mussolini Canal

xxx Panzer LXXVI

U.S. Rangers

U.S. III TRUSCOTT

xxx U.S. VI LUCAS — 22 January 1944

Latina

Frascati

Alban Hills

Albano

Velletri

Campoleone

Cori

Cisterna

Valmontone

0   7.5 miles

0   10 kms

98b. Anzio:
22 January - 23 April 1944

→ Allied attack from 22 January

--- front line, 24 January

-·-·- front line, 30 January

→ German counterattacks

•••• Caesar line of defense

-·-·- Allied advance from 23 April

Brenner Pass

Bolzano

Udine   7 May 1945

Lavariano

Trieste   ⊕

Forzia   Ⓜ

Lake Como

Valtellina

Lake Garda

Salo   Verona

Venice

Milano

Como

Turin

Po R.

Genoa   Ⓜ

Emilia   Lake Comacchio

Bologna   Ravenna

15 Jan.-8 April 1945

Pesaro

Massa   ②

Lucca   Florence

Pisa   Ⓜ

Arno R.

Arezzo   Ancona

Cortona

Lake Trasimeno, 17 June 1944

Elba

Grosseto   Ⓜ

Gran Sasso

January-May 1944

Abruzzi

①

Rome

5 June 1944   Caesar line, 6 June 1944

Anzio   Monte Cassino

Liri R.   Volturno R.

Garigliano R.

Foggia, 27 September 1943   Ⓜ

Bari, 22 September 1943

6th U.S. Corps (LUCAS) 22 May 1944

Caserta

Naples   ⊕   14 Sept. 1943   Ⓜ

Salerno   14 Sept. 1943

U.S. 5th Army (CLARK) 9 September 1943

14 Sept. 1943

Brindisi, 11 September 1943

14 Sept. 1943

Taranto, ⊕ 9 September 1943

Catanzaro, 10 September 1943

Tyrrhenian Sea

Palermo

Messina

Reggio di Calabria

Str. of Messina

Sicily

British 8th Army (MONTGOMERY) 3 September 1943

Ionian Sea

—N→

0   150 miles

0   200 kms

SWITZERLAND (NEUTRAL)

FRANCE

GERMANY

HUNGARY

YUGOSLAVIA

Ljubljana

Zagreb

7 May 1945

7 May 1945

Adriatic Sea

ITALY

Corsica

Adige R.

A l p s

forced the Allies to evacuate in mid-February. The beachhead held, but continuing efforts by British, French, New Zealand, and Indian units to reach Anzio and to drive on to Rome ran into stiff opposition.

Finally, on 11 May, after several months of preparation, the Allies once again made an all-out attempt to break through the Gustav Line. Both the Germans and the Allies had approximately twenty-three divisions in Italy, but this time the Americans and British could not be halted. French troops advanced through the mountains to high ground overlooking the Liri Valley, forcing the Germans to start withdrawing from the southern sector toward Rome. The Gustav Line collapsed, and Montgomery's Eighth Army drove forward in the valley, while Clark's Fifth Army advanced along the west coast, linking up with the Anzio formations on 25 May. In spite of conflicts between the American and British commanders over the honor of liberating Rome, by 4 June, the Eternal City was in Allied hands.

The Allies did not pause long to celebrate, and by 23 July, Allied forces reached the River Arno, 175 miles north of Rome. But, then, the Allies' progress slowed noticeably because their supply lines were stretched to the limit, their troops were exhausted, and some divisions had been removed for operations elsewhere. Shortly after crossing the Arno in force, the Allies came up against Germans dug in along the Gothic Line, which ran 180 miles from Massa in the west through the Apennines north of Florence to Pesaro on the Adriatic. Although the Allies pierced the Gothic Line in several places and some units even reached the Lombardy Plain, they became bogged down by autumn rains and settled into

the northern Apennines for another winter of discontent.

Offensive of 1944

In the east, the Soviets' pace quickened during 1944. The Red Army had already made substantial gains after the tank battle at Kursk the year before. While advances on that front continued, Stalin's forces relieved Leningrad in the north and started moving south and west toward the Reich. In the center on 22 June, three years to the day after Germany had attacked the Soviet Union, the Red Army and air force unleashed a murderous assault against German forces holding a line in Byelorusssia and the Ukraine. The front of Germany's Army Group Center collapsed and the Soviets did not stop until they were well inside the Polish border. On the southern front, the Russian armies sped into Romania and Bulgaria, thus forcing two of Hitler's satellites out of the war.

For the Americans and the British, 1944 was filled with stunning victories in the west, but their elation was tempered by enough defeats to preclude bringing the European war to a successful conclusion by the end of the year. The most momentous campaign was Operation Overlord, the Allied landings launched along the Normandy coast from England on 6 June 1944. The author Stephen Ambrose has described it as "the climactic battle of World War II."

Operation Overlord

Although it began on 6 June 1944, Operation Overlord had been in preparation for more than two years and it was the biggest amphibious assault in both size and complexity ever undertaken. Prior to the D-Day landings, the German forces

All sections of the Atlantic Wall were not alike, but most included anti-ship, anti-tank, and anti-personnel obstacles. From the sea to the land, these included rafts carrying mines just beneath the surface, backed by anti-ship stakes topped with mines. Next came anti-tank obstacles, e.g., steel tetrahedrons and concrete "dragon's tooth blocks." At the high water mark were barbed-wire and mine fields to stop personnel, and concrete pillboxes positioned to provide flanking machine gun fire. Then came an anti-tank wall and trenches for infantry

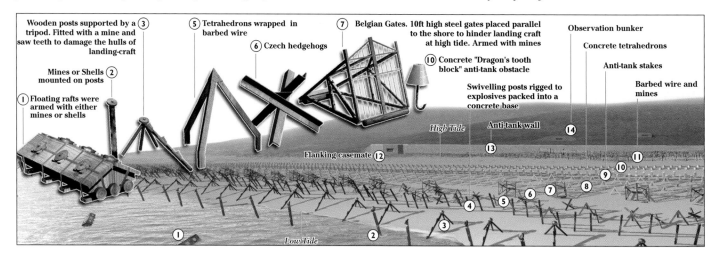

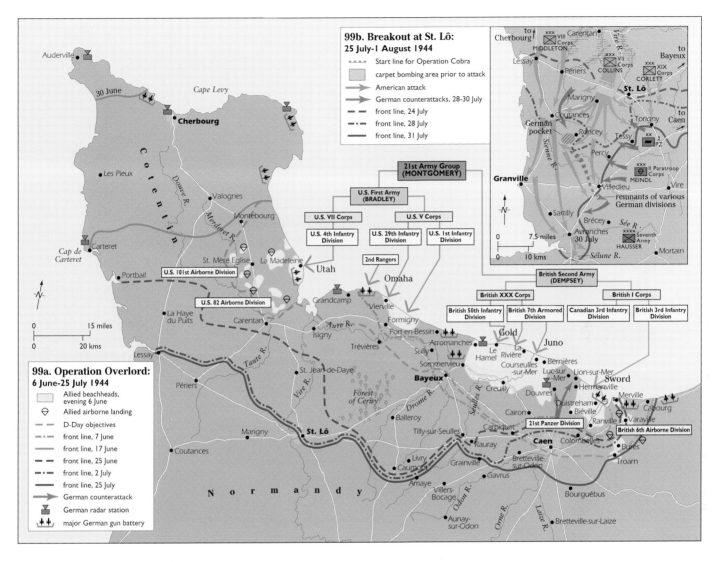

99b. Breakout at St. Lô:
25 July-1 August 1944

- ···· Start line for Operation Cobra
- carpet bombing area prior to attack
- → American attack
- → German counterattacks, 28-30 July
- --- front line, 24 July
- ···- front line, 28 July
- — front line, 31 July

21st Army Group (MONTGOMERY)

U.S. First Army (BRADLEY)

U.S. VII Corps — **U.S. 4th Infantry Division**

U.S. V Corps — **U.S. 29th Infantry Division** — **U.S. 1st Infantry Division** — **2nd Rangers**

British Second Army (DEMPSEY)

British XXX Corps — **British 50th Infantry Division** — **British 7th Armored Division**

British I Corps — **Canadian 3rd Infantry Division** — **British 3rd Infantry Division**

21st Panzer Division

British 6th Airborne Division

remnants of various German divisions

99a. Operation Overlord:
6 June-25 July 1944

- Allied beachheads, evening 6 June
- ⊖ Allied airborne landing
- --- D-Day objectives
- — front line, 7 June
- — front line, 17 June
- --- front line, 25 June
- ·-·- front line, 2 July
- — front line, 25 July
- → German counterattack
- ▽ German radar station
- ✦✦ major German gun battery

in France (and they now included many non-Germans among their ranks) were subjected to incessant bombing. By the spring of 1944, General Rommel, the overall tactical commander in the area, and Field Marshal Gerd von Rundstedt, the theater commander, realized that the Allies were conducting a highly effective interdiction campaign against the Normandy transportation network, especially the River Seine bridges. But they could not tell if the expected invasion would take place north or south of the Seine and when it would occur. In addition, as in other operations, Allied deceptions played a part. In this instance, the Allies carried out a number of elaborate diversions such as dummy paratroopers, misleading naval feints and radio traffic, and a bogus army in Britain, commanded by, of all people, Lieutenant General Patton. Measures, such as these, helped the Allies achieve tactical surprise.

Roosevelt and Churchill made General Eisenhower the supreme commander of the operation. He brought with him a number of subordinate commanders from Italy, including Air General Carl Spaatz to command U.S. Strategic Forces in Europe, and generals Bernard Montgomery and Omar Bradley to lead their respective ground forces. Allied forces in Britain consisted of 39 divisions and about 2,900,000 personnel. There were 7,000 ships and landing craft and an astounding 12,837 aircraft (including transports) available for the operation. The Germans, in comparison, had 58 divisions and 1,900,000 military personnel in the west, only 561 ships, and 919 aircraft, many of which were not in commission when the Allied invasion began on 6 June.

The invasion began just after midnight with airborne drops designed to link up with the amphibious forces and to gain control of vital bridges. The Allied gliders and paratroopers were more widely scattered than had been hoped, but by morning parts of the units, including the U.S. 82nd and 101st Airborne divisions, had gathered themselves and were moving

The two artificial harbors or, "mulberries," secretly constructed in England and assembled in Normandy, lacked sufficient capacity to support the Allied armies during Operation Overlord. For the next month, supplies had to be brought ashore across open beaches. The complexity of such operations is reflected in this photograph of "Easy Sector" at Omaha Beach, photographed just after 6 June 1944. Note the freighters standing offshore, landing craft on the beach, barrage balloons overhead, and the trucks snaking their way to and from the beach.

toward their bridge or beach-exit objectives. Pre-dawn naval and air bombardments continued to pound the coast until about 6 A.M. At 6:30 A.M., on a rising tide, the seaborne forces began streaming ashore on five main beaches along a 60-mile front. The Americans were on the right, with the 4th Infantry Division landing at Utah Beach, and the 1st and 29th Infantry at Omaha Beach. Two British and one Canadian division started disembarking on Gold, Juno, and Sword, the three beaches on the left.

Only at Omaha were great difficulties encountered. German artillery and small arms fire were heavy, the foreshore obstacles had not been cleared sufficiently, and the American assault teams and shore parties remained pinned down on the beaches for approximately four hours. But by 11 A.M., with the help of

naval gunfire, the Germans' deadly barrages started to abate, and U.S. soldiers began to move across the beach and to establish themselves among protected dunes and other defensive positions. By noon, the American commanders were confident that Omaha could be held.

Throughout the afternoon, the Americans, British, and Canadians consolidated their beachheads and, except at Omaha, advanced steadily inland. By nightfall, some of the assault forces had linked up with the airborne units and had penetrated as far as six miles (only one mile at Omaha) from the coast. This distance was still short of the transportation hub of Caen, a D-Day objective, which was 8 miles inland, but on that first day, 155,000 Allied soldiers (including 23,400 airborne) had landed and the Allies were on the Continent to stay.

The relatively weak German response can be attributed, in part, to the inclement weather in the invasion zone which had forced Eisenhower to delay the invasion by a day, and to Allied bombing and strafing attacks which were particularly devastating during the daylight hours. Allied deception measures also contributed to the German response, for while the Germans were aware that the landings in Normandy marked the long-awaited western front, they refused to believe it was not a feint that would be followed by an assault in the Pas de Calais, north of Normandy. The Germans were convinced that the Allies had more divisions in Britain than was actually the case, that these forces would be employed in the Calais area, and, accordingly, the Wehrmacht did not move its coastal divisions out of the Calais area until the end of July.

During the next six weeks, and according to plan, the Allies expanded their beachhead and built up their forces, though against strong opposition. During the expansion British and U.S. armies achieved operational objectives, including the joining of British and American unit sectors near Port-en-Bessin on 9 June. Although the Germans knew American intentions through radio interceptions, U.S. divisions then fought through the difficult-to-traverse hedgerows of the Normandy countryside and sealed off the Cotentin Peninsula on 17 June. Next they moved northward and took the port of Cherbourg on the tip of the peninsula by 27 June. The capture of Cherbourg proved disappointing, however, since German demolition of the harbor and the city's defenses prevented it from being used as a landing port until September.

During the fighting, American small unit commanders demonstrated great resolve and ingenuity. Not only did they come up with innovations, such as bulldozers with "teeth" to cut through the hedgerows, but they also effectively used combined arms—a mix of infantry, armored, and artillery units, assisted by air, engineering, and tank destroyer formations—to deal the enemy a series of setbacks. To the east, the British Second Army experienced serious difficulties. Its divisions tried repeatedly, but were unable to capture Caen until 8 July, and they did not get into a war of movement until the end of the month, when a breakout in the American sector relieved the pressure on the British portion of the front.

Despite substantial German reinforcements, including eight *Panzer* divisions, by 25 July, the Allies had built up their forces to thirty-six divisions and 1,452,000 troops (812,000 U.S. and 640,000 British). They were assisted by two factors, which continued to be Allied advantages until the end of the war. One was Ultra, which with other intelligence sources, gave the Allies a great advantage. On occasion, Allied cryptographers were able to decode German messages within an hour-and-a-half after they were sent. Only a week after the Normandy landings, Montgomery, Bradley, and the other commanders

had precise information on the location of enemy land, sea, and air formations throughout the region. Moreover, Ultra at times allowed the Allies to influence the tactical course of a battle. On 13 June, for instance, it permitted American units to snuff out a German *Panzer* attack at Carentan, and it helped in the capture of Cherbourg two weeks later. In other words, Ultra had an effect at both the strategic and the tactical levels.

The other factor was air power. It had a devastating impact on German troop movements, and with the assistance of the French Resistance, which was sabotaging German supply operations, air attacks delayed the arrival of German supplies to the western front, sometimes for days. In addition, the Allied tactical air force began to be used effectively to provide close air support for ground troops. The success of air coverage led the Allies to pair a tactical air force with each of its land armies, a valuable addition with which to pursue combat operations.

Operation Cobra

On 25 July, the Americans launched their breakout from the Normandy lodgment starting with an advance south from St. Lô, after carpet bombing west of the town tore an opening in the German lines. Seven days later, the Third Army, with Patton as its commander, became operational. Its original mission was to exploit a gap at Avranches and to move west to capture Brittany's valuable ports, which would provide a logistical base

The distinctive hedgerows of Normandy, called bocages *in French, traditionally planted to divide farmland into small parcels, provided excellent cover for German defenders. The level of the fields enclosed by the hedgerows was often two to three feet below the soil supporting the roots of the bushes, making up the hedgerows. When tanks climbed the mounds of soil, their unarmored bottoms were exposed, making them susceptible to light, anti-tank weapons. Hedgerows significantly slowed Allied advances in Normandy.*

for eventual offensives toward Paris and beyond. But on 3 August, Bradley, commanding the Twelfth Army Group, became aware, through Ultra, that the German forces to the east were in disarray, except near Mortain, where the First Army was alerted to prepare for a German counteroffensive. Given the favorable situation, Bradley ordered Patton to clear Brittany with only one of his three corps, and to use his other two corps to push south and east toward the Loire and Seine rivers as rapidly as possible. Patton did not have to be told twice (he had already surmised the possibility). At about the same time, the German position in Normandy began to fall apart as its lines of defense were penetrated and units of varying size were isolated. The Allied offensive across France was ready to commence. It soon became a dash as portions of Patton's troops, with the support of General O.P. Weyland's XIX Tactical Air Command, advanced up to 160 miles in eleven

days between 3 and 14 August.

Meanwhile, on 10 August, one of Patton's corps struck north from Le Mans through Alençon to Argentan hoping to link up with elements of the Canadian army attacking southward and to trap up to twenty-one German divisions in a pocket east of Falaise. Hard fighting ensued, but the Allies were unable to close the gap between American, Canadian, and Polish forces in time to prevent a number of Germans from eluding capture. The Germans lost thousands of troops and hundreds of artillery pieces, tanks, and vehicles in the battle, and although it was a serious defeat for the Wehrmacht, it was not as decisive a battle as it might have been had the Allies coordinated their operations more closely. On 20 August, Patton's army crossed the upper Seine, and on 25 August, with the assistance of French forces and the Resistance, the Allies liberated Paris.

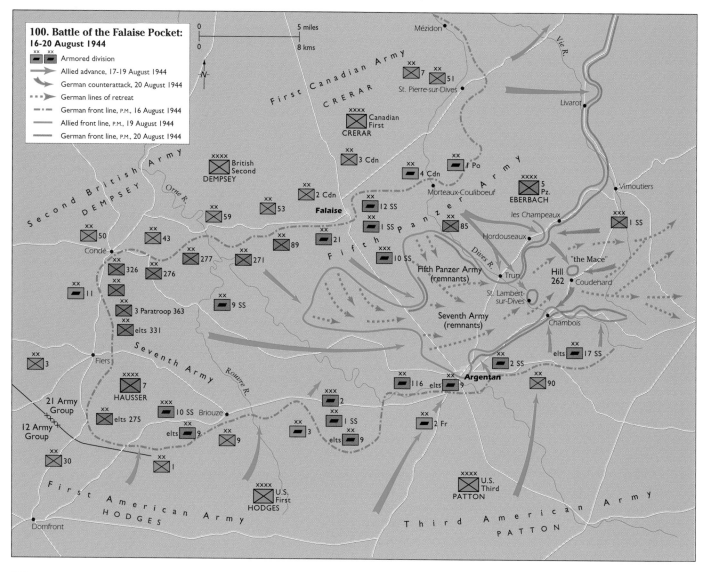

Operation Dragoon

Ten days earlier, another Allied invasion was launched against southern France, code-named Operation Anvil. First suggested in early 1943 after Operation Torch opened up the western Mediterranean, it had been approved at the Teheran Conference in November of that year, but then postponed because of problems on the Italian front and the priority given to Operation Overlord. U.S. leaders refused to abandon the operation.

Renamed Dragoon, the operation was launched along the French Riviera on 15 August, when troops of the Seventh Army landed on the Riviera between Toulon and Nice, commanded by General Alexander Patch, Jr. His force of 250,000 comprised ten U.S. and French divisions, seven of which had fought in Italy. There were 2,250 ships and naval craft, and over 4,000 aircraft. Opposing them were eight-and-two-thirds German divisions, mostly second-rate troops, scattered throughout the area, and only 75 ships and 175 aircraft. Even though the Germans had learned the exact day and the approximate location of the invasion between Toulon and Nice, there was little they could do to stop it.

Following the same pattern used in Normandy, paratroopers and glider forces began landing at 3:15 A.M. At 8:00 A.M., three American divisions—the 3rd, the 45th, and the 36th—began disembarking along a forty-five mile front centering on St. Tropez. The next day, seven French, follow-up divisions came ashore as well. With overwhelming air and naval superiority, the ground formations moved quickly into the interior, and on the night of 17-18 August, the German theater commander ordered his troops to start withdrawing from all of southern France.

The Allies, assisted by Ultra and by the French Resistance, attempted to trap portions of the German forces during the retreat on two occasions: Along the Rhône River north of Montélimar and near Besançon in eastern France. But, in both instances, the enemy eluded capture. By 11 September, the Germans had made contact with other German units setting up a defensive barrier in the approaches to the Vosges Mountains in the east. By this time, the American and French troops had stretched their lines of logistics to the limit, and on 15 September, Allied commanders brought the French Riviera campaign to an end.

Farther north, Patton's Third and Lieutenant General Courtney Hodges' First armies moved into eastern France and toward the German frontier. But in early September, their momentum began to slow, as a lack of supplies and stiffening German resistance were taking their toll on the Americans. On 25 September, General Eisenhower ordered the Third Army to halt its offensive operations and to assume a defensive posture, thereby ending Patton's nearly 400-mile dash across France.

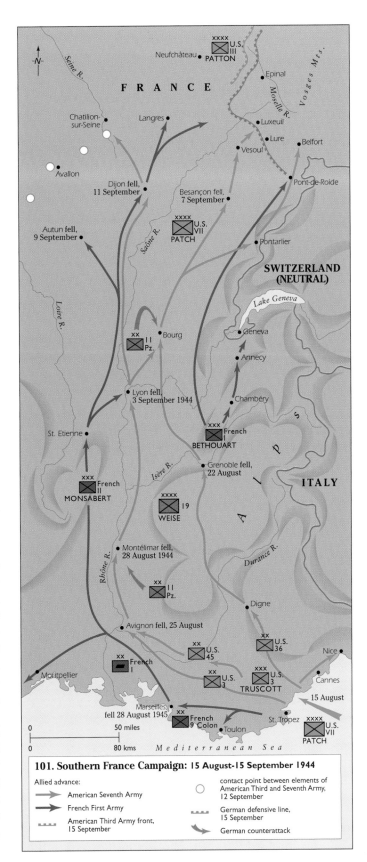

101. Southern France Campaign: 15 August–15 September 1944

Allied advance:

→ American Seventh Army

→ French First Army

···· American Third Army front, 15 September

○ contact point between elements of American Third and Seventh Army, 12 September

···· German defensive line, 15 September

→ German counterattack

Dwight Eisenhower poses amid the generals who directed the U.S. advance across France and into Germany. In the front row, from the left, sit Lieutenant General William H. Simpson, 9th Army; General George S. Patton (in the chrome helmet), 3rd Army; General Carl A. Spaatz, U.S. Strategic Air Forces in Europe; Eisenhower; Lieutenant General Omar N. Bradley, 12th Army; Lieutenant General Courtney H. Hodges, 1st Army; and Lieutenant General Leonard T. Gerow, 15th Army. In the rear, left to right, stand Air Force commanders Brigadier General Ralph P. Sterling, Lieutenant General Hoyt S. Vandenberg, Major General O. P. Weyland, and Brigadier General Richard E. Nugent, who flank Walter Bedell Smith, Ike's chief of staff.

Germany had been dealt a number of other setbacks in the summer and early fall of 1944. There had been an unsuccessful attempt on Hitler's life on 20 July, engineered by disenchanted German officers. His response had been a widespread purge of individuals involved or suspected in the plot to kill him. Furthermore, the German army had suffered numerous defeats as the territory it held in the east, France, and most of Belgium had been lost. The Germans also had suffered three million casualties on all fronts. Despite these setbacks, the Nazi regime continued to hold on.

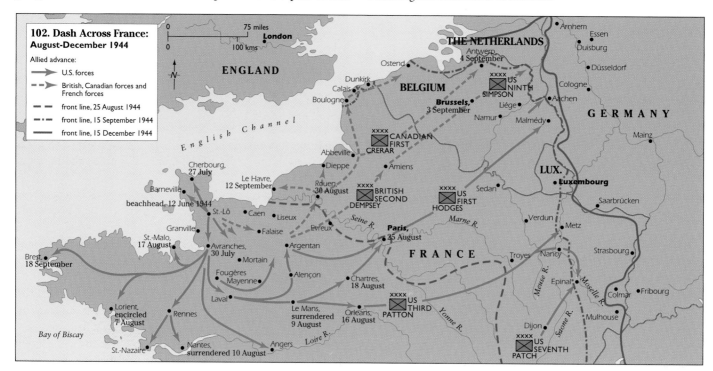

Operation Market Garden

In a bold move designed to bring the European war to a conclusion, possibly before the end of 1944, the Allies attempted in mid-September to launch a narrow thrust through Belgium into the Netherlands and across the Rhine River at Arnhem. The operation, later known as a "bridge too far," called for airborne troops—the U.S. 82nd and 101st and one British division—to seize and hold five key bridges, the last of which spanned the Rhine at Arnhem. A column of British armor was to exploit the situation by advancing rapidly along a narrow front, crossing the bridges, and opening a corridor for ground troops. Montgomery's forces in the Netherlands would

During Operation Market Garden, paratroopers from the U.S. Airborne Division disarm captured German troops as civilians look on in Eindhoven, the Netherlands. British Field Marshal Bernard Montgomery proposed the audacious plan, but Eisenhower approved it as supreme commander and, thus, had to bear responsibility for the failure of the overly ambitious operation.

attempt to outflank the German defenses in France, so that his formations might then be able to drive into northern Germany and secure a rapid victory. But, a combination of unexpectedly strong German resistance and poor Allied planning and execution, doomed the operation to failure. The war continued into 1945.

The Ardennes Campaign

Despite its victory at Arnhem, Germany was in a difficult position, so difficult that some of Hitler's commanders advised him to surrender. But Hitler would not listen to defeatist talk, and during August, he began to contemplate another offensive, this one in the west, since he considered the British and Americans less capable adversaries than the Russians. This was the genesis of the Ardennes offensive, also called the Battle of the Bulge.

The German plan called for two *Panzer* armies, supported by two regular armies on the flanks, to break through the Ardennes forest, as the Germans had done in 1940, then to move rapidly across the Meuse River and capture the port of Antwerp, thus cutting the Allied forces in two. On 16 December, aided by overcast skies, the Germans struck. It was a fortunate choice, for only inexperienced or badly battered American divisions were deployed in the area. The Allies were surprised. They knew that the Germans had been massing their forces, but it was thought that the enemy was merely strengthening its defenses. American intelligence also knew

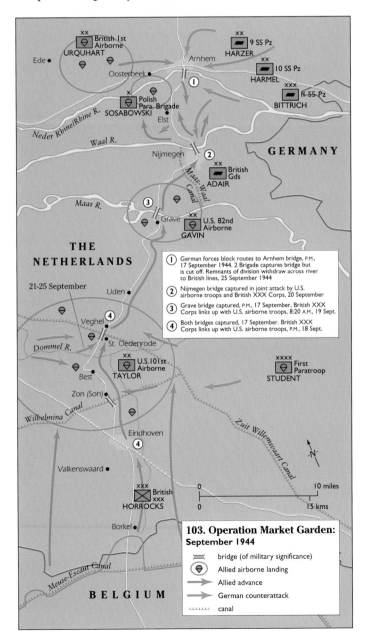

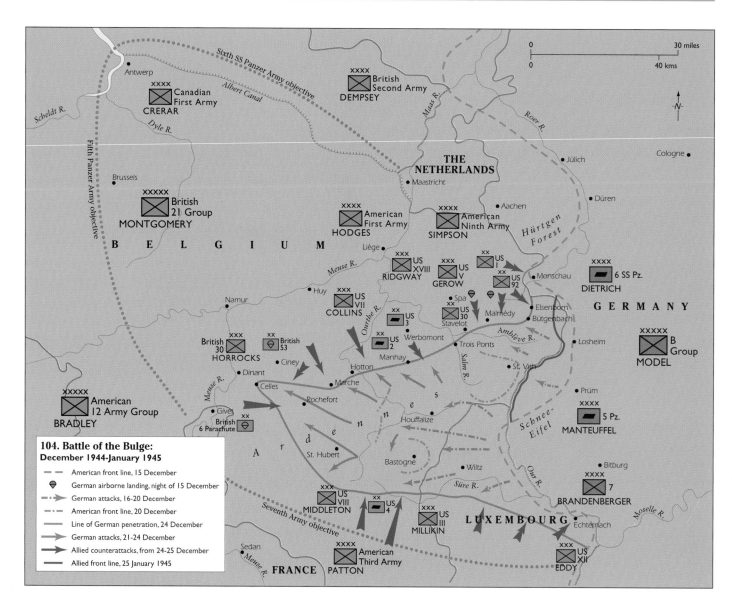

104. Battle of the Bulge:
December 1944-January 1945

- – – American front line, 15 December
- German airborne landing, night of 15 December
- German attacks, 16-20 December
- American front line, 20 December
- Line of German penetration, 24 December
- German attacks, 21-24 December
- Allied counterattacks, from 24-25 December
- Allied front line, 25 January 1945

that the Germans were conserving oil, but they concluded that their Nazi opponent was merely running short, and not saving oil for an attempted breakthrough.

The Germans gained early successes, but the Americans responded well, and the Wehrmacht failed to reach the River Meuse. The battle came to hinge on the transportation hubs at St. Vith and Bastogne, where in the face of intense German pressure, the Americans held out. At Bastogne, the acting commander of the 101st Airborne, Brigadier General Anthony McAuliffe, gave his famous cryptic reply to a German demand for the Americans to surrender. "Nuts!" he replied. His troops fought on.

McAuliffe's response was not as courageous as one might think. He knew help was on the way. Eisenhower had ordered Patton to shift the focus of his forces to deal with the German

offensive, and the Third Army commander rapidly readied his units for a 50-to-75-mile drive north to engage the enemy. When the skies cleared on Christmas Day, German units were subjected to incessant bombing and strafing attacks. The American troops under the British Field Marshal Montgomery in the northern portion of the invasion sector also helped to blunt the attack.

Having stopped the Germans, the Americans now began to collapse the bulge. Although there was hard fighting, by 28 January, the Allies had fought the Germans back to the line of the start of the offensive near the Belgian-German border. Eisenhower was so distressed by the fighting in the Ardennes battle, which was followed up by German offensives on other fronts in the west, that he cabled Washington requesting that any reserves that remained in the United States be dispatched to Europe. Although those reserves had been earmarked for the Pacific, they were shipped to France instead.

Victory Achieved

All of the 1945 Allied campaigns, including punishing bombing attacks, became controversial because of the Cold War that followed the war. But at the outset of 1945, the main concern of Allied military leaders continued to be the defeat of Germany. Increasingly unrealistic, Hitler refused to negotiate or surrender, and despite many problems, continued to fight on. But the Red Army and Soviet air force soon made significant progress and dealt a series of grave setbacks to the Germans. The Russians started an offensive on 12 January, took Warsaw on 17 January, captured Budapest in mid-February, and entered Vienna in early April. The forces under marshals Georgi Zhukov and Ivan Konev continued to face stiff opposition, but by the end of March they came within thirty-eight miles of Berlin.

In Italy, the Allies might merely have held their ground, but the British and the Americans in the theater insisted that they undertake their own offensive, and on 9 April, it began. After meeting initial resistance, the well-prepared and rested British Eighth and American Fifth armies pushed through the lines of the dispirited German and Italian soldiers, and the Allies finally captured Bologna on 21 April. The Allied offensive turned into a pursuit of the broken German armies. By 29 April, the German commanders, facing an impossible situation, contacted the Allies and signed the necessary documents for a surrender, which took effect on 2 May.

The major fighting for the Allies in 1945 still remained in the west. Concentrated near the German border were seven armies. In the north were the Canadian First and the British Second armies. In the center were the Americans—Lieutenant General William Simpson's Ninth Army, Lieutenant General Courtney Hodges' First, Lieutenant General George Patton's Third, and Lieutenant General Alexander Patch's Seventh Army. On the extreme southern flank was the First French Army.

Eisenhower resisted British pressure for a single thrust into Germany and decided to continue his strategy of advancing on a broad front. The initial goal for Allied forces was to close to the Rhine. On 19 January, a series of offensives started to unfold. By early March, several units were within sight of the river. Allied commanders expected they would have to prepare carefully before attempting to cross the last major barrier to the heart of Germany, but on 7 March, a railway bridge at Remagen was taken intact. Elements of the U.S. 9th Armored Division crossed to the eastern side of the river, where they secured a substantial bridgehead and erected several pontoon bridges, before the original bridge gave way and collapsed ten days later. This unforeseen good fortune certainly relieved

some of the pressure for Patton's Third Army, which managed to cross the Rhine near Oppenheim on the night of 22 March, and Montgomery's 21st Army Group, which followed suit farther north the next night. The battle for the Rhine was won.

The battle for Germany was about to enter its final phase when U.S. forces surrounded the Ruhr industrial region and captured it in early April. Despite continuing German resistance, by mid-month, the Americans crossed the River Elbe. Eisenhower, at this point, decided not to "race" the Red Army, whose main forces were a lot closer to Berlin. He based his decision on a number of factors. A key factor was that the Soviets had more troops in Germany than the British and Americans—one-and-a-quarter million versus one million western troops. Equally important was the fact that the United States expected to need Russian assistance in the war against Japan and wished to avoid straining relations with Stalin. In fact, U.S. soldiers in Europe were already being pulled out of the front lines and being shifted to the United States for deployment to the Pacific. Moreover, with the death of President Franklin Roosevelt on 12 April, the new president, Harry Truman, was reluctant to make changes to zone boundaries that the Allies had agreed for the occupation of Germany, which had placed Berlin inside the Soviet zone.

As Soviet troops pressed on toward Berlin, Germany collapsed. General Patch's divisions raced into southern Germany to preclude the Nazis from setting up a possible redoubt

Always the showman, the flamboyant George S. Patton posed on a pontoon bridge at Oppenheim when his 3rd Army finally reached the Rhine River on 24 March 1945. Before crossing into the German homeland, Patton stopped to urinate in the Rhine, commenting, "I have been looking forward to this for a long time." After crossing the river, Patton led his troops on a rapid drive across southern Germany to the prewar border of Czechoslovakia, where he was ordered to halt.

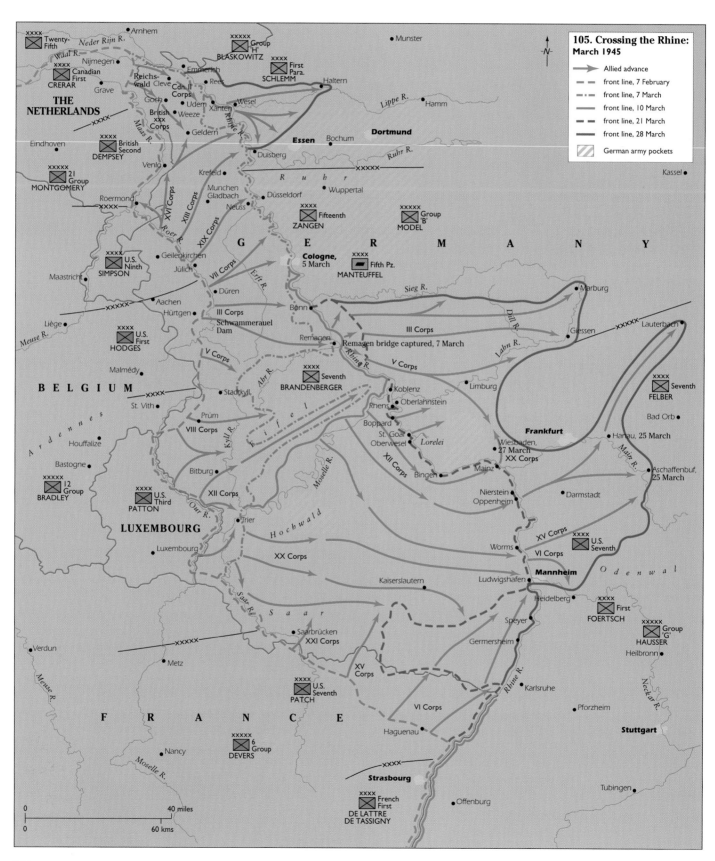

German P.O.W.s file past Americans pouring into Germany in 1945 (above). General George C. Marshall (below) presided over U.S. victory as the army's chief of staff.

106. The Collapse of Germany: April-May 1945

→ Allied advance
⇢ German retreat
– – – front line, April 1945
—— front line, May 1945

German army pockets
① 1. Remnants of Eleventh Army surrender, 19 April 1945
② 2. Remnants of Army Group B surrender, 21 April 1945

▨ German-held territory at time of surrender, 8 May 1945

---

in the Bavarian Alps. Hodges' and Patton's troops moved into central Germany and American units established contact with the Red Army at Torgau on 25 April. The Allied forces of the east and west had met.

As the American and British forces moved into Germany, they began to liberate a number of German concentration camps. The Allies had been aware of their existence for years, but these visual reminders of German bestiality—the Soviets had already seen a number of camps in the east—were almost more than the Allies could bear. What has become known as the Holocaust showed Nazi Germany at its worst.

With the end in sight, on 30 April, Hitler killed himself in his bunker in Berlin. The next day, the Red Army captured Berlin, Germany's capital city. The new government of Admiral Karl Dönitz quickly arranged for a surrender. On 7 May, at Eisenhower's headquarters, a schoolhouse in Reims, France, the German military signed the surrender documents. The Allies declared victory in Europe on 8 May, and the next day, surrender proceedings, similar to those that took place in Reims, were staged for the benefit of the Soviets in Berlin. The European war was over.

Over the years, historians have largely attributed the Allies' victory to their industrial power which, in the end, overwhelmed the opposition. But, more recently, historians have begun to emphasize other factors. The Allied triumph was a result of economic might, combined with technological ability, a realistic strategy, combat prowess especially during the later stages of the war, and a superior moral tone. World War II was certainly a very bloody war: 405,399 American lives were lost. Only the American Civil War, with its 618,222 deaths, surpassed it in terms of Americans killed. Winning the war in Europe has had a tremendous impact on the United States, and on the world since World War II, and it set the stage for the nearly half-century-long Cold War that followed.

The Korean War: 1950-53

The Korean War was a seminal event in U.S. history. One of the least studied of American wars, it is often known as "the Forgotten War." It was a key event in the Cold War and a prime example of the U.S. policy of full militarized containment of Communism. Militarily, it is significant both for its two-phase nature of maneuver and stalemate, and for the restrictions placed on the conduct of the war by political leaders. Korea was the first limited war in the nuclear age. It was also the only time since World War II that the armies of two major powers, China and the United States, met on the battlefield. Diplomatically the war is interesting for the miscalculations and misperceptions on both sides that led up to it. Korea was also the first United Nations (U.N.) war.

General Background
In 1950, Korea was a poor country with few roads. Most of the country is mountainous, especially in the north, and there are extremes of climate. Korea is remarkably homogeneous, with no dispossessed racial or ethnic minorities. For most of its history, it has been a single entity. The 38th parallel, thus, arbitrarily divides a single geographic, economic, linguistic, and ethnic entity. The only social divisions are by class and clan.

Both sides in the Korean War fought hard and sustained high casualties. Following a battle in the Haktong-ni area of Korea on 28 August 1950, a U.S. soldier comforts his comrade while a corpsman fills out casualty forms.

The division of Korea into two hostile states had its origins in an agreement reached between the United States and the Soviet Union in August 1945, with the defeat of Japan in World War II. Under this agreement, Korea, which had been part of the Japanese empire since 1905, was split into two along the 38th parallel, with the U.S. occupying the southern part of the peninsula, and the Soviet Union's Red Army holding the northern area. Each power then installed its own Korean leaders, strongly anticommunist in the American zone and procommunist in the Soviet zone. The advent of the Cold War made this temporary division permanent. In late 1947, the U.N. General Assembly recognized Korea's claim to independence and laid plans to establish a unified government and the withdrawal of occupation forces.

Formation of New Governments
A United Nations' commission arrived in Seoul to supervise national elections for a constituent assembly in January 1948. When the commission was refused admission to the Soviet zone, it recommended that elections proceed in the South. In August 1948, the Republic of Korea (R.O.K.) was officially proclaimed, headed by seventy-year-old, dedicated Korean nationalist, Syngman Rhee, strongly conservative and widely detested by most democratic elements in Korea for his strong-arm methods and persecution of political opponents.

During the following month, a Korean Peoples' Democratic Republic (D.P.R.K.), which also claimed authority over the entire country, was organized in the North under the presidency of veteran Communist Kim Il Sung. Kim led guerrilla raids against Japanese outposts in North Korea. Fleeing a Japanese crackdown, he and his followers settled in Siberia in 1941. In 1945, he surfaced as a major in the Red Army that took the Japanese surrender in Korea above the 38th parallel. In December, the U.N. General Assembly endorsed the Republic of Korea as the only lawfully elected government, and that same month, the Soviet Union also announced that it had withdrawn all its forces from North Korea. The United States completed withdrawal of its occupation forces in June 1949.

U.S. Hands-Off Policy
Beginning in May 1948, sporadic fighting had broken out along the 38th parallel, and in September 1949, the U.N. Commission on Korea warned of civil war. The U.S. State Department, worried that Rhee might instigate a war, went out of its way to disassociate itself from these border clashes and President Harry S. Truman issued a policy statement, in April 1948, warning that actions in Korea would not automatically involve the United States in a war. Unfortunately, this attempt at a hands-off policy only served to lead Kim to

0   75 miles
0   100 kms

N

SOVIET UNION

MANCHURIA

to Harbin ↑

Vladivostok

C H I N A

to Mukden

Tunghwa

Chongjin

Yalu R.

Kanggye

Chosan

Chosin
Reservoir

Chosin

Iwon

Chongchon R.

Hagard

Sea of Japan

Sinuiju

Hungnam

NORTH
KOREA

Yongdok

Wonsan

Pyongyang

Imjin R.

Iron
Triangle

Ongjin
Peninsula

Pyonggang

Pork Chop Hill

Kumhwa

Chorwon

Yangyang

38th Parallel

Kaesong

Panmunjom

Chunchon

Kimpo
airfield

SOUTH
KOREA

Samchok

Seoul

Inchon

Suwon
airfield

Taebaek Mts.

Osan

Han R.

Yellow

Sea

Kum R.

Taejon

Sobaek Mts.

Yondok

Kumchon

Pohang

Kunsan

Naktong R.

Taegu

Yonil airfield

Chiri
Mts.

Masan

Pusan

Mokpo

Koje-do
Island

Korea Strait

Tsushima
(Japan)

Tsushima Stait

J A P A N

107. The Korean War: 1950-53

Limit of North Korean advance,
June-September 1950

Limit of United Nations advance,
November 1950

Limit of Chinese advance,
January 1951

Armistice line, 27 July 1953

battle site

principal railroads

principal Chinese railroad
supply lines

principal roads

major airfields

international boundary

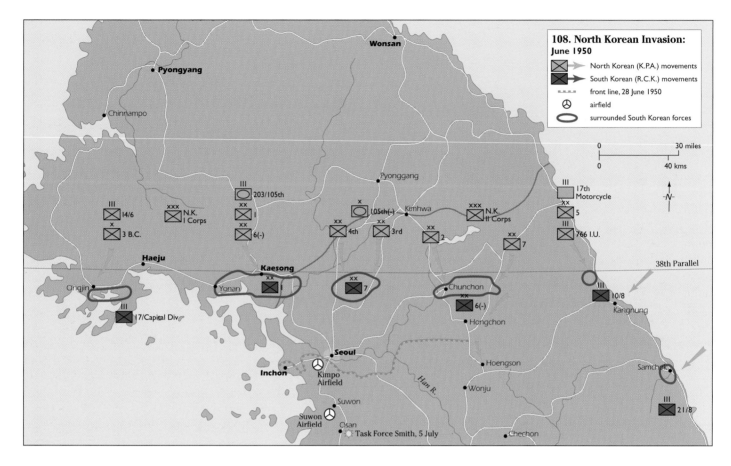

108. North Korean Invasion: June 1950

North Korean (K.P.A.) movements

South Korean (R.C.K.) movements

front line, 28 June 1950

airfield

surrounded South Korean forces

0   30 miles

0   40 kms

-N-

38th Parallel

believe that the United States would not fight for Korea. U.S. Secretary of State Dean Acheson, in January 1950, specifically excluded both Korea and Taiwan from the Asian "defensive perimeter" vital to American interests. Acheson remarked that Korea was not within the direct defense perimeter of the United States, although he made it clear that the United States had a strong interest in the country. His decision was not intended to invite a Communist response.

The Military Situation in June 1950

By June 1950, when North Korea invaded the South, the Korean Peoples Army (K.P.A.) was equipped with weapons surrendered by the Japanese and with Russian weapons left behind when the Soviets departed Korea. In the spring of 1950, the Russians supplied the North with additional modern arms, including 120 mm, heavy artillery; 120 T-34 tanks; trucks; automatic weapons; and about 180 new aircraft. The North Korean Army numbered about 135,000 men in ten divisions.

South of the 38th parallel, the military situation was very different. By the end of 1949, fewer than half of sixty-seven R.O.K. battalions had passed the battalion phase of their training. The R.O.K. had only 105 mm guns and no heavy artillery,

no tanks, no antitank weapons, and its air force consisted of only a few training and light, unarmed aircraft for liaison purposes. The R.O.K. had 95,000 men in eight divisions, only four of which were at full strength.

Washington was aware of the massive buildup in the North but failed to pay sufficient attention to Kim's intentions to reunify the peninsula by force, if necessary. Because of the quiet nature of the border in early 1950, U.S. leaders believed that the Communist powers were not ready to risk atomic war by resorting to armed aggression. The U.S. military was also very weak. It had been reduced from 12 million troops under arms in 1945 to only 1.5 million in 1950. It was short of combat ships, planes, and arms, and ammunition stockpiles were very low.

War Begins

North Korea invaded the South on 25 June 1950. The reasons behind the North Korean invasion were shrouded in mystery until the breakup of the Soviet Union in the 1980s to 1990s. Some believed it was a diversionary attack by the Communists to draw U.S. attention from Europe, where the Russians had just suffered a rebuff in the Berlin Blockade of 1948-49. Others thought it was staged to test U.S. resolve, a demonstration to show the world that America was a "paper tiger," or an elaborate plot by Josef Stalin to help unseat Mao Zedong in China. The long held claim of the Communist bloc and some sympathetic U.S. historians that the war was begun with a South Korean attack on the North, initiated by Rhee to reunite the two Koreas under his leadership, has been disproved by modern scholarship.

The reasons behind the invasion were local, not global. Just before the invasion, Rhee's government suffered an election reversal, and given the American position regarding Korea and Kim's own attitude, the moment seemed ripe to invade the South. Moscow and Beijing were actively involved in preparations for the invasion as early as the spring of 1949, and Soviet military advisors helped with the planning. Kim Il Sung consulted Josef Stalin in March and April 1950 concerning an invasion and provided Stalin with exaggerated promises of military success, eventual Communist dominance in the South, and American abstention from intervention. Stalin assured Kim of sufficient Soviet support to make the invasion succeed, but he also ruled out direct Soviet intervention. In addition, Stalin ordered the North Koreans to desist from any action that might precipitate war before the North was ready. There was a consequent diminution in border clashes between October 1949 and June 1950 when North Korea invaded the South. Stalin also insisted that Kim meet with Mao Zedong to secure his assent, which was forthcoming at the end of 1949, when Mao Zedong released the 164th and 166th Divisions of People's Liberation Army (P.L.A.) to return to Korea. These units were made up of Korean volunteers who had fought against the Japanese and the Nationalists in China. Their arrival in North Korea provided the K.P.A. with about 30 to 40 thousand well-trained troops that could be used to spearhead the invasion of the South.

U.N. and U.S. Support for the South

At the time of the invasion, the Soviet Union was boycotting the U.N. Security Council over its refusal to admit Communist China. Because of the absence of the Russians, the Security Council moved quickly to call for an immediate end to hostilities and the withdrawal of North Korean forces from the South. Then, on 27 June, U.N. member states were asked to furnish "every assistance" to R.O.K. forces.

President Truman broadened the range of U.S. air and naval operations, previously restricted to south of the 38th parallel, to include North Korea, and he authorized U.S. forces to protect Pusan, the country's only modern port. General Douglas MacArthur flew to Korea from Japan and recommended that U.S. ground forces be immediately committed, which President Truman authorized on 30 June.

The conflict caught MacArthur and Washington completely by surprise. Truman later described his decision to use force in Korea as the toughest he had to make while in office. But U.S. intervention was virtually certain, given the determination of the United States to contain Communism, the regional threat posed by the 1949 Communist victory in the Chinese civil war, the anticommunist hysteria fomented by U.S. Senator Joseph McCarthy, and the lessons learned from the appeasement of Adolf Hitler at Munich in 1938.

U.S. strength in the Far East was woefully inadequate. All four U.S. divisions in Japan were below authorized strength; the men were poorly trained; and there were serious shortages of equipment, including rifles. By cannibalizing the 7th Division, MacArthur was able to get the 24th, 25th, and 1st Cavalry Divisions to Korea quickly, within two weeks of the start of the war.

The fighting went badly for Korea. Seoul fell in only three days, on 28 June. R.O.K. forces had to abandon most of their equipment when bridges over the Han River on the southern edge of the city were blown up. On 5 July, the first American force went into battle against the North Korean Army at Osan, fifty miles south of Seoul. This operation was named Task Force Smith. It numbered only 540 Americans, who were expected to stop an entire North Korean division of approximately 12,000 men, spearheaded by Russian T-34 tanks. Not surprisingly, the K.P.A. quickly engulfed the American force. The Americans' largest and most powerful antitank weapon was the 2.36-inch bazooka. Its round, however, could not

U.S. forces were poorly armed at the beginning of the Korean War, with few anti-tank weapons and no heavy artillery. Here, men of the 7th U.S. Infantry Division fire a 75-mm recoilless rifle against Communist forces.

Early in the war, U.S. and R.O.K. troops could do little to delay the more numerous and better armed North Korean forces. A group of U.S. engineers in this photograph set charges to prepare to blow up a bridge as Korean refugees continued to cross it in their trek southward. Destruction of rail and road bridges often left civilians at the mercy of the North Koreans.

penetrate T-34 tank armor. One daring American soldier fired twenty-two bazooka rounds at K.P.A. tanks, not stopping one. Task Force Smith had only thirteen armor-piecing rounds, the total issued for the Pacific theater.

The U.S. Navy and Air Force provided invaluable assistance. Most U.N. supplies came to Korea by sea, and the U.S. Navy kept the sea lanes open and provided gunfire and carrier aviation support. Later in the war, it carried out amphibious operations and evacuations. The U.S. Air Force obtained domination over the Korean skies early in the war, providing invaluable tactical air support to retreating troops and by bombing and strafing the K.P.A. Within weeks, it had taken out all strategic targets in North Korea.

At the same time, following the request of the U.N. Security Council, a United Nations Command (U.N.C.) was set up and seventeen countries contributed military assistance. Washington insisted on a U.S. commander, and on 10 July, President Truman appointed MacArthur to head the U.N.C. At peak strength, U.N.C. forces totaled nearly 700,000 men: About 400,000 R.O.K. troops, 250,000 U.S. troops, and 35,000 from other nations (including two United Kingdom and one Canadian brigade, forming the 1st Commonwealth Division; a brigade from Turkey; and troops from Australia, Thailand, the Philippines, Colombia, Ethiopia, France, Greece, Belgium, Luxembourg, the Netherlands, and New Zealand). Other states sent medical units.

Over the next weeks, the United States rushed more troops to Korea. Many American draftees were brought into the service, issued an M-1, and found themselves in combat in Korea ten days later. Inadequate stocks and faulty equipment were a constant problem for U.S. troops. The North Koreans used civilians as human shields and shot prisoners. All of this contributed to low U.S. morale and poor combat effectiveness.

Battle for the Pusan Perimeter

For a month, U.N.C. troops were being steadily pushed back, until mid-July, when they were restricted to the so-called Pusan Perimeter—an area approximately 30-50 miles around the vital port of Pusan on the southeastern tip of the Korean peninsula. Until mid-September, U.S. and R.O.K. forces bought valuable time, holding the perimeter as the U.N.C. raced to build up its strength. U.N.C. control of the skies, heavy artillery fire, and U.S. Lieutenant General Walton

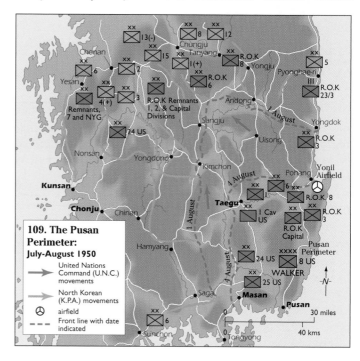

109. The Pusan Perimeter: July-August 1950

→ United Nations Command (U.N.C.) movements
→ North Korean (K.P.A.) movements
Ⓜ airfield
--- Front line with date indicated

Walker's brilliant maneuvering are all to be credited for this important stand. Walker shifted his Eighth U.S. Army around the perimeter in a superb example of mobile defense. Fortunately the K.P.A. played into Walker's hands by failing to mount simultaneous attacks. By early September, the perimeter had been stabilized and U.N.C. forces outnumbered the K.P.A. by three to two.

Inchon

As the Battle of the Pusan perimeter raged, General MacArthur was preparing an amphibious assault deep behind enemy lines to cut the main K.P.A. line of supply and communications at Inchon and Seoul. Confident Walker could hold the Pusan Perimeter, MacArthur weakened the Eighth Army in order to build up an invasion force. MacArthur selected Inchon, just fifteen miles from Seoul, for the landing, because the Inchon-Seoul area was the main K.P.A. communications and supply line center. Cutting the supply lines there would starve the K.P.A. on the Pusan Perimeter and lessen pressure on the Eighth Army. Inchon was also Korea's second largest

Among the difficulties in the Inchon landing was a high sea wall. Here, men of the 1st U.S. Marine Division use scaling ladders to climb the sea wall in the landing of 15 September 1950.

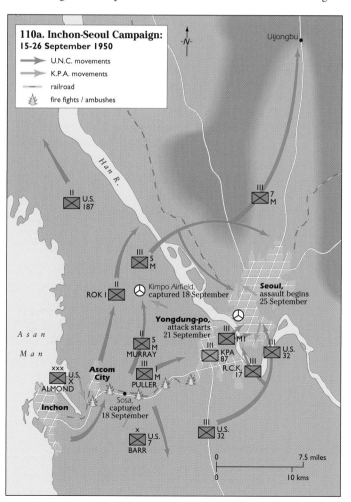

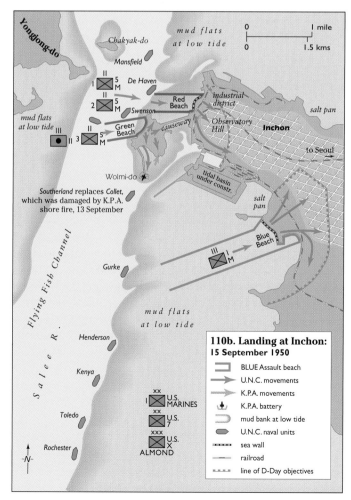

port and its Kimpo Airfield was one of the few hard-surface runways in Korea. Taking Inchon would also lead to the rapid recapture of Seoul, which would deliver a heavy psychological and political blow to North Korea.

Everyone in authority agreed on an amphibious assault, but only MacArthur felt it should be at Inchon. The Joint Chiefs of Staff and most subordinate commanders opposed it, and with good reason. Tides at Inchon, the second highest in the world, could range to as high as thirty-two feet. There would be only six hours in twenty-four that invaders could be resupplied. The only entrance to the port was a narrow and winding channel, a perfect location for mines; one ship sunk there would block all traffic, and strong currents associated with the tides would pose problems for assault craft. Finally, the attackers would have to scale high sea walls. Despite this, MacArthur overrode the opposition.

On 15 September, American Major General Edward Almond's X Corps carried out the invasion. It consisted of the 1st U.S. Marine Division (a heavy division of 20,000 men) and the 7th U.S. Army Division. Welcoming the operation, the U.S. Marine Corps saw it as an opportunity to prove that it was not obsolete in the nuclear age. Inchon was taken on 25 September with relatively light casualties and Seoul fell on 26 September.

Concurrent with the landing, U.N.C. forces broke out from the Pusan Perimeter, driving north. On 26 September, the two forces made contact and MacArthur then called on North Korean forces to surrender. The North Koreans ignored this, despite the fact that only one-fourth to one-third of the K.P.A. forces escaped to the north across the 38th parallel.

On 1 October, General Walker's R.O.K. I Corps crossed the 38th parallel and advanced toward Wonsan on the east coast of Korea. The U.N. General Assembly adopted a new resolution on 7 October, calling for a unified, independent, and democratic Korea. MacArthur ordered the crossing of the 38th parallel by U.S. troops on 7 October. The North Korean capital of Pyongyang fell to U.N.C. forces on 19 October, while the remnants of the K.P.A. and D.P.R.K. officials fled north toward the Yalu River. Little attention was paid, at this point, to the possibility of Chinese intervention.

The Push North

The U.N.C. was slow in pursuing the defeated K.P.A. forces. The decision to cross the 38th parallel had been taken in Washington and was only communicated to MacArthur on 27 September, delaying planning by a week. To carry out the drive to the Yalu River in North Korea, on the border with Manchuria, MacArthur chose to mount another amphibious assault, dividing his forces in an unfortunate fashion. X Corps would be transported by sea to Wonsan on the east coast. The

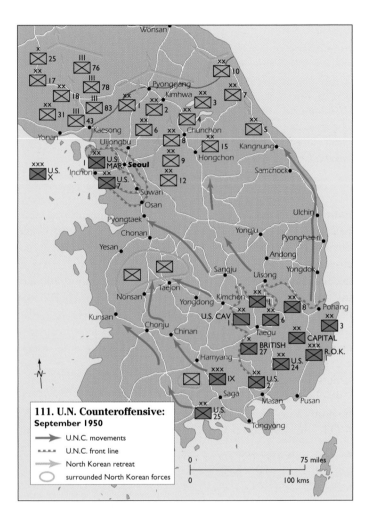

111. U.N. Counteroffensive:
September 1950

→ U.N.C. movements

---- U.N.C. front line

→ North Korean retreat

◯ surrounded North Korean forces

0 _____ 75 miles

0 _____ 100 kms

R.O.K. I Corps, advancing by land, would then join X Corps in clearing northeastern Korea by sending columns up the coast and through the mountains to the Yalu River. The U.S. Eighth Army, meanwhile, would remain on the west coast for the drive into northwest Korea. This meant that the two commands would be separated by a gap of twenty to fifty miles. Although staff generals and General Walker protested, MacArthur justified this decision on the basis of geography. The Taebaek mountain range ran north and south and made an advance on two axes the only practical means of overcoming the geographical difficulty. MacArthur assumed, wrongly as it turned out, that terrain in the gap was too rough to permit Communist forces to mount large-scale operations.

Meanwhile, X Corps embarked from Inchon on 7 October. It arrived at Wonsan on 19 October, waiting a week on board ship until the U.S. Navy cleared minefields laid by the North Koreans. Meanwhile, the R.O.K. had taken Wonsan by land.

The two-pronged advance north exacerbated MacArthur's developing contest of wills with Washington. A 27 September

U.S. naval warships, from destroyers to battleships, performed important shore bombardment duties during the Korean War. Here, the battleship New Jersey *fires her 16-inch guns with great accuracy against Communist shore installations.*

Joint Chiefs of Staff directive forbade the presence of non-Korean forces in the provinces contiguous to China and the Soviet Union in an attempt to mollify China, which was already alarmed. MacArthur ignored that directive by ordering his commanders to drive forward with "all speed and full utilization of their forces." The Joint Chiefs of Staff complained, but MacArthur cited Secretary of Defense George C. Marshall's statement that he was to be "unhampered" in his operations, and he claimed that the weakness of R.O.K. forces necessitated pushing American units forward. The Joint Chiefs of Staff acquiesced.

Walker's Eighth Army crossed the Chongchon River (at Sinanju) and, on 26 October, a reconnaissance platoon of the R.O.K. 6th Division reached the Yalu River at Chosan. By the

In the Korean War, the United States made extensive use of helicopters. They were employed in a variety of missions, including the rescue of downed pilots, resupply, observation, and deployment of troops. But perhaps their most important role was in medical evacuation. Here, a Sikorsky H-5 helicopter lifts off with a wounded soldier in a litter capsule, while a corpsman gives the soldier plasma. Rapid evacuation of casualties by helicopter saved many U.N.C. lives.

end of October, the North Korean Army had all but dissolved and the U.N.C. had taken 135,000 prisoners.

China Intervenes

From Mao Zedong's perspective, Chinese intervention was necessary for national security reasons. With U.S. bombers based in North Korea, China's most important industrial area of Manchuria would be vulnerable to attack. Entering the war was also an opportunity for China to secure recognition as a great power.

After South Korean forces crossed the 38th parallel, Chinese Foreign Minister Zhou Enlai stated that if American troops followed, China would fight. When Pyongyang fell,

**112. Invasion of North Korea:
October-November 1950**

→ U.N.C. movements

→○ Chinese (C.P.V.A.) movements and areas of troop concentration

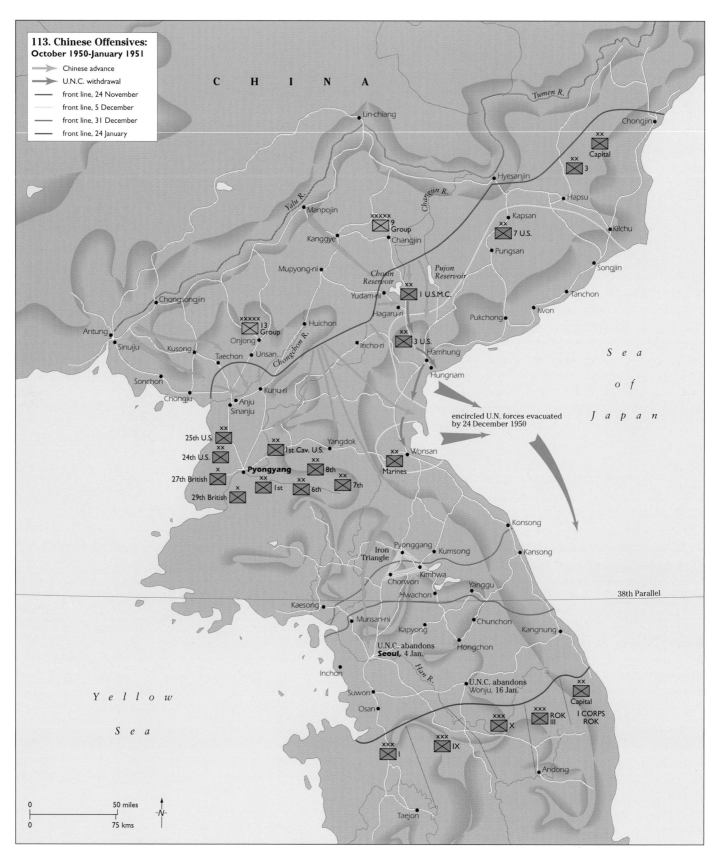

113. Chinese Offensives:
October 1950-January 1951

Chinese advance
U.N.C. withdrawal
front line, 24 November
front line, 5 December
front line, 31 December
front line, 24 January

C H I N A

Tumen R.

Lin-chiang

Chongjin

Yalu R.

Manpojin

Hyesanjin

Changjin R.

Hapsu

Kilchu

Kapsan

xxxxx
9 Group

Kanggye

Changjin

Pungsan

xx
7 U.S.

Songjin

Mupyong-ni

Huichon

Chosin Reservoir

Pujon Reservoir

Tanchon

Chongsongjin

xxxxx
13 Group

Yudam-ni

xx
I U.S.M.C.

Hagaru-ri

Pukchong

Iwon

Antung

Onjong

Chongchon R.

Incho-ri

xx
3 U.S.

Sinuiju

Kusong

Taechon

Unsan

Hamhung

S e a

Sonchon

Kunu-ri

Hungnam

o f

Chongju

Anju
Sinanju

J a p a n

xx
25th U.S.

encircled U.N. forces evacuated
by 24 December 1950

xx
24th U.S.

xx
1st Cav. U.S.

Yangdok

xx
Marines

Wonsan

x
27th British

Pyongyang

xx
1st

xx
8th

xx
7th

Konsong

x
29th British

xx
6th

Kansong

Pyonggang

Iron Triangle

Kumsong

Chorwon

Kimhwa

Yanggu

Hwachon

38th Parallel

Kaesong

Chunchon

Kangnung

Munsan-ni

Kapyong

Hongchon

U.N.C. abandons
Seoul, 4 Jan.

Inchon

U.N.C. abandons
Wonju, 16 Jan.

xx
Capital

Suwon

xxx
X

xxx
ROK
III

I CORPS
ROK

Osan

Y e l l o w

xxx
I

xxx
IX

S e a

Andong

Taejon

0 _____ 50 miles
0 _____ 75 kms

-N-

Beijing warned that U.S. invasion of the North was a direct threat to China's security. Although there was concern in Washington, there was also a belief that this was mere posturing.

In fact, Mao Zedong had begun contingency planning well before June 1950. He and Marshal Peng Du-hai, who would command Chinese forces in the field, believed that its world-wide commitments would prevent the United States from putting sufficient troops in the field to counter the Chinese advantage. Also, he regarded the Americans as soft and untrained in night-fighting techniques. Chinese preparations were well advanced by August 1950, before the Inchon invasion. On 2 October, Mao Zedong informed Josef Stalin that the Chinese were entering the war to drive the United States out of Korea and to assist in the expansion of world Communism.

Soviet Support

Moscow promised Beijing air support in the form of deploying MiG-15 jet fighter units already in China to cover Chinese forces massing along the border and to prevent U.S. air attacks on Manchurian targets. Soviet pilots began flying MiG-15 missions against the U.N.C. on 1 November. Although Chinese and North Korean pilots also became involved in the aerial combat over the area known as "MiG Alley," the Soviets bore the brunt of the air combat throughout the war. Soviet units also trained their Chinese counterparts and turned over aircraft to newly formed units. In this process, the U.S.S.R. helped China establish the third largest air force in the world.

Recently secured Soviet documents indicate that Stalin never planned to use his MiG-15s and antiaircraft forces for anything other than defending Chinese industry and supply lines. However, the Chinese claim that Stalin promised complete air support for their ground forces. Nonetheless, the Chinese went into the war in late October without air cover or bomber support. This alleged betrayal by Stalin was an important factor in the eventual breakdown in Sino-Soviet relations.

Early Chinese Activities

In a meeting with President Truman at Wake Island on 15 October, MacArthur played down the possibility of Chinese entry into the war. He assured Truman that the war was all but won. On 25 October, however, troops from the Chinese People's Volunteer Army (C.P.V.A.) attacked and defeated the R.O.K. 6th Division. A U.S. regiment sent to support the South Koreans was overwhelmed in fierce fighting at Unsan on 1-3 November. General Walker now wisely brought the bulk of his forces back behind the Chongchon River. Gradually, the positions stabilized and the Chinese offensive slackened.

The Chinese had also been active in the east, where the

Control of the skies over Korea gave United Nations forces an important advantage over Communist forces, especially in resupply over the difficult, mountainous terrain that marks much of Korea. Helicopters proved invaluable. A Sikorsky HRS-2 delivers supplies to U.N.C. troops in the rugged mountains of North Korea.

R.O.K. 3rd Division ran into a heavy Chinese force. But, as in the west, the Chinese suddenly halted operations and broke contact. Meanwhile, the first jet, air battle of history took place on 8 November, when an F-80 of the U.S. 5th Air Force shot down a MiG-15 over Sinanju in North Korea.

Unanswered Questions

This initial Chinese intervention, from 25 October to 7 November, raised questions that neither MacArthur nor Washington could answer. MacArthur believed the two-week-long intervention was only an attempt to save what remained of the shattered K.P.A. and to hold part of the country. Washington was not so certain. One of the great puzzles of the Korean War is how MacArthur could have misread the Chinese so badly and placed his command in such a vulnerable position. MacArthur seemed to have had complete confidence that U.N.C. air power could smash any large-scale Chinese intervention. Yet from 1 November 1950 to October 1951, Soviet MiGs so dominated the Yalu River area that U.S. B-29 bombers had to be withdrawn from daylight bombing.

Blinded by his own optimism and relying on inadequate intelligence, MacArthur and his staff were slow to grasp the measure of the Chinese move. His intelligence estimates of Chinese strength were far off the mark. Undetected, in part because of bad weather, by mid-November the Chinese had thirty divisions totaling 300,000 men in North Korea ready to resume the offensive.

MacArthur ordered his air force commander, General George Stratemeyer, to destroy the twin bridges over the Yalu River linking Sinuiju and Antung. This promoted another contest of wills with Washington, which canceled the order and limited bombing to five miles from the frontier. MacArthur raged that this threatened the destruction of his forces, and Washington gave way. On 8 November, nearly 400 U.N.C. aircraft struck bridges and towns on either side of the Yalu River. The effect of this bombing was minimal, however, as the Chinese were by that time secure in their positions in North Korea. In any case, the Yalu River was soon frozen and, thus, no barrier to resupply efforts.

Washington prohibited MacArthur from striking Manchuria or sending reconnaissance flights there but he could take other military steps he found advisable. This included a renewed advance by the U.N. forces. While U.S. forces were forbidden to attack Manchuria, it is also worth noting that the Soviets and Chinese did not attack Pusan by air. With the exception of some antiquated Soviet PO-2 biplanes, known as "Bed Check Charlies" because they sometimes bombed U.N. positions at night, Communist air power remained north of Pyongyang. U.S. convoys could travel, lights blazing at night, without fear of air attack. Nor did Communist forces make any effort to disrupt Allied sea communications. This was critical for U.N.C. prosecution of the war, and should be remembered by those who claimed that only U.S. forces were required to fight with restrictions placed on their operations by political leaders.

MacArthur's Obstacles

MacArthur wanted an immediate resumption of the offensive. But, X Corps was dependent logistically on the Eighth Army, rather than on Japan, and this meant a critical shortage of petroleum and other supplies. Weather was now also a serious problem, with temperatures already below freezing. In addition to the cold, there was the gap between the Eighth Army and X Corps. Walker insisted on holding his army along the Chongchon River until the supply problem could be rectified. Finally, he agreed to attack on 24 November.

At the eastern end of the U.N. line, X Corps was widely dispersed. Along the coast, divisions of the R.O.K. I Corps were pushing toward the Soviet frontier; the American 7th Division was moving through Pungsan toward the Yalu and two regiments of the 1st U.S. Marine Division in the center were pushing toward the Changjin (Chosin) Reservoir, sixty miles from the China border.

MacArthur was supremely confident of victory when he announced the final drive to the northernmost limit of the peninsula. Major General O. P. Smith, commanding the 1st U.S. Marine Division, was so concerned by MacArthur's decision that he communicated this to Washington. Smith slowed his advance and established a base at Hagaru-ri, which in all probability saved the division from annihilation in the weeks

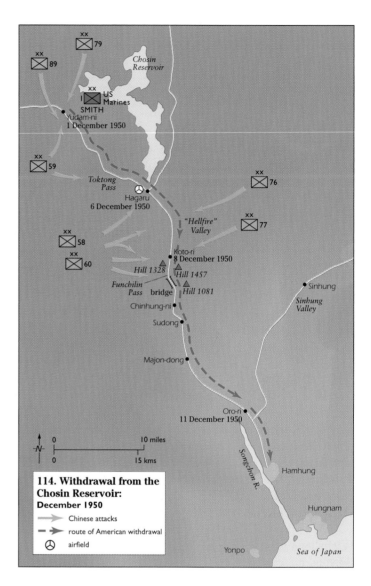

114. Withdrawal from the Chosin Reservoir: December 1950

→ Chinese attacks

-→ route of American withdrawal

Ⓜ airfield

to follow. Nonetheless, MacArthur seemed unfazed by the reticence of his field commanders.

The Eighth Army in Jeopardy

But within twenty-four hours of the offensive, the situation changed dramatically. On the night of 24–25 November, the Chinese attacked the Eighth Army in full force. The Americans held, but their advance was halted. Then, on 26 November, the R.O.K. II Corps of three divisions on the Eighth Army's right flank disintegrated under Chinese attack. Into the gap the Chinese poured eighteen divisions in six armies. Its right flank gone, the Eighth Army was in jeopardy.

The U.S. Army 2nd Division staved off disaster. At Kunu-ri it bought time for the 24th and 25th Divisions and the 1st R.O.K. Division to cross over the Chongchon River and reach safety south of the river. An important factor in this forty-

General of the Army Douglas MacArthur (above) generated strong concerns over his decision to divide his army for the drive into North Korea. His critics' fears were justified when Communist Chinese forces drove into the gap separating the Eighth Army and X Corps and forced U.N.C. withdrawal. At left, men of the U.S. 7th Infantry Division of X Corps board landing craft at Hungnam for evacuation south by sea.

eight-hour delaying action was the 2nd Division's artillery, which inflicted heavy casualties on the advancing Chinese. The division could not hold indefinitely, and on 29 November it withdrew. The Eighth Army was now in full retreat, its rear guard under heavy Chinese pressure. MacArthur then ordered a retirement, just below the 38th parallel, to protect Seoul.

Withdrawal from North Korea

Washington was also worried about X Corps and ordered MacArthur to pull it out of northeastern Korea to prevent it from being flanked. Under heavy Chinese attack, X Corps fought a heroic retirement to the east coast for seaborne evacuation along with the R.O.K. I Corps. The most dramatic aspect of this withdrawal was the movement from the Chosin Reservoir of the 1st Marine Division under Major General Oliver Smith. The Chinese committed twelve divisions (three armies) to the fight, but, thanks to artillery, air power, and their own tenacity, the U.S. Marines completed what is rightly regarded as one of the most masterful military withdrawals in history. By mid-December, X Corps was secure in the Hamhung-Hungnam area.

A total of 105,000 officers and men were evacuated at Hungnam in more than 100 ships. Everything of value was carried off, along with about 91,000 Korean refugees. When the evacuation was completed on Christmas Eve 1950, engineers blew up the waterfront. North Korea was then left to the Communists.

Defeat in the North

For all practical purposes, the Korean War was over; the U.N.C. was now fighting China. The reversal in the first phase of the war surprised Washington almost as much as it had MacArthur, but the general never believed in limited war and, to his way of thinking, a decisive confrontation with Communism was better sooner than later. He now began to publicize this view to friends in the United States. MacArthur alluded to the "extraordinary inhibitions" placed on him and emphasized that no blame should be attached to him or to his staff for the defeat in the North.

Rethinking of Policy and Strategy

Strategically the U.N.C. defeat forced a drastic rethinking of plans and operations in Korea. There was a loss of confidence in the U.N.C. leadership, exacerbated by Walker's death in a jeep accident on 22 December. Not until Lieutenant General Matthew Ridgway arrived to replace Walker did the command situation improve. The political leadership in Washington and the Joint Chiefs had always held Europe as the strategic priority. The administration thus decided to seek only the preservation of South Korea, rather than attempt to conquer the entire country.

The Chinese New Year Offensive

U.N.C. forces were again forced to retreat when the Chinese

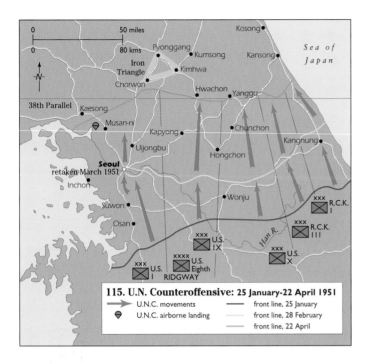

115. U.N. Counteroffensive: 25 January–22 April 1951

→ U.N.C. movements   —— front line, 25 January
● U.N.C. airborne landing   —— front line, 28 February
                                                 —— front line, 22 April

launched their New Year's offensive. The U.N.C. abandoned Seoul on 4 January and Wonju in the middle of the month. But, with their extended supply lines, the C.P.V.A. offensive ground to a halt and Ridgway went over on the offensive. One of the premier leaders of the war, he rebuilt the Eighth Army, which now included X Corps, insisting his commanders lead by example from the front. Ridgway's offensive was designed to inflict maximum punishment on the Communists rather than capture ground. In a methodical, limited advance, by the end of March, U.N.C. forces had retaken Seoul, and by the end of April they were advancing slightly north of the 38th parallel.

Removal of General MacArthur

On 11 April 1951, President Truman relieved MacArthur from his military posts, appointing Ridgway to take his place. Lieutenant General James Van Fleet flew out from the United States to command the Eighth Army. MacArthur's removal was extremely unpopular at the time, but Truman was exercising his legal prerogative as commander-in-chief and his decision was fully supported by the Joint Chiefs of Staff. MacArthur was not in sympathy with limiting the war to Korea and had not concealed his thoughts on the issue. He wanted to bomb Manchuria, and he advocated the use of Chinese Nationalist troops in Korea and the "unleashing" of Nationalist troops on the Chinese mainland. Although MacArthur returned to the United States to receive a hero's welcome and address a joint session of U.S. Congress, the wave of support for him died quickly.

The Chinese Counterattack

Meanwhile the Chinese had counterattacked in Korea on 22 April. Rather than expend forces in a defensive stand, Van Fleet ordered a step-by-step withdrawal to permit the full use of artillery and air support. Chinese pressure pushed the U.N.C. south of the 38th parallel, but the offensive was brought to a halt by 19 May, largely as the result of massive artillery fire.

U.N.C. forces rolled forward beginning on 20 May. By the end of May, the front was practically restored to Line Kansas, natural defensive positions across the peninsula, generally, just above the 38th parallel. The Joint Chiefs of Staff limited the Eighth Army to the vicinity of that line, although some latitude was allowed. Attacks were directed toward the Iron Triangle in the center of the front and in the direction of the Punch Bowl in the east.

After a year of fighting, the war became a stalemate. On 23 June, U.S.S.R. representative to the U.N., Jacob Malik, proposed a cease-fire. With the Chinese indicating an interest in a truce, Truman authorized Ridgway to negotiate. Meetings began on 10 July at Kaesong with an understanding that hostilities would continue until an armistice was signed. Washington saw Communist interest in negotiations as a belief that the other side wanted to end the war; Beijing saw the talks as another form of battle.

For the most part, U.N.C. military operations from this

U.N.C. Commander General of the Army Douglas MacArthur is seen with other officers near Suwon, South Korea. Lieutenant General Matthew B. Ridgway (third from right) took over the Eighth Army in December 1950 and restored morale after the death of Lieutenant General Walton Walker. In April 1951, Ridgway succeeded MacArthur as commander of U.N.C. forces.

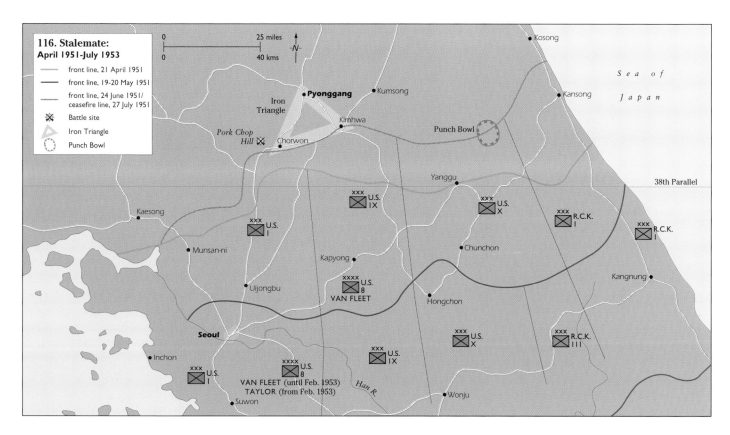

116. Stalemate:
April 1951-July 1953

front line, 21 April 1951
front line, 19-20 May 1951
front line, 24 June 1951/
ceasefire line, 27 July 1951
✳ Battle site
△ Iron Triangle
⬭ Punch Bowl

point were sharply limited. Each side had deep defensive lines that would have been very difficult to pierce. Gradually the fighting decreased in intensity. In August, talks broke down and, late that month, the Battle of Bloody Ridge began. It grew into the Battle of Heartbreak Ridge, which ended on 14 October with U.N.C. forces in possession of the ridge which they retained until the war's end. Later that month, negotiations finally resumed, this time at Panmunjom, but the fighting continued. Indeed, half of the war's casualties occurred during the period of the armistice negotiations.

On 12 November 1951, Ridgway ordered Van Fleet to cease offensive operations. Fighting devolved into raids, limited local attacks, combat patrols, and artillery fire. Van Fleet retired in February 1953 and was succeeded as Eighth Army commander by Lieutenant General Maxwell D. Taylor.

Intensification of Air Combat

With the ground fighting diminished, air combat intensified. Antiaircraft artillery and ground fire took by far the greatest toll of U.N.C. pilots over the battlefield, and close air support and night-flying B-26 and B-29 pilots flew more missions and died in greater numbers than did their fellow airmen, the high-flying F-86 Sabre pilots. Beginning in April 1952, on their own initiative, F-86 pilots began crossing the Yalu River to pursue MiG-15s in Manchuria.

When armistice talks broke down in August 1951, U.N.C. forces launched an offensive aimed at taking strategic terrain north of Seoul. This last major U.N.C. ground offensive of the war centered on the high ground that came to be named Heartbreak Ridge and Bloody Ridge. Prolonged battles there were reminiscent of World War I trench warfare. The rugged terrain changed hands several times before the U.N.C. secured control of both ridges. Armistice talks resumed shortly thereafter.

Although U.S./U.N.C. air power could never completely cut off the flow of supplies from China to Communist forces in Korea, it did reduce this so that it was hard for Communist forces to sustain offensive operations. Also, strikes against the Suiho hydroelectric facilities up the Yalu River from Andong in 1952 helped accelerate the peace talks at Panmunjom.

Ending the War

In November 1952, General Dwight D. Eisenhower was elected President of the United States. He had campaigned on the promise that, if elected, he would go to Korea. Somehow the American public believed this meant that he had a plan to end the war. With casualties running at about 2,500 a month, the war had become politically impossible in the United States. In effect, Eisenhower was elected to end the conflict. He immediately instructed the Joint Chiefs of Staff to draw up plans to end the war militarily, including the possible use of nuclear weapons. At the same time, Secretary of State John Foster Dulles threatened China and the D.P.R.K. with strong steps if the war was not settled by negotiation. There were no worthwhile nuclear targets in Korea, and the only case in which nuclear weapons would have been used there was to cover the withdrawal of the Eighth Army, but planning for their use was made known. This strategy of bluff by a new, more determined administration was part of the solution. Another key to the war's end was the death of Stalin on 5 March 1953 and the consequent internal unrest in the Communist world which led to the Communists putting out peace feelers.

As armistice negotiations entered their final and decisive phase in May, the Chinese stepped up the action. Twice the Chinese initiated attacks, in mid-June and mid-July, to remove bulges in the line. The U.N.C. gave up a few miles of ground but inflicted heavy casualties in the process.

The chief stumbling block at Panmunjom was the repatriation of prisoners of war. Under the terms of the Geneva Convention and the precedents of previous wars, all prisoners should have been returned home once the fighting ended. The issue in Korea was complicated because the North Koreans had captured and drafted into their army many South Korean soldiers and civilians, and thousands of these had subsequently been captured by the U.N.C. If all K.P.A. prisoners were repatriated, then those South Korean citizens would be sent to North Korea instead of to their real homes in the South. In addition, many captured Chinese preferred to go to Taiwan, rather than return to the Communist mainland. By the time negotiations had begun on this issue at the start of 1952, President Truman had become convinced that no prisoners should be repatriated against their will. Despite arguments that this would prolong the negotiations and also the end of the war, Truman held firm to this view for the rest of his presidency.

Although they initially rejected the concept of voluntary repatriation, the C.P.V.A./K.P.A. might have accepted voluntary repatriation in early 1952 if the majority of the Chinese and North Korean soldiers had elected to return. But, a screening of prisoners carried out in April 1952 to determine their repatriation desires had revealed that only 70,000 of more than 170,000 desired repatriation. C.P.V.A./K.P.A. negotiators declared this to be unacceptable and the talks turned hostile. It was not until intense air strikes on North Korean hydroelectric facilities and the capital of Pyongyang, in March 1953, that the Communists finally yielded on this point. A face-saving formula was found whereby a neutral commission would deal with prisoners refusing repatriation.

On 17 June 1953, Syngman Rhee released North Korean prisoners from U.N.C. prisoner of war camps, bringing negotiations to a halt and almost derailing the armistice. Rhee finally agreed to abide by the armistice after receiving a pledge of future U.S. support, a mutual security treaty, and an aid package. Rhee's acceptance removed the final obstacle to a truce, and an armistice was signed at Panmunjom on 27 July 1953.

Results of the War

The R.O.K. put its casualties during the war at 901,656 killed, wounded, or missing. The U.S. losses were 140,200 and U.N.C. losses ran to 15,488. North Korean casualties are uncertain, although the R.O.K. claims the K.P.A. lost 294,931 dead alone. Estimates of Chinese losses range to one million dead. Perhaps three million Korean civilians died from causes directly related to the war.

A Fifth U.S. Air Force F-86 Sabre jet flies over North Korea. The first U.S. swept-wing jet and the world's first air superiority fighter, the F-86 arrived in Korea in December 1950, replacing the obsolete F-80 Shooting Star in an air superiority role. During the course of the war, F-86s destroyed 792 MiGs while suffering only 110 losses.

In the position warfare that typified the second phase of the Korean War, both sides dug into the earth creating extensive systems of earthworks and trenches resembling those of World War I. A steady progression of artillery barrages, probing raids, and patrols inflicted growing numbers of casualties on both sides as the armistice talks continued, seemingly without result. Here, a member of the 5th U.S. Marine Regiment scans Communist lines with his binoculars.

The war devastated Korea. It hardened the divisions between North and South, adding to the existing enmity between the two Koreas. The Chinese gained greatly from their intervention, at least in a diplomatic sense. China came to be regarded as the major military power in Asia, and a decade later, the threat of Chinese military intervention haunted American planners and was one of the principal factors precluding a U.S. invasion of North Vietnam during the Vietnam War.

Ironically, the Korean War may have been a mistake for the Communist world. In the past, after each war, the U.S. military had demobilized to a small force. After Korea, it remained strong. The U.S. defense budget quadrupled, and the United States emerged with the world's most powerful military, a state which has continued to the present.

The war led to militarization of the policy of containment. Until 1950, Marshall Plan aid had been almost entirely non-military; now it shifted over heavily to military rearmament. The war also solidified the role of the United States as the world's policeman and strengthened the country's relationship with its western European allies. The North Atlantic Treaty Organization (N.A.T.O.) underwent fundamental change, as it facilitated the rearmament of the Federal Republic of Germany. A divided Germany seemed to many observers all too reminiscent of Korea before the Communist invasion.

The Korean War also had an impact on Vietnam, for when President Truman announced that the United States would aid Korea, he also said that Washington was for the first time sending direct military assistance to the French in Indochina. The war also had an impact on Japan, fueling that nation's economy as the principal base for the U.S. resupply efforts.

Militarily, the war was interesting for the extensive use of the helicopter. Its potential was clearly demonstrated in reconnaissance, evacuation, and rescue work. It was a reminder that air power alone cannot bring about a final decision in land warfare, and it revealed the importance of command of the sea.

Fifty years later, the two Koreas remained divided and perhaps the world's most dangerous flash point. At the end of the Cold War, the reduction of Russian economic support for North Korea and the improvement of U.S.-Chinese relations increased the isolation of North Korea and led its leaders to pursue the development of nuclear weapon's technology. Despite a decline in its economy and the threat of mass starvation, North Korea continued to support a one-million-man army, equipped with modern weapons and long-range missiles. South of the demilitarized zone, the R.O.K. countered with a 500,000-man army and the United States has maintained 37,000 troops. This was the largest deployment of U.S. forces abroad since the 1991 Gulf War. The United States offered the North humanitarian aid in exchange for its abandonment of development of nuclear weapons and, at the same time, threatened to construct an antimissile defense system capable of nullifying North Korea's nuclear threat.

The Vietnam War: 1959-75

The Vietnam War was the most divisive conflict in the U.S. experience since the American Civil War. U.S. involvement in Vietnam began with financial aid and military advice to the French during the First Indochina War (1946-54), and continued unabated through 1975, when Saigon, the capital of the U.S.-supported Republic of Vietnam (R.V.N.), was finally conquered by the Communist People's Army of Vietnam (P.A.V.N.). U.S. combat units first entered the conflict between North and South Vietnam in March 1965 and remained until March 1973, making Vietnam the longest foreign deployment in the history of American arms. Accompanying these forces was a huge logistical supporting establishment on land, sea, and in the air, along with a welter of civilian and governmental agencies engaged in "nation building" in South Vietnam. U.S. military personnel numbered a mere 760 in November 1959—the time of the first American deaths in the war and the date often used as the beginning of the American war by the U.S. military. By 1969, at the peak of American involvement, 543,000 Americans were "in-country." One measure of the complexity of the war is that U.S. forces never lost a multi-battalion engagement to Communist forces on the battlefield, and yet the core objective of the war—the establishment of an independent, noncommunist state in South Vietnam—was never achieved.

Issues Still Debated

The conflict's lessons and legacies remain hotly debated today. Most historians agree that the war wrenched the social fabric of the United States and had an enormous impact on the military, foreign policy, and the national psyche in the years since the guns fell silent. Some 2.7 million Americans served in Vietnam. They encountered a remarkably diverse terrain and climate. Indeed, "For those who served there," writes veteran and analyst Colonel Harry G. Summers, Jr., the locale "made an enormous difference, for the swamps of the Mekong Delta were as different from the mountains of the Central Highlands and the trenches of the D.M.Z. [Demilitarized Zone at the 17th parallel separating North and South Vietnam] as the terrain of the European-African-Middle Eastern battlefields of World War II were different from those of the South Pacific."

The Vietnam War Memorial in Washington D. C. lists the names of 58,000 Americans killed in the conflict. The Vietnamese on both sides, civilian and military alike, lost four million people. Debates over the conflict's efficacy, the motives of the various administrations who made policy, and the strategy developed by the U.S. military to carry out those policies will continue for decades, but few serious students of the war would quarrel with historian Stanley Karnow's description of the event as "a tragedy of epic dimensions."

Containment of Communism

The roots of the conflict lie in the guiding foreign policy principle of containment of Communism, for it was containment that drew the U.S. into the struggle between Ho Chi Minh's Communists and the French, who had colonized Vietnam in the nineteenth century and were anxious to reassert their control after Japan's defeat and withdrawal from Indochina after World War II. In the wake of such "free world" setbacks as the fall of China to Mao Zedong in 1949 and the invasion of democratic South Korea by Soviet-sponsored North Korea, the Truman administration weighed in with massive support for the French war against Vietnamese Communism—albeit after the French agreed to grant Vietnam quasi-independence under Emperor Bao Dai on 8 March 1949.

The dramatic defeat of the French at Dien Bien Phu engineered by Viet Minh General Vo Nguyen Giap in May 1954 did not lesson the determination of the Eisenhower administration to preserve a noncommunist state in Vietnam. The 1954 Geneva conference divided Vietnam at the 17th parallel and established a ceasefire until national elections could be held. But neither the United States nor Bao Dai's government signed the Geneva accords, and the Americans pressed forward in South Vietnam, providing the government with ever more military and economic aid (the U.S. had provided three billion dollars to the French war effort already), and ensuring that no nationwide referendum was ever held. The ardent

The tropical conditions of Indochina—oppressively high humidity and temperatures, plagues of insects, and flood conditions during the monsoon season in the Mekong River Delta (below)—combined with boredom and frustration, produced serious adjustment and morale problems among U.S. servicemen stationed in Vietnam.

anticommunist Catholic Ngo Dinh Diem assumed the mantle of South Vietnam's leadership and announced the creation of the Republic of Vietnam with Washington's blessing in 1955, thus beginning an uneasy and complicated partnership between Diem and the United States that would result in the first military defeat in U.S. history.

An Adroit In-Fighter

Saigon at this time, writes journalist Frances Fitzgerald, "was a political jungle of warlords, sects, bandits, partisan troops, and secret societies." Diem proved to be an adroit political in-fighter, defeating soundly the Binh Xuyen crime syndicate and two religious sects that attempted to overthrow him in April 1955 and declaring himself president. Diem siphoned off a good percentage of the U.S. funds earmarked for land reform and economic development to family and friends, thereby insuring that his power base remained very narrow indeed outside of Saigon, where political cadres left behind by the Communists began to indoctrinate the peasantry in the Communist cause. Between 1955 and 1960 only about 2 percent of U.S. aid went to land reform. The Agroville program (1959), in which large numbers of peasants were wrenched from their villages and placed in fortified hamlets to protect them from the depredations of Communist cadres, proved a dismal failure, for the peasantry resented being torn from their ancestral lands and the restrictions on their movement.

Meanwhile, despite a vast increase in the number of U.S. military advisers, and intense pressure to reform from Washington, the Army of the Republic of Vietnam (A.R.V.N.) continued to perform badly as a result of poor leadership and corruption. Senior positions were awarded not to the ablest soldiers, but to those who proved themselves personally loyal to Diem and his advisers. Catholics dominated the officer corps in an army of Buddhists. It was for good reason that Americans in Vietnam came to see the South Vietnamese President as "a puppet who pulls his own strings." Utterly dependent on the United States, he nonetheless refused to undertake the political, military, and economic reforms that would secure the peoples' loyalty.

Hanoi and the National Liberation Front

In December 1960 came a critical development: Hanoi organized the National Front for the Liberation of South Vietnam (N.L.F.), and shifted its strategy regarding the unification of the country from *dau tranh chinh tri* (political struggle) to *to dau tran vu trang* (armed struggle). The N.L.F. presented itself throughout the war as an organization of native southerners, and its success in concealing Hanoi's tight control won it support in world opinion. By 1961, well trained Communist guerrillas, called Vietcong by the A.R.V.N. and American advisers,

Anti-war protests spread across America and throughout the world in the mid-1960s. The National Commission on the Causes and Prevention of Violence reported there were 104 U.S. antiwar demonstrations organized between 1963 and 1968. This peace rally was staged in Los Angeles in 1966. The next year saw some of the largest anti-war gatherings; the one held in Washington in November 1967 attracted more than 50,000 protestors who surrounded the Pentagon.

were conducting terrorist operations and small unit attacks all over South Vietnam, and it was increasingly clear to the new American president, John F. Kennedy, that the A.R.V.N. was incapable of crushing the insurgency without significant additional U.S. military assistance. About 4,000 A.R.V.N. officials were killed by Vietcong attacks in 1961 alone.

Kennedy and Counterinsurgency

In May 1961, shortly after assuming office, President Kennedy moved to increase American assistance to South Vietnam. There were 1,364 U.S. advisors in the country when he took office. In May 1961, he sent 400 Special Forces Green Berets into the Central Highlands to train non-ethnic Vietnamese tribesmen, known as Montagnards, in counterinsurgency and he tripled the level of aid to Saigon. A new, higher level military command was created under General Paul Harkins called Military Assistant Command, Vietnam (M.A.C.V.). Kennedy, under pressure from Communist adversaries in Cuba, Berlin, and elsewhere, resolved to hold the line in Vietnam. To bolster

The U.S. military developed several new weapons systems in Vietnam, including the armored monitor, photographed here leading two armored amphibious landing craft through a canal in the Mekong Delta. The monitors, which got their name because they resembled the Civil War-era ironclads, were generally equipped with a 20-mm and a 40-mm cannon, two to three .50-caliber and six M-60 machine guns, and an 81-mm mortar.

the South Vietnamese, he sent amphibious, armored personnel carriers and helicopter gunships to the A.R.V.N., authorized the use of new technology, including napalm and defoliants designed to deny coverage to the Vietcong, and ordered U.S. destroyers operating along the coasts of both North and South Vietnam to interdict supplies being sent south by North Vietnam to support the Vietcong air surveillance and reconnaissance flights to provide the A.R.V.N. with the location of enemy troop and supply concentrations, and helicopters from U.S. carriers off the coast to fly combat support missions. In an effort to assist the government in "winning the hearts and minds" of the people, Kennedy also supported Diem's strategic hamlet program. This was essentially a more ambitious Agroville program, run by Diem's brother, Ngo Dinh Nhu. Like its predecessor, the strategic hamlet program was corrupt and unpopular with the people.

Rhetoric was inflated along with aid: One Kennedy administration official even referred to Diem as "the Churchill of Southeast Asia." Indeed, by the early 1960s, South Vietnam had become what historian George Herring has called "a test case of America's determination to uphold its commitments in a menacing world and of its capacity to meet the new challenge posed by guerrilla warfare in the emerging nations." In the fall of 1961, Kennedy sent General Maxwell Taylor on a fact-finding tour. An alarmed Taylor called for more advisors and even the introduction of combat troops to preserve the integrity of

South Vietnam. Kennedy demurred on the latter suggestion. But he increased the number of U.S. military advisors from 3,200 in December 1961 to 16,300 in December 1963.

The Situation Deteriorates

The situation in South Vietnam continued to deteriorate over the next year. On 2 January 1963, a Vietcong battalion of 320 men soundly defeated some 3,000 A.R.V.N. troops at Ap Bac, southwest of Saigon, despite the presence of American UH-1 "Huey" helicopters, tactical air support, and armored personnel carriers. In the fall of 1963, with tacit U.S. support, a group of South Vietnamese generals staged a *coup d'etat* against Diem in the wake of increasingly strident Buddhist protests against government oppression. Three weeks later, Kennedy was assassinated in Dallas, and Lyndon Baines Johnson assumed the presidency.

By the summer of 1964, the new administration faced a dilemma: Johnson felt bound by the containment policy and domestic political pressure to defend South Vietnam against an increasingly effective Vietcong insurgency, yet he did not want the United States fully engaged in a land war in southeast Asia for fear of provoking a wider conflict with China, the Soviet Union, or both. He also feared that war would jeopardize his programs to rout out poverty and racial discrimination at home. In June of 1964, Lieutenant General William Westmoreland, one of the Army's most accomplished officers, was

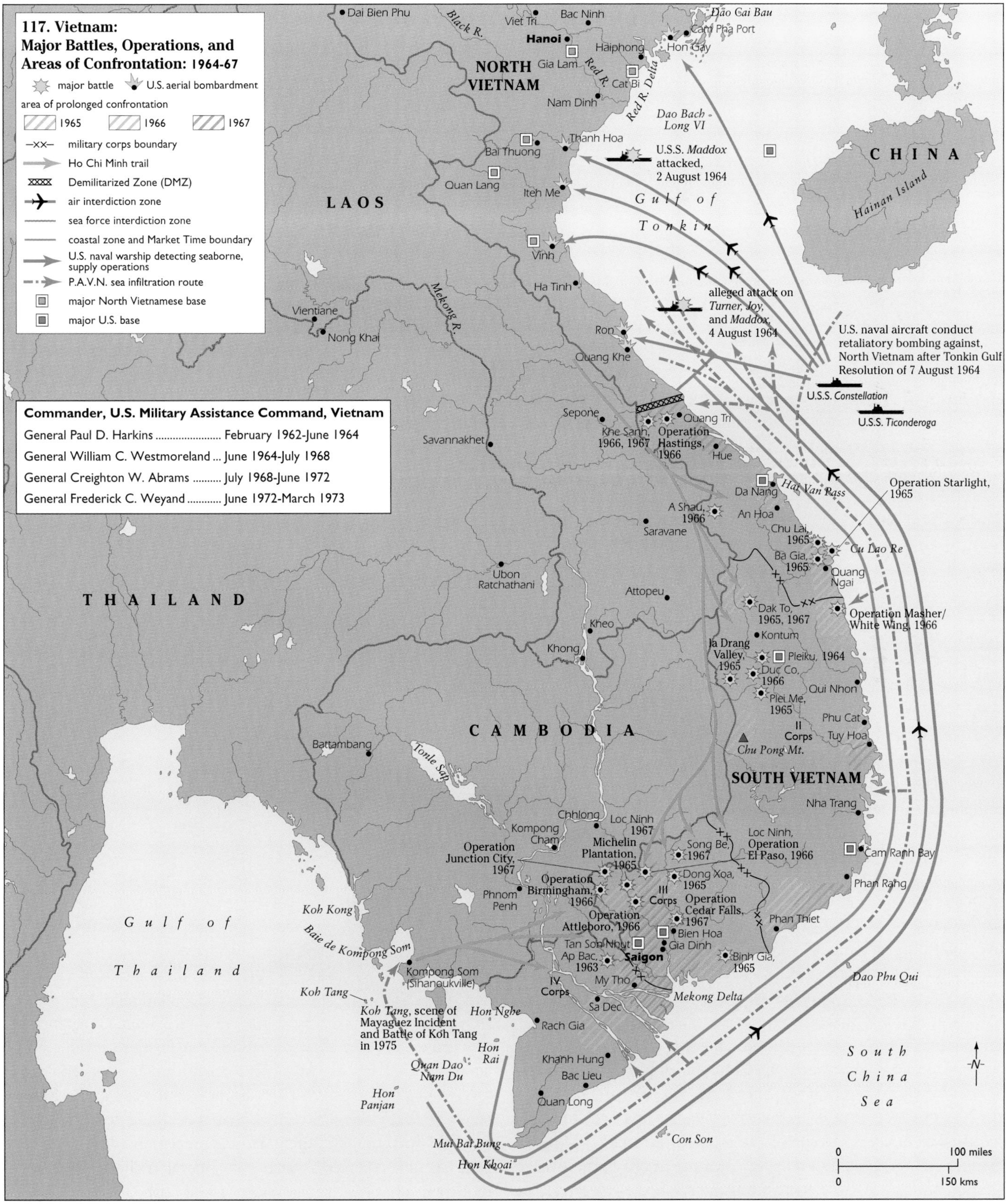
117. Vietnam:
Major Battles, Operations, and Areas of Confrontation: 1964-67
major battle
U.S. aerial bombardment
area of prolonged confrontation
1965
1966
1967
military corps boundary
Ho Chi Minh trail
Demilitarized Zone (DMZ)
air interdiction zone
sea force interdiction zone
coastal zone and Market Time boundary
U.S. naval warship detecting seaborne, supply operations
P.A.V.N. sea infiltration route
major North Vietnamese base
major U.S. base
Commander, U.S. Military Assistance Command, Vietnam
General Paul D. Harkins .... February 1962-June 1964
General William C. Westmoreland ... June 1964-July 1968
General Creighton W. Abrams .... July 1968-June 1972
General Frederick C. Weyand .... June 1972-March 1973
Dai Bien Phu
Black R.
Viet Tri
Bac Ninh
Hanoi
Gia Lam
Haiphong
Red R.
Cat Bi
Red R. Delta
Dao Gai Bau
Cam Pha Port
Hon Gay
NORTH VIETNAM
Nam Dinh
Dao Bach Long VI
Thanh Hoa
Bai Thuong
U.S.S. Maddox attacked, 2 August 1964
CHINA
Hainan Island
Quan Lang
Iteh Me
LAOS
Gulf of Tonkin
Vinh
Ha Tinh
alleged attack on Turner, Joy, and Maddox, 4 August 1964
Mekong R.
Vientiane
Nong Khai
Ron
Quang Khe
U.S. naval aircraft conduct retaliatory bombing against, North Vietnam after Tonkin Gulf Resolution of 7 August 1964
U.S.S. Constellation
U.S.S. Ticonderoga
Sepone
Quang Tri
Khe Sanh, 1966, 1967
Operation Hastings, 1966
Savannakhet
Hue
Da Nang
Hai Van Pass
Operation Starlight, 1965
A Shau, 1966
An Hoa
Saravane
Chu Lai, 1965
Cu Lao Re
Ba Gia, 1965
Quang Ngai
Ubon Ratchathani
THAILAND
Attopeu
Dak To, 1965, 1967
Operation Masher/ White Wing, 1966
Kheo
Kontum
Khong
Ia Drang Valley, 1965
Pleiku, 1964
Duc Co, 1966
Qui Nhon
Plei Me, 1965
Phu Cat
CAMBODIA
II Corps
Tuy Hoa
Chu Pong Mt.
Battambang
Tonle Sap
SOUTH VIETNAM
Nha Trang
Chhlong
Loc Ninh 1967
Kompong Cham
Michelin Plantation, 1965
Song Be, 1967
Loc Ninh, Operation El Paso, 1966
Cam Ranh Bay
Operation Junction City, 1967
Operation Birmingham, 1966
Dong Xoa, 1965
Phan Rang
Phnom Penh
III Corps
Operation Cedar Falls, 1967
Koh Kong
Gulf of Thailand
Operation Attleboro, 1966
Bien Hoa
Phan Thiet
Baie de Kompong Som
Tan Son Nhut
Gia Dinh
Saigon
Ap Bac, 1963
Binh Gia, 1965
Kompong Som (Sihanoukville)
IV Corps
My Tho
Dao Phu Qui
Koh Tang
Mekong Delta
Koh Tang, scene of Mayaguez Incident and Battle of Koh Tang in 1975
Hon Nghe
Sa Dec
Rach Gia
Hon Rai
Khanh Hung
South China Sea
N
Quan Dao Nam Du
Bac Lieu
Hon Panjan
Quan Long
Mui Bai Bung
Con Son
Hon Khoai
0
100 miles
0
150 kms

appointed commander of M.A.C.V. and quickly promoted to full general—a clear sign of the conflict's increasing importance.

The Tonkin Gulf Incident

Under the Pentagon's OPLAN 34A, the U.S. Navy conducted intelligence-gathering patrols in support of South Vietnamese commando raids on the North Vietnamese coast. These patrols produced the event that opened the door to all future U.S. involvement: The 2 August 1964 Tonkin Gulf Incident. The destroyer U.S.S. *Maddox* was approached by three North Vietnamese patrol boats while monitoring People's Republic of Vietnam radio transmissions and there was a brief exchange of ship-to-ship gunfire. U.S. Navy jets joined in the pursuit, damaging one boat. A second attack against the *Maddox* and another destroyer, the U.S.S. *Turner Joy*, was reported by the patrol commander two days later. It is now generally accepted that this second attack never transpired. Rough weather apparently caused an instrument misreading, and the Pentagon was unsure of what happened.

Washington quickly ordered retaliatory air strikes against North Vietnam on 5 August. Far more important than the strikes, however, was the passage on 7 August of the Tonkin Gulf Resolution by the U.S. Congress, authorizing the President to do whatever he felt necessary to assist South Vietnam in the event of aggression by the North Vietnamese. Although administration spokesmen reassured Congress at the time that deployment of U.S. combat forces was not seen as a live option, the resolution did indeed provide the legal support for "Johnson's war."

Johnson and Conventional Warfare

President Johnson considered the February 1964 Vietcong attack on the U.S. garrison at Pleiku a calculated show of contempt for the United States. Twelve hours later, he ordered U.S. aircraft to bomb North Vietnam for the first time. In March 1965—a watershed month in the history of the American war in Vietnam—Johnson responded to a request for U.S. troops from General Westmoreland by ordering two battalions of the 9th U.S. Marine Expeditionary Brigade to land at Danang, ninety-five miles south of the D.M.Z., and to protect that sprawling air base from rocket attacks. Elsewhere, however, the Vietcong continued to inflict defeats on the A.R.V.N. Thus, Westmoreland's request to send 150,000 U.S. troops to South Vietnam to take up the offensive was approved. The entire 3rd U.S. Marine Division arrived in Vietnam in force in May 1965, along with the U.S. Army's 173rd Airborne Brigade. By June, Westmoreland had articulated the strategy of attrition followed by the U.S. military until the summer of 1968: Using their superior mobility and firepower, U.S. forces were to find, fix, and destroy the enemy's combat units in such

numbers that they could not continue to resupply the battlefield with men and material. Thus, the "body count" became an index of U.S. success, along with other quantifiable measures, such as the number of tons of supplies captured or destroyed along the network of roads, trails, and supply depots known as the Ho Chi Minh Trail. To implement the attrition strategy, U.S. combat battalions were deployed in "search and destroy" missions beginning in June 1965.

Operation Starlite

The first multi-battalion offensive engagement of the U.S. war was conducted by the marines in Operation Starlite (18-24 August). The objective was the destruction of the 1st Vietcong Regiment, which had inflicted heavy casualties on an A.R.V.N. garrison at Ba Gia village near Chu Lai, on the South Vietnamese coast, about forty miles south of Danang. The scheme of maneuver called for the 3rd Battalion of the 3rd U.S. Marine Regiment to land two companies abreast at Green Beach along with eight tanks about two miles south of Van Tuong, suspected command post of the Vietcong force, and to block that unit's escape to the south. M company of the 7th U.S. Marines would come down from Chu Lai and set up blocking positions north of the area of operations. The 2nd

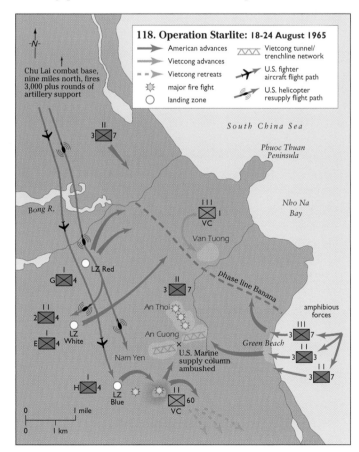

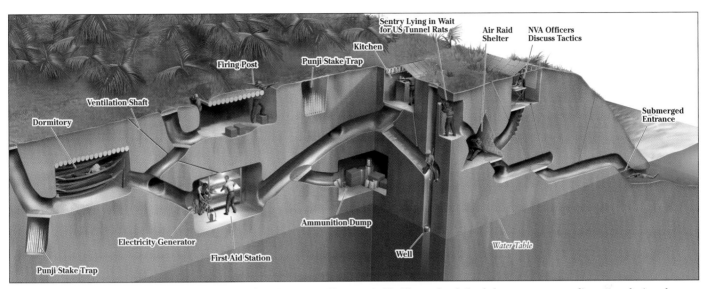

This cutaway drawing of a tunnel complex, a type found in many Vietcong-held villages that helped the enemy seem to disappear, depicts the mastery of Vietcong and North Vietnamese "engineers." General William Westmoreland wrote that, "No-one has ever demonstrated more ability to hide his installations than the Vietcong. They were human moles."

Battalion of the 4th Regiment would be transported by helicopter to three landing zones about a mile inland and sweep northeast through a series of Vietcong-held hamlets, driving the enemy toward the sea. The amphibious landing went off on schedule at 6:30 a.m. against light resistance.

At LZ Blue, one mile inland from the coast, however, the marines landed right on top of a Vietcong battalion and fierce fighting ensued throughout the day. It was particularly tough for the marines to drive through the fortified village of An Cuong, which had camouflaged trenchlines connected by tunnels. A Huey helicopter gunship was downed and a U.S. Marine supply column of tracked landing vehicles (L.V.T.s) was ambushed by the Vietcong, who possessed recoilless rifles, mortars, machine guns, and small arms. But with expertly coordinated supporting fires from U.S. Marine jets and two destroyers, the Leathernecks were indeed able to drive the Vietcong toward the coast and inflict heavy casualties on them in the process. Most of the heavy fighting was over by nightfall, and the remnants of organized resistance were eliminated by noon on 19 August. From 19 to 24 August, the marines systematically cleaned out the tunnels, along with a few stragglers from the 1st Vietcong Regiment. Six hundred and fourteen Vietcong were killed in the action—more than seventy of them had been killed by well-aimed artillery strikes when marine infantry spotted them assembling at a distance. The marines lost 45 men killed in action and 203 wounded.

Search and Destroy Tactics

Operation Starlite was typical of hundreds of offensive sweeps run by the U.S. Army and U.S. Marines between 1965 and 1968 against the Vietcong guerrillas in its use of superior mobility and firepower to drive the enemy from its enclaves—albeit temporarily. But U.S. infantry units also experienced frustration and monotony during endless patrolling in swamps, jungles, and one-hundred-degree heat, against an enemy which was indistinguishable from the general civilian population, and whose favored tactics were ambush and hit and run attacks. It was the Vietcong, not the Americans, who chose the time and place of most small unit combat in Vietnam.

In addition to ground combat operations, extensive naval and air assets were used to cut off supplies intended for Vietcong political and military cadres. The "brown water Navy" prowled the extensive network of rivers in the Mekong Delta. In Operation Market Time (1965-1972) the U.S. Navy interdicted seaborne supplies along South Vietnam's 1,200-mile coastline.

Operation Rolling Thunder

March 1965 also witnessed the beginning of Operation Rolling Thunder (2 March 1965-31 October 1968). In that operation, U.S. Navy and Air Force jets flew about one million sorties against key bridges, radar sites, fuel depots, and power plants with a view to crippling North Vietnam's capacity to support the insurgency in the south. Although about three-quarters of a million tons of bombs rained down on North Vietnam, destroying more than half the bridges and two-thirds of the power plants, the resourceful North Vietnamese began to disburse their critical war-making supply depots. They also developed an exceptionally effective antiaircraft campaign, deploying Soviet-made surface-to-air missiles, as well as thousands of conventional antiaircraft batteries. Nine hundred and

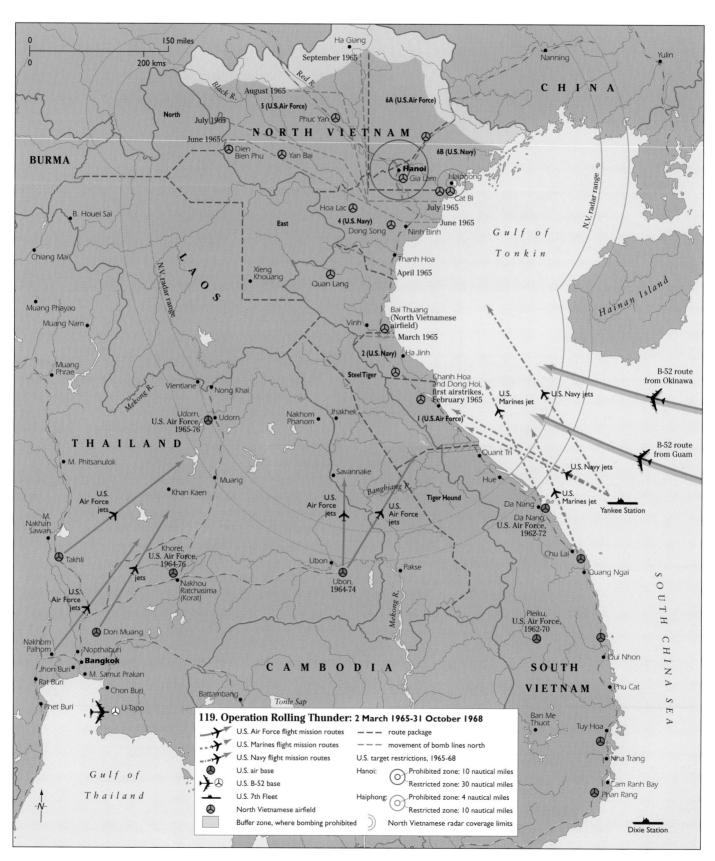

ninety U.S. planes were lost over North Vietnam during Operation Rolling Thunder, and Hanoi was adept at displaying the collateral damage of the air attacks to gain world sympathy. An estimated 52,000 civilians died as a result of the bombings. Operation Rolling Thunder failed to accomplish its objective in the end, for it hardly persuaded Hanoi to call a halt to operations against the R.V.N. Indeed, according to M.A.C.V.'s own estimates, the flow of both supplies and troops moving down the Ho Chi Minh Trail increased markedly during each year of Rolling Thunder.

Battle of the Ia Drang Valley

Escalation of the war in 1965 by the United States prompted Hanoi to deploy its own regular army into the conflict in the south. Well trained and equipped, the People's Army of Vietnam first clashed with the U.S. forces in the rolling hills and jungle of the Central Highlands in October of 1965 in the Battle of the Ia Drang Valley, where they sought to drive east to the coast, cutting South Vietnam in half. The battle began when two P.A.V.N. regiments attacked the U.S. Army Special Forces camp at Plei Me on 19 October. Those troops were forced to disengage and withdraw to the southwest, into the Ia Drang Valley when General Westmoreland ordered the powerful First Air Cavalry Division into the fight. On 14 November, the 430-man 1st Battalion of the 7th Cavalry made a heliborne assault right into the assembly area of the 66th P.A.V.N. Regiment. One U.S. platoon was isolated from the rest of the force and the Americans were nearly overrun in the early hours of the battle. Lieutenant Colonel Harold Moore brought in reinforcements to LZ X-Ray, fourteen miles

east of Plei Me Special Forces Camp, in time to prevent the P.A.V.N. units from completing a flanking maneuver. Despite withering fire on the approaching helicopters, the U.S. Cavalrymen had inflicted heavy casualties on the enemy by nightfall.

At 6:30 a.m. on 15 November, the 7th Battalion of the 66th P.A.V.N. Regiment attacked the U.S. perimeter and got into the lines before being repulsed. Reinforcements arrived in the form of the 2nd Battalion of the 5th U.S. Cavalry, and crushing artillery fire was called down on suspected P.A.V.N. positions. U.S. B-52s began six days of strikes against suspected enemy assembly areas in the Chu Pong Massif. The fighting throughout the day was savage, in some cases hand-to-hand, for the North Vietnamese had been ordered to stand and fight the Americans close in so as to neutralize the effectiveness of U.S. close air and artillery support.

Another P.A.V.N. attack came on the morning of 16 November, but it was easily repulsed and the North Vietnamese withdrew from the battlefield later that day. Casualties were estimated at 1,215 killed, while U.S. losses were 79 killed and 121 wounded over three days of fighting. On 17 November, the U.S. victory was marred by disaster as the 2nd Battalion, 7th U.S. Cavalry moved overland toward LZ Albany, about two miles northeast of LZ X-Ray, and stumbled into an ambush set up by the 8th Battalion, 66th P.A.V.N. and other units. Of the 400 U.S. soldiers in the column, 155 were killed and 124 wounded. General Westmoreland considered the battle to be a validation of air, mobile, and search-and-destroy tactics, but others, including Moore, viewed it more as a sign of just how tenacious the enemy could be. In any case, the P.A.V.N.'s attempt to sever South Vietnam had been thwarted.

While soldiers, like those of the 1st Cavalry Division (left), slogged through rice paddies in South Vietnam, the air force, directed by Chief of Staff John P. McConnell (above), conducted an air campaign aimed at breaking the will of North Vietnam to continue the war.

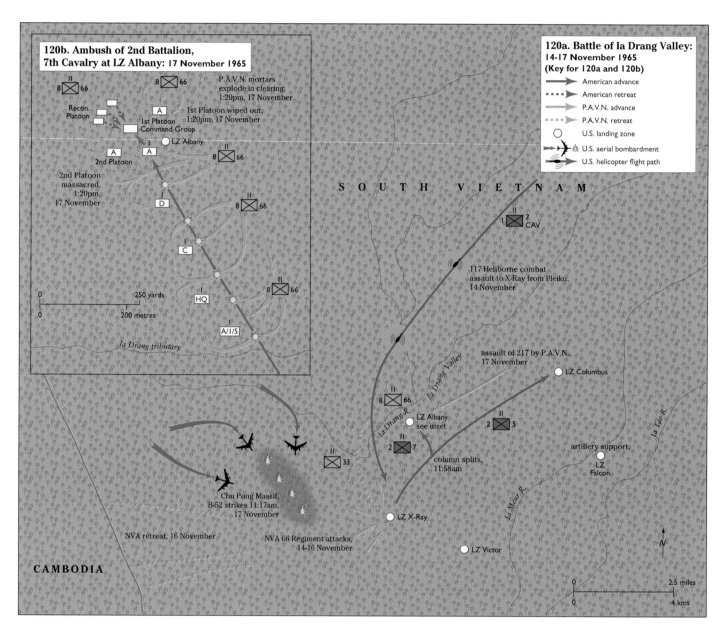

**120b. Ambush of 2nd Battalion,
7th Cavalry at LZ Albany: 17 November 1965**

P.A.V.N. mortars
explode in clearing,
1:20pm, 17 November

8 ⊠ 66   8 ⊠ 66

Recon.
Platoon

A   1st Platoon wiped out,
1:20pm, 17 November

1st Platoon
Command Group

A   LZ Albany

A   8 ⊠ 66

2nd Platoon

2nd Platoon
massacred,
1:20pm,
17 November

D   8 ⊠ 66

C   8 ⊠ 66

0   250 yards
0   200 metres

HQ

A/1/5

Ia Drang tributary

**120a. Battle of Ia Drang Valley:
14-17 November 1965
(Key for 120a and 120b)**

→ American advance
⇢ American retreat
→ P.A.V.N. advance
⇢ P.A.V.N. retreat
○ U.S. landing zone
➤ U.S. aerial bombardment
➤ U.S. helicopter flight path

S O U T H   V I E T N A M

1 ⊠ 7 CAV

117 Heliborne combat
assault to X-Ray from Pleiku,
14 November

assault of 217 by P.A.V.N.,
17 November

8 ⊠ 66

LZ Columbus

Ia Drang R.

LZ Albany
see inset

2 ⊠ 7

2 ⊠ 5

column splits,
11:58am

artillery support,
LZ Falcon

Ia Tae R.

33

Chu Pong Massif,
B-52 strikes 11:17am,
17 November

LZ X-Ray

Ia Meur R.

NVA retreat, 16 November

NVA 66 Regiment attacks,
14-16 November

LZ Victor

CAMBODIA

0   2.5 miles
0   4 kms

Operation Cedar Falls

During 1966, American troops took on a greater burden of the combat, and A.R.V.N. units were increasingly deployed in pacification and occupation of the countryside. By the end of the year, some 385,000 U.S. military personnel were in Vietnam, organized into seven divisions plus other specialized forces, including airborne brigades, engineers, and logistical support. The largest operations of the war to date took place in 1967, as 30,000 U.S. troops assaulted the large enemy base area forty miles north of Saigon known as the Iron Triangle in Operation Cedar Falls (8-26 January). Cedar Falls was a classic "hammer and anvil" operation, as "anvil" forces were positioned along the western side of the Saigon River and the village

of Ben Suc, the Vietcong command center in the area, was air-assaulted by the 2nd Brigade of the 1st U.S. Infantry Division which was dropped in from sixty UH-1 helicopters. Then various American units swept through the Iron Triangle from the north and east. The Vietcong chose to retreat from the area rather than stand and fight. Large quantities of arms and equipment were uncovered, and some parts of a vast tunnel network in the area were uncovered. The evacuation of the 6,000 villagers of Ben Suc, however, became a rallying point for the antiwar movement and was widely criticized by world opinion. U.S. television viewers saw American troops setting thatched huts alight with cigarette lighters. The Vietcong moved back into the area soon after the Cedar Falls operation concluded.

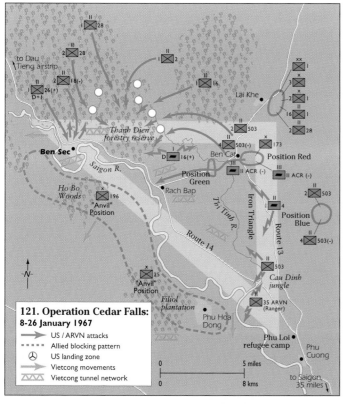

121. Operation Cedar Falls:
8-26 January 1967

US / ARVN attacks
Allied blocking pattern
US landing zone
Vietcong movements
Vietcong tunnel network

0   5 miles
0   8 kms

Dak To

In fall 1967, General Vo Nguyen Giap, Defense Minister of the D.R.V. and chief military strategist, ordered the 1st P.A.V.N. Division into the sparsely populated area around Dak To in Kontum Province in the Central Highlands. Their mission: Destroy the U.S. Special Forces camps near the Laotian and Cambodian borders that both monitored and threatened the infiltration routes used by the Communists. By drawing U.S. combat battalions from the populated areas along the coast, Hanoi also hoped to ensure the success of the countrywide Tet Offensive planned for the end of January 1968. Dak To sits in a mist-shrouded valley floor surrounded by rugged peaks as high as 4,000 feet. The peaks and saddles in the area are covered with lush, triple-canopy jungle.

Fierce fighting had begun in June 1967, when the 2nd Battalion of the 503rd U.S. Airborne Brigade encountered the 6th Battalion of the 24th P.A.V.N. Division and fought to a stalemate. Sporadic fighting continued in the area until the first week of November, when the 8th and 12th U.S. Infantry of the 4th Division and the 173rd U.S. Airborne Brigade engaged in intense fighting which commenced around Hill 823, southwest of Dak To. The Third Battalion of the 12th Infantry assaulted Hill 1338, also southwest of Dak To, and drove the 32nd P.A.V.N. Regiment from the area. On 11 November, various

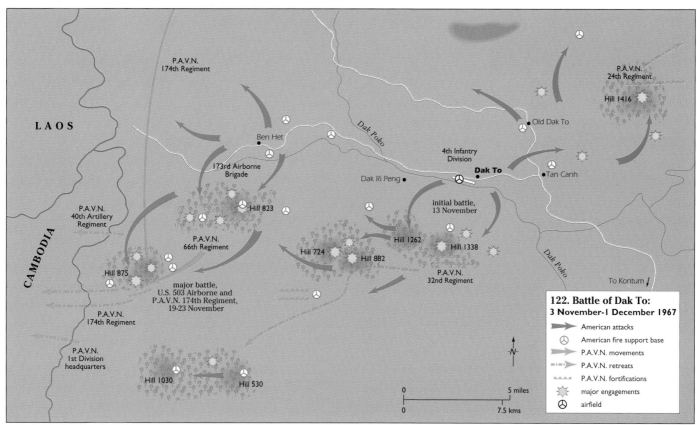

122. Battle of Dak To:
3 November-1 December 1967

American attacks
American fire support base
P.A.V.N. movements
P.A.V.N. retreats
P.A.V.N. fortifications
major engagements
airfield

0   5 miles
0   7.5 kms

As U.S. commander in Vietnam (1964-68), General Westmoreland (above) ordered the establishment of scores of Special Forces bases along the Cambodian border. Camps such as this one (right) were set up to cut the flow of enemy supplies into South Vietnam.

U.S. units fought off an attack by the 66th P.A.V.N. Regiment successfully on Hill 724, approximately four miles west of Hill 1338. A.R.V.N. units also managed to drive the P.A.V.N. 24th Regiment from Hill 1416 in the northeastern corner of an expanded battlefield.

The climax of the battle commenced when the P.A.V.N. committed their reserve forces, the 174th Regiment, to block U. S. and A.R.V.N. forces ten miles southwest of Hill 724, on Hill 875, as other P.A.V.N. units moved west into Cambodia. The 2nd Battalion of the 503rd U.S. Airborne assaulted the heavily fortified hill complex on 19 November and were summarily turned back. Two U.S. platoons were hit unexpectedly by P.A.V.N. attacks and obliterated, but the battalion held on through the night. Tragedy struck when a U.S. Air Force fighter dropped a bomb into the 503rd's line, killing and wounding a number of American soldiers. The 2nd Battalion of the 503rd Airborne was relieved, due to heavy casualties on 20 November, by the 4th Battalion, 503rd Airborne Infantry. On 21 November, Hill 875 was pummeled for seven hours by artillery fire and napalm, but the 174th Regiment held tenaciously to their positions. Individual reinforced bunkers had to be taken in detail, as they had on Iwo Jima in the Pacific during World War II, with flame throwers and satchel charges. The hill was finally seized on 23 November. Enemy losses were placed at 1,644 killed. U.S. losses amounted to 289 killed in action. The A.R.V.N. lost a total of 89 men killed.

The Antiwar Movement

The hard-fought victories of 1967 by the U.S. Army in the Central Highlands and by the U.S. Marines in the D.M.Z. war in Quang Tri Province in no sense diminished the fervor of the antiwar movement in the United States or the growing unease over the course of the war among the American public. In the wake of an October march on the Pentagon by 50,000 demonstrators and the resignation of Defense Secretary Robert McNamara, President Johnson recalled Westmoreland to the United States in November, hoping to inject a dose of optimism about the war on the home front. The general spoke with authority before U.S. Congress: Attrition was working. U.S. operations were grinding down the will of the Communists to carry on. "We have about got them on the ropes," he reported, and the country could expect to see "light at the end of the tunnel." The North Vietnamese took a different view: Hanoi was well along in its plans to launch an offensive on a major scale on 31 January 1968, during Tet, the Vietnamese new year.

The Tet Offensive

The Tet Offensive brought simultaneous attacks against all of South Vietnam's major cities and many military installations and district capitals. Rooted in Communist doctrine, the offensive sought to crush major units of the A.R.V.N. and precipitate an uprising on the part of the people. Another objective was psychological: The P.A.V.N. could not hope to defeat U.S. forces on the battlefield; instead, Hanoi hoped it would crack the Americans' confidence in their ability to continue to wage a limited war.

Hanoi's preparations for the attack went largely undetected, but one Communist unit conducted its assault twenty-four hours too early, prompting a recall of many A.R.V.N. troops

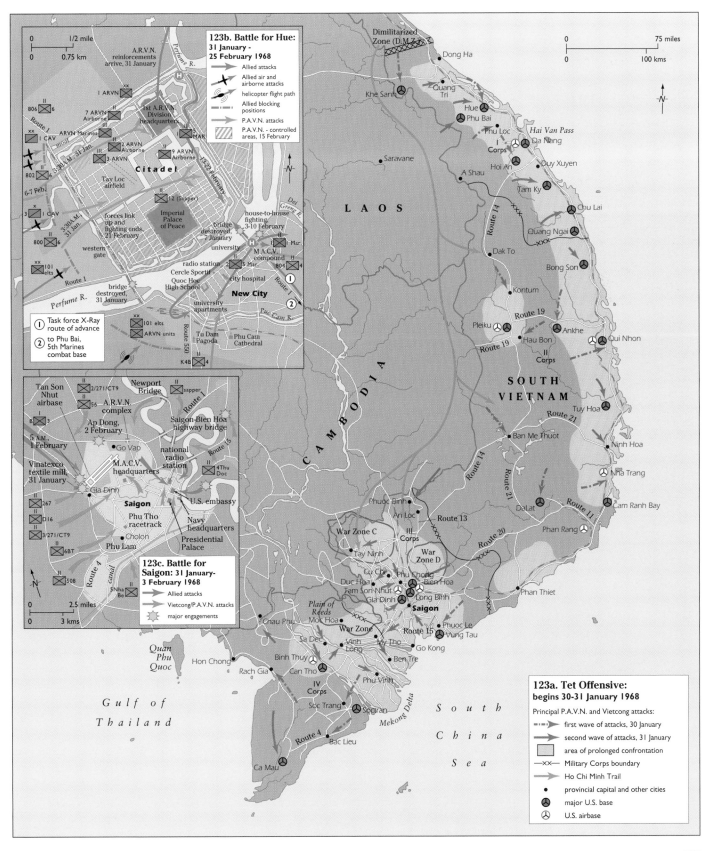

Viet Cong dead line a wall at the entrance to the U.S. Embassy in Saigon, after an attack on 31 January 1968. Such photographs shocked American civilians during the Tet Offensive.

who had been given leave for the holiday, and U.S. troops were placed on high alert. Still, General Westmoreland and his M.A.V.C. staff in Saigon never imagined that the Communists could engineer such an ambitious offensive.

Within twenty-four hours of the opening attack against the Presidential Palace in Saigon at 1:30 A.M. on 31 January, five of six autonomous cities and thirty-nine of forty-four provincial capitals were under siege. A Vietcong sapper team penetrated the U.S. Embassy and the compound was nearly overrun before reinforcements arrived to dispense with the enemy there—a small group of Vietcong volunteers among the 84,000 Vietcong and P.A.V.N. troops engaged in the offensive. In most cases, the attacks were quickly repulsed once the A.R.V.N. and U.S. units regained their balance, but the fighting in the cities and towns was immensely destructive. At Ben Tre in the Mekong Delta, a U.S. Army major told

reporter Peter Arnett that "It became necessary to destroy the town in order to save it."

The Fight for Hue

The fighting in Saigon lasted three days. It was in the ancient Vietnamese capital of Hue that the P.A.V.N. held out the longest—some twenty-five days. Hue was a very bloody affair for the civilian population. Soon after the initial attacks by the 800th and 802nd P.A.V.N. divisions, most of the city was controlled by the Communists. N.L.F. political cadres quickly rounded up government officials, Catholic priests, men of fighting age, and other "cruel tyrants and reactionary elements," and executed them without trials. The corpses of 2,800 civilians—many bludgeoned with shovels—were uncovered after the battle and another 3,000 civilians simply disappeared during the Communists' brief tenure in the city.

Initially, the fight for Hue was exclusively an A.R.V.N. concern, as Lieutenant General Ngo Quang Truong of the A.R.V.N. 1st Division counterattacked from his besieged headquarters in the northern corner of the Citadel. On 4 February, the 1st marine Regiment and the 2nd Battalion of the 5th U.S. Marines began a bitter and frustratingly slow, five-day, house-to-house battle to clear the enemy-infested south bank where M.A.C.V. headquarters troops had rebuffed repeated assaults by the 804th P.A.V.N. Regiment on their compound. The 1st Battalion, 5th U.S. Marines was thrown into the fighting for the Citadel on 11 February after the 1st A.R.V.N. Division took heavy casualties.

As the U.S. Marines struck against well-fortified enemy positions on both sides of the Perfume River, the 1st U.S. Cavalry Division's 3rd Brigade and the 101st U.S. Airborne's 501st Infantry attempted to block P.A.V.N. reinforcements from reaching the city. In the second week of February, these units attacked P.A.V.N. positions in the Citadel. The combined A.R.V.N.-U.S. response did not effectively cut off the P.A.V.N. supply line from the A Shau Valley, southwest of Hue, long a Communist stronghold, for almost three weeks. The initial restrictions on the use of artillery and tanks to protect the city's beautiful architecture greatly slowed the pace of reducing the enemy redoubts. Finally, on 21 February the 1st U.S. Cavalry closed off the Communist supply route, but house-to-house fighting continued until 25 February, when U.S. Marine units entered the Citadel without resistance. The enemy had fled the previous night. Mopping-up operations continued until 2 March. U.S. casualties were heavy: 216 men were killed in action—142 of them U.S. Marines—and 1,364 soldiers and marines were wounded.

Outcome of the Tet Offensive

Paradoxically, the Tet Offensive was a great tactical failure for

Hanoi but a strategic disaster for the United States and South Vietnam. More than 58,000 Communist troops were killed. By attacking everywhere, the Communists enjoyed superior battlefield strength nowhere. The Vietcong units that had spearheaded many of the attacks were utterly decimated. In fact, for the remainder of the war, the fighting was carried out largely by North Vietnamese regulars. There was no uprising of the South Vietnamese people against the Americans and the R.V.N. Yet, in the wake of the previous November's sunny assessment by General Westmoreland, the American people and the Johnson administration were deeply shocked by the enemy's capacity to undertake such an ambitious attack, and in the wake of Tet, victory seemed a distant possibility. More and more Americans questioned the wisdom of the Johnson administration's policies in Vietnam.

Khe Sanh

Contributing to the sense of frustration and pointlessness was the P.A.V.N.'s siege of the U.S. Marine combat base at Khe Sanh in the northwestern corner of Quang Tri Province. There, Colonel David Lownds's 26th Regiment was surrounded by some 20,000 crack P.A.V.N. troops for well over two months and had to be supplied exclusively by air, as the North Vietnamese controlled Route 9—the only road supply route in the area. Khe Sanh was the western anchor of a series of American bases along the D.M.Z. General Westmoreland had ordered the U.S. Marines there against their wishes, in part, to monitor enemy infiltration into South Vietnam and in the hope of luring a significant number of enemy troops into a large, setpiece battle in the area.

In April and May 1967, the 3rd U.S. Marine Regiment had driven off P.A.V.N. units from the hills surrounding the base. Soon after the 26th U.S. Marines replaced the 3rd Regiment in the fall of 1967, signs of a P.A.V.N. buildup were detected on a regular basis. The siege commenced on 20 January when I Company, 3rd U.S. Marine Battalion came under heavy fire as it approached Hill 881 North during a reconnaissance in force mission. Twenty marines were killed or wounded. That night a P.A.V.N. deserter reported that a major attack was planned against Hill 861, northwest of the combat base. Colonel Lownds immediately ordered the hill reinforced. The attack was launched that night, and part of the marines' perimeter was overrun. A counterattack retook the lost ground. The next night, a crisis developed when a P.A.V.N. shell landed in the base's ammunition dump, setting off 90 percent of the contents stored there. But, no major attack was launched on the base itself thereafter. Instead, the Communists fired as many as 1,000 rounds of artillery into the base on a daily basis from remote artillery batteries in Laos. Small unit attacks against the U.S. Marines on the hills around the base continued.

On 4-5 February, E Company, 2nd Battalion 26th Marines withstood a fierce assault on Hill 861A by a battalion from the 325C P.A.V.N. Division. One platoon was overrun, and the fighting soon turned, in the words of one participant, into "uncontrolled pandemonium." E Company held on through the night, and in the morning, 109 P.A.V.N. corpses were counted. Seven marines died and thirty-five were evacuated

To many civilians watching television reports of the seventy-seven days of combat around the U.S. Marine base at Khe Sanh, the stubborn resistance of the embattled Americans became a symbol of the nation's will to win the Vietnam War. Other viewers were more impressed with the ability of the North Vietnamese to shell the encampment for weeks on end, and the battle conjured up memories of the 1954 French defeat at Dien Bien Phu that resulted in the French withdrawal from all of Indochina. This is a view of Hill 861.

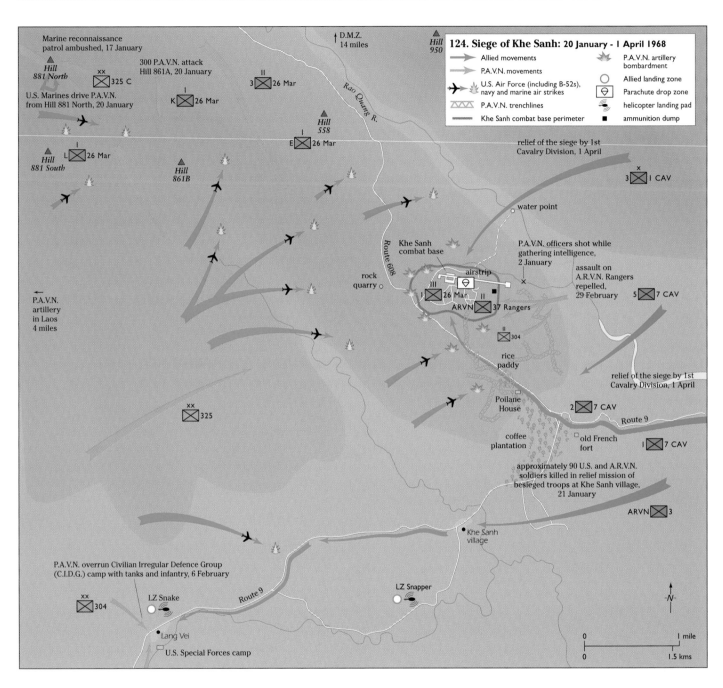

Marine reconnaissance
patrol ambushed, 17 January

Hill
881 North

XX 325 C

U.S. Marines drive P.A.V.N.
from Hill 881 North, 20 January

300 P.A.V.N. attack
Hill 861A, 20 January

K 26 Mar

3 26 Mar

I 26 Mar

Hill
558

E 26 Mar

Hill
881 South

L 26 Mar

Hill
861B

Rao Quang R.

D.M.Z.
14 miles

Hill
950

124. Siege of Khe Sanh: 20 January - 1 April 1968

→ Allied movements	P.A.V.N. artillery bombardment
→ P.A.V.N. movements	○ Allied landing zone
U.S. Air Force (including B-52s), navy and marine air strikes	Parachute drop zone
P.A.V.N. trenchlines	helicopter landing pad
Khe Sanh combat base perimeter	■ ammunition dump

relief of the siege by 1st
Cavalry Division, 1 April

3 1 CAV

water point

P.A.V.N. officers shot while
gathering intelligence,
2 January

Khe Sanh
combat base

Route 608

rock
quarry

airstrip

III
I 26 Mar
II

ARVN 37 Rangers

II 304

assault on
A.R.V.N. Rangers
repelled,
29 February

5 7 CAV

P.A.V.N.
artillery
in Laos
4 miles

XX 325

rice
paddy

Poilane
House

2 7 CAV

Route 9

relief of the siege by 1st
Cavalry Division, 1 April

coffee
plantation

old French
fort

1 7 CAV

approximately 90 U.S. and A.R.V.N.
soldiers killed in relief mission of
besieged troops at Khe Sanh village,
21 January

ARVN 3

Khe Sanh
village

P.A.V.N. overrun Civilian Irregular Defence Group
(C.I.D.G.) camp with tanks and infantry, 6 February

XX 304

LZ Snake

Route 9

LZ Snapper

Lang Vei

U.S. Special Forces camp

-N-

| 0 | 1 mile |
| 0 | 1.5 kms |

with wounds. An extraordinary five Navy Crosses were awarded—the highest decoration awarded for bravery to U.S. Marines with the exception of the Congressional Medal of Honor. Meanwhile, President Johnson had become so obsessed with the fate of the U.S. Marines that he had reports sent to him hourly and had a replica of the battlefield built in the White House basement. American B-52s struck at regular intervals against suspected enemy troop concentrations: Between 60,000 and 75,000 tons of bombs had fallen in the area by the siege's end on 1 April.

End of the Siege

In early March, P.A.V.N. units began to withdraw from the area, and the siege was officially lifted with the advent of the 1st Cavalry's relief of the U.S. Marines, commencing on 1 April. The official casualty tally indicates that 205 marines were killed and 1,600 wounded, although many veterans think that those figures are too low. M.A.C.V. estimated that 10,000 to 15,000 P.A.V.N. soldiers were killed, the vast majority by air strikes. The battle remains controversial. General Vo Nguyen Giap claimed that the siege was a feint—a diversion to keep

M.A.C.V.'s attention and resources away from cities he planned to attack during the Tet Offensive. In any event, the absence of an unambiguous victory for the U.S. Marines—and the abandonment of the base at Khe Sahn in June 1968—seemed to demonstrate the futility of war to an American public that was transfixed by the battle along with their president.

Reviewing U.S. Options

In response to a request from General Westmoreland and Joint Chiefs of Staff Chairman Earle G. Wheeler that an additional 206,000 U.S. troops be sent to Vietnam, Johnson asked his Secretary of Defense, Clark Clifford and a group of foreign policy "wise men," such as former Secretary of State Dean Acheson and General Omar Bradley, to review the U.S. options. The clear consensus was that the request for more troops should be turned down. The United States should not expand its commitment in Vietnam. The American public, in the estimation of the wise men, would not accept an expanded war in the wake of the Tet Offensive. A war-weary Johnson concurred, telling Saigon that the A.R.V.N. would have to assume a greater burden of the fighting. On 31 March, Johnson went further: He announced that he would seek to negotiate with Hanoi and restrict the bombing of North Vietnam as a signal of his resolve to end the war. And he shocked the nation with another statement: He would not seek reelection in the upcoming presidential election. A critical turning point had been reached, but the pace of combat did not slacken appreciably during the rest of 1968. The Communists launched the so-called Mini-Tet Offensive in May, exacerbating the refugee problem in South Vietnam. Altogether, some 14,000 Americans died in Vietnam in 1968. Peace talks opened in May, but quickly ground to a halt.

A Change in Tactics

In July 1969, General Creighton Abrams assumed command of M.A.C.V. An exceptionally capable and intelligent officer, he seemed to have a more subtle grasp of the limits of U.S. military power to affect events in the complex political struggle that was unfolding in Vietnam than his predecessor. Abrams set about making U.S. forces more tactically flexible and, like many senior U.S. Marine officers, he thought greater emphasis had to be placed on the pacification of South Vietnam's 14,000 hamlets. He urged greater restraint on his commanders in calling in highly destructive artillery and air support in combat.

Pacification Efforts

The government of South Vietnam, of course, had implemented an array of pacification programs designed to bring security

and economic opportunity to the villages and loyalty to the G.V.N.—and to prevent the formidable Vietcong political infrastructure from expanding its hold over the country's 14,000 villages. The success of these programs, ranging from the Agroville and strategic hamlet initiatives, requiring the peasants to move to forlorn, protected communities, resembling concentration camps, to the establishment of local and regional security forces, was limited by lackluster execution, corruption, and studied indifference to the welfare of the peasantry that characterized all of South Vietnam's political regimes from that of Diem to the military government of Nguyen Cao Ky and Nguyen Van Thieu. The United States financed most of these programs and provided both civilian and military advisors at all levels.

No small degree of acrimony arose in Washington over the South Vietnamese government's failure to implement these programs effectively. Initially the U.S. Ambassador to South Vietnam was expected to integrate the disparate programs, working directly with local South Vietnamese officials. But turf disputes arose and the various services and agencies involved worked at cross purposes. In May 1967, President Johnson appointed Robert Komer as Westmoreland's deputy in charge of pacification. Komer established the Civilian Operations and Revolutionary Development program (C.O.R.D.) to unify U.S. pacification efforts. Komer saw to it that G.V.N. programs were given access to more advisors and supplied with military resources such as engineers and medical personnel.

Among the many programs supervised by C.O.R.D., the joint U.S.-G.V.N. Phoenix program was almost certainly the most successful at inflicting serious damage on the Vietcong infrastructure. Phoenix was supported and directed by the Central Intelligence Agency (C.I.A.). Begun in 1968, its success lay in the remarkable effectiveness of its Intelligence Coordination and Exploitation program, which produced accurate lists of Vietcong political operatives that were turned over to various military units charged with "neutralizing" those operatives. Many Phoenix missions were carried out by Vietnamese police, U.S. Navy S.E.A.L. teams, or C.I.A. covert operations people. The program was controversial because it employed a favorite Communist practice against the Vietcong: Assassination. Thirty-four thousand Vietnam operatives were taken prisoner before Phoenix came to a halt after the Easter Offensive of 1972. According to Komer's successor William Colby, most of the 20,000 Vietcong operatives that had been killed had died in conventional combat operations, not as a result of assassination.

Nixon and Vietnamization

Richard M. Nixon won the November 1968 presidential election on the promise to end the war. Once in office,

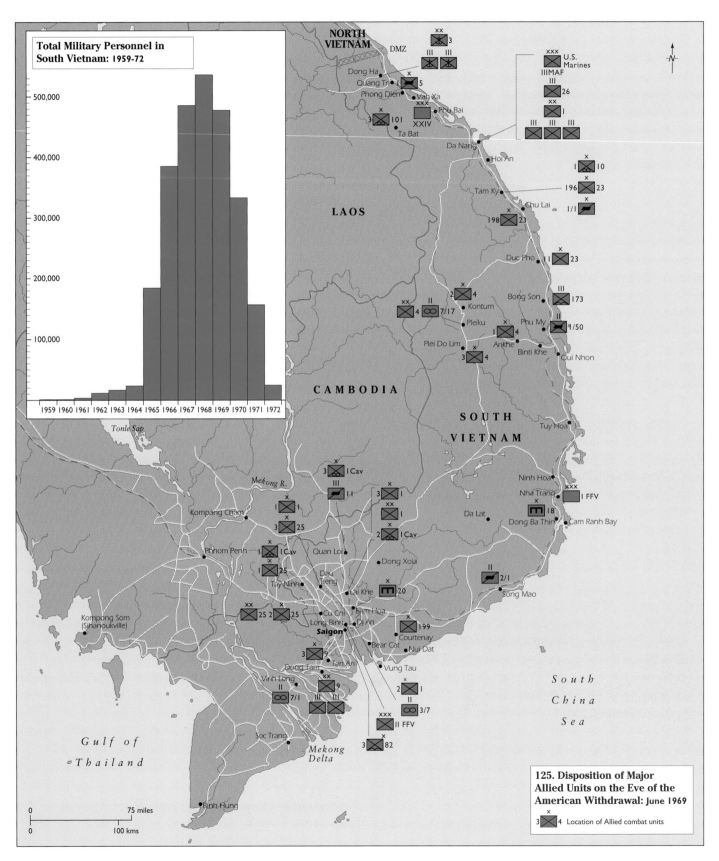

Total Military Personnel in South Vietnam: 1959-72

125. Disposition of Major Allied Units on the Eve of the American Withdrawal: June 1969

Location of Allied combat units

however, Nixon and his chief foreign policy architect, National Security Advisor (and later Secretary of State) Henry Kissinger showed themselves more than ready to press the attack against Hanoi, albeit along different lines than those pursued before Johnson's critical decisions of March 1968. Nixon formalized the decision to turn over more of the ground fighting to the A.R.V.N., when he announced the policy of Vietnamization—U.S. troops would be withdrawn from Vietnam gradually as the A.R.V.N. expanded and modernized its weaponry and equipment. The withdrawal began in August 1969 with the departure of some 25,000 troops. To protect the shrinking U.S. force and relieve pressure on the A.R.V.N., Nixon approved Operation Menu (March 1969)—the secret bombing of P.A.V.N. base camps in Cambodia.

While accepting that a negotiated settlement was now the primary objective for the United States, Nixon and Kissinger time and again sought to show Hanoi that the U.S. would not countenance the outright defeat of the A.R.V.N. on the battlefield during or after the drawdown of U.S. forces: Nixon unleashed highly damaging bombing campaigns over North Vietnam at several junctures to signal that resolve, most dramatically in the wake of the Communist Easter Offensive of spring 1972. The Nixon administration also sought, with some success, to circumscribe Hanoi's military initiatives by improving diplomatic relations with China and the Soviet Union, its suppliers of military hardware. All these policies were undertaken against a background of an increasingly strident antiwar movement that saw Nixon's effort to achieve "peace with honor" as highly suspect.

Morale Problems

The shift in America's objective from battlefield victory to negotiated settlement and withdrawal had deleterious effects on the performance and the morale of U.S. forces. Drug abuse and incidents of fragging, the killing of officers and noncommissioned officers by subordinates, increased markedly during the war's later years. (The term derives from the fragmentation grenade—the weapon of choice in these incidents—but officers were also killed by other means.) The U.S. Army reported 126 fragging incidents in 1969. In 1971 there were 333 such incidents. Racial incidents increased alarmingly as well. The steady influx of inadequately trained junior officers was another source of morale problems. More and more combat troops saw themselves as pawns in a game the politicians had already given up on winning. Thus, the troops turned to drugs, particularly marijuana, and were increasingly reluctant to engage the enemy.

My Lai

The Nixon era saw a diminution in the number of big unit

As the war in Vietnam dragged on, U.S. political and military leaders had to deal with a serious deterioration of morale among troops in Vietnam, brought on by the conditions "in country" and by the lack of support for the war back home. Cynicism, drug abuse, racial conflict, fragging, and a sense of hopelessness became part of the daily life for most soldiers stationed in Vietnam. These members of the U.S. 9th Infantry Division look anything but confident and ready for battle while they wait for artillery support prior to attacking an enemy machine gun bunker in Dinh Tuong Province on 4 April 1968.

combat operations due to the drawdown of U.S. forces and the growing body of media stories emphasizing the pointlessness of combat in Vietnam. A dark shadow was cast over the U.S. Army following revelations of the massacre of between 200 and 500 unarmed civilians in the hamlet of My Lai in Quang Tri Province by troops of Company C, 1st Battalion, 20th Infantry, 23rd Division. Only Lieutenant William Calley, a mere platoon commander, was convicted of murdering civilians, and his sentence was cut short by President Nixon on the grounds that he had been used as a scapegoat. The incident, brought to light in spring 1969, had occurred on 16 March 1968. Many on the left thought that the atrocities committed at My Lai confirmed their view that the war was both immoral and illegal.

The Battle of Hamburger Hill

The ten-day operation conducted by the 101st Airborne Division against entrenched P.A.V.N. positions on Ap Bia Mountain in the A Shau Valley in May 1969 became an infamous symbol of the waste of American lives. Assaults on 12 and 13 May by the 3rd Battalion of the 187th Infantry failed to dislodge the enemy. Two additional battalions were deployed for attack along with a battalion from the 3rd A.R.V.N. Regiment. A two-battalion frontal assault against a torrent of grenades and machine guns took the summit on the 18 May, but torrential rains forced the U.S. and A.R.V.N. troops to withdraw to the base of the mountain. Finally a four-battalion assault on 20 May forced the North Vietnamese off Ap Bia and into the safety of Laos. But the P.A.V.N. units quickly returned to the moun-

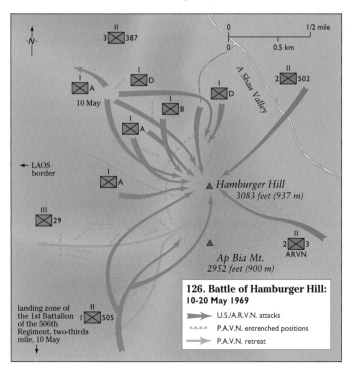

landing zone of the 1st Battalion of the 506th Regiment, two-thirds mile, 10 May

126. Battle of Hamburger Hill:
10-20 May 1969
→ U.S./A.R.V.N. attacks
- - - P.A.V.N. entrenched positions
→ P.A.V.N. retreat

tain when the Americans departed. A *LIFE* magazine article published the pictures of the 241 Americans who died in Vietnam during the week of the battle. Forty-six of them had died at Ap Bia, and the engagement became known across the United States as the Battle of Hamburger Hill—a symbol of the pointlessness of continuing to fight in Vietnam. General Abrams was ordered to avoid such "meatgrinder" engagements in the future.

Invasion of Cambodia

Under continual pressure to disengage at home, Nixon nonetheless widened the scope of the war in April 1970, when he ordered an invasion of Cambodia to eradicate the Communists' longstanding sanctuaries there and, thus, reduce their capacity to attack U.S. and A.R.V.N. forces in South Vietnam. The first phase of the Cambodian incursion was largely an A.R.V.N. operation, in which various units struck into the Parrot's Beak area where a number of base camps and supply depots were located. On 1 May, A.R.V.N. units, joined by the 11th U.S. Armored Cavalry and other elements of the 1st U.S. Air Cavalry Division attacked in the Fishhook area of Cambodia where they encountered little resistance but a great many weapons and supplies. On 2 May, the 2nd Brigade of the First Cavalry uncovered "The City," a gigantic Vietcong supply depot and training base. On 6 May, that same unit deployed to Enemy Base Area, while A.R.V.N. units and the 1st Armored Cavalry attacked Enemy Base Area 350. By 4 June, the entire 1st Air Cavalry Division was in operation in Eastern Cambodia, where it made frequent contact with P.A.V.N. units, but never fought a protracted battle.

All U.S. units pulled out of Cambodia by 30 June. During the incursion, U.S. and A.R.V.N. units captured weapons and war materiel sufficient to support more than fifty P.A.V.N. battalions for a full year. Many of the supply depots were restocked once the Americans and South Vietnamese left the area and the major long-term effect of the incursion was a congressional prohibition on deploying U.S. forces or advisors to Laos or Cambodia.

Operation Lam Son

Despite the congressional prohibition, the U.S. provided logistical support to an A.R.V.N. invasion into Laos during Operation Lam Son in February 1971. That operation initially caught P.A.V.N. units off guard, but it ended with an undignified retreat and withdrawal that cast doubt on the capacity of the A.R.V.N. to fight protracted engagements against the more highly motivated troops of North Vietnam.

Operation Linebacker I

At best, Lam Son forestalled for a few months General Giap's

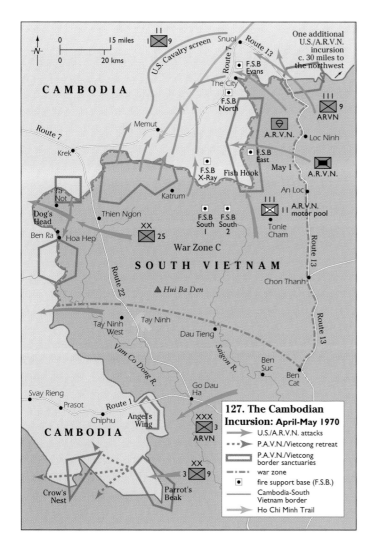

127. The Cambodian Incursion: April-May 1970

→ U.S./A.R.V.N. attacks
┅► P.A.V.N./Vietcong retreat
▭ P.A.V.N./Vietcong border sanctuaries
┅ war zone
⊡ fire support base (F.S.B.)
— Cambodia-South Vietnam border
➤ Ho Chi Minh Trail

ed the bombing to the area south of the 20th parallel. When the negotiations stalled again in December, Nixon ordered an all-out bombing of the area around Hanoi in Operation Linebacker II. The world had not seen so extensive an air campaign since World War II, as B-52 bombers began the systematic destruction of oil storage facilities, bridges, railroad lines, and other military targets. The North Vietnamese quickly exhausted their supply of surface-to-air missiles, but Nixon nonetheless continued to bomb North Vietnam in an effort to get Hanoi to negotiate seriously and in good faith.

The Paris Peace Agreement

Nixon's tactic worked, for Hanoi, fearing that its dike system and civilian neighborhoods would become the object of American attack, did return to the table with a more flexible attitude. On 27 January 1973, the United States, North Vietnam, and representatives of the N.L.F. and the R.V.N. signed the Paris Peace Agreements. In a concession to the United States and the R.V.N., President Nguyen Van Thieu's government would continue in Saigon; there would be no coalition formed. All American P.O.W.s would be returned. Ominously, all P.A.V.N. units inside South Vietnam were allowed to remain. Nixon claimed to have achieved "peace with honor" for the United States. In fact he had managed to extricate the United States well in advance of the final collapse of South Vietnam.

Agreement Violations

Violations of the agreement by both sides commenced almost immediately, lending credence to Colonel Harry G. Summers' assertion that the peace agreement marked not an end to the Vietnam war, but merely a prelude to its next phase. The next phase was not long in coming. When Hanoi decided to launch its Ho Chi Minh Campaign—a twenty-plus armor-infantry *blitzkrieg* attack in January 1975, neither President Ford, who succeeded Nixon after he resigned in disgrace, nor the American people showed much of an appetite to assist Saigon in its death throes. The Watergate scandal, which had its origins in the secret bombings of Cambodia, and the lies and misrepresentations of both the Johnson and Nixon administrations concerning the war, had eviscerated the country's will to preserve an independent South Vietnam. Indeed the U.S. Congress had by that point placed strict limits on the president's power to deploy U.S. forces without its consent in the War Powers Act of 1973. So South Vietnam stood alone, despite a written promise from Nixon to Thieu that the U.S. would commit troops again in the event of an invasion by the North Vietnamese.

Easter Offensive, which began on 30 March 1972. A.R.V.N. units in Quang Tri were decimated by Hanoi's fourteen-division offensive, replete with a heavy complement of tanks. Nixon and Kissinger, furious that Hanoi would undertake such a major military initiative while simultaneously negotiating a settlement, responded with a massive air attack. Operation Linebacker I (10 May-23 October 1972) sought to interdict the flow of the D.R.V.'s supplies to the battlefield and destroy critical targets inside North Vietnam. U.S. Navy A-6 and A-7 fighter bombers dropped mines at the entrance to Haiphong Harbor—Hanoi's port and the source of a huge percentage of its war-making materiel—and laser-guided bombs were used for the first time in history to destroy North Vietnam's infrastructure and to isolate it from its suppliers. Imports in September were half what they had been in May.

Operation Linebacker II

In response to progress at the Paris negotiations, Nixon limit-

The Final Offensive of the War

P.A.V.N. General Van Tien Dung led the final offensive of the

Vietnam War. Striking with three divisions into the Central Highlands at Ban Me Thuot, south of the Ia Drang Valley, he sought to cut the country in half, just as Hanoi had attempted to do in the 1965 Ia Drang campaign. R.V.N. President Nguyen Van Thieu unwisely decided to abandon the Central Highlands and concentrate his forces in the south. Dung then launched another prong of his attack across the D.M.Z. and drove down the coast, capturing South Vietnam's important cities and towns in succession. By late March, Danang and Hue had fallen, and A.R.V.N. soldiers began to desert en

128. The Final Offensive:
March - April 1975

→ P.A.V.N. advance

∙∙∙▶ A.R.V.N. movements

masse. The last major battle of the war was fought at Xuan Loc, thirty-five miles east of Saigon. That city fell after savage fighting, and the road to Saigon was clear. The capital city came under direct attack on 26 April. The U.S. Embassy was evacuated hurriedly by U.S. Marines in Operation Frequent Wind on 29 April, and on 30 April, Soviet-made tanks of the P.A.V.N. rolled though the gates of the Presidential Palace. Hanoi's thirty-year war to unify all Vietnam came to an end.

The War's Legacies

Thousands of books and articles have tried to explain how and why the United States lost in Vietnam. Discussions show no signs of abating. Leftist historians, such as Gabriel Kolko and Howard Zinn, have interpreted U.S. involvement as over-reaching by an imperialist superpower, blind to Ho Chi Minh's nationalist appeal and bent on extending capitalist domination among the developing nations. The more convincing interpretation, and the dominant one in the scholarship today, is by such writers as George Herring and Stanley Karnow. They see the war as a tragic and avoidable blunder by a succession of U.S. administrations. Imbued with an arrogant belief in their ability to shape world politics, they were blind to the growing body of evidence that South Vietnam was a nation of questionable legitimacy. And they grossly underestimated the strength of will and purpose of Hanoi, its people, and their army. Seeing the world through the lens of postwar, Communist containment, and utterly ignorant of Vietnamese culture, they stumbled forward into a quagmire. The key decision makers simply could not imagine that a country with the resources of the U.S.—political, military, and moral—could be defeated by, what Henry Kissinger called, a "fourth rate power."

The war's legacies have been profound and varied. In the immediate aftermath of the conflict, many U.S. military officers left the service with bitterness, feeling betrayed by politicians who forced them to fight with one hand tied behind their backs. But others, including generals Colin Powell and H. Norman Schwarzkopf, dedicated themselves to understanding what went wrong and why. They brought about a revolution in U.S. military doctrine, culture, and organization that reestablished pride and discipline in a demoralized military that departed Vietnam in a state of crisis. One of many critical post-Vietnam developments was the creation of a new force structure that depended on marrying the reserves with regulars, so that even a regional war would require the call-up of reserves—something that never transpired in Vietnam.

It would be difficult to quarrel with Arnold R. Isaacs' remark in 1997 that Vietnam "lingers in the national memory, brooding over our politics, our culture, and our long unfinished debate over who we are and what we believe." The war's

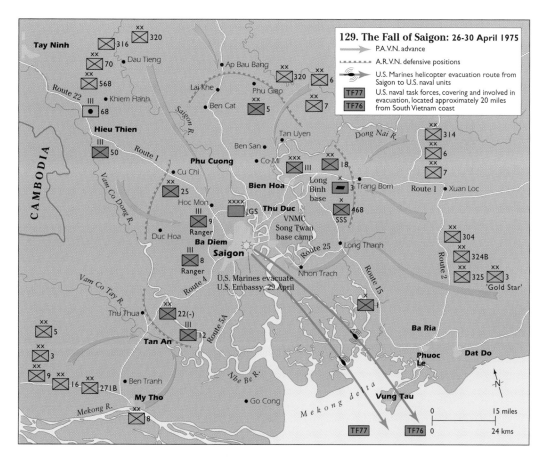

129. The Fall of Saigon: 26-30 April 1975

→ P.A.V.N. advance

- - - A.R.V.N. defensive positions

↝ U.S. Marines helicopter evacuation route from Saigon to U.S. naval units

TF77
TF76
U.S. naval task forces, covering and involved in evacuation, located approximately 20 miles from South Vietnam coast

An A-6 Intruder from the U.S.S. Constellation, above, is shown being loaded with ordnance. The Intruder was the primary all-weather, close air support plane flown by the marines, whose ground troops depended on significantly more fixed wing air support than did U.S. Army ground units because they generally had less artillery and helicopter support. Marine, navy, and air force jets supported army operations. U.S. pilots also flew the tough A-4 Skyraider and the sleek F-4B Phantom.

cost contributed to federal budget deficits and the first significant downturn in the U.S. economy since the Great Depression of the 1930s. Coupled with Watergate—the product of the rancorous relations between Nixon and the antiwar supporters—the conflict undermined the American people's faith in government, particularly the presidency and the foreign policy-making apparatus. The U.S. Congress, in the wake of Vietnam, exercised increasing restraint on American military involvement abroad, prompting Richard Nixon to coin the term, "Vietnam syndrome." Since Vietnam, policy makers have been required to be more concrete about missions, objectives, and risks inherent in any deployment of the military abroad.

The impact of the conflict on the national ethos and spirit is hard to overestimate, for it brought to an end what historian James Patterson has called the era of "grand expectations." The belief that the U.S. could accomplish unilaterally whatever it set out to do in the world died in the jungles and villages of Vietnam. The war, in short, brought about a period of national soul-searching. The most prescient of Lyndon Johnson's advisers, George Ball, put it this way: Vietnam was a "defeat for our political authority and moral influence abroad and for our sense of mission and cohesion at home."

When Khmer Rouge soldiers seized the Mayaguez on 12 May 1975, President Ford ordered marines to retake the ship and to rescue the crew thought to be on Koh Tang Island. When the marines boarded, they found the ship abandoned. By the time U.S. officials learned that the 39 crewmen had been released, 15 U.S. servicemen were dead, 50 wounded, and 3 were missing. To critics, the operation was precipitous, but its supporters believed America had to protect the free use of international waters in Southeast Asia.

The Global Cold War: 1946-90

The Cold War was a period of political, ideological, strategic, and military conflict between the United States and the Soviet Union. The term "cold war" was first applied to this struggle in 1947 by newspaper writer Herbert Swope, who used it in a speech he wrote for American financier and political advisor, Bernard Baruch, that was delivered to the State Legislature of South Carolina. Rarely marked by outright war between the two superpowers, the Cold War nevertheless affected many regions of the world. Political and social differences between these two nations after World War II produced different views of internationalism which, in turn, produced competing foreign policies in the late 1940s. Essentially, the United States envisioned a world dominated by Democratic governments and free market economies while the former U.S.S.R. saw that American view of the world as a poorly disguised plan to dominate them. Although Cold War tension was felt first in Europe, where U.S. and Soviet policy-makers clashed over the political and economic reconstruction of countries devastated by the war, the struggle for postwar dominance soon spread to all corners of the globe. In the end, the Cold War was a global struggle as many nations in the east and the west, Democratic and Communist, came to compete for influence in shaping the developing world into nations compatible and friendly with their own political systems.

Resistance to Join the Struggle

Some countries resisted the temptation to join the Cold War struggle. The Non-Aligned Movement (N.A.M.) was a loose coalition of developing nations that adopted a nonaligned foreign policy during the Cold War. Prominent among early members of this movement were Yugoslavia, India, and Indonesia, although by 1980 the N.A.M. included most Third World nations. Some N.A.M. members, such as India or Indonesia, pursued genuinely nonaligned foreign policies, but many nations did not. In fact, some N.A.M. nations played different and often opposing roles in the rivalry between the east and west, with some displaying consistently pro-west or pro-east tendencies, such as the Philippines, a nation with close ties to the United States, or Cuba, a country with a formal alliance with the Soviet Union. Perhaps because of this trend, the N.A.M. met with only limited success, especially as the Cold War lengthened. Generally speaking, most countries, in all regions of the world, found it difficult to navigate within the community of nations absent from the Cold War calculations of diplomacy, power, and policy.

Fractures in the Wartime Alliance

Important fractures in the wartime alliance of the United States and the Soviet Union first surfaced in disagreements about the occupation of Poland and Germany as well as the governmental structure in Yugoslavia and Czechoslovakia immediately following World War II. The U.S.S.R., invaded twice in as many generations by western European nations, was determined to dictate the shape and form of governments in central and eastern Europe. The U.S.S.R., in part through the presence of the Red Army, was able to impose its will in Poland, Czechoslovakia, and, to a lesser extent, Yugoslavia. But in the former Third Reich, an impasse among the occupying nations of Germany (Great Britain, France, the Soviet Union, and the United States) eventually led to the partition of that country into West and East Germany by 1949.

By 1947, this standoff between east and west had spilled

General Curtis LeMay (above) helped organize the Berlin Airlift, when the Soviet Union cut land links to the West. For a year, U.S. and British cargo planes (right) flew in an average of 4,500 tons of supplies a day.

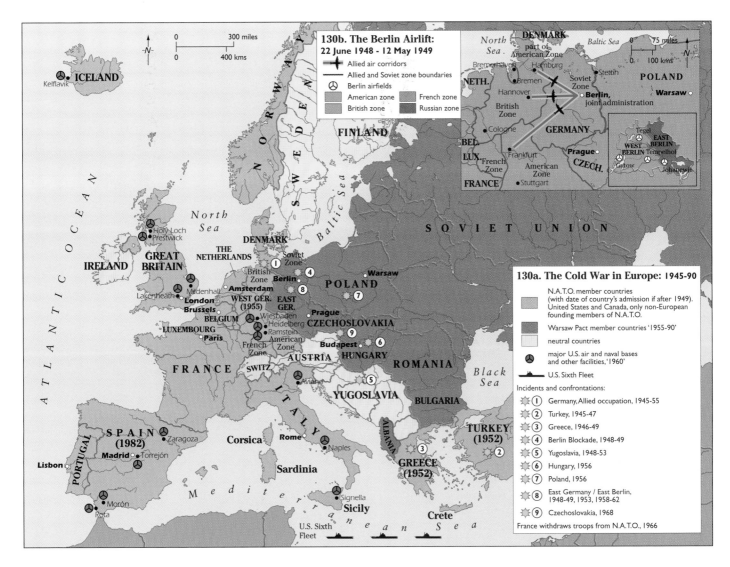

**130b. The Berlin Airlift:
22 June 1948 - 12 May 1949**
- Allied air corridors
- Allied and Soviet zone boundaries
- Berlin airfields
- American zone
- British zone
- French zone
- Russian zone

130a. The Cold War in Europe: 1945-90

N.A.T.O. member countries (with date of country's admission if after 1949). United States and Canada, only non-European founding members of N.A.T.O.

Warsaw Pact member countries '1955-90'

neutral countries

major U.S. air and naval bases and other facilities,'1960'

U.S. Sixth Fleet

Incidents and confrontations:
1. Germany, Allied occupation, 1945-55
2. Turkey, 1945-47
3. Greece, 1946-49
4. Berlin Blockade, 1948-49
5. Yugoslavia, 1948-53
6. Hungary, 1956
7. Poland, 1956
8. East Germany / East Berlin, 1948-49, 1953, 1958-62
9. Czechoslovakia, 1968

France withdraws troops from N.A.T.O., 1966

into neighboring nations, most notably Greece, where a Communist insurgency threatened the government, and Turkey, where the Soviets pressured for transit rights connecting the Black Sea with the Mediterranean. The United States responded to these developments with economic and military aid worth 400 million dollars enunciated in the Truman Doctrine, as President Harry S. Truman declared the incipient Cold War a struggle between free institutions and representative governments, on the one hand, and nations forcibly ruled by small, evil cabals, on the other hand. In 1948, the United States followed this aid package with the Marshall Plan, which poured billions of dollars into the economies of European nations to combat the spread of Communism that had traditionally been bred on social and economic turmoil. With American assistance, the Greeks defeated their Communist insurgents, and in Italy the Christian-Democratic party defeated the Communist-Socialist party in national elections.

Tension Escalates Over Germany

At the same time tension over Germany escalated. The city of Berlin had been occupied by both Soviet and Allied (American, British, and French) troops since World War II and in the summer of 1948 the Soviets tried to force the withdrawal of the United States and other western allies by blockading the city. This led to the improvised and massive Berlin Airlift using both U.S. and British cargo planes to feed and support western troops and civilians in the city. The airlift, which began on 22 June 1948 and ended on 12 May 1949, was a seminal event in the early Cold War because it established the precedent of east-west confrontation that fell just short of outright war. In fact, the Berlin Airlift might have done more than anything to ensure that the Cold War became cold rather than hot. The drama of the conflict also prodded Belgium, Canada, Denmark, France, Iceland, Italy, Luxembourg, the Netherlands, Norway, Portugal, the United Kingdom, and the

217

INDONESIA Java
MALAYA
SOUTH VIETNAM
BORNEO
THAILAND
CELEBES
7,000
Tan Son Nhut
Bangkok 4,000
EAST PAKISTAN
Bien Hoa
Cam Ranh Bay Sattahip
Nha Trang Ta Khli
Ankhe Udon
Chu Lai Nakhon
Da Nang
BURMA
INDIA
PHILIPPINES
5 10,000
Sangley Point Subic Bay
Clark
Tainan
NORTH VIETNAM
TIBET
PAKISTAN
Peshawar
Okinawa
TAIWAN
Taipei
5 50,000
C H I N A
AFGHANISTAN
Kadena
Naha
SOUTH KOREA
40,000 11
IRAN
Dhahran
SAUDI ARABIA
ETHIOPIA
Sasebo
Kunsan
Osan
Kimpo
MONGOLIA
IRAQ
JAPAN
14 40,000
NORTH KOREA
Incirlik
SUDAN
Yokosuka Yokota
Atsugi Tachikawa
Misawa
Sea of Japan
Krasnodar
Ankara
TURKEY
2 8,700
Cigli
Iraklion
LIBYA
14,000 1
EGYPT
CHAD
S O V I E T   U N I O N
Ural Mts.
Moscow
GREECE
Mediterranean
Naples
2 35,000
Wheelus
ITALY
10,000 6
TUNISIA
PACIFIC
Leningrad
Pacific Fleet
10 55,000
Shemya
White Sea
Murmansk
FINLAND
West Berlin
6,500 1
SWEDEN
NORWAY
260,000 14
FRANCE
50,000 18
SPAIN
5 10,000
ALGERIA
5,000 6
Kenitra
Adak
ARCTIC OCEAN
North Pole
WEST GERMANY
U.K.
35,000 18
Keflavik
PORTUGAL
MOROCCO
Bering Strait
Cape Lisburne
GREENLAND
6,000 3
ICELAND
1 4,000
Alaska
5 31,000
Thule
Azores
2 1,900
Lajes Field
Clear Eielson
Kodiak Elmendorf
Distant Early Warning Line (D.E.W.)
Sondrestrom
Cape Dyer
Pearl Harbor
Hawaii
42,000 6
Wheeler
Hickham
Bellows
Mid-Canada Line
C A N A D A
Goose
ATLANTIC OCEAN
Pine Tree Line
0   1500 miles
0   2000 kms
Argentia

131. U.S. Global Defense and the Disposition of Its Forces at the Height of the Cold War: 1962

	Countries allied with the United States and the West
	Communist-bloc countries
	non-aligned countries
6	Number of U.S. bases and facilities in area
5,000	Number of U.S. forces in area
⟨	Ballistic Missile Early Warning System
- - -	Radar coverage of continental United States
—	other warning system lines
⊕	major U.S. air base

U N I T E D   S T A T E S
1,800,000
U.S. Naval Space surveillance system
Kindley
Bermuda (British)
MEXICO
Puerto Rico (U.S.)
Roosevelt Roads
Ramey
CUBA
Caribbean
HAITI
DOM. REP.
9 20,000
Guantanamo Bay (U.S.)
GUATEMALA
EL SALVADOR
NICARAGUA
Coco Solo
VENEZUELA
COSTA RICA
PANAMA
COLOMBIA
B R A Z I L

In August 1961, the German Democratic Republic and the Soviet Union began constructing the Berlin Wall to stop the flow of refugees to the West that threatened to cripple the East German economy. First barbed wire, then a concrete wall, were put in place. President John F. Kennedy, who visited the Berlin Wall on 26 June 1963 (left) was criticized for not defying the Soviets and bulldozing it. Over the next thirty years, minefields, automatic machine guns, and other additions made the Berlin Wall impassable. The Berlin Wall and "Checkpoint Charlie," one of the few places to cross the barrier, quickly became vivid symbols of the Cold War. The dismantling of the wall and the reunification of Germany in 1990 are commonly cited as marking the end of that conflict.

United States to formalize a mutual defense pact treaty, when they founded the North Atlantic Treaty Organization (N.A.T.O.) in 1949. In 1955, the Soviet Union along with Albania, Bulgaria, Czechoslovakia, East Germany, Hungary, Poland, and Romania responded to the establishment of N.A.T.O. and the rearmament of West Germany in 1954 by founding the Warsaw Treaty Organization, sometimes known as the Warsaw Pact. Henceforth, Cold War conflicts, at least in Europe, were managed through these two opposing military alliances.

An Uneasy Truce

Beyond a few high profile crises like the Soviet crushing of the Hungarian Revolution in 1956 or the building of the Berlin Wall by Communist East Germany in 1961, both aggressive Soviet acts, Europe settled into an uneasy armed truce for the rest of the Cold War. Tensions calmed after 1949, in part because, after that year, both the United States and the Soviet Union possessed nuclear weapons and the consequences of total war could not be contemplated. With Europe essentially in political stalemate, in 1949, the United States adopted a policy, embodied in National Security Council Paper 68, which focused on the third or developing world as an important battleground in the Cold War.

Tension in Latin America and the Caribbean

Latin America and the Caribbean Sea, geographically close to the United States, witnessed much Cold War tension and military activity. The United States had a military history of involvement in the region dating from the articulation of the Monroe Doctrine in 1823. The Mexican-American War (1846-48), the Spanish-American-Cuban War (1898), the construction of the Panama Canal (1904-14), and at least twenty instances of U.S. military intervention in Latin American nations in the first third of the twentieth century all underscored American interests in the region. Over time, Central American nations came to regard the behavior of the United States in the area as heavy-handed, and considered U.S. policy in the region an affront to their respective sovereignties.

In 1933, President Franklin D. Roosevelt initiated a "Good Neighbor" policy that accepted a principle of U.S. nonintervention in Latin American nations. Subsequent improvements in inter-American relations contributed to a united hemispheric solidarity against Germany and Japan in World War II. Following the war, the Inter-American Treaty of Reciprocal Assistance in 1947 pledged signatories to a mutual defense pact, and the Organization of American States (O.A.S.), formed in 1948 and consisting of the United States and twenty Latin American nations, codified Roosevelt's non-interventionism and aimed to promote common interests, resolve disputes, and provide a mechanism for collective behavior in matters requiring military action.

The onset of Cold War tensions aborted these improvements in relations, however. Shaky governments, persistent social and economic unrest, and a history of intimidation by the United States in Latin America made the region receptive to Communist overtures. When various countries calculated their own security and strategic interests differently than did the United States, Latin America became a smoldering hotbed of Cold War animosity, competition, covert action, and revolution.

Protecting U.S. Interests

Unable to persuade the O.A.S. to compromise the principle of nonintervention in the name of anti-Communism, the United States returned to a pattern of unilateral action to protect its interests in the region. Employing the Central Intelligence Agency, the United States covertly destabilized the left-leaning governments in Guatemala in 1954 and Brazil in 1965. Also in 1965, political instability in the Dominican Republic bred American fears of a Communist takeover there, and President Lyndon B. Johnson authorized an outright invasion of the nation. As he did so, Johnson publicly repudiated the O.A.S. charter on nonintervention and insisted that the United States would not accept the existence of Communist governments in the Western Hemisphere. Beginning in 1970, the United States covertly worked to overthrow the Marxist president of Chile, Salvador Allende Gossens, and in 1973 General Augusto Pinochet replaced him following a bloody military coup.

The Bay of Pigs and Its Consequences

This renaissance of American activity in the internal affairs of Latin American nations rekindled regional concerns of an overbearing neighbor to the north. The renewed animosity toward the United States was most dramatically expressed in Cuba where, since 1902, United States policy had often served the economic interests of U.S. firms operating in Cuba at the expense of indigenous social and economic reforms. In 1959, a revolution propelled Fidel Castro into power, and for the first time Cuba, just ninety miles from the coast of Florida, became an important strategic problem for the United States.

In 1961, the new U.S. president, John F. Kennedy, authorized U.S. sponsorship of a hastily conceived plan to overthrow Castro's government using 1,300 Cuban exiles trained in the United States. On 18 April, this force, code-named Brigade 2506, waded ashore in Cuba at the Bahia de los Cochinos (Bay of Pigs), backed up by a joint U.S. Marine-U.S. Navy task force. Although Castro easily repulsed this invasion with 20,000 militiamen, his subsequent fury toward the United States carried important consequences.

After the Bay of Pigs, Castro courted the assistance of the Soviet Union to balance U.S. threats to his government. The Soviets, seeing an opportunity to counter U. S. military assets in Europe close to their own borders, leaped at the chance for a presence so near the territorial United States. By the spring of 1962, Cuba hosted a Russian base as well as intelligence-gathering units; by that summer, a task force of 40,000 Soviet soldiers and advisors were in Cuba as Fidel Castro and Soviet Premier Nikita Khrushchev laid plans to construct a nuclear missile base in Cuba.

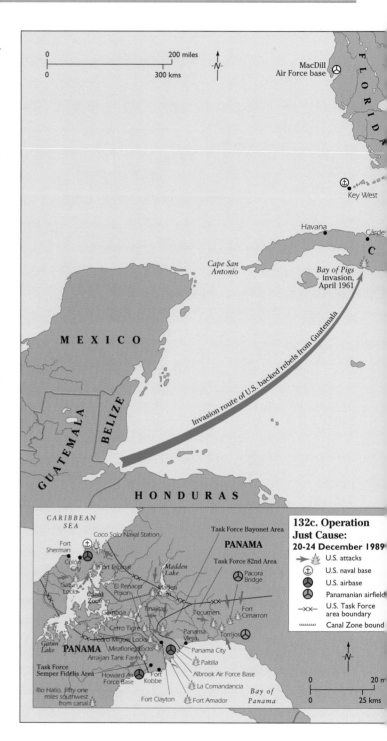

The Cuban Missile Crisis

Castro's and Khrushchev's last move precipitated the most dramatic and dangerous crisis of the Cold War. On 15 October 1962, U.S. Air Force U-2 intelligence aircraft discovered the Soviet missile base under construction in Cuba. Following a week of secret deliberations with his advisors, President Kennedy declared a "naval quarantine" on shipments of

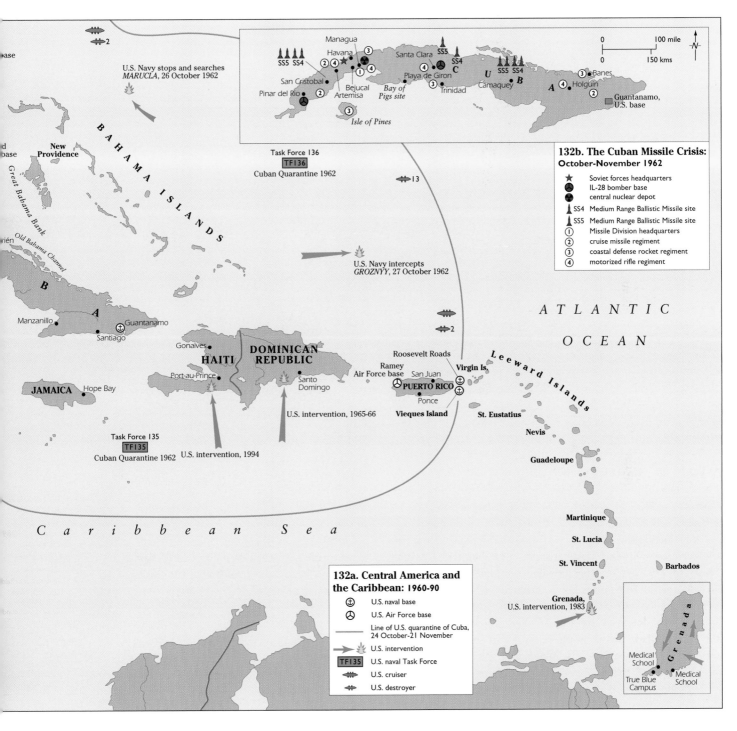

U.S. Navy stops and searches *MARUCLA*, 26 October 1962

Managua
Havana
SS5 SS4
Santa Clara
SS5 SS4
San Cristobal
Bejucal
Artemisa
Pinar del Rio
Playa de Giron
Bay of
Pigs site
Trinidad
Camaquey
Banes
Holguin
Guantanamo,
U.S. base
Isle of Pines

0 ——— 100 mile
0 ——— 150 kms

132b. The Cuban Missile Crisis:
October-November 1962

★ Soviet forces headquarters
● IL-28 bomber base
☣ central nuclear depot
⚰ SS4 Medium Range Ballistic Missile site
⚰ SS5 Medium Range Ballistic Missile site
① Missile Division headquarters
② cruise missile regiment
③ coastal defense rocket regiment
④ motorized rifle regiment

Task Force 136
TF136
Cuban Quarantine 1962

U.S. Navy intercepts
GROZNYY, 27 October 1962

New
Providence

B A H A M A   I S L A N D S

Great Bahama Bank
Old Bahama Channel

A T L A N T I C

O C E A N

Manzanillo
Santiago
Guantanamo

Gonaives
HAITI
Port-au-Prince

DOMINICAN
REPUBLIC
Santo
Domingo

U.S. intervention, 1965-66

Roosevelt Roads
Ramey
Air Force base
San Juan
PUERTO RICO
Ponce
Vieques Island

Virgin Is.
L e e w a r d   I s l a n d s
St. Eustatius
Nevis
Guadeloupe

JAMAICA
Hope Bay

Task Force 135
TF135
Cuban Quarantine 1962

U.S. intervention, 1994

C a r i b b e a n   S e a

Martinique
St. Lucia
St. Vincent
Barbados

Grenada,
U.S. intervention, 1983

132a. Central America and
the Caribbean: 1960-90

⊕ U.S. naval base
⊗ U.S. Air Force base
—— Line of U.S. quarantine of Cuba,
24 October-21 November
→ U.S. intervention
TF135 U.S. naval Task Force
⊷ U.S. cruiser
⊶ U.S. destroyer

Medical
School
True Blue
Campus
Medical
School
Grenada

offensive weapons to Cuba, effective 24 October, and demanded the Soviets abandon the missile base. Kennedy dispatched naval vessels in the sea around Cuba and won an unusual endorsement for his decision to create the blockade from the O.A.S. Khrushchev viewed these U.S. actions as a flagrant interference in Soviet-Cuban relations and a violation of international laws relating to freedom of navigation. As the world

sat on the brink of nuclear exchange, a settlement emerged whereby the Soviets agreed to abort their missile plans in Cuba in exchange for the public promise by the United States not to invade Cuba. The Soviets also received the private promise from the Americans to remove equivalent Jupiter nuclear missiles from Turkey. The acute phase of the crisis ended on 28 October, although Kennedy did not lift the naval

This photo, taken by an American U-2 spy plane, proved that the Soviets, despite their denials, were constructing a missile base at San Cristóbal, Cuba, in 1962. Deployed there, Soviet missiles would be able to strike U.S. cities, so President Kennedy ordered Cuba blockaded until the Soviets dismantled the sites. The Cuban Missile Crisis was a turning point in the Cold War. After the Soviets agreed to U.S. demands, and Premier Khrushchev agreed to remove the missiles from Cuba on 26 October, leaders of both nations sought to reduce tensions.

quarantine until 21 November, when he was finally satisfied the Russians had abandoned their plans.

A Thaw in Tensions

The Cuban Missile Crisis was as close as the two superpowers came to nuclear blows in the Cold War. Scholars continue to debate its causes and the performance of the respective leaders, but one clear consequence of the sobering showdown was a general thaw in east-west tensions. The Limited Test Ban Treaty of 1963 marked the start of a series of arms reduction accords, while the Hot Line Agreement of 1963 improved communication capacity between the U.S. and Soviet leaders. The military defeat in the Vietnam War which ended in 1975 left the United States more sanguine about interventions abroad. At the same time this broader détente, marked by the passage of the Strategic Arms Limitation Treaty (S.A.L.T. I), cooled global Cold War tensions. In Latin America, a general absence of international animosity and a series of treaties in 1978, passing eventual control of the Panama Canal to the Panamanians, marked a period of good feelings.

The Revival of Old Concerns

Détente, however, was short-lived. As early as 1979, left-leaning revolutions in Nicaragua, Grenada, and El Salvador revived old concerns about Communist hegemony in the area. Throughout the 1980s, U.S. President Ronald Reagan, a solid

Cold War warrior, built up U.S. military strength and used both overt and covert action to counter developments in Latin America that he believed to have been guided by operatives from the Soviet Union. In 1983, the United States invaded the small island nation of Grenada in the Caribbean to protect large numbers of U.S. students there and to abort a Soviet-funded and controlled airstrip from operating in the Western Hemisphere. Elsewhere, low level and often covert U.S. involvement in the region, most notably in El Salvador (from 1979 to 1984) and Nicaragua (from 1980 to 1985), where bloody civil wars pitted entrenched powers friendly to the United States against leftist revolutionary movements, met with varying degrees of success. In particular, the Reagan Administration's secret support of anti-Communist forces in Nicaragua involved financial intrigues that fostered an ugly political scandal in 1986 and 1987, marred the Reagan Administration, and hurt the standing of the United States in the world.

The ebb of the Cold War in the late 1980s allowed President Reagan's successor, George Bush, to see political and social developments in Latin America without the thick lens of east-west competition. The interest of the United States in the region predated the Cold War by 150 years, of course, and the Monroe Doctrine continued to shape the actions of the United States in Latin America. But Cold War fears of falling dominos and Communist takeovers have played a decreasing role as other concerns, most notably a vigorous drug trade between

Latin American suppliers and U.S. drug users, continued to fuel political and military activity in the region. These actions included the invasion of Panama by the United States in 1989 to bring General Manuel Noriega to trial and continuing U.S. military activity in Colombia beginning in the early 1990s.

Cold War Influences in Africa

Policy makers in the United States and the Soviet Union viewed events in Africa through the prism of the Cold War. Africa had been colonized by west European nations over four centuries, from the sixteenth century to the late nineteenth century. After World War II, a wave of nationalist sentiment swept across Africa, in part stimulated by the experiences of African troops in the war. Independence movements grew in which Democratic and Communist ideals of government competed to replace old colonial administrations in various African colonies.

In June 1960, in the region known loosely as the Congo (the Republic of Zaire after 1971), for example, indigenous forces won independence from Belgium, but these quickly dissolved into factions, some of them secessionist, fighting for control of the country. From July 1960 to November 1965, constantly changing coalitions maneuvered for power, assisted at times by the United Nations, Belgium, France, and the United States, on the one hand, and the Soviet Union and Communist China on the other. On 25 November 1960, Mobutu Sese Seko, a former army colonel generally aligned with the western nations, declared himself head of state following a coup, and began to consolidate power.

From 1965 until the end of the Cold War, Mobutu proved adept at exploiting global Cold War tensions and competition to curry favor with the United States, while amassing a personal fortune through corruption, near-dictatorial exercise of power, and widespread human rights abuses. Reflecting a disturbing pattern of U.S. foreign policy in developing nations during the Cold War, the United States overlooked these problems, and the C.I.A. continued covert support to Zaire as long as Mobutu stood symbolically against Communism. With the end of the Cold War, east-west tensions that had aided Mobutu's hold on power faded, and an international voice of condemnation forced him to allow democratic elections in Zaire in 1992.

This pattern was repeated in South Africa, where concerns about Communist influence among the black population and the banned Marxist-oriented African National Congress, led the United States to support the all-white ruling class in its efforts to forestall the creation of a multiracial government and society there. The end of the Cold War caused U.S. policy in that country also to change. International pressure, including a U.S.-backed economic embargo, compelled white South Africans by 1994 to include their black countrymen in political life and dismantle white-enforced racial barriers.

Conflict in Asia

Cold War competition also shaped and influenced conflict in east Asia. Indeed, the two major wars of the Cold War era occurred there: Korea and Vietnam. But these struggles were not the region's only flash points during the Cold War. Unlike Europe, the United States and the Soviet Union were unable to agree on the political shape of Asia following World War II, a fact that underscored the Cold War importance of a civil war in China. Internal strife in China between Mao Zedong's Communist forces and the nominally Democratic forces of Chaing Kai-shek's Nationalists predated World War II, and this fight reached a crescendo in the years immediately after Japan's surrender. Despite aid from the United States to the Nationalists, Mao's troops forced Chiang's government from power in 1949 and proclaimed the Communist People's Republic of China. As Chiang set up a government-in-exile on the island of Formosa (Taiwan), Mao's victory in the world's most populous nation heightened U.S. fears of a global movement toward Communism and led to the establishment of the U.S. Seventh Fleet which on several occasions positioned units between Formosa and the Chinese mainland to shield the Nationalists.

First Chinese Encounters

The first of several encounters with the Chinese began in September 1954 when Communist shore batteries shelled

After the United States contacted Chinese diplomats in Paris, indicating its wish to establish regular contact with the People's Republic of China, several months of secret negotiations led President Nixon, shown here toasting Chinese leader Zhou Enlai, to make an historic visit to China in February 1972, marking a dramatic thaw in Cold War relations between the two countries.

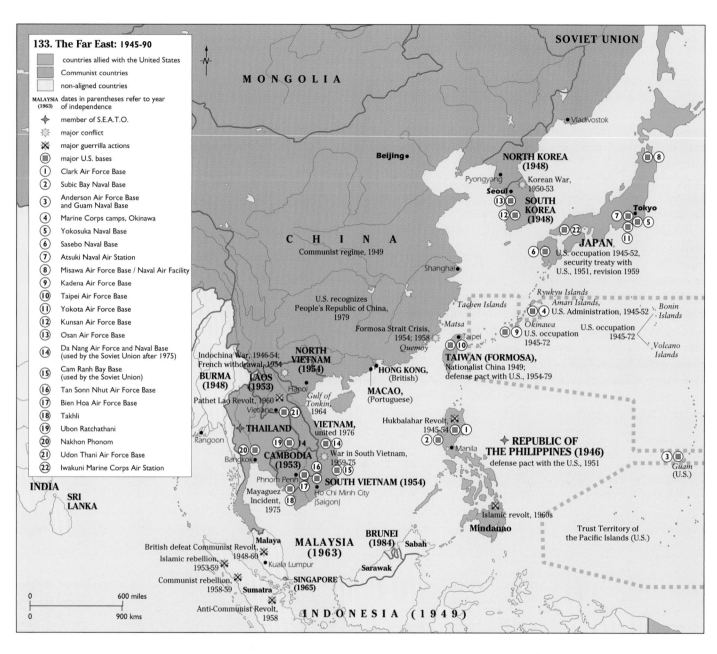

133. The Far East: 1945-90

- countries allied with the United States
- Communist countries
- non-aligned countries

MALAYSIA (1963) dates in parentheses refer to year of independence

- ✦ member of S.E.A.T.O.
- ☼ major conflict
- ✕ major guerrilla actions
- ▣ major U.S. bases

1. Clark Air Force Base
2. Subic Bay Naval Base
3. Anderson Air Force Base and Guam Naval Base
4. Marine Corps camps, Okinawa
5. Yokosuka Naval Base
6. Sasebo Naval Base
7. Atsuki Naval Air Station
8. Misawa Air Force Base / Naval Air Facility
9. Kadena Air Force Base
10. Taipei Air Force Base
11. Yokota Air Force Base
12. Kunsan Air Force Base
13. Osan Air Force Base
14. Da Nang Air Force and Naval Base (used by the Soviet Union after 1975)
15. Cam Ranh Bay Base (used by the Soviet Union)
16. Tan Sonn Nhut Air Force Base
17. Bien Hoa Air Force Base
18. Takhli
19. Ubon Ratchathani
20. Nakhon Phonom
21. Udon Thani Air Force Base
22. Iwakuni Marine Corps Air Station

Quemoy, one of the larger islands in the Straits of Formosa under Nationalist control. Fearing an attack on Formosa itself, the United States strengthened its ties to Chiang Kai-shek's government, concluding a mutual defense pact treaty with Formosa in December 1954. The United States increased fleet patrols in the straits and, in January 1955, the U.S. Congress passed the Formosa Resolution which authorized the president to commit American forces to Formosa's defense.

In April 1955, President Dwight D. Eisenhower threatened to use nuclear weapons in the event of a Communist assault on Quemoy or nearby Matsu. This time the United States sent several aircraft carrier battle groups into the area and war

between Communist China and the United States appeared a real possibility until diplomats in both Washington and Beijing diffused the situation. Since the 1950s, tempers in the region have flared periodically, with aggressive moves on either side of the Straits of Formosa and persistent patrolling by U.S. naval vessels, but tensions never again escalated into a similar crisis.

The Southeast Asia Treaty Organization

In 1954, the United States, Great Britain, Australia, New Zealand, France, Pakistan, Thailand, and the Philippine Islands formed the Southeast Asia Treaty Organization (S.E.A.T.O.) to block the spread of Communist influence in the region. The Philippine Islands became an important outpost for U.S. strategic interest in Asia after the Communist triumph in China. Because of this, the U.S. military maintained an active presence in the Philippines, most notably at Clark Air Force Base and Subic Bay Naval Base, even after Philippine independence from the United States in 1945. From 1946 to 1954, the U.S. military assisted Philippine forces in the suppression of the Communist Huk rebellion, one of the few instances of successful U.S. intervention in an indigenous civil uprising. After that time, the Philippine Islands became a critical cog in the U.S. defense perimeter and a key staging point for American forces during the Vietnam War (1959-75).

A belief that the Soviet Union directed civil unrest in Asia motivated U.S. strategic behavior during the Cold War in places like the Formosan Straits, the Philippines, and to a lesser extent, along the Malay Peninsula. In retrospect, however, the Soviet invasion of Afghanistan in 1979 was perhaps the sole overt, aggressive military action by the Russians in this part of the world; other struggles may have been more the function of nationalist impulses against colonialism and less about global Communism. But the strong lens of the Cold War, on both sides of the struggle, colored these conflicts with broader meaning and higher stakes for both the Soviet Union and the United States.

The Middle East

Something akin to this dynamic worked in the Middle East as well. As in other parts of the world, the involvement of the United States and the Soviet Union in the Middle East predates the Cold War. The United States sent naval warships into the Mediterranean as early as 1801, for example, to protect national interests against the Barbary corsairs and Russia had long meddled in the region to protect her strategic and security interests in the eastern Mediterranean. Sustained involvement in the region dates from the late 1940s, however, when three factors combined to elevate the region's importance to the superpowers: Mounting tensions between Arab nations and the Israelis, growing Cold War rivalry between Washington and Moscow, and an increasing western dependence on Persian Gulf oil.

The controversial partition of Palestine in 1947, and the swift recognition by the United States of the new Jewish nation of Israel in 1948, prompted concerns of Soviet adventurism in the region among U.S. policy makers. Accordingly, the United States established the Sixth Fleet in the Mediterranean Sea, which, henceforth, almost constantly patrolled Middle Eastern waters in an effort to discourage Russian activism in the area. At the same time, the United States worked to reduce the possibility of east-west clashes in the area by limiting its

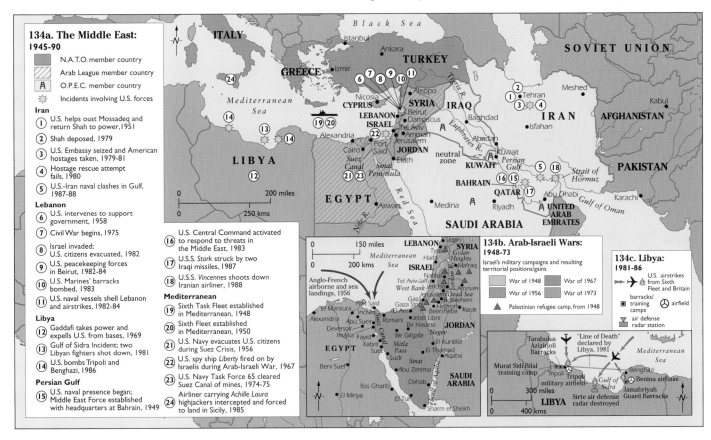

own involvement in the region. In 1950, western nations agreed to the Tripartite Declaration, which placed tight limits on the sale of American, British, and French arms in the Middle East. Six years later, when Israel attacked Egypt with British and French help during a broader dispute over control of the Suez Canal, the United States used diplomatic and economic leverage to force the invaders to withdraw, believing the seizure of the Suez Canal would disrupt the region's precarious balance of power. The pressure from the United States on its European friends during the Suez Canal Crisis in 1956 was a rare departure from western solidarity during the early Cold War period.

Iran

United States policy turned more aggressive after Soviet aid poured into various Arab nations in the late 1950s. Iran, with oil vital to the west and a 1,300-mile border with the Soviet Union that blocked Moscow's search for a warm water port in the area, was a perennial diplomatic battleground. In 1953, the C.I.A. helped overthrow Mohammed Mossadeq, the pro-Soviet Prime Minister of Iran, to strengthen the power of the ruler, Mohommed Reza Shah Pahlevi. By the early 1960s, the United States had extended 200 million dollars in military weaponry to Iran, a move that angered conservative Islamic opponents of the secular Shah. Ten years later, when the Nixon Doctrine shifted the burden of regional defense onto key allies, the Shah of Iran received even more U.S. assistance;

16.2 billion dollars of U.S. aid flowed into Iran from 1972 to 1977. This overt western aid increased nationalist resentment of the Shah and helped trigger the fundamentalist revolution directed by the Ayatollah Khomeini in 1978, that led to, among other things, the seizure of the U.S. Embassy in Iran and fifty-three American hostages in November 1979. In 1980, the Carter Administration authorized a daring scheme to rescue the U.S. hostages held in Iran, a plan that ended in tragedy when helicopters and planes of the rescue mission collided at a secret airstrip outside Tehran, killing eight U.S. Marines. In Iran, strong anti-American attitudes continued through the 1990s, when feelings began to calm with the election of a more moderate Iranian leadership.

Other U.S. Involvement in the Middle East

The activism of U.S. military policy in the region was evident in other nations as well. On 15 July 1958, when a bloody left-wing coup in neighboring Iraq threatened Lebanese President Camille Chamoun, the United States sent 15,000 U.S. Marines to Beirut. These soldiers helped restore order and arrange a truce between warring Christian and Muslim factions. They had not suffered a single casualty by the time they left three months later and their experience of deployment helped establish U.S. precedent in the region as peacekeepers.

In 1963, the Americans stationed a squadron of U.S. jet fighters in Saudi Arabia in response to a left-leaning coup in Yemen. That nation lacked advanced aircraft, but Russia had

The U.S. government plan to rescue American hostages detained in Iran in April 1980 failed. Shortly after helicopters lifted off from the deck of the U.S.S. Nimitz *(below) to rendezvous with six C-130 transports, a dust storm forced two pilots to turn back. Another experienced mechanical problems. The mission was aborted, but not before a helicopter collided with a C-130, killing eight American personnel.*

When peace talks between Israel and Egypt stalled, President Jimmy Carter (center) invited Egyptian President Anwar Sadat (left) and Israeli Prime Minister Menachem Begin (right) to his presidential retreat, Camp David, and there brokered the Camp David Accords in which Israel agreed to withdraw from the Sinai in return for Egyptian recognition of Israel as a nation. In addition, Israel agreed to negotiate "new arrangements" with the Palestinians for the West Bank.

supplied Egypt with modern jets, and the Egyptian and U.S. aircraft engaged in a dangerous game of cat and mouse until early 1964, when President Johnson ordered the U.S. jets to remain well within Saudi airspace.

U.S. Support for Israel

In 1958, the United States, perceiving threats to Israeli security, moved to strengthen the Jewish nation's defense by supplying Israel with recoilless rifles. The United States sent antiaircraft missiles in 1962, battle tanks in 1965, and jet fighters in 1966. Enraged at aggressive Egyptian moves limiting Israeli navigation through the Strait of Tiran and enabled by U.S. aid, on 5 June 1967, Israel's defense forces attacked Egypt and Jordan, which had allied with Cairo. Five days later, the Israelis invaded Syria, and in quick succession, Israel occupied the Sinai Peninsula, the West Bank, and the Golan Heights. When the Soviet Union threatened to intervene in the Six-Day War to prevent the defeat of its Arab client states, the United States sent the Sixth Fleet into the region as a show of support for Israel and to discourage Moscow.

In mirror image, this war was repeated in October 1973 when Egypt and Syria attacked Israel in an attempt to regain the lost territory in the Sinai Peninsula and along the Golan Heights. The attack caught the Israelis by surprise and the tide did not turn in its favor until the United States agreed to airlift critical war materials to Israel in Operation Nickel Grass in late October. Moscow once again threatened to intervene militarily. In response,

the United States placed its strategic forces on a heightened state of readiness and dispatched Secretary of State Henry Kissinger to the Middle East to broker a peace agreement. Kissinger's efforts yielded a truce in 1975, and subsequent efforts in the region led to the Camp David Accords in 1978 which gave some semblance of a stable peace in the area for a time.

The general thaw in Cold War tensions in the late 1970s and early 1980s meant less active conflict in the Middle East. But as the 1980s lengthened, so too did the odds of a stable period of tranquillity. After Israel's invasion of Lebanon in June 1982, President Ronald Reagan agreed to station U.S. Marines in Beirut once again. This decision met with disaster when, in October 1983, Iranian-backed terrorists detonated a bomb near the U.S. Marine barracks in Beirut and killed 241 soldiers. This tragedy weakened the U.S. appetite for direct involvement in the region, but it did not stop U.S. Air Force strikes against Muamar Gaddafi's left-leaning Libya in April 1986 after evidence linked Libyan terrorists to a bombing near a U.S. military base in Germany.

The Persian Gulf War

The Middle East witnessed a spectacular episode of violence as the Cold War ebbed in the late 1980s and early 1990s. In August 1990, the Iraqi leader, Saddam Hussein, invaded Kuwait over long-standing border and financial disputes. This lead to a broad coalition of nations, including many western states, as well as Arab stalwarts, such as Saudi Arabia and Egypt, acting to reverse the Iraqi invasion. But with the end of the Cold War, this Persian Gulf War did not have the same east-west overtones of earlier fights in the region. In fact, the Soviet Union, which had begun dissolving into numerous states beginning in the late 1980s, exerted diplomatic pressure in concert with the United States-led coalition seeking to oust Iraq from Kuwait. More than Cold War ideology, the Middle East's immense oil reserves and traditional balance of power equations relating to Israel and Arab nations were the factors which dominated the geopolitical landscape of the Persian Gulf War in 1991.

End of the Cold War

In the Middle East and elsewhere, the breakup of the Soviet Union in the late 1980s and early 1990s effectively ended the Cold War struggle. The crumbling of the Berlin Wall in 1989, after the fall of the Communist regimes of eastern Europe the same year, and German reunification in 1990 further marked the end of the Cold War. Armed violence, diplomatic tension, and international competition did not cease with the end of east-west rivalry, of course, but power equations, henceforth, were no longer influenced by traditional Cold War policy calculations in the rest of the world.

The Post-Cold War Era: 1990–

When the downfall of Communism in the Soviet Union brought the Cold War to an end, many Americans anticipated a "peace dividend" in the form of decreased defense spending and thus lower taxes. President George H. Bush encouraged such expectations when he announced that the agreement he signed with Russian leader Mikhail Gorbachev marked the start of a "new world order," an era of greater stability and peace than at any time during the previous century.

In fact, the United States had little time to celebrate the end of the Cold War. Within months it found its armed forces engaged in other conflicts that differed from those of the Cold War, but that were equally troubling. Ironically, the absence of a struggle between the two post-World War II superpowers, the United States and the Soviet Union, seemed to encourage other countries to settle old antagonisms with violence. Over the next decade, the United States deployed its armed forces to carry out conventional war, humanitarian missions, nation building, and peacekeeping. Although not as threatening as global or nuclear warfare, these contingencies presented a wide variety of challenges and outcomes.

The Invasion of Kuwait

At 1:00 A.M., 2 August 1990, Iraq, led by dictator Saddam Hussein, astonished the world by invading and occupying Kuwait. A day later U.S. President Bush launched a diplomatic offensive aimed at isolating Iraq and ordered the U.S.S. *Eisenhower* Carrier Battle Group to sail from the Mediterranean into the Red Sea and the U.S.S. *Independence* Carrier Battle Group to proceed from the Indian Ocean into the Persian Gulf. Within the U.S. military command system, the Iraq invasion fell under the geographical auspices of U.S. Central Command (CENTCOM), commanded by General Norman H. Schwarzkopf. On 6 August, General Schwarzkopf and U.S. Secretary of Defense Dick Cheney met with Saudi Arabia's King Fahd, who requested that U.S. ground forces be sent to his country. Two days later, President Bush ordered the largest deployment of American forces since the Vietnam War.

Formation of a United Nations Coalition

Undeterred, Saddam Hussein declared Kuwait to be Iraq's nineteenth province on 8 August 1990. Although Saddam Hussein had little difficulty taking Kuwait, he set the stage for one of the most dramatic victories in the history of warfare. That same day, on 8 August, forward elements of the U.S. 82nd and 101st Airborne Divisions arrived in Saudi Arabia, along with twenty-three combat-ready F-15C Eagles from the 1st U.S. Tactical Fighter Wing, Langley Air Force Base, in the United States. The U.S. military in the region were joined by air and ground units from Kuwait, Saudi Arabia, Bahrain, Qatar, the United Arab Emirates, Oman, and major contingents from the United Kingdom, France, Egypt, and Syria that formed the United Nations' Coalition opposed to Iraq's actions. On August 8, President Bush ordered the U.S.S. *Enterprise* Carrier Battle Group to sail from the U.S. military base on the island of Diego Garcia in the Indian Ocean to the Gulf of Hormuz on the eastern end of the Persian Gulf.

To put economic pressure on Saddam Hussein, Turkey and

Lieutenant General Charles A. Horner (above) commanded both U.S. Air Force and Navy forces in the air campaign against Iraq. The photograph, at right, of an air force KC-135E and a navy A-6E refueling navy EA-6Bs en route to Iraq, symbolizes the joint operations conducted during the Gulf War.

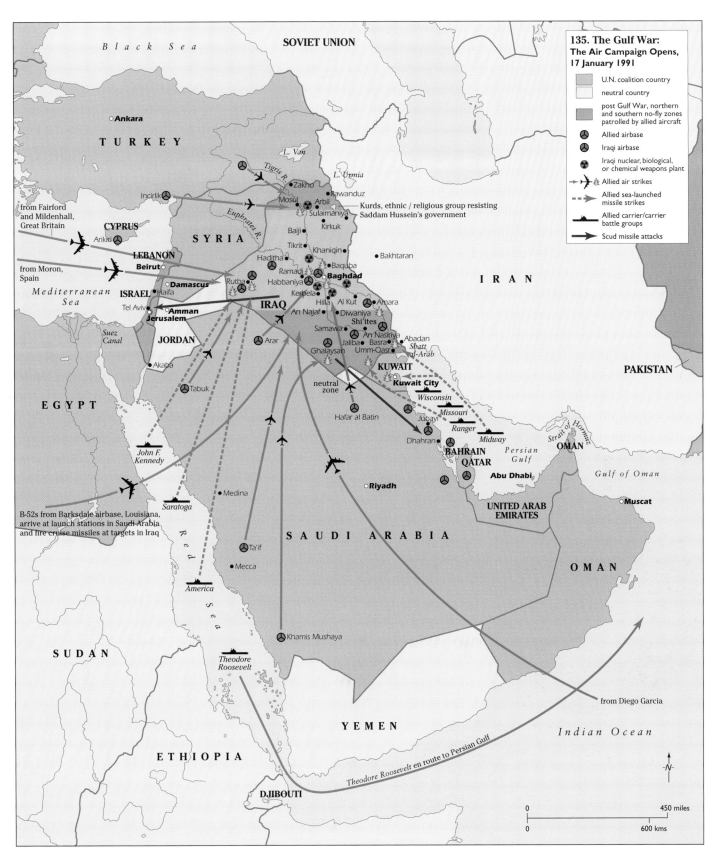

135. The Gulf War:
The Air Campaign Opens,
17 January 1991

- U.N. coalition country
- neutral country
- post Gulf War, northern and southern no-fly zones patrolled by allied aircraft
- Allied airbase
- Iraqi airbase
- Iraqi nuclear, biological, or chemical weapons plant
- Allied air strikes
- Allied sea-launched missile strikes
- Allied carrier/carrier battle groups
- Scud missile attacks

Black Sea

SOVIET UNION

Ankara

TURKEY

L. Van

L. Urmia

Tigris R.

Incirlik

Zakho
Rawanduz
Mosul
Arbil
Sulaimaniya — Kurds, ethnic / religious group resisting Saddam Hussein's government

from Fairford and Mildenhall, Great Britain

CYPRUS

Arikiri

Euphrates R.

SYRIA

Baiji
Kirkuk

from Moron, Spain

LEBANON
Beirut

Tikrit
Khaniqin
Haditha
• Bakhtaran

Damascus

Ramadi
Baquba

Habbaniya
Baghdad

Mediterranean Sea

ISRAEL • Haifa
Rutba

Tel Aviv
Kerbela
I R A N

Amman
Jerusalem

IRAQ
Hilla
Al Kut
Amara

An Najaf
Diwaniya

Suez Canal

JORDAN

Arar

Samawa
Shi'ites

An Nasiriya
Abadan

• Akaba

Jaliba
Basra

Ghalaysan
Umm-Qasr
Shatt al-Arab

PAKISTAN

neutral zone

KUWAIT

E G Y P T

Tabuk

Kuwait City
Wisconsin

Hafar al Batin

Missouri

Jubayl
Ranger

John F. Kennedy

Dhahran
Midway

BAHRAIN
Persian Gulf

OMAN

QATAR

Strait of Hormuz

• Medina

Abu Dhabi

Saratoga

Riyadh

Gulf of Oman

B-52s from Barksdale airbase, Louisiana, arrive at launch stations in Saudi Arabia and fire cruise missiles at targets in Iraq

UNITED ARAB EMIRATES

Muscat

Red Sea

S A U D I   A R A B I A

O M A N

America

Ta'if
• Mecca

Theodore Roosevelt

S U D A N

Khamis Mushaya

from Diego Garcia

Y E M E N

Indian Ocean

E T H I O P I A

Theodore Roosevelt en route to Persian Gulf

N

DJIBOUTI

| 0 | | 450 miles |
| 0 | | 600 kms |

A U.S. Navy F-14 Tomcat fighter flies over the remains of an Iraqi radar installation. The forty-two days of bombing by the U.S.-led coalition shattered the infrastructure of Iraq, damaging, among other things, its power generation plants, telecommunication and sanitation systems, and crippling the oil and gas facilities of the country.

Saudi Arabia shut off the pipelines which Iraq used to export oil and the U.S. Navy clamped a quarantine on Iraqi-controlled ports. On 14 September, multinational enforcement of the blockade began when men from U.S. and Australian frigates boarded an Iraqi tanker. Hussein's refusal to leave Kuwait led President Bush to call 46,700 military reservists into active duty on 22 August, with the number later increased to 125,000. CENTCOM's principal force was the XVIII Airborne Corps comprised of the 82nd Airborne Division, the 101st Airborne Division, and the 24th Mechanized Infantry Division. As the Iraqi order of battle increased, on 8 November, President Bush announced the deployment of the U.S. Army's VII Corps, based in Germany, to Saudi Arabia. The VII Corps' 1st Infantry Division (Armor), 1st Armor Division, and 1st Cavalry Division (Mechanized) would provide the heavy armor force to counter Hussein's Republican Guard Corps. On 29 November 1990, the U.N. Security Council authorized the use of "all necessary means" if Iraq did not leave Kuwait by 15 January 1991. By the start of the air war, the U.N. Coalition had gathered over 600,000 soldiers, airmen, sailors, and marines, including 430,000 Americans, to push Iraq out of Kuwait.

The Air Campaign

The Persian Gulf War, also known as Operation Desert Storm, was a turning point in the history of warfare. The U.N. Coalition that attacked Iraqi forces displayed a breathtaking feat of military arms that culminated in a one hundred-hour ground war that routed the reputed fourth largest army in the world. The Allies conducted twenty-four-hour, all-weather

operations, and used combined arms, rapid maneuver, and technological innovations that isolated and destroyed an army tested and hardened by the Iraq-Iran War (1980-88).

On 8 January 1991, President Bush sought authorization from the U.S. Congress to employ force to eject Iraqi forces from Kuwait. Approval was given on 12 January 1991, and Desert Storm began five days later, on 17 January 1991, when the U.N. Coalition launched a massive air campaign against Iraq. At 2:34 A.M. local time, Task Force Normandy—U.S. Army A-64 Apache attack helicopters led by two MH-53J U.S.A.F. Pave Lows, specially equipped, pathfinding helicopters—fired Hellfire missiles at an Iraqi radar site to clear a path in the early warning network and allow a U.S. Air Force strike force into Iraq. The U.S. Air Force and Navy launched cruise missiles while U.S. Air Force F-117A Nighthawks attacked communication and leadership targets in Baghdad. The synchronized strikes and targeting reflected a revolution in the application of air power gleaned from the lessons learned in Vietnam and the application of the technology revolution to military systems since 1975.

The Strength of the Coalition's Campaign

U.N. Coalition air forces confronted a formidable enemy, although Iraq's 300 combat aircraft never posed a sustained threat to Allied forces. On the first night of the air campaign, the U.N. Coalition possessed 1,736 aircraft from twelve different countries which flew missions from bases located in neighboring countries and from six aircraft carrier battle groups. The biggest danger for attacking Allied aircraft lay in Iraq's interwoven, antiaircraft weapons and modern air-warning system. Designed by France, KARI (Iraq spelled backwards in French) consisted of a central Air Defense Operations Center (ADOC) in Baghdad and a network of Sector Operations Centers (SOC) and Intercept Operation Centers (IOC), dispersed in concentric circles around Baghdad and other vital cities. The ADOC coordinated information to over 8,000 antiaircraft pieces, 300 interceptor aircraft, SA-2s, SA-3s, SA-8s, and ROLAND I/II surface-to-air missile batteries. To attack targets in Iraq, the Allies first had to disable or destroy KARI.

In the first two days of the air campaign, U.N. Coalition aircraft virtually shut down Iraq's electrical power system and disabled the Iraqi air defense network. Allied aircrews attacked targets in Baghdad, airfields throughout Iraq, and nuclear, chemical, and biological facilities with resounding success. Aircrews dropped precision-guided munitions in the heart of Iraq's capital with minimal collateral damage. Next, the air attacks turned their attention to Iraqi ground forces with the goal of reducing their combat effectiveness by 50 percent. During Desert Storm, the U.N. Coalition air forces flew a total of 112,000 combat and support sorties, including vital airlift, tanker, surveillance, and reconnaissance flights. 23,430 of the missions, the largest category, were directed against Iraqi ground forces. The next highest categories of targets attacked were Scud mobile ground missile launchers and airfields at 1,460 and 2,996 respectively. Although relatively insignificant as a military weapon, a Scud nonetheless killed twenty-eight Americans in an attack on Dhahran. The ballistic missiles caused much more destruction when Hussein launched them against Israel, but they did not bring Israel into the war.

Allied aircrews severely damaged Iraq's command and control system, supply depots, roads, and bridges. Attacks degraded Hussein's communication system so badly that many front line units lost contact with their headquarters. By G-Day, day one of the ground conflict, CENTCOM estimated that Allied air power had reduced Iraqi front-line divisions to 50 percent of their combat effectiveness and the Republican Guards divisions by 25 percent. The opening of the ground war found a severely demoralized Iraqi army suffering from lack of food, water, and leadership. Thousands of Iraqi front-line soldiers surrendered to U.N. Coalition forces and those that fought were overwhelmed by Allied armor, artillery, and air power.

The Ground Campaign

By the beginning of the ground war, Iraq had approximately 43 divisions composed of 545,000 troops in the Kuwait theater. Its well-equipped forces had an estimated 4,280 tanks, 3,100 artillery pieces, and 2,800 armored personnel carriers. The U.N. Coalition had approximately 540,000 troops in seven U.S. Army divisions, two U.S. Marine Corps divisions, a British armored division, one French light armored division, and the equivalent of more than four Arab/Islamic divisions. Schwarzkopf's original plan called for XVIII Corps to attack directly north from Saudi Arabia toward Kuwait City. However, the addition of VII Corps gave Schwarzkopf the option of avoiding a costly frontal attack for a huge flanking movement.

The week prior to the beginning of the ground war, U.N. Coalition forces probed Iraqi defenses while the air campaign

This Soviet-made Iraqi tank (left) was destroyed by Allied forces near Kuwait City. U.S. Marines, commanded by Lieutenant General Walter E. Boomer (above), spearheaded the attack on the capital, but halted on its outskirts, so Arab forces could be the first to enter the city.

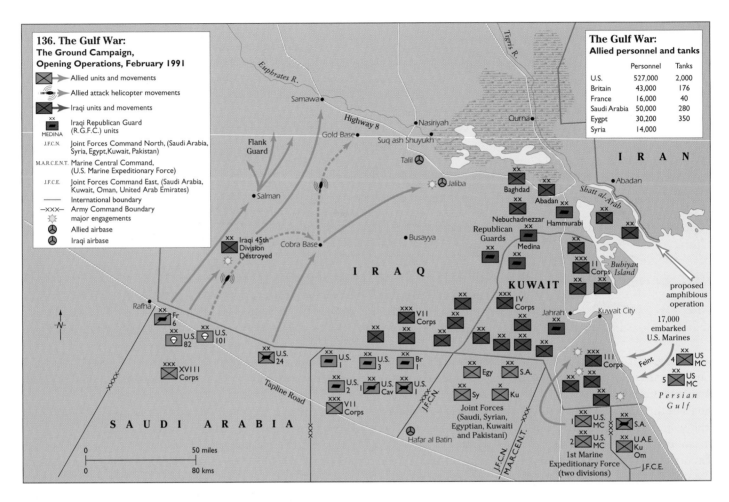

136. The Gulf War:
The Ground Campaign,
Opening Operations, February 1991

- Allied units and movements
- Allied attack helicopter movements
- Iraqi units and movements
- Iraqi Republican Guard (R.G.F.C.) units
- J.F.C.N.   Joint Forces Command North, (Saudi Arabia, Syria, Egypt, Kuwait, Pakistan)
- M.A.R.C.E.N.T.   Marine Central Command, (U.S. Marine Expeditionary Force)
- J.F.C.E.   Joint Forces Command East, (Saudi Arabia, Kuwait, Oman, United Arab Emirates)
- International boundary
- Army Command Boundary
- major engagements
- Allied airbase
- Iraqi airbase

The Gulf War: Allied personnel and tanks		
	Personnel	Tanks
U.S.	527,000	2,000
Britain	43,000	176
France	16,000	40
Saudi Arabia	50,000	280
Eygpt	30,200	350
Syria	14,000	

increasingly focused on the Iraqi army. At 4:00 A.M. on 24 February (G-day), the ground war commenced, after Saddam Hussein ignored an ultimatum to remove his forces from Kuwait. Coalition forces advanced along a front stretching from the Persian Gulf westward to Rafha, while U.S. Marine amphibious forces cruised off the Kuwaiti coast tying up four Iraqi divisions, as advance elements of the U.S. 101st Airborne Division flew into Iraq and established an airhead.

In one of the two main thrusts, U.S. Marine and Arab Coalition forces attacked directly toward Kuwait City, with the 1st U.S. Marine division advancing along the Kuwaiti coastal road, while Joint Forces Command North, comprised of Kuwaiti, Saudi, Egyptian, and Syrian forces, pushed into Kuwait to their left. Meanwhile, in the second main thrust, XVIII Corps, 250 miles to the west, attacked north–northeast toward the Euphrates River, and then cut off Highway 8. This action screened VII Corps' left flank, severed Iraqi lines of communications, and cut off the Iraqi army's escape route. VII Corps held their position for approximately twelve hours while XVIII Corps, the U.S. Marines, and Arab Coalition forces breached defense lines and gave the Iraqis a false view of

Allied intentions. Once XVIII and VII Corps broke out of the Iraqi defense lines, each turned east to cut off the Republican Guards and remnants of the Iraqi front-line divisions. The entire operation, resembling a giant wheeling motion, was initially called the "Hail Mary" attack and later, more appropriately, the "Left Hook."

By 25 February, elements of the 101st U.S. Airborne established a blocking position about twenty-seven miles south of the Euphrates River and attacked traffic trying to reinforce or flee the Kuwaiti area. The airborne armada moved 155 miles in thirty-one hours to cut off the Iraqi main supply line. The 24th U.S. Infantry joined the 101st Airborne in its attack on Highway 8 after recording the fastest armor attack in history. By 26 February, the 1st U.S. Marine Expeditionary Force and Joint Forces advanced to the outskirts of Kuwait City and waited for Kuwaiti forces to enter the city.

The Liberation of Kuwait

Early on 27 February, VII Corps turned right to advance on the Tawakalna, the Al-Madinah, and the Hammurabi divisions of the Republican Guards. The movement initiated the largest

137. The Gulf War: The Ground Campaign, The "Left Hook," February 1991

After the provisional ceasefire of 28 February 1991, U.S. General Norman Schwarzkopf (left) and Saudi General Khalid Bin Sultan al-Saud (second from left) met with Iraqi generals in a tent near Safwan to explain the terms for a permanent end to hostilities.

series of tank battles since World War II. In the initial VII Corps contact with the Republican Guards, the 2nd U.S. Armored Cavalry Regiment destroyed the Tawakalna Division's 18th Mechanized Brigade in the Battle of 73 Eastings (the map grid-line location), and set up a defensive position. In an eighty-mile line from north to south, the U.S. 1st Cavalry, 1st Armor, 3rd Armor, 1st Infantry, 2nd Armored Cavalry Regiment, and the 1st British Armoured divisions bore down on the Iraqis. In a dazzling display of combined arms, U.N. Coalition armor, aviation, and artillery crushed the Republican Guards. On the same day, Kuwaiti forces liberated their capital.

President Bush ordered a cease-fire at 8:00 A.M. on 28 February. In one hundred hours, U.N. Coalition forces devastated the Iraqi armed forces. By the end of the operation, CENTCOM estimated that only five to seven of Iraq's forty-three combat divisions remained effective. U.N. Coalition forces captured approximately 86,000 enemy prisoners-of-war. The Allied effort destroyed or captured 3,847 tanks, 1,450 armored personnel carriers, and 2,917 artillery pieces. The U.N. Coalition had executed a relentless air campaign and a powerful ground assault to carry out one of the fastest and most dramatic wars in history.

Somalia

By early 1992, civil war, famine, and the collapse of the government in the East African country of Somalia had killed more than one-half million people. These conditions also left an estimated one million Somali children malnourished and another 4.5 million people urgently requiring food aid.

Heavily armed clans ruled as de facto government officials and demanded payment from humanitarian organizations before they were permitted to distribute food and aid supplies in Somalia. In April 1992, the United Nations created the first U.N. Operations in Somalia (UNOSOM I) to provide humanitarian aid and end the fighting. President Bush ordered U.S. forces to assist the effort. Phase I of Operation Provide Relief, in which U.S. forces airlifted approximately 28,000 metric tons of relief supplies from air bases in Kenya to Somalia, was

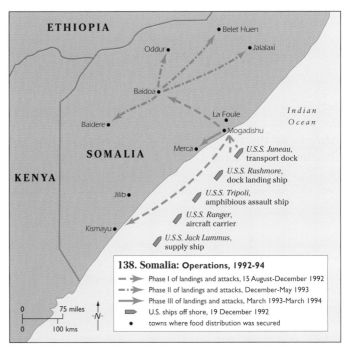

138. Somalia: Operations, 1992-94

staged from 15 August to 9 December 1992. Despite the airlift, the fighting and food shortages continued.

Phase II of Operation Restore Hope, 9 December 1992 to 4 May 1993, was a U.N.-sponsored, limited military, nation-building effort under U.S. leadership, designed to enforce peace and continue the humanitarian mission in Somalia. This humanitarian operation began with the landing of a U.S. Marine Corps expeditionary force in the Somali capital of Mogadishu and the eventual deployment of 30,000 U.S. military personnel and 10,000 troops from U.N. Coalition nations. In March 1993, the U.N. took over Phase III of Operation Restore Hope under the auspices of UNOSOM II while the U.S. continued to provide logistical support.

U.N. policing efforts angered the chief warlord in Mogadishu, Mohammed Farah Aidid. Aidid ambushed Pakistani-U.N. soldiers on their way to seize Aidid's radio station killing twenty-four Pakistanis. After the killings, the U.N. set out to debilitate Aidid's organization. On 3 October 1993, acting on a tip from a spy, Task Force Ranger, an American Quick Reaction Force, raided a clan leader's meeting and captured several of Aidid's lieutenants. The raid sparked a brutal street battle that cost eighteen American lives and downed two Black Hawk helicopters. Americans were shocked to see on their television screens a U.S. soldier's corpse dragged through the city. U.S. involvement in the operations ended on 4 March 1994 when American troops were withdrawn.

Haiti

In February 1990, Haitian President-elect Jean-Bertrand Aristide took office, only to be overthrown in September by elements in the island's army led by Lieutenant General Raoul Cedras. In response, the United Nations imposed an economic and arms embargo and brought the Haitian military leader to the negotiating table. In the United Nations-brokered Governor's Island Agreement in July 1993, the *junta* agreed to place Aristide back in office, but then refused to carry out the accord. When conditions within Haiti deteriorated because of the embargo, impoverished Haitians fled the country, many for the United States. In response to this exodus, the United States led a multinational force to carry out the United Nations' mandate and restore the country's legitimate government.

On 19 September 1994, the United States initiated Operation Uphold Democracy, deploying 3,900 82nd Airborne paratroopers, a naval task force, including the aircraft carriers U.S.S. *America* and U.S.S. *Eisenhower*, and U.S. Army, Navy, and Air Force special operations units for a forced entry into the country. However, as forces moved into position for the invasion, a delegation led by former President Jimmy Carter negotiated an agreement for a nonviolent transition of power

When U.S. troops entered Haiti in September 1994 to force Raoul Cedras to return control of Haiti to President Jean-Bertrand Aristide, they learned that former President Jimmy Carter had already negotiated a peaceful shift in power. Troops of the 10th U.S. Mountain Division are pictured with a Haitian-American translator.

and peaceful entry of approximately 20,000 American and 2,000 U.N. troops for peace-keeping and humanitarian operations. On 31 March 1995, the U.S. transferred operational responsibility to the United Nations.

Bosnia

Until 1991, Yugoslavia was comprised of six independent republics: Slovenia, Croatia, Bosnia-Herzegovina, Serbia, Montenegro, and Macedonia. With the end of the Cold War in 1990, nationalism and ethnic distrust erupted in the Balkans.

139. The Former Yugoslavia:
The Bosnian Crisis, 1991-
— international boundary
boundaries of the six Yugoslav republics
○ U.N. "safe areas"
Operation Deliberate Force: N.A.T.O. air strikes, 30 August-21 September 1995
Dayton Peace Accords for Bosnia: November/December 1995
area of Bosnian Serb Republic
area of Bosnian Muslim/Croat Federation
0   75 miles
0   100 kms

It had been suppressed by the former Communist leader, President Josip Broz Tito, who had led Yugoslavia from the end of World War II until his death in 1980. During the next decade the region fought three separate bloody civil wars, as republics fought to establish their independence or to expand their borders at the expense of their neighbors. The fighting caused many deaths and brought about ethnic cleansing, forced dislocation which often led to rape, torture, imprisonment, and mass extermination of whole populations. In 1993, the U.N. sought to stem the fighting by declaring six safe enclaves and a no-fly zone over Bosnia-Herzegovina.

On 28 August 1995, a Serbian mortar exploded in the Bosnian capital of Sarajevo, a designated U.N. safe area, killing thirty-eight people and wounding more than eighty-five. The attack came after a warning from the United States for the Bosnian Serbs to stop attacking the city. Two days later, the North Atlantic Treaty Organization (N.A.T.O.) unleashed Operation Deliberate Force, when sixty N.A.T.O. aircraft, flying from bases in Italy and the U.S. aircraft carriers positioned in the Adriatic Sea, struck Bosnian Serb army targets around the besieged city. Deliberate Force ended on 21 September when the Serbs finally agreed to meet in Dayton, Ohio, to negotiate regional peace accords.

The United States flew 65.9 percent of the total 3,515 sorties in Operation Deliberate Force. N.A.T.O. allies flew the remaining missions. The Allied aircraft struck 60 percent of their targets with precision-guided bombs. Most importantly, the aerial attacks brought the belligerents to the bargaining table, resulting in completion of the Dayton Peace Accords in November. In December 1995, the United States and Allied nations deployed peacekeeping forces on the ground in Bosnia to support Operation Joint Endeavor. Task Force Eagle, comprised of 20,000 American soldiers, implemented the military elements of the Dayton Peace Accords in support of Operation Joint Endeavor. This operation marked the first commitment of forces in N.A.T.O.'s history and, for the first time since World War II, American and Russian soldiers shared a common mission.

Operation Allied Force

From 24 March to 10 June 1999, N.A.T.O. air forces attacked targets in Serbia in an effort to halt the ethnic cleansing carried out by Serbian President Slobodan Milosevic against the Albanian ethnic majority in Kosovo. In 1987, from Kosovo, Milosevic had launched his Serbian nationalistic attack on ethnic groups in Serbia. In early 1998, violence escalated between Serbs and the Albanian ethnic majority in Kosovo, resulting in the displacement of 300,000 people. Milosevic agreed to a cease-fire in October, but on 15 January 1999, he gave the orders for the massacre of forty-five ethnic Albanians by Serb

140. Kosovo: Operation Allied Force, 24 March–10 June 1999 and subsequent occupation

✳ principal N.A.T.O. bombing targets	▮ ① Germany (Sector South)
—— international boundary	▮ ② France (Sector North)
—— Yugoslav republic boundary	▮ ③ Italy (Sector West)
- - - provincial boundary	▦ ④ United States (Sector South East)
—— U.N./N.A.T.O. Kosovo Peacekeeping Force Sectors, August 1999	⊕ ⑤ Great Britain (Sector East)

forces at Racak. When the Serbian president ignored one last U.S. appeal for the cessation of violence against the Kosovars, N.A.T.O. launched Operation Allied Force on 24 March 1999.

The effort against Serbia was one of the most successful air campaigns in history. U.S. and N.A.T.O. air forces flew 38,000 sorties with only two aircraft lost and both crewmembers recovered. Since Operation Desert Storm, the United States had emphasized developing and procuring a new generation of standoff, precision-guided munitions like the Joint Direct Attack Munition (JDAM), and the Joint Stand Off Weapon. The B-2 Spirit stealth bomber made its combat debut by dropping the Global Positioning System-assisted, JDAM weapon on the first night of the operation. Thirty-eight percent of the munitions the Allied air forces used against Serbian targets during this operation were precision-guided.

After seventy-eight days of aerial attack against army, command and control, industry, and transportation targets, Serbia

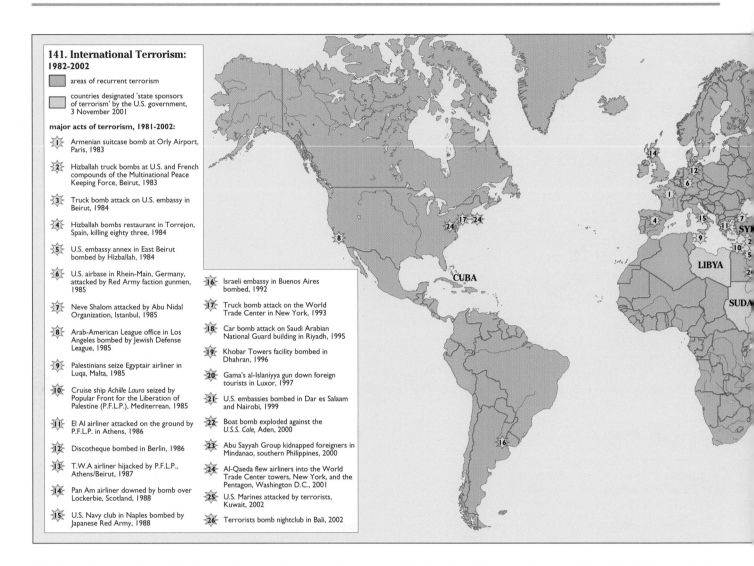

141. International Terrorism: 1982-2002

▨ areas of recurrent terrorism

▢ countries designated 'state sponsors of terrorism' by the U.S. government, 3 November 2001

major acts of terrorism, 1981-2002:

1. Armenian suitcase bomb at Orly Airport, Paris, 1983

2. Hizballah truck bombs at U.S. and French compounds of the Multinational Peace Keeping Force, Beirut, 1983

3. Truck bomb attack on U.S. embassy in Beirut, 1984

4. Hizballah bombs restaurant in Torrejon, Spain, killing eighty three, 1984

5. U.S. embassy annex in East Beirut bombed by Hizballah, 1984

6. U.S. airbase in Rhein-Main, Germany, attacked by Red Army faction gunmen, 1985

7. Neve Shalom attacked by Abu Nidal Organization, Istanbul, 1985

8. Arab-American League office in Los Angeles bombed by Jewish Defense League, 1985

9. Palestinians seize Egyptair airliner in Luqa, Malta, 1985

10. Cruise ship *Achille Lauro* seized by Popular Front for the Liberation of Palestine (P.F.L.P.), Mediterrean, 1985

11. El Al airliner attacked on the ground by P.F.L.P. in Athens, 1986

12. Discotheque bombed in Berlin, 1986

13. T.W.A airliner hijacked by P.F.L.P., Athens/Beirut, 1987

14. Pan Am airliner downed by bomb over Lockerbie, Scotland, 1988

15. U.S. Navy club in Naples bombed by Japanese Red Army, 1988

16. Israeli embassy in Buenos Aires bombed, 1992

17. Truck bomb attack on the World Trade Center in New York, 1993

18. Car bomb attack on Saudi Arabian National Guard building in Riyadh, 1995

19. Khobar Towers facility bombed in Dhahran, 1996

20. Gama's al-Islaniyya gun down foreign tourists in Luxor, 1997

21. U.S. embassies bombed in Dar es Salaam and Nairobi, 1999

22. Boat bomb exploded against the *U.S.S. Cole*, Aden, 2000

23. Abu Sayyah Group kidnapped foreigners in Mindanao, southern Philippines, 2000

24. Al-Qaeda flew airliners into the World Trade Center towers, New York, and the Pentagon, Washington D.C., 2001

25. U.S. Marines attacked by terrorists, Kuwait, 2002

26. Terrorists bomb nightclub in Bali, 2002

halted attacks on ethnic Albanians and removed its army from Kosovo. A weakened Milosevic held on to power, but under increasing domestic pressure, agreed to an election in September 2000 that ultimately led to his downfall and arrest for war crimes committed in Kosovo.

The Twenty-First Century

The last decade of the twentieth century witnessed operations by U.S. air, sea, and land forces on three continents. It opened in 1990 with Saddam Hussein's brutal aggression against Kuwait that paved the way for Operation Desert Storm, the largest U.S. wartime engagement since the Vietnam War. After a punishing forty-three day, U.N. Coalition air campaign, Allied ground forces enveloped and destroyed a heavily armoured Iraqi army in one hundred hours. After the Gulf War, while Hussein continued to menace the Persian Gulf region, controversy raged over whether the Allies should have attacked Baghdad with ground forces. Similarly, subsequent political and military actions in Somalia, Haiti, and the Balkans defied clear cut victories or political settlements. As the United States entered the twenty-first century, units of its armed forces continued their half-century long deployment on the Korean Peninsula, and naval forces remained in the Persian Gulf, while allied air units enforced no-fly zones over Iraq. United States-backed N.A.T.O. operations continued over the simmering Balkans. Conventional and terrorist threats in the Middle East, Europe, Pacific Rim, Africa, and Latin America intensified, exemplified by incidents such as the attack on the U.S.S. *Cole* in Yemen and the midair collision of a U.S. surveillance plane and a Chinese fighter, followed by the emergency landing of the U.S. plane on Hainan Island off the coast of China.

Terrorism took on a more international dimension in this period, but Americans still felt safe from its threat, assuming a sense of invulnerability from direct assault. The 11 September 2001 terrorist attacks on the World Trade Center and the

Pentagon shattered that myth. Stunned Americans watched helplessly as small groups of suicide bombers hijacked airliners and used them with deadly effect to not only kill thousands, but literally shake the country's economic and military foundations. Allies quickly rallied to America's side, and on 7 October 2001, they joined U.S. air, sea, and land forces in attacking terrorist targets in Afghanistan. Operations in this rugged, mountainous country with little modern infrastructure, industry, or political stability, demonstrated that the new century might prove even more diplomatically and militarily challenging than the last.

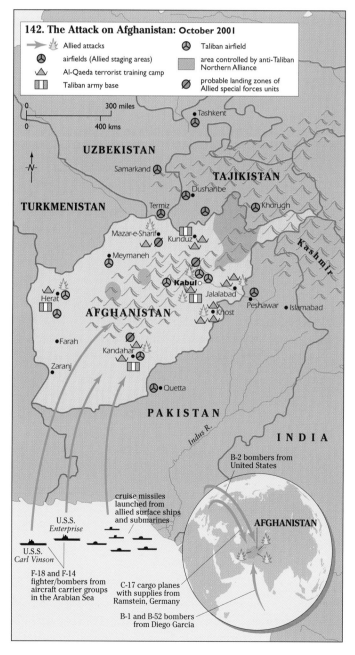

142. The Attack on Afghanistan: October 2001

- Allied attacks
- airfields (Allied staging areas)
- Al-Qaeda terrorist training camp
- Taliban army base
- Taliban airfield
- area controlled by anti-Taliban Northern Alliance
- probable landing zones of Allied special forces units

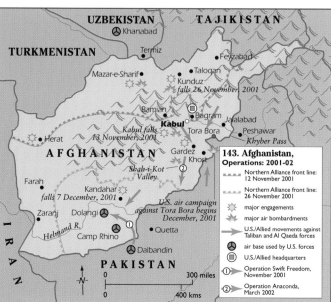

143. Afghanistan, Operations: 2001-02

- Northern Alliance front line: 12 November 2001
- Northern Alliance front line: 26 November 2001
- major engagements
- major air bombardments
- U.S./Allied movements against Taliban and Al Qaeda forces
- air base used by U.S. forces
- U.S./Allied headquarters
- ① Operation Swift Freedom, November 2001
- ② Operation Anaconda, March 2002

About the Editor and Contributors

Editor

James C. Bradford is Associate Professor of History at Texas A & M University. He specializes in naval history and the American Revolutionary War and is the author or editor of eight books on naval and military history.

Contributors

Merrill Bartlett is an independent scholar and the author or editor of seven works on amphibious warfare and the U.S. Marine Corps.

Graham Cosmas is Chief, Joint Staff History Branch, Joint History Office, Joint Chiefs of Staff. Dr. Cosmas is the author of books on the U.S. Army's role in the Spanish-American War and a history of the Military Assistance Command in Vietnam.

Joseph G. Dawson III is Professor of History at Texas A&M University. He focuses his research on mid-nineteenth century American military history.

R. David Edmunds is Watson Professor of History at the University of Texas at Dallas and the author of seven books including biographies of the Shawnee Prophet and Tecumseh.

Don Hickey is Professor of History at Wayne State College, has written a history of the War of 1812 and is writing a history of the Quasi-War.

Thomas Alexander Hughes is Associate Professor of Strategy and International Security at the U.S.A.F.'s Air War College, Montgomery, Alabama, author of a biography of General Pete Quesada and is writing a biography of Admiral William Halsey.

James Kirby Martin is Distinguished University Professor of History at the University of Houston. His is the author or editor of nine books including two on the American Revolutionary War.

Dennis Mills is an historian at the Air Armament Center, Eglin Air Force Base, Florida.

Carol Reardon is Associate Professor of History and Scholar-in Residence of the Civil War Era Center at Pennsylvania State University. She serves as adjunct faculty of the Marine Corps Command and Staff College at Quantico and has written books on the American Civil War.

Jack Shulimson is the former Head of the Histories Section and Senior Vietnam Historian at the Marine Corps History and Museums Division. He is the author of several books on the U.S. Marine Corps.

Christopher Smith is currently completing his doctoral studies at the University of Houston.

David Smurthwaite is Assistant Director, National Army Museum, London and has been an extra-mural lecturer on Military Studies at the University of London. He has written a book on World War II in the Pacific and a number of other works on military topics.

Ian Steele is Professor of History at the University of Western Ontario and the author or editor of eight books on colonial America including two about relations between Europeans and Amerindians.

David Trask, is the former Chief of Military History, U.S. Army Center of Military History and the author or editor of fifteen books, including books on the Spanish-American War and World War I.

Spencer Tucker is the John Biggs Professor of Military History at the Virginia Military Institute. He specializes in European and military history and has written or edited twenty books, the most recent of which is an encyclopedia of naval warfare.

James Warren is an independent scholar who has written books on the war in Vietnam, the Cold War, and the history of the U.S. Marines.

Samuel Watson is Assistant Professor of History at the U.S. Military Academy, West Point, and specializes in the history of the U.S. Army and military history from 1750 to 1918.

Alan F. Wilt is Professor Emeritus of History at Iowa State University and the author of three books on World War II in Europe.

Robert Wooster is Professor of History at Texas A & M University-Corpus Christi and is the author of five books on the frontier army in the late nineteenth century.

Select Bibliography

GENERAL WORKS

Love, Robert W. Jr. *History of the U.S. Navy*, 2 vols. Harrisburg, PA: Stackpole, 1992.

Mahon, John K. *History of the Militia and National Guard*. New York: Macmillian, 1983.

Millett, Alan R. *Semper Fidelis: The History of the United States Marine Corps*. New York: Macmillan, 1980.

Millett, Allan R., and Peter Maslowski. *For the Common Defense: A Military History of the United States of America*. New York: Free Press, 1984.

Millis, Walter. *Arms and Men: A Study in American Military History*. New York: Putnam, 1956.

Potter, E. B., ed. *Sea Power: A Naval History*. Englewood Cliffs, NJ: Prentice-Hall, 1960.

Symonds, Craig L. *The Naval Institute Historical Atlas of the U.S. Navy*. Annapolis, MD: Naval Institute Press, 1995.

Weigley, Russell. *American Way of Making War: A History of United States Military Strategy and Policy*. New York: Macmillan, 1973.

_____. *of the United States Army*. New York: Macmillan, 1967.

THE COLONIAL WARS: 1512-1774

Anderson, Fred. *Crucible of War: The Seven Years' War and the Fate of Empire in British North America, 1754-1766*. New York: Alfred A. Knopf, 2000.

Eccles, William John. *The Canadian Frontier, 1534-1760*. New York: Holt, Rinehart and Winston, 1969.

Ferling, John E. *Struggle for a Continent: The Wars of Early America*. Arlington Heights, IL: Harlan Davidson, 1993.

Galay, Alan. *Colonial Wars of North America, 1512-1763: An Encyclopedia*. New York: Garland, 1996.

Gipson, Lawrence H. *The British Empire Before the American Revolution*, 15 vols. Caldwell, ID: The Caxton Printers, Ltd., 1936-70.

Leach, Douglas Edward. *Arms for Empire: A Military History of the British Colonies in North America, 1607-1763*. New York: Macmillan, 1973.

Lepore, Jill. *The Name of War: King Phillip's War and the Origins of American Identity*. New York: Alfred Knopf, 1998.

Starkey, Armstrong. *European and Native American Warfare, 1675-1815*. Norman, OK: University of Oklahoma Press, 1998.

Steele, Ian K. *Warpaths: Invasions of North America*. New York: Oxford University Press, 1994.

Vaughn, Alden T. *New England Frontier: Puritans and Indians, 1620-1675*. Boston: Little, Brown, 1965.

Weber, David J. *The Spanish Frontier in North America*. New Haven, CT: Yale University Press, 1992.

THE AMERICAN REVOLUTIONARY WAR: 1775-83

Allen, Gardner W. *A Naval History of the American Revolution*, 2 vols. New York: Russell & Russell, Inc., 1913.

Barnes, Ian, and Charles Royster, eds. *The Historical Atlas of the American Revolution*. New York: Routledge, 2000.

Calloway, Colin G. *The American Revolution in Indian Country: Crisis and Diversity in Native American Communities*. New York: Cambridge University Press, 1995.

Conway, Stephen. *The War of American Independence, 1775-1783*. London: Edward Arnold, 1995.

Dull, Jonathan R. *A Diplomatic History of the American Revolution*. New Haven, CT: Yale University Press, 1985.

Fowler, William M., Jr. *Rebels Under Sail: The American Navy During the Revolution*. New York: Charles Scribner's Sons, 1976.

Higginbotham, Don. *The War of American Independence: Military Attitudes, Policies, and Practice, 1763-1789*. New York: Macmillan, 1971.

Hoffman, Ronald, and Peter J. Albert, eds. *Arms and Independence: The Military Character of the American Revolution*. Charlottesville, VA: University Press of Virginia, 1984.

Mackesy, Piers. *The War for America, 1775-1783*. Cambridge, MA: Harvard University Press, 1964.

Martin, James Kirby, and Mark Edward Lender. *A Respectable Army: The Military Origins of the Republic, 1763-1789*. Arlington Heights, IL: Harlan Davidson, Inc., 1982.

Neimeyer, Charles Patrick. *America Goes to War: A Social History of the Continental Army*. New York: New York University Press, 1996.

O'Donnell, James H., III. *Southern Indians in the American Revolution*. Knoxville, TN: The University of Tennessee Press, 1973.

Royster, Charles. *A Revolutionary People at War: The Continental Army and American Character, 1775-1783*. Chapel Hill, NC: University of North Carolina Press, 1979.

Shy, John. *A People Numerous and Armed: Reflections on the Military Struggle for American Independence*. New York: Oxford University Press, 1976.

Syrett, David. *Shipping and the American War, 1775-1783: A Study of British Transport Organization*. London: University of London, Athlone Press, 1970.

Ward, Christopher. *The War of the Revolution*, 2 vols. New York: Macmillan, 1952.

FOREIGN WARS OF THE EARLY REPUBLIC: 1798-1815

The Quasi-War

Allen, Gardner W. *Our Naval War with France*. Hamden, CT: Archon Books, 1967.

De Conde, Alexander. *The Quasi-War: The Politics and Diplomacy of the Undeclared War with France, 1797-1801*. New York: Scribners, 1966.

Ferguson, Eugene S. *Truxton of the Constellation: The Life of Commodore Thomas Truxton, U.S. Navy, 1755-1822*. Baltimore, MD: Johns Hopkins, 1956.

Palmer, Michael A. *Stoddert's War: Naval Operations During the Quasi-War with France, 1798-1801*. Columbia, SC: University of South Carolina Press, 1987.

The Barbary Wars

Allen, Gardner W. *Our Navy and the Barbary Corsairs*. Boston: Houghton-Mifflin, 1905.

Field, James A., Jr. *America and the Mediterranean World, 1776-1882*. Princeton, NJ: Princeton University Press, 1969.

McKee, Christopher. *Edward Preble: A Naval Biography, 1761-1807*. Annapolis, MD: Naval Institute Press, 1972.

Tucker, Glen. *Dawn Like Thunder: The Barbary Wars and the Birth of the U.S. Navy*. Indianapolis, IN: Bobbs-Merrill, 1963.

Wright, Louis B., and Julia H. Macleod. *The First Americans in North Africa: William Eaton's Struggle for a Vigorous Policy Against the Barbary Pirates, 1799-1805*. Princeton, NJ: Princeton University Press, 1945.

The War of 1812

Hickey, Donald R. *The War of 1812: A Forgotten Conflict*. Urbana, IL: University of Illinois Press, 1989.

Horsman, Reginald. *The War of 1812*. New York: Alfred A. Knopf, 1969.

Mahan, A.T. *Sea Power and Its Relations to the War of 1812*, 2 vols. Boston: Little, Brown, 1905.

Mahon, John K. *The War of 1812*. Gainesville, FL: University of Florida Press, 1972.

Quimby, Robert S. *The U.S. Army in the War of 1812: An Operational and Command Study*, 2 vols. East Lansing, MI: Michigan State University Press, 1997.

Roosevelt, Theodore. *The Naval War of 1812*. New York: G. P. Putnam, 1882.

Stagg, J.C.A. *Mr. Madison's War: Politics, Diplomacy, and Warfare in the Early American Republic 1785-1830*. Princeton, NJ: Princeton University, 1983.

Tucker, Glenn. *Poltroons and Patriots: A Popular Account of the War of 1812*, 2 vols. Indianapolis, IN: Bobbs-Merrill, 1954.

AMERICAN INDIAN WARS: 1790-1859

Covington, James W. *The Seminoles of Florida*. Gainesville, FL: University Press of Florida, 1993.

Gilpin, Alec R. *The War of 1812 in the Old Northwest*. East Lansing, MI: Michigan State University Press, 1958.

Hagan, William T. *The Sac and Fox Indians*. Norman, OK: University of Oklahoma Press, 1958.

Mahon, John. K. *History of the Second Seminole War, 1835-1842*. Gainesville, FL: University of Florida Press, 1967.

Prucha, Francis Paul. *Sword of the Republic: The United States Army on the Frontier, 1783-1846*. Toronto: The Macmillan Co., 1968.

Sword, Wiley. *President Washington's Indian War: The Struggle for the Old Northwest, 1790-1795.* Norman, OK: University of Oklahoma Press, 1985.

THE GROWTH OF THE PROFESSIONAL ARMY: 1815-60

Bauer, K. Jack. *Zachary Taylor: Soldier, Planter, and Statesman of the Old Southwest.* Baton Rouge, LA: Louisiana State University Press, 1985.

Cunliffe, Marcus. *Soldiers and Civilians: The Martial Spirit in America, 1776-1865.* 2nd ed. New York: The Free Press, 1973.

Gillett, Mary C. *The Army Medical Department, 1818-1865.* Washington, D.C.: Government Printing Office, 1987.

Johnson, Timothy D. *Winfield Scott: The Quest for Military Glory.* Lawrence, KS: University Press of Kansas, 1998.

Morrison, James L., Jr. *"The Best School in the World". West Point in the Pre-Civil War Years, 1833-1866.* Kent, OH: Kent State University Press, 1986.

Moten, Matthew. *The Delafield Commission and the American Military Profession.* College Station, TX: Texas A&M University Press, 2000.

Ness, George T., Jr. *The Regular Army on the Eve of the Civil War.* Baltimore, MD: Toomey Press, 1990.

Pappas, George S. *To the Point: The United States Military Academy, 1802-1902.* Westport, CT.: Praeger, 1993.

Silver, James W. *Edmund Pendleton Gaines, Frontier General.* Baton Rouge, LA: Louisiana State University Press, 1949.

Skelton, William B. *An American Profession of Arms: The Army Officer Corps, 1784-1861.* Lawrence, KS: University Press of Kansas, 1992.

THE TEXAS REVOLUTION AND THE U.S.-MEXICAN WAR: 1835-48

Bauer, K. Jack. *The Mexican War.* New York: Macmillan, 1974.

_____. *Surfboats and Horse Marines: U.S. Naval Operations in the Mexican War.* Annapolis, MD: Naval Institute Press, 1969.

Dawson, Joseph G., III. *Doniphan's Epic March: The First Regiment of Missouri Volunteers in the Mexican War.* Lawrence, KS: University Press of Kansas, 1999.

Frazier, Donald S., ed. *The United States and Mexico at War.* New York: Macmillan, 1998.

Hardin, Stephen L. *Texian Iliad: A Military History of the Texas.* Austin, TX: University of Texas Press, 1994.

Winders, Richard B. *Mr. Polk's Army: The American Military Experience in the Mexican War.* College Station, TX: Texas A&M University Press, 1997.

THE AMERICAN CIVIL WAR: 1861-65

Alexander, E.P. *Military Memoirs of a Confederate.* New York: Charles Scribner's Sons, 1907.

Bern, Anderson. *By Sea and By River: The Naval History of the Civil War.* New York: Alfred A. Knopf, 1962.

Bradley, Mark L. *This Astounding Close: The Road to Bennett Place.* Chapel Hill, NC: University of North Carolina Press, 2000.

Castel, Albert. *Decision in the West: The Atlanta Campaign of 1864.* Lawrence, KS: University Press of Kansas, 1992.

Coddington, Edwin B. *The Gettysburg Campaign: A Study in Command.* New York: Scribner's, 1968.

Freeman, Douglas Southall. *R.E. Lee: A Biography*, 4 vols. New York: Scribner's, 1934-35.

Gallagher, Gary. *The Confederate War.* Cambridge, MA: Harvard University Press, 1997.

Grant, U.S. *The Personal Memoirs of U.S. Grant*, 2 vols. New York: C.L. Webster, 1894.

Harsh, Joseph L. *Confederate Tide Rising: Robert E. Lee and the Making of Southern Strategy, 1861-1862.* Kent, OH: Kent State University Press, 1998.

Haskell, Frank. *The Battle of Gettysburg.* Madison, WI: Wisconsin History Commission, 1910.

Hattaway, Herman, and Archer Jones. *How the North Won: A Military History of the Civil War.* Urbana, IL: University of Illinois Press, 1983.

Hennessy, John. *Return to Bull Run: The Campaign and Battle of Second Manassas.* New York: Simon & Schuster, 1993.

Johnson, R.U., and C.C. Buel. *Battles and Leaders of the Civil War.* New York: Century Co., 1887-88.

McPherson, James M. *Battle Cry of Freedom: The Civil War Era.* New York: Oxford University Press, 1988.

Porter, Edward A. *Fighting for the Confederacy: The Personal Recollections of General Edward Alexander Porter.* Chapel Hill, NC: University of North Carolina Press, 1989.

Rhea, Gordon. *The Battle of the Wilderness, May 5-6, 1864.* Baton Rouge, LA, Louisiana State University Press, 1994.

Robertson, James I., Jr. *Stonewall Jackson: The Man, the Soldier, the Legend.* New York: Macmillan, 1997.

Roland, Charles P. *Albert Sidney Johnston: Soldier of Three Republics.* Austin, TX: University of Texas Press, 1964.

Sears, Stephen W. *Chancellorsville.* Boston: Houghton Mifflin Co., 1996.

_____. *Landscape Turned Red: The Battle of Antietam.* New Haven, CT: Ticknor & Fields, 1983.

Weigley, Russell F. *A Great Civil War: A Military and Political History, 1861-1865.* Bloomington, IN: Indiana University Press, 2000.

AMERICAN INDIAN WARS: 1866-90

Tate, Michael L. *The Frontier Army in the Settlement of the West.* Norman, OK: Oklahoma Press, 1999.

Utley, Robert M. *Frontier Regulars: The United States Army and the Indian, 1866-1891.* New York: Macmillan, 1973.

Wooster, Robert. *The Military and United States Indian Policy, 1865-1903.* New Haven, CT: Yale University Press, 1988.

THE SPANISH-AMERICAN WAR: 1898

Chadwick, French Ensor. *The Relations of the United States and Spain: The Spanish-American War*, 2 vols. New York: Scribner's, 1911.

Cosmas, Graham A. *An Army for Empire: The United States Army in the Spanish-American War.* 2d rev. ed. Shippensburg, PA: White Mane Publishing Company, 1994.

Crawford, Michael J., et al. *The Spanish-American War: Historical Overview and Select Bibliography.* Washington, DC: Naval Historical Center, 1998.

Trask, David F. *The War with Spain in 1898.* New York: Macmillan, 1981.

AMERICA'S RISE TO WORLD POWER: 1867-1917

Beale, Howard K. *Theodore Roosevelt and the Rise of America to World Power.* Baltimore: Johns Hopkins, 1956.

Bradford, James C., ed. *Admirals of the New Steel Navy.* Annapolis, MD: Naval Institute Press, 1990.

Campbell, Charles S. *The Transformation of American Foreign Relations, 1865-1900.* New York: Harper & Row, 1976.

Karsten, Peter. *The Naval Aristocracy: The Golden Age of Annapolis and the Emergence of Modern American Navalism.* New York: Free Press, 1972.

LaFeber, Walter. *The New Empire: An Interpretation of American Expansion, 1860-1898.* Ithaca, N.Y.: Cornell University Press, 1963.

Seager, Robert, II. *Alfred Thayer Mahan: The Man and His Letters.* Annapolis, MD: Naval Institute Press, 1977.

Shulman, Mark Russell. *Navalism and the Emergence of American Sea Power, 1882-1893.* Annapolis, MD: Naval Institute Press, 1995.

RISE OF THE UNITED STATES AS AN ASIAN POWER: 1899-1922

Braisted, William Reynolds. *The United States Navy in the Pacific, 1897-1909.* Austin: University of Texas Press, 1958.

_____. *The United States Navy in the Pacific, 1909-1922.* Austin: University of Texas Press, 1971.

Challener, Richard D. *Admirals, Generals, and American Foreign Policy.* Princeton, NJ: Princeton University Press, 1973.

Duiker, William J. *Cultures in Collision: The Boxer Rebellion.* Novato CA: Presidio Press, 1978.

Graves, William S. *America's Siberian Adventure.* New York: Jonathan Cape & Harrison Smith, 1931.

Hagedorn, Hermann. *Leonard Wood*, 2 vols. New York: Harper, 1931.

Hoyt, Edwin Palmer. *The Boxer Rebellion.* London: Abelard-Schuman, 1968

Linn, Brian McAllister. *The U.S. Army and Counterinsurgency in the Philippine*

War, 1899-1902. Chapel Hill, NC: University of North Carolina Press, 1989.

Maddox, Robert James. *The Unknown War with Russia: Wilson's Siberian Intervention.* Novato, CA: Presidio Press, 1977.

Miller, Stuart C. *"Benevolent Assimilation": The American Conquest of the Philippines, 1899-1903.* New Haven: Yale University Press, 1983.

Reckner, James R. *Teddy Roosevelt's Great White Fleet.* Annapolis, MD: Naval Institute Press, 1988.

Unterberger, Betty. *America's Siberian Expedition, 1918-1920.* Durham, NC: Duke University Press, 1956.

INTERVENTION IN CENTRAL AMERICA AND THE CARIBBEAN: 1903-35

Eisenhower, John S. D. *Intervention: The United States and the Mexican Revolution, 1913-1917.* New York: Norton, 1993.

Healy, David. *Drive to Hegemony: The United States in the Caribbean, 1898-1917.* Madison, WI: University of Wisconsin Press, 1982.

Langley, Lester D. *The Banana Wars: An Inner History of American Empire, 1900-1934.* Lexington, KY: University Press of Kentucky, 1983.

_____. *Mexico and the United States: The Fragile Relationship.* Boston: Twayne, 1991.

_____. *The United States and the Caribbean in the Twentieth Century.* Athens, GA : University of Georgia Press, 1980.

Schmidt, Hans. *Maverick Marine: General Smedley D. Butler and the Contradictions of American Military History.* Lexington, KY: The University Press of Kentucky, 1987.

_____. *The United States Occupation of Haiti, 1915-1934.* New Brunswick, NJ: Rutgers University Press, 1971

Smythe, Donald. *Guerrilla Warrior: The Early Life of John J. Pershing.* New York: Scribner's, 1973.

Sweetman, Jack. *The Landing at Veracruz: 1914.* Annapolis, MD: Naval Institute Press, 1968.

Vandiver, Frank E. *Black Jack: The Life and Times of John J. Pershing,* 2 vols. College Station, TX: Texas A & M University Press, 1977.

THE UNITED STATES IN WORLD WAR I: 1917-18

Braim, Paul F. *The Test of Battle: The American Expeditionary Forces in the Meuse-Argonne Campaign.* Newark, DE: University of Delaware Press, 1987.

Coffman, Edward M. *The War to End All Wars: The American Military Experience in World War I.* New York: Oxford University Press, 1986.

Halpern, Paul G. *A Naval History of World War I.* Annapolis, MD: Naval Institute Press, 1994.

Smythe, Donald. *Pershing: General of the Armies.* Bloomington, IN: University of Indiana Press, 1986.

Trask, David F. *The AEF and Coalition Warmaking, 1917-1918.* Lawrence, KS: University Press of Kansas, 1993.

_____. *Captains and Cabinets: Anglo-American Naval Relations, 1917-1918.* Columbia, MO: University of Missouri Press, 1972.

THE UNITED STATES IN WORLD WAR II IN THE PACIFIC: 1941-45

Costello, John. *The Pacific War.* New York: Rawson Wade, 1981.

Cutler, Thomas J. *The Battle of Leyte Gulf, 23-26 October 1944.* New York: Harper-Collins, 1994.

Dull, Paul S. *A Battle History of the Imperial Japanese Navy, 1941-1945.* Annapolis, MD: Naval Institute Press, 1978.

Foster, S. *Okinawa 1945. Final Assault on the Empire.* London: Hodder and Stoughton, 1994.

Frank, Richard B. *Guadalcanal.* New York: Random House, 1990.

Fuchida, Mitsuo, and Matasuke Okumiya. *Midway. The Battle That Doomed Japan, the Japanese Navy's Story.* Annapolis MD: Naval Institute Press, 1955.

Long, Gavin. *Australia in the War of 1939-1945.* Series One. Army. Volume VII. Canberra, AUST: Australian War Memorial, 1963.

Morison, Samuel Eliot. *History of United States Naval Operations in World War II,* 15 vols. Boston: Little Brown, 1947-1962.

Morton, Louis. *United States Army in World War II. The War in the Pacific. Strategy and Command: The First Two Years.* Washington: Center for Military History, 1962.

Prange, Gordon W. *At Dawn We Slept. The Untold Story of Pearl Harbor.* New York: Viking, 1991.

Shaw Henry I. Jr., et al. *History of the U.S. Marine Corps Operations in World War II,* 5 vols. Washington: Historical Branch, HQMC, 1958-1968.

Smurthwaite, David. *The Pacific War Atlas 1941-1945.* New York: Facts On File, 1995.

Spector, Ronald. *Eagle Against the Sun. The American War with Japan.* New York: Vintage, 1985.

Willmott, H.P. *Empires in the Balance: Japanese and Allied Pacific Strategies to April 1942.* Annapolis, MD: Naval Institute Press, 1982.

_____. *The Barrier and the Javelin; Japanese and Allied Pacific Strategies February to June 1942.* Annapolis, MD: Naval Institute Press, 1983.

THE UNITED STATES WORLD WAR II IN EUROPE: 1941-45

Ambrose, Stephen E. *D-Day, June 6, 1944: The Climactic Battle of World War II.* New York: Simon & Schuster, 1994.

_____. *The Supreme Commander: The War Years of General Dwight D. Eisenhower.* Garden City, NY: Doubleday, 1970.

Bennet, Ralph. *Ultra in the West: The Normandy Campaign, 1944-1945.* New York: Scribners, 1979.

Crane, Conrad. *Bombs, Cities, and Civilians: American Airpower Strategy in World War II.* Lawrence, KS: University of Kansas Press, 1992.

D'Este, Carlo. *Patton: A Genius for War.* New York: Harper Collins, 1995.

Gardner, W.J.R. *Decoding History: The Battle of the Atlantic and Ultra.* Annapolis, MD: Naval Institute Press, 1999.

Graham, Dominick, and Shelford Bidwell. *Tug of War: The Battle for Italy, 1943-1945.* New York: St. Martin's Press, 1986.

MacDonald, Charles B. *A Time for Trumpets: The Untold Story of the Battle of the Bulge.* New York: William Morrow, 1985.

Murray, Williamson, and Allan R. Millett. *A War to Be Won: Fighting the Second World War, 1937-1945.* Cambridge, MA: Harvard University Press, 2000.

Overy, Richard. *Why the Allies Won.* New York: W. W. Norton, 1995.

Ryan, Cornelius. *A Bridge Too Far.* New York: Simon & Schuster, 1974.

Van der Vat, Dan. *The Atlantic Campaign: World War II's Great Struggle at Sea, 1939-1945.* New York: Harper & Row, 1988.

THE KOREAN WAR: 1950-53

Appleman, Roy E. *South to the Naktong, North to the Yalu.* Washington, D.C.: Office of the Chief of Military History, 1961.

Barclay, C. N. *The First Commonwealth Division: The Story of British Commonwealth Land Forces in Korea, 1950-1953.* Aldershot, U.K.: Gale and Polden, 1954.

Blair, Clay. *The Forgotten War: America in Korea, 1950-1953.* New York: Times Books, 1987.

Cagle, Malcolm W., and Frank A. Manson. *The Sea War in Korea.* Annapolis, MD: U.S. Naval Institute, 1957.

Crane, Conrad C. *American Airpower Strategy in Korea, 1950-1953.* Lawrence, KS: University Press of Kansas, 2000.

Ent, Uzal W. *Fighting on the Brink: Defense of the Pusan Perimeter.* Paducah, KY: Turner Publishing, 1996.

Futrell, Robert F. *The United States Air Force in Korea, 1950-1953.* Washington, DC: Office of the Chief of Air Force History, 1983.

Goncharov, Sergei, et al. *Uncertain Partners: Stalin, Mao, and the Korean War.* Stanford, CA: Stanford University Press, 1993.

Hastings, Max. *The Korean War.* New York: Simon & Schuster, 1987.

Hermes, Walter G. *United States Army in the Korean War: Truce, Tent, and Fighting Front.* Washington, DC: Office of the Chief of Military History, 1966.

Lowe, Peter. *The Origins of the Korean War.* London: Longman, 1986.

Montross, Lynn, et al. *U.S. Marine Operations in Korea, 1950-1953,* 5 vols. Washington, DC: U.S. Marine Corps Historical Branch, 1954-72.

Mossman, Billy C. *U.S. Army in the Korean War: Ebb and Flow, November 1950-July 1951.* Washington, DC: U.S. Army, Center of Military History, 1990.

Paik, Sun Yup. *From Pusan to Panmunjom.* Washington: Brassey's, 1992.

Republic of Korea, Ministry of National Defense. *The History of the United Nations Forces in the Korean War*, 6 vols. Seoul: War History Compilation Commission, 1967-1975.

Ridgway, Matthew B. *The Korean War: How We Met the Challenge, How All Out Asian War Was Averted, Why McArthur Was Dismissed, Why Today's War Objectives Must Be Limited.* Garden City, NY: Doubleday, 1967.

Sandler, Stanley. *The Korean War: No Victors, No Vanquished.* Lexington, KY: University Press of Kentucky, 1999.

Schnabel, James F. *United States Army in the Korean War: Policy and Direction, the First Year.* Washington, DC: Office of the Chief of Military History, Department of the Army, 1972.

THE VIETNAM WAR: 1959-75

Karnow, Stanley. *Vietnam: A History.* New York: Viking, 1983.

Neu, Charles, E., ed. *After Vietnam: Legacies of a Lost War.* Baltimore, MD: Johns Hopkins University Press, 2000.

Tucker, Spencer, ed. *The Encyclopedia of the Vietnam War.* New York: Oxford University Press, 1998.

Stanton, Shelby L. *Rise and Fall of an American Army.* Novoto, CA: Presidio, 1985.

Summers, Col. Harry G., Jr. *Vietnam War Almanac.* New York: Facts On File, Inc., 1985.

_____. *Historical Atlas of the Vietnam War.* Boston: Houghton Mifflin, 1995.

THE GLOBAL COLD WAR: 1946-1990

Blasier, Cole. *The Hovering Giant: U.S. Responses to Revolutionary Change in Latin America, 1910-1985.* Pittsburgh: University of Pittsburgh Press, 1986.

Chang, Gordon. *Friends and Enemies: The United States, China, and the Soviet Union, 1948-1972.* Stanford, CA.: Stanford University Press, 1990.

Frankel, Benjamin. *The Cold War, 1949-1991.* Detroit: Gale Research, 1992.

Fursenko, Alexandr, and Timothy Naftali. *One Hell of a Gamble: Krushchev, Castro, and Kennedy, 1958-1964.* New York: W. W. Norton, 1997.

Gaddis, John Lewis. *The United States and the Origins of the Cold War, 1941-1947.* New York: Columbia University Press, 1972.

_____. *Strategies of Containment: A Critical Appraisal of Post-War American National Security Policy.* New York: Oxford University Press, 1982.

Kaufman, Burton. *The Arab Middle East and the United States: Inter-Arab Rivalry and Superpower Diplomacy.* New York: Twayne, 1996.

Kolko, Gabriel. *Confronting the Third World: United States Foreign Policy, 1945-1990.* New York: Pantheon Books, 1988.

Lafeber, Walter. *Inevitable Revolutions: The United States and Central America.* New York: W. W. Norton, 1983.

_____. *America, Russia, and the Cold War.* New York: McGraw Hill, 1993.

LeoGrande, William. *Our Own Backyard: The United States in Central America.* Chapel Hill, NC: University of North Carolina Press, 1998.

May, Ernest and, Philip Zelikow. *The Kennedy Tapes: Inside the White House During the Cuban Missile Crisis.* Cambridge, MA: Harvard University Press, 1997.

Schoenbaum, David. *The United States and the State of Israel.* New York: Oxford University Press, 1993.

Zubok, Vladislav, and Constatnine Pleshakow. *Inside the Kremlin's Cold War: From Stalin to Kruschev.* Cambridge, MA: Harvard University Press, 1996.

POST-COLD WAR ERA: 1990-

Ballard, John R. *Upholding Democracy: The United States Military Campaign in Haiti, 1994-1997.* Westport, CT: Praeger, 1998.

Bowden, Mark. *Black Hawk Down: A Story of Modern War.* New York: Atlantic Monthly Press, 1999.

Cohen, Eliot A., ed. *United States Air Force Gulf War Air Power Survey*, vols. I-V. Washington, DC: Government Printing Office, 1993.

Cordesman, Anthony H., and Abraham R. Wagner. *The Lessons of Modern War: The Gulf War.* Boulder, CO: Westview Press, Inc., 1990.

Delong, Kent. *Mogadishu! Heroism and Tragedy.* Westport, CT: Praeger, 1994.

Department of Defense. *Conduct of the Persian Gulf War: Final Report to Congress.* Washington, DC: Government Printing Office, 1992.

_____. *Kosovo/Operation Allied Force After-Action Report: Report to Congress.* Washington, DC: Government Printing Office, 2000.

Gordon, Michael R., and Bernard E. Trainor. *The General's War: The Inside Story of the Conflict in the Gulf.* Boston: Little, Brown, and Company, 1995.

Holbrooke, Richard C. *To End a War.* New York: Random House, 1998.

Hutchinson, Kevin D. *Operation Desert Shield/Desert Storm: Chronology and Fact Book.* Westport, CT: Greenwood Publishing Group, Inc., 1995.

Kretchik, Walter E., et al. *Invasion, Intervention, "Intervasion": A Concise History of the U.S. Army in Operation Uphold Democracy.* Fort Leavenworth, KS: U.S. Command and General Staff College Press, 1999.

Owen, Robert C. *Deliberate Force: A Case Study in Effective Air Campaigning.* Maxwell Air Force Base, AL: Air University Press, 2000.

Pokrant, Marvin. *Desert Storm at Sea: What the Navy Really Did.* Westport, CT: Greenwood Publishing Group, Inc., 1999.

Summers, Harry G. *Persian Gulf Almanac.* New York: Facts On File, Inc., 1995.

PHOTO CREDITS

Index